DICKENS STUDIES ANNUAL

Robert B. Partlow, Jr., *Editor*

Sub-editors:

William Axton   Robert Patten

Jerome Meckier   Richard Stang

Advisory Board:

Trevor Blount   Madeline House

Philip Collins   J. Hillis Miller

Ross Dabney   Steven Marcus

Earle Davis   Sylvère Monod

George Ford   Harry Stone

K. J. Fielding   Graham Storey

DICKENS STUDIES ANNUAL

VOLUME
3

Edited by

ROBERT B. PARTLOW, JR.

SOUTHERN ILLINOIS UNIVERSITY PRESS

Carbondale and Edwardsville

FEFFER & SIMONS, INC.

London and Amsterdam

Contents

List of Illustrations

Preface

THE EDITORS are most pleased that finally, after the delay of almost a year, they are able to publish this third volume of the *Dickens Studies Annual* series. Both the University of Alberta, which originally planned to publish the papers of the Dickens Centennial Conference of 1970 as a separate monograph, and Southern Illinois University, which has supported the *Annual* generously since 1969, have been hampered by the present financial crisis. Only the loyalty to scholarship of a few administrators and the publisher have enabled us to issue this book so long prepared and, we hope, so useful to students and critics.

The papers in Part Two were originally delivered during the Dickens Centennial Conference sponsored by the Department of English of the University of Alberta on 1 and 2 October 1970. Professor Rowland McMaster was the director of the Conference, ably assisted by his wife, Professor Juliet McMaster, by Professor Norman Page, Professor J. D. W. Crowther, and Professor J. M. Nelson. The Canada Council, the British Council, and the French Ministry of Foreign Affairs all offered significant support. The Conference was one of the more successful in the busy Centennial year, not least in that it attracted many of the best-known Dickens scholars in the United States and Canada as audience and discussants, and even more in that Professor McMaster induced several of the most exciting and advanced Dickens critics to speak.

Initially the plan was to publish the proceedings of the Conference, the papers and the discussions they triggered, as a separate book—and a very fine contribution it would have been. Unfortunately, however, the financial pressure was already on Professor McMaster; he had to relinquish his plan. The editors of the *Annual,* hearing this, offered to publish the papers, not as a separate volume but as part of the series scheduled to appear in the fall of 1972. Professor McMaster agreed to collect the papers, edit them, and oversee their production. But as Southern Illinois University also fell into the slough of despond, production was pushed back, and back, and back, so that a whole year was lost. Even more, two highly interesting papers had to be withdrawn: Professor Steven Marcus decided to offer his "Pickwick Revisited" to another journal and of course it was accepted, and Professor J. Hillis Miller used his remarks on *Bleak House* as the introduction to his fine edition of that novel. Also missing are the impossible-to-print, inimitable readings of Dickens offered by Professor Philip Collins.

What remains is still riches. Ian Watt's "Oral Dickens" deals with three aspects of the oral in Dickens: the celebrated richness of his treatment of food and drink, beginning with their moral and structural significance in the early novels and moving on to larger psychological and social implications in the later works; Dickens' interest in the satisfactions of language; and the oral character types that abound in his novels. The paper handles its load of probing psychoanalytic theory gracefully and wittily.

No one has explored Dickens' public readings more thoroughly than Philip Collins. In his paper he examines the pressures and attractions that led Dickens to become a reader, and he then considers the relationship of the readings to the novels from which they came, the changes that were made, and the reasons why certain passages were retained or omitted. Professor Collins, drawing upon many contemporary reactions, suggests what Dickens was like as a reader.

John M. Robson's paper was probably the most traditional and most provocative of all those delivered. Taking as his text the first number of *Our Mutual Friend,* Professor Robson applied a traditional rhetorical analysis and demonstrated how such analysis could provide new insights into the ambiguities of the maskings, transformations through naming, and games that generate multiple networks of interpretation.

Professor Sylvère Monod's confession of his high regard for G. K. Chesterton was, like all his work, witty, urbane, and far-reaching. While admitting Chesterton's love of paradox and fine phrases, Professor Monod argued that there is in Chesterton an acuity, a breadth of interest, a sense of wonder, and an exhilaration too rarely found in our usual academic criticisms. Like Guinness, the Chestertonic is good for us.

Part One of this volume of the *Annual* was designed to supplement the admirable studies of the Centennial Conference, and so the editors' emphasis was on the work of younger scholars. We found, however, that Mr. Greaves' beautiful tour of the London of "Gone Astray" could not be omitted; it is an artfully contrived balancing of the past that Dickens knew, the London of Dickens' day, and the London of today, written with the authority and love of a lifelong Dickensian. The other inclusion by an older scholar was Henri Talon's "Space, Time, and Memory in *Great Expectations,*" perhaps the last piece he wrote before his untimely death last year. In this article Professor Talon explores with his usual acumen and depth of understanding the philosophical and psychological *Grundlagen* of a novel often analyzed on quite other grounds and so offers a fresh and provocative interpretation.

The other studies in Part One constitute a cross-section of the various techniques of analysis and critical approaches now being used by graduate students and young scholars. Lance Schachterle, for example, places *Oliver Twist* in the tradition of serial novels and explains how skillfully Dickens adapted the form to his peculiar needs and genius. Angus Easson also adapts the older technique of analysis of Dickens' "sources," in this case his knowledge of the Marshalsea and of unhappy prisoners like a certain Giles Hemans, in order to study the creative projection of character and situation.

Two of the articles in this issue were written when the authors were graduate students moving toward their doctorates—and very nice articles they are, of professional caliber. Roopnaraine set himself the task of exploring the implications of the metaphor of circularity in *Little Dorrit,* the "wheel of life," as set against the flow of actual time, and he succeeds brilliantly; it is to be hoped that he will continue this study of time, both real and lived, in Dickens' novels. Mrs. Thomas set herself a completely different, but perhaps more difficult task: a reassessment of "George Silverman's Explanation," that late and largely neglected story.

Stanley Tick and Anthony Winner both use the apparently old-fashioned techniques of "character analysis" with great tact and insight to dig into the central meanings of *Little Dorrit* and *Great Expectations.* Harland Nelson studies anew, and with renewed understanding, what railroads meant to Dickens: a disquiet that he could put a name to, a symbol of speed and transformation, the triumph of dehumanizing industry. Alan Burke reaches much the same conclusion in his detailed study of the city in *Martin Chuzzlewit:* the architectural city as Dickens' image of hypocrisy generated by selfishness.

In the editors' estimation this third volume of the *Annual* is, therefore, a judicious blend of the traditional and the new, of scholarly research and critical insight, and of tight analysis and broad generalization. Since we could select only a relatively small proportion of the many articles submitted to us for consideration, and since so many of those returned were eminently worthy of publication (indeed some of them have been accepted elsewhere), the editors are convinced that Dickens studies are hale and hearty. There has been little falling off, either in number of articles and books or significance, since we wondered if the Centennial year marked the apogee of interest in Charles Dickens—quite the reverse. The quarterly bibliography printed in the *Dickens Studies Newsletter* indicates that more articles and books about Dickens are being published now than ever before. And that's as it should be.

Finally, as Senior Editor of the *Annual,* I wish to express my deep gratitude to Professor Rowland McMaster. Not only did he generously offer the studies published in Part Two, but he edited them carefully and judiciously. Without him, this volume would be a good deal slighter than it now is.

Carbondale, Illinois
February 1973

Robert B. Partlow, Jr.

Notes on Contributors

ALAN R. BURKE is an Associate Professor at the University of Arizona. He has published several articles on Dickens and is presently completing a book on Dickens' urban poetics.

PHILIP COLLINS is Professor and Head of the Department of English, University of Leicester. He has written *Dickens and Crime, Dickens and Education;* edited *Dickens: The Critical Heritage,* the Public Reading version of *A Christmas Carol;* and published many essays and studies on Dickens and the Victorian period.

ANGUS EASSON taught at Newcastle University after receiving his Oxford doctorate with a dissertation entitled *Dickens and the Marshalsea;* he is now at Royal Holloway College, London University. He has published articles on Dickens and Joyce and edited *The Old Curiosity Shop* and Mrs. Gaskell's *North and South.* He is currently working on an introductory study of Mrs. Gaskell.

JOHN GREAVES has served as Hon. Secretary of the Dickens Fellowship since 1948. He gave Dickens character recitals during World War I, and he has been giving public readings of Dickens since 1945. An authority on the reading tours, he is also the author of *Who's Who in Dickens* and joint author of *The London of Dickens.*

SYLVÈRE MONOD, Professor at the Université de la Sorbonne Nouvelle, is the author of *Dickens the Novelist,* a French history of modern English literature, and many articles, primarily on Dickens. He has translated and edited five Dickens novels and coauthored a critical edition of *Hard Times.* Among his forthcoming publications are a similar edition of *Bleak House* and French editions of the *Christmas Stories* and Edward Lear's limericks.

HARLAND S. NELSON is a Professor at Luther College. He has published articles on Dickens, Stephen Crane, and Steinbeck.

JOHN M. ROBSON is Principal and Professor of English, Victoria College, University of Toronto. Thirteen of a projected twenty-four volumes of the *Collected Works of John Stuart Mill,* of which he is general and textual editor, have appeared, the most recent being *A System of Logic* (2 vols., 1973). His writings on the Victorian period include *The Improvement of Mankind: The Social and Political Philosophy of J. S. Mill.* A collection of humorous pieces, mainly on academia, appeared in 1970. An essay on narrative transitions in *Middlemarch* will soon be published. He is currently working on rhetoric in the nineteenth century.

R. RUPERT ROOPNARAINE, now an Assistant Professor of Comparative Literature at Cornell University, was a doctoral candidate when the present article was accepted. He has articles on Cesare Pavese and on Dickens forthcoming. He is now at work on reflexive procedures in the modern novel.

LANCE SCHACHTERLE is Assistant Professor of English at the Worcester Polytechnic Institute. He is a member of the Committee on Serial Fiction of the Research Society for Victorian Periodicals. At present he is preparing a definitive textual edition of Cooper's *The Pioneers.*

HENRI TALON, late Professor of English at the Université de Dijon, wrote eight major books, including works on Bunyan, Thackeray, and Lawrence. At the time of his death last year, he was working on extended studies of Tennyson and Thackeray.

DEBORAH ALLEN THOMAS was a graduate student at the University of Rochester when she wrote this article. She is now at Fairleigh Dickinson University in Madison.

STANLEY TICK, Professor of English at California State University, San Francisco, has published studies of Melville, George Eliot, James, Conrad, and Faulkner. Recently he has paid increasing attention to Dickens and is therefore spending the 1972-73 year in England studying Dickens' characterization.

IAN WATT, Eli Jackson Reynolds Professor of Humanities at Stanford University, is best known as the author of *The Rise of the Novel* and numerous articles and reviews and editor of *The Victorian Novel: Modern Essays in Criticism.* His Goldentree bibliography of *The British Novel: Scott through Hardy* is forthcoming. Currently he is writing a study of Joseph Conrad.

ANTHONY WINNER is an Associate Professor at the University of Virginia. He has edited *Great European Short Novels,* and has published articles on Dos Passos, the image of Italy in American fiction, and Richardson's Lovelace. The latter belongs, with the essay on Jaggers, to a series of studies devoted to the topic of fallen omniscience in the novel.

PART ONE

Recent Critical Studies

Lance Schachterle

OLIVER TWIST AND ITS SERIAL
PREDECESSORS

THE ORIGINAL readers of Charles Dickens' second novel, *Oliver Twist*, found the story of the orphan boy parcelled out over twenty-four installments in *Bentley's Miscellany*, instead of in the conventional novel form of three separate volumes.[1] Consequently, instead of reading the story from cover to cover at their pleasure, *Oliver's* first audience had to wait in suspense for over two years to enjoy the young hero's final triumph over Fagin and Bill Sikes. In publishing *Oliver Twist* serially, Dickens was working within the minor literary tradition of the magazine serial, a tradition which dates back at least to Smollett's *Sir Launcelot Greaves* (1760-61). Just as no consideration of the form of *Pickwick Papers* should ignore such precedents as the humorous accounts of sporting life which (like Pierce Egan's *Life in London*) were published in monthly parts, no view of *Oliver Twist* can be complete without some account of the kinds of fiction which had appeared in magazines immediately before Dickens' novel.

In terms of its design for magazine serialization, the form of *Oliver Twist* is quite different from that of *Pickwick Papers,* which appeared in the significantly different format of pamphlet parts. To be sure, magazine serialization and publication in pamphlet parts have in common the need to divide a narrative into segments appearing periodically. But in the early nineteenth century these two kinds of serial novels were distinct enough to be spoken of separately. Because of tighter space restrictions, the individual installments in magazine serials were often shorter than issues of a publication in parts; commonly in magazine stories the author restricted the number of characters to a young hero and his friends and simplified the narrative by concentrating on the hero's adventures from childhood to early maturity. Perhaps because periodical tales appeared as features to maintain sales, magazine serials often rely as stock in trade on installment parts whose suspenseful conclusions might encourage continued magazine purchases. On the other hand, publication in parts with its longer installments *(Pickwick's* installments averaged 18,500 words, *Oliver's* averaged 9,000) was better

[1]

suited to the rambling improvisations of humorous narratives like those of Combe and Egan.

The distinction between the two kinds of serialization appears clearly in the structural and sylistic differences between *Oliver Twist* and *Pickwick Papers.* Dickens eschews comic digressions in the spare and rapidly paced *Oliver Twist,* focusing on the serious story of a young orphan's eventual discovery of his real family; in *Pickwick Papers,* which is twice *Oliver's* length, the author delights in relaxed comic digressions and in a genial panorama of characters and incidents organized only by a simple plot. Certainly other kinds of distinctions enter into the differences between Dickens' first two novels, but the important matter of modes of serialization should not be overlooked.

Any novel consisting of installments separately published and read, yet judged by posterity in its continuous form, provides a serious dilemma for the would-be serial novelist. The demands made upon him pull in opposing directions: each part, read by itself, must be varied and substantial enough to stand by itself, and must bring the reader to a satisfactory resting-point; yet each part must also open into its sequel in order to maintain the reader's interest and to insure overall continuity when the whole novel is complete. The problems of serialization are magnified by the complexity of the narrative; in a novel like *Oliver Twist* where events in one installment have consequences in sequels, the author must exert great care to keep the threads of causality within the plot from becoming tangled.

In order to examine *Oliver* in the context of some of its magazine predecessors, a few criteria for comparing magazine serials are in order. 1) Does each installment within the serial stand well by itself, maintaining the reader's interest by weaving together the different strands of the plot? Or is the installment patently a fragment of a larger tale, ripped clumsily out of context? 2) If the installments end suspensefully, does the conclusion arise naturally out of the story and touch upon its significant themes? Or does it seem a gratuitous addition calculated only to end the installment with an appropriate flourish? 3) Does the serial as a whole convey a sense of narrative progression with incidents developing as natural consequences of earlier events? Or does each installment seem a mere improvisation which does not relate its subject matter to events narrated earlier or later?

By attending to these criteria in the following survey of some of the magazine serials which appeared immediately before *Oliver Twist,* we may see with greater certainty wherein lay the superiority of Dickens' first magazine serial over its predecessors.

Whether Dickens had read any of these early serials attentively enough to learn from their techniques is not possible to determine. Harry Stone's study of Dickens' reading mentions none of these serials as works known to have been perused by the young author.[2] But Dickens' youthful appetite for fiction might well have led him to *Blackwood's Magazine* or Marryat's

Metropolitan Magazine; in any case, by comparing the achievement of serializing *Oliver Twist* with the level of competence shown in earlier magazine serials, Dickens' mastery early in his career of the serial craft will be made quite clear.

Early writers of serial prose fiction found that the easiest solution to the difficult demands of serialization was simply to tell a series of separate tales joined by a common storyteller, as in the *Canterbury Tales.* The individual magazine sketch was a popular form of early Victorian prose fiction; both Dickens and Thackeray began their literary careers by contributing sketches to magazines. Given the currency of such periodical vignettes, a group of related sketches naturally presented a simple solution to the problems of maintaining consistency in an extended work of serialized prose fiction; Dickens himself was to use this method in the short stories of *Master Humphrey's Clock.* The variety of narratives in each installment insured a pleasing contrast of moods within the part and within the whole work, while the presence of the same storyteller throughout each part provided rudimentary continuity. Such simple works of fiction, however, can lay few claims for consideration as novels, and though Dickens was undoubtedly familiar with series of separate tales like *Jorrocks's Jaunts and Jollities,* he could have learned from them little of significance for *Oliver Twist.*

In its serial form *Oliver* resembles most closely the type of pre-Dickensian magazine serial which I shall call the *adventure serial.* Instead of building a long work from a series of short tales, the author of an adventure serial divided a continuous and exciting story into suitable installment units. Ideally, he could take a finished narrative and break it up into effective units, each ending at a point which would rouse the reader's curiosity and insure his purchase of the sequel. In actual practice adventure serial tales at times seem as extemporized as collections of anecdotes. Nonetheless, an adventure story centering the reader's attention on a hero had the advantage over a series of vignettes that interest in a chief character insured narrative continuity throughout the serial. In terms of the three criteria for judging magazine serials, the adventure story has possibilities not inherent in a series of short tales for fulfilling the demands of periodical publication. The exciting narrative helped to make each part independent, for the hero's adventures could be prorated over the various parts in order to sustain interest in each installment. And individual magazine installments might counterpoint different characters or themes selected from the whole tale to present a richer narrative within the part. Exciting action also offered the possibilities of cliff-hangers: suspenseful installment conclusions which placed the hero in jeopardy and aroused the reader's curiosity as he waited in suspense for the resolution of the adventure. Such cliff-hangers need not be merely sensational, for by intelligent choice of incidents at the end of an installment, the author might emphasize his important themes.

Finally, it is most significant that a continuous adventure story, no matter how picaresque, offered not a simple consecutive series of episodes, but instead a consequential plot in which events in past installments often influence action in the sequels. Thus the reader turned to a sequel to observe in a progressively complicated plot what the consequences of a developing series of related events would be. In a good adventure serial—and *Oliver Twist* is that and more—action was not repetitive but cumulative. Sequel by sequel, excitement built up as the reader waited to see how a young hero would overcome the obstacles placed in his path.

An early example of the adventure serial is George R. Gleig's *The Subaltern,* which ran in seven issues of *Blackwood's* from March to September 1825. The subaltern's perils in the Peninsular campaigns against the French provide the necessary adventure; the simple chronological progression of his year's service provides a coherent narrative. Rather surprisingly, Gleig makes no attempt to adapt his tale to the serial medium, for installments often end simply with the hero falling asleep after a busy day, instead of in moments of possible jeopardy. By centering the narrative wholly around the young subaltern and excluding other significant characters, Gleig ignored the possibility of playing characters off against each other for contrast within each installment. Nor did he make much attempt to develop a consequential plot; events narrated in one month neither arise from nor develop into other incidents. Only the excitement of the war and the possibility of the central character's injury kept the serial reader's curiosity alive.

The cliff-hanger was not ignored in another *Blackwood's* serial, David Stewart's *The Man-of-War's Man* (September 1821-June 1826).[3] In tracing the sea adventures of his hero, Stewart's style is often clumsy and obtuse, but he did glimpse the possibility of intensifying the reader's interest by ending an installment with a goad to his curiosity. Unlike Gleig, Stewart was able in at least one respect to adapt his narrative to the special medium of the magazine serial, for he ends at least one installment in a way which forces the reader to await the sequel for the line of action to continue. The fifth installment concludes with this passage:

> We would gladly indulge our readers with some brief specimens of what was passing in this two hours' terror-stirring confabulation [the ship's crew are exchanging ghost stories], had we not unfortunately left ourselves neither room nor leisure. In our next, however, we pledge ourselves to serve up to them one of the most popular of the host. . . . We are the more inclined to make this promise at once, because while it rids us for the time of what we confess to think rather a broad-bottomed subject, it conducts us, at the same time, with an eclat quite astonishing, to the end of our Seventh Chapter.[4]

Clumsy as this installment conclusion is, it is the first sign in *Blackwood's* that a serialized adventure story required an occasional fillip of suspense at a part ending. But the serial techniques of *The Man-of-War's Man* are a far cry from those of *Oliver Twist*. Stewart's novel presents nothing but an episodic plot, and such coy and studied installment conclusions as that to the fifth part arouse no interest in the characters or the plot.

Far superior to Stewart as a serial writer was Michael Scott, author of *Tom Cringle's Log* (*Blackwood's*, September 1829-August 1833) and *The Cruise of the Midge* (*Blackwood's*, March 1834-June 1835). Scott's earlier serial falls into self-contained units, each of which describes a naval engagement or an encounter with the colorful natives of a Caribbean port. Scott began the novel he later called *Tom Cringle's Log* as a series of autobiographical sketches, called simply by various titles appropriate to the scenes they delineate. Only at the seventh installment (June 1831) did the serial receive its permanent title. The sketches were well received, and William Blackwood urged Scott to develop the vignettes into a full-length book, which Blackwood printed part by part in his magazine. Each installment of *Tom Cringle's Log* is a complete episode in itself, and the novel has the advantage of a rudimentary plot running through all the parts. Yet *Tom Cringle's Log* never shakes off its episodic origin; the separate installments stand well alone, but when read together have (unlike *Oliver Twist*) no cumulative effect of mounting suspense. Our interest is not aroused by the development from installment to installment of a consequential plot.

The irregular publication of his first novel did not encourage Scott to put his serial medium to fullest use. *The Cruise of the Midge* bears greater witness to Scott's power as a serialist. His second serial, like so many other magazine adventure novels, is the story of a young hero, Benjamin Brail, on an exotic naval voyage. But in *The Cruise of the Midge* the serial junctures fall less at random. Scott attempted here to make the installment parts read less like independent magazine sketches and more like elements in an articulated serial novel. To adapt his story for serial publication, Scott used the technique of stimulating the reader's curiosity with suspenseful conclusions in at least five of the sixteen parts. The first number (March 1834) ended with Benjie's being knocked unconscious; he recovers only with the coming of the sequel. At the end of the sixth installment (August) he falls ill, and at the end of the seventh (September) the serial's Byronic villain apparently dies during a violent storm (in a "curtain" straight from the melodramatic stage). The tenth installment (December) concludes with a drunken sea-captain discovering the disappearance of his ship, and, most spectacular of all, the penultimate installment (May 1835) ends with a pirate ship caught by a huge wave—and left there until the next month, when the reader learned of its destruction.

Unlike *Tom Cringle's Log*, *The Cruise of the Midge* has a villain, Adderfang, who recurs in episode after episode to harass Benjamin Brail. The opposition of Brail and Adderfang supplies the give-and-take of a dramatic plot, and helps to insure the continuation of the reader's interest through the various installments. Just as in some of the installments of *Oliver Twist* Dickens heightened the narrative interest by counterpointing the evil of Fagin and Bill Sikes against the goodness of Oliver, so Scott in some installments played off Benjie's kindness and naïveté against Adderfang's villainy. The greater significance of a train of consequential events and the carefully crafted installment conclusions make *The Cruise of the Midge* a more coherent and exciting serial, and less the episodic miscellany of landscape sketches Scott presented in his earlier novel. The installment junctures do not fall at random in his second novel, but at points which mark out integral serial units. And, as we have seen, these units often end with spectacular "curtains" carefully contrived to encourage the reader to buy the sequel so that he may see what happens next.

Besides *Blackwood's,* Dickens might have encountered magazine serials in a second periodical, the *Metropolitan Magazine* (London, 1831-50), which, under the editorship of Frederick Marryat, serialized novels regularly before 1837. In the pages of the *Metropolitan Magazine,* four novels by Marryat himself appeared before *Oliver Twist* began publication.[5] Marryat offered his readers much the same fare of adventure serials that Michael Scott provided for the subscribers of *Blackwood's,* though Scott's *The Cruise of the Midge* surpassed Marryat's serials in the skill with which suspense was built up at the end of installments. Marryat's adventure stories offer frequent opportunities for suspenseful endings, but only in *Snarleyyow* (January 1836-June 1837) did he avail himself of the opportunity to rouse suspense by interrupting the narrative at critical points. In his three earlier serials, the installment junctures fall more or less at random—but at least succeed in putting off the novel's denouement for many months.

Like his predecessors but unlike Dickens, Marryat did not construct well-made plots which turn upon an accumulation over the months of hints concerning the interrelation of characters. His stories are usually picaresque adventure tales in which events pile on top of one another with only slight causal relationship, and his novels consequently lack the climactic force of *Oliver Twist,* where the last installments work out the clues about Oliver's heritage which have been appearing from the first portion of the tale.

The first of Marryat's novels to appear serially in his magazine was *Peter Simple,* part of which ran from June 1832 to September 1833. Peter's progress from family fool to lordship is interrupted monthly, but only once, at the end of the first installment (when Peter is challenged to a duel), does the serial juncture occur at a point which rouses the audience's curiosity. *Peter Simple* is not lacking in excitement, but installment conclusions rarely fall at a suspenseful moment. Incidents with potential suspense like the near-fatal storm (No. VII, December 1832) or Peter and O'Brien's escape from a French prison (No. X, March 1833) are contained within a single part, and the reader closes the *Metropolitan* knowing the outcome of these episodes instead of having to wait a month to learn what happens next.

In September 1833, Marryat rather casually announced that the publication of *Peter Simple* was suspended, and that the whole novel would appear in three volumes shortly. In an apology for serialization at the end of *Peter Simple's* last installment, the author proceeded to "take this opportunity of defending the system of having one or two of the papers [parts of the novel] in the magazine as continuations." Marryat's remarks about "continuations" are remarkable for anticipating the comments which later critics of serialization from Dickens to Mrs. Tillotson have made. Marryat first defended serialization for providing a suitably large canvas for the magazine author "to delineate character truly, and give that effect which, as writers, we feel that our reputation demands." He then went on to remark significantly:

> Perhaps there is another reason which we, as story-tellers, claim as our privilege, that of imparting a degree of prospective interest to our work, and inducing the public to look forward to the ensuing number. When the Kessehgou, or story-teller of the East, has entered upon the most effective part of his narrative, and his audience are breathless with interest and impatience, he drops his cap and his story at one and the same time, and until he perceives that his cap is replete with the small coin of the country—until, in short, Avarice has been vanquished by Curiosity, he proceeds no further. Why, then, may we not claim the same privilege, and wish to excite that interest which will occasion the purchase of the ensuing number? The praise which has been so flatteringly bestowed upon "Peter," has invariably been mixed up with diatribes against continuations; but these are flattering proofs of the interest which it has excited, and may be construed rather to the dislike of being obliged to leave off.[6]

Not only does Marryat's reference to the Kessehgou remind us of Kathleen Tillotson's explanation of serialization in terms of Chaucer, the spellbinding storyteller,[7] but his desire "to excite that interest which will occasion the purchase of the ensuing number" clearly anticipates Dickens' similarly keen appreciation of the commercial advantages of serial publication. And later in the same paragraph, Marryat anticipates Trollope's famous remark that serialization keeps the author on his toes: "A narrative may appear in three volumes, and if there is one good chapter out of three, the public are generous and are satisfied, but when every portion is severally presented to be analyzed and criticized for thirty days, the author dare not flag."[8] As the last clause indicates, Marryat, like George Eliot, appreciated the fact that serial presentation exposed each of the installments to a month's careful and thoughtful scrutiny.[9] Though Marryat did not use the serial form to stimulate curiosity as fully as Michael Scott did, he thoroughly understood how serial publication—even if it abstained from overdone cliff-hangers—maintained an audience's interest.

As a good editor, Marryat was anxious to keep up the sales of the *Metropolitan Magazine* by having a popular novel running in it—just as the editorial Dickens later maintained sales of *Master Humphrey's Clock, Household Words,* and *All the Year Round* by infusions of his own serials. As a result of his desire for a good tale to take up the slack from the unfinished *Peter Simple,* Marryat moved immediately in the September issue of the *Metropolitan* to the first chapter of a new novel, *Jacob Faithful,* which he ran through to its completion in October 1834. Like *Peter Simple, Jacob Faithful* is a picaresque story in which exciting episodes fall into single installments instead of being spread out over two or more parts. Marryat did, however, allay the anxiety of readers who feared that he might arrest the serialization of *Jacob Faithful* just when interest was at its peak, for in the fifth installment (January 1834) he printed this reassuring notice: "In reply to several letters requesting to know if 'Jacob Faithful' will be finished in the 'Metropolitan,' we state, that such is our intention."[10]

Marryat's third serial novel, *Japhet, in Search of a Father* (November 1834-January 1836), resembles its two predecessors in tracing the maturation of a young man. One installment, however, does end suspensefully: No. VIII (June 1835) closes with Japhet distraught at having apparently killed a man in a duel. Not until July did readers learn that his opponent was merely wounded. *Snarleyyow* (January 1836-June 1837) further diverges from Marryat's earlier formula. His fourth serial is comic and pseudo-Gothic, not heroic and adventurous; Captain Vanslyperken, his dog Snarleyyow, and his wretched ship's crew mock rather than praise the British navy. The plot is again improvisatory, but not based on the development of a central hero. Smallbones' feud with the fiendish Snarleyyow provides the central thread of interest running through a collection of facetious episodes. But to a greater extent than before, the author acknowledges the special form of the magazine serial by ending two of the eighteen parts with dramatic "curtains": No. VI (June 1836) and No. XII (December 1836). Furthermore, No. VII (July 1836) ends so as to suspend a line of action until the next month, just as *The Cruise of the Midge* had on occasion done earlier.

No one could take the installments of Marryat's novels—as one might *Tom Cringle's Log*—for wholly separate magazine sketches, tied together only by a common interest in the hero's life. Each part of a Marryat serial contributes, though at times rather vaguely, to a developing plot. Unlike *Tom Cringle's Log,* description never gets the upper hand over narrative in Marryat's serials, though the author was often enough willing to fill an installment by allowing a minor character to contribute his life's story or to amuse the audience with his conversation. However, such changes of pace are not clumsy space-fillers. Marryat, like Dickens after him, apparently felt the need to vary the moods of the individual installments by introducing a diversity of characters and switching between adventure and comedy.

Despite his appreciation of the potential which suspense had for intensifying the reader's interest, Marryat rarely employed climactic or suspenseful installment conclusions. But his gift for storytelling served the purpose of creating suspense well enough. His novels have steadily unfolding plots which readers could tell were going in the direction of the heroes' success in life—but thanks to the serial presentation they could not tell when that success would arrive. Simply by arresting these unfolding plots at serial junctures, Marryat aroused widespread curiosity among the English reading public. Lionel Stevenson records an anecdote about *Japhet, in Search of a Father* which might well be told about his great successor, Dickens: "It was typical of the interest in his stories that when *Japhet* was coming out serially an American ship stopped a British merchantman in mid-ocean and ran up a flag-signal to ask, 'Has Japhet found his father yet?' "[11]

Editorial enthusiasm aside, Marryat's remarks about "the praise which has been so flatteringly bestowed upon 'Peter,' " his ready assurance that *Jacob Faithful* would run to its conclusion in the *Metropolitan,* and the anecdote of the sailors anxious about *Japhet* suggest that before *Oliver Twist* the public demand for novels in magazines was considerable. Serialization in these pre-Dickens novels often amounted only to breaking up an exciting narrative at intervals not greatly affected by a demand for the integrity of an installment or for smooth transitions from part to part. At best, the serialist divided into appropriate sections a simple, adventurous narrative unencumbered and unenriched by symbolic or thematic resonances; at worst, serialization meant a collection of sketches or episodes unrelated save by the reappearance of significant characters in the various numbers. But the existence of magazine novels like *The Cruise of the Midge* and *Jacob Faithful* proves that immediately before *Oliver Twist* authors and readers alike were aware of the serial form. *Oliver,* at least in terms of its structure, did not fall from the heavens upon an audience wholly unfamiliar with the techniques of magazine serialization.

Though Dickens, always reticent about his ideas of art, published fewer remarks about serial techniques than Marryat did, he applied the devices of serialization more rigorously. *Oliver Twist* uses all the serial techniques we have examined, but with greater effectiveness. Like Marryat and Michael Scott, Dickens in *Oliver Twist* draws upon the tradition of the adventure serial in which the growth of a young hero is traced through a series of exciting events. But unlike some earlier writers of magazine adventure stories, in *Oliver* Dickens took care to involve his serial readers in a tale where all the episodes are related by a causal plot so that events in earlier installments have consequences in later ones. Installment conclusions often arrest the narrative at points in the unfolding serial which direct the reader's attention to the consequences of a long chain of related events. Episode does not follow upon episode with improvisatory nonchalance. Nor are suspenseful installment conclusions gratuitous, as is often the case in earlier serials like *The Cruise of the Midge.*

Furthermore, in addition to the superiority of style and narrative inherent in his genius, in *Oliver Twist* Dickens imparted a new element to the magazine serial: mystery. In the following remarks on *Oliver,* let me suggest that Dickens went beyond handling individual installments with unprecedented skill, making suspense grow naturally out of the narrative, and giving his serial a sense that events were linked together by a series of credible consequences. He improved upon earlier magazine serials by arousing the reader's interest in the mystery of Oliver's birth, by putting before his audience over the months all the clues necessary to encourage their solution of the puzzle presented by the narrative. One might speculate that without the element of working out the answer to the mystery imbedded in the serial installments, neither *Oliver Twist* nor its host of successors might have enjoyed their popularity.

But before considering Dickens' handling of suspense, let us examine how he surpassed the serial techniques of his predecessors. In the matter of suspenseful installment conclusions, Dickens avoids the embarrassing clumsiness of writers like Michael Scott. He takes care not to overwrite installment conclusions, abstaining from drubbing into the reader the fact that serial junctures at times put off the outcome of an episode for a month or two. Indeed, in the rather tentative remarks about his serial methods in chapter xvii of *Oliver Twist,* the author scorns contrived cliff-hangers and digressions: "I am anxious to disclaim at once the slightest desire to tantalise my readers by leaving young Oliver Twist in situations of doubt and difficulty, and then flying off at a tangent to impertinent matters, which have nothing to do with him."[12] No doubt because *Oliver* was a serious examination of the hardships of a parochial orphan, written with eventual publication as a triple-decker novel in mind, Dickens avoided egregious crowd-catching devices of serialization like the blatant appeals to the reader's curiosity found in *The Man-of-War's Man.*

Only once did Dickens conclude an installment—the first one *(Bentley's Miscellany,* London, February 1837)—with a specific remark in the editorial first person about the sequel: "As I propose to show in the sequal whether the white-waistcoated gentleman was right or not, I should perhaps mar the interest of this narrative (supposing it to possess any at all), if I ventured to hint, just yet, whether the life of Oliver Twist will be a long or a short piece of biography" (12). Here the conclusion is purposely vague, refusing to tell whether Oliver is hanged as the "white-waistcoated gentleman" predicted. Most installments end simply with an appropriate dramatic curtain, like Noah running for Bumble after being beaten by Oliver (No. III, April 1837), Messrs. Brownlow and Grimwig awaiting Oliver's return from the bookseller (No. VII, September 1837), or the revelation that Monks has been the mysterious man talking with Bumble about the circumstances surrounding the death of Oliver's mother (No. XVI, July 1838).

Usually each installment of *Oliver Twist* is self-contained to the extent that information about Oliver is not withheld from month to month. However, in addition to the first part, two other important exceptions occur. In the seventeenth installment (August 1838), Nancy overhears Fagin and Monk's conversation. But the monthly portion ends before the reader learns what Nancy has heard: "If she [Nancy] betrayed any agitation, by the time she presented herself to Mr. Sikes, he did not observe it; for merely inquiring if she had brought the money, and receiving a reply in the affirmative, he laid his head upon his pillow and resumed the slumbers which her arrival had interrupted" (265-66). In Nancy's confession to Rose Maylie in the next installment the reader learns of the content of Fagin and Monk's conversation.

The other example of suspense is more complex and concerns Oliver's unwilling participation in Bill Sikes' attempted robbery of Mrs. Maylie. The theft is planned at the end of the ninth installment (December 1837), and carried out in the tenth (January 1838), which concludes with Oliver's being shot by Mrs. Maylie's servant. Rather than relieve suspense immediately in the eleventh part (February 1838), the first two chapters revert to the Bumbles, revealing that Oliver's mother owned a gold locket. While Oliver is left bleeding as a robber, the reader is offered a significant clue about his genteel origins. Not until the last chapter of the installment do we hear of Oliver, but only indirectly through Toby Crackit's surprise at learning that Oliver and Bill have not returned to London. Again, Dickens directs the reader's interest to the wounded child without letting the serial reader know of his actual state.

Without being coy or artificial, the twelfth installment (March 1838) does exactly what the eleventh did—it keeps Oliver to the fore without revealing the consequences of his being wounded. Only in chapter xxviii, at the beginning of the thirteenth installment (April 1838), does Dickens drop back to Oliver and Bill to record what actually passed after the robbery was foiled. By means of these carefully constructed delays, Dickens managed without being unduly opaque to keep up suspense about Oliver for three months. In Michael Scott's magazine serials suspense was always resolved early in the immediate sequel, for Scott—unlike Dickens—never developed subsidiary characters to the point where they might occupy the reader's interest for several installments while the hero remained offstage. Suppressing Oliver's fate was a significant mark not only of Dickens' sense of how much suspense the audience could bear, but also a tribute to his countrapuntal skill in weaving other characters into the story so as to fill up the vacuum left by the hero's absence. Never before had nineteenth-century magazine readers been subjected to such purposeful and carefully designed delays in a serial novel.

By cleverly stretching out suspense, Dickens encouraged the serial reader to look forward. But he had also to make each unit self-sufficient by supplying a variety of moods in each installment. Marryat had rather casually balanced humor and excitement in his serials by introducing comic char-

acters (Domine Dobbs in *Jacob Faithful*, Cophagus in *Japhet*) who are useful not only for entertainment but also as sources for letterpress which help
to put off the denouements of the adventure plots. Dickens, however, was
less willing than Marryat to introduce comic scenes into his serial with the
blatant purpose of increasing suspense. In fact, in one instance he felt the
need for an apology for straying from the straight and narrow path of
Oliver's story. In the eighth installment (November 1837), the narrative returns to Bumble who was left behind in Oliver's native town in the fourth
part (May 1837); the author defends the ensuing comic description which
interrupts the advance of Oliver's history as a natural foil to the hero's
troubles, just as "the layers of red and white in a side of streaky, well-
cured bacon" meet "in . . . regular alternation" (105). Though Bumble provides much-needed comedy throughout the middle installments of the serial
(which concern Oliver's part in Bill Sikes' housebreaking expedition), and
though Bumble's involvement with the nurse of Oliver's mother eventually
connects his story again to the hero's, Dickens' defense of alternating melodramatic and comic scenes suggests his fear that a return to Bumble might
unwarrantably disturb the steady unfolding of Oliver's narrative. Thus he
assures his readers that he has "good and substantial reasons for making
the journey" (106, n. 3) back to the town of the orphan's birth.

Such clumsy explanatory intrusions, however, are absent in the middle
installments (Nos. X-XIII) in which Dickens was quite prepared to alternate between Bumble, Fagin, and Oliver without prior editorial assurance
that the unity of the serial was not being violated. Earlier serialists solved
the problem of providing variety simply by using the rough-and-tumble of
adventure as an excuse to bring in new characters as needed, but the cumulative force of their serials was consequently impaired. Dickens, by alternating between the streaks of the bacon, provided a pleasing change of pace in
his novel, but not at the cost of abandoning the order imposed by a tightly
constructed plot.

Alternation among a variety of characters also helps to keep the reader
in suspense concerning what happens to Oliver. Anticipation in *Oliver
Twist* is not, however, the mere interest in what comes next in a collection of
funny stories, as in *Jorrocks's Jaunts and Jollities;* rather it is the more fascinating concern to see what the consequences of past action would be. The
pattern of causality that art imposes upon everyday life (in which the consequences of actions are often not apparent) is no doubt one of the chief
attractions of the novel. Such consequentiality is rare even in the best adventure serials before Dickens but omnipresent in *Oliver Twist*. Oliver's resemblance to Mr. Brownlow's picture in the sixth part (August 1837), the
golden locket in the eleventh installment (February 1838), and Monk's remark in the eighteenth installment (October 1838) that Rose would be surprised to learn of her relation to Oliver, all implant suggestions which have
great bearing on Oliver's fate—if the audience has the wit to seize them.

Much of *Oliver's* great fascination as a serial results from its being, unlike earlier serials, in part a mystery story.

In *Oliver Twist* for the first time magazine serial readers were presented with an elaborate puzzle to work out—Oliver's relation to genteel society —and the working out of this puzzle held the reader's attention in a more compelling way than do the slighter plots of the loose, picaresque adventure stories which preceded it. The skillful foreshadowings in *Oliver Twist* of events months before they occurred in the serial suggest that Dickens had a control over his narrative far surer than that of his improvising predecessors. Dickens aroused the reader's curiosity and imagination by stretching out Oliver's story over twenty-four installments with greater deliberation than Michael Scott or Marryat ever manifested. Employing with greater skill all the devices of serialization—the variety of moods of the collections of anecdotes, the suspenseful endings of *The Cruise of the Midge,* and the adventurous narratives of Marryat—Dickens created in *Oliver Twist* a serial which challenged the audience to assemble a complex pattern of relationships, installment by installment, in an imaginative effort to detect for themselves what happens next.

Alan R. Burke

THE HOUSE OF CHUZZLEWIT AND THE ARCHITECTURAL CITY

EDEN, AS we are told when Martin Chuzzlewit and Mark Tapley first peruse Mr. Scadder's elaborate wall plan, is a city, "an architectural city":

> There were banks, churches, cathedrals, market-places, factories, hotels, stores, mansions, wharves; an exchange, a theatre; public buildings of all kinds, down to the office of the Eden Stinger . . . all faithfully depicted in the view before them. (xxi, 355)[1]

Martin's subsequent journey to the architectural city of Eden to establish himself as an architect and land surveyor is as frustrating and strange as the mission of Kafka's land surveyor, K., to the Castle of Count Westwest. Indeed, in Eden, Martin's "air-built castle" is quickly razed by the discovery that the architectural city is, after all, only a malarial swamp (xxiii, 379). This discovery by the would-be architect and land surveyor that the architectural city of Eden is as chimerical as the self-flattering architectural projects of his imagination is central to the theme of selfishness and to the attendant theme of hypocrisy—that strategy of selfishness which designs and constructs for itself gorgeous façades of unselfishness. The architectural city of Eden is emblematic of Dickens' conception and use in *Martin Chuzzlewit* of that infinitely greater architectural city, London.

The London of the novel, it will be remembered, is dominated by an architectural memorial commemorating the Great Fire of 1666 and the subsequent rebuilding of the city by Sir Christopher Wren and other architects —the Monument near Todgers'.[2] Of the Monument and of the Great Fire it commemorates, Dickens writes in *A Child's History of England:*

> It broke out at a baker's shop near London Bridge, on the spot on which the Monument now stands as a remembrance of those raging flames. It spread and spread, and burned and burned, for three days. . . . Church steeples fell down with tremendous crashes; houses crumbled into cinders by the hundred and the thousand. . . . Nor

[14]

did it stop until the whole way from the Tower to Temple Bar was a desert, composed of the ashes of thirteen thousand houses and eighty-nine churches. (xxv, 502-3)

The Monument then is a perpetual reminder to Londoners of the time when that "terrible visitation" spread through and engulfed the architectural structure of the densely-packed city, the streets of which "were very narrow, and the houses mostly built of wood and plaster" (xxxv, 503).

As Dickens goes on to indicate in *A Child's History,* however, the Monument is more than a reminder of the architectural follies of the past; it is also a celebration of the rebuilding of the city: "But the Fire was a great blessing to the City afterwards, for it arose from its ruins very much improved—built more regularly, more widely, more cleanly and carefully, and therefore much more healthily" (xxxv, 503). But, in spite of these improvements, the rebuilding of the city, as Dickens comments, was seriously flawed:

It might be far more healthy than it is, but there are some people in it still—even now at this time, nearly two hundred years later—so selfish, so pig-headed, and so ignorant, that I doubt if even another Great Fire would warm them up to do their duty. (xxxv, 503)

The important word here is *selfish.* The city could have been rebuilt more efficaciously if it had not been for the selfishness of landowners and speculators. Samuel Pepys, one of Dickens' sources for *A Child's History,* remarks of the inflated prices of land after the Great Fire: "So much some will get by having the City burned! Ground . . . that was not 4*d.* a-foot before, will now, when houses are built, be worth 15*s.* a-foot."[3] Such was the selfishness which led to the crowded, labyrinthine city Dickens depicts in *Martin Chuzzlewit.*

This selfishness and hypocrisy inherent in the rebuilding of the city extended even to the Monument itself, which periodically was made to bear hypocritical inscriptions accusing the Catholics of starting the Fire. This Monumental bit of hypocrisy provoked Alexander Pope's couplet:

Where London's column, pointing at the skies,
Like a tall bully, lifts the head, and lyes.[4]

It also provoked Dickens to write in *A Child's History:* "An inscription on the Monument long attributed it to the Catholics; but it is removed now, and was always a malicious and stupid untruth" (xxxv, 503). Because these inscriptions were expunged by an act of Common Council in 1831, they could no longer be used by Londoners to transfer the blame for the "most dreadful burning of this Protestant city" from themselves to "ye treachery & malice of ye Popish faction."[5]

In *Martin Chuzzlewit*, the Monument, a lively embodiment of these meanings—the folly of previous overbuilding and the selfishness and hypocrisy which marred the otherwise admirable rebuilding of the city—looms over Todgers' and London "with every hair erect upon his golden head, as if the doings of the city frightened him" (ix, 130). And well might the Monument express fright at the doings of the city which are objectified in the "nervous" chaos of the surrounding architecture, an architecture imaged by Dickens in terms of the complementary metaphors, *wilderness* and *labyrinth* (ix, 130, 127).[6] This wilderness or labyrinth, with the Monument at its center, is comprised of countless versions of the "house" of Chuzzlewit (lii, 804). The house of Chuzzlewit, as old Martin Chuzzlewit pronounces, is afflicted with the "curse" of "the love of self" (lii, 804). It contains thereby many lesser houses and almost all of the characters in the novel, most of whom are, in one way or another, architects. Their "Plans" and designs, their "workings and windings," and their "building fortunes on the weaknesses of mankind," are expressed spatially and temporally in the labyrinthine configurations of the architectural city (v, 82; xliv, 677, 683). This architectural city is Dickens' unifying image of hypocrisy generated by self-love.

— *1* —

The house of Chuzzlewit is a house of architects. It contains, in Alexander Welsh's words, "the builders of the earthly city" which "was founded on the love of self."[7] Mr. Pecksniff, of course, is preeminent among these builders. When he is first introduced to young Martin Chuzzlewit, he poses with "a pair of compasses in his hand" and with his eye glancing over "a vast number of mathematical diagrams, of such extraordinary shapes that they looked like designs for fireworks" (v, 79). His pose is reminiscent of the allegorical bas-relief sculpted on the west base of the London Monument. The bas-relief depicts Charles II in the act of commanding his three attendants (Science, Architecture, and Liberty) to raise London (depicted as a languishing female) from her ruins. Architecture is portrayed as "holding in the right hand a plan, and in the left a square and compasses."[8] Thus, with his "plans, elevations, sections," Mr. Pecksniff poses throughout the novel as an allegorical figure of Architecture similar to the one represented on the base of the Monument (v, 82). His attitudinizing is enhanced by the subordinate symmetry of his two allegorical daughters, Charity and Mercy—the three of them forming a charming *tableau vivant*. As such, Mr. Pecksniff and his daughters comprise the chief architectural ornaments of the house of Chuzzlewit.

Although Mr. Pecksniff designs and builds nothing of his own, he speaks often of architectural matters and fills his language with architectural references and terms. For example, when he prepares to leave for London, he warns young Martin jocularly to take care "that the house does not run away in our absence" and informs him generously that he is "forbidden to enter no corner of this house," but is encouraged to make himself "perfectly at home in every part of it" (vi, 87). Such is Mr. Pecksniff's largess in offering Martin the freedom of his cramped and uncomfortable house. The hypocrisy of his generosity is compounded in his parting request that Martin rearrange a pile of bricks and flowerpots into "any form" which will remind him of "St. Peter's at Rome, or the Mosque of St. Sophia at Constantinople" (vi, 88). Any form which reminds him of such grandiose structures will do. And this is true also of his own architecture-laden language. He protests to Mrs. Todgers, for example, that his feelings "will not consent to be entirely smothered, like the young children in the Tower" (ix, 149). He informs old Martin Chuzzlewit that Mercy is "constructed on the best models"; and he assures Jonas Chuzzlewit that his conscience is his "bank" (x, 164; xx, 328). Even when Mr. Pecksniff's language is devoid of specific architectural terms and references, it is contrived so as to be "ornamental"—a verbal equivalent of St. Peter's and St. Sophia's (iv, 59).

Mr. Pecksniff's architectural plans, projects, and student exercises are also ornamental. He puts his pupils to work "making elevations of Salisbury Cathedral from every possible point of sight; and in constructing in the air a vast quantity of Castles, Houses of Parliament, and other Public Buildings" (ii, 14). These airy monuments, of course, are meant for show. Similar showpiece exercises are assigned to young Martin when Mr. Pecksniff asks him for his idea of "a monument to a Lord Mayor of London; or a tomb for a sheriff; or . . . of a cowhouse to be erected in a nobleman's park," or of "a pump," "a lamp-post," or an "ornamental turnpike" (vi, 87). Not only are these projects ornamental and monumental and thus suggestive of the London Monument, but they are discrete entities which bear no relationship to one another. Mr. Pecksniff's cataloging of previous student projects is illustrative of this disconnection:

"Salisbury Cathedral from the north. From the south. From the east. From the west. From the south-east. From the nor'-west. A bridge. An alms-house. A jail. A church. A powder-magazine. A wine-cellar. A portico. A summer-house. An ice-house." (v, 81)

This arbitrary listing of discrete views and structures which have no architectural interrelationships reveals the disconnectedness inherent in the selfish and hypocritical individual and anticipates the architectural chaos of London as seen from the top of Todgers'.

Mr. Pecksniff, however, does contrive certain plans and attempts to put them into operation. By the "workings and windings" of hypocrisy, by "walking up and down the narrow ways and by-places" of life, and by worming himself "through dirty ways" into favor, he creates and attempts to execute various projects (xlviv, 677; xx, 328; x, 162). He attempts "to wall up" old Martin Chuzzlewit for his own selfish purposes (xxx, 475). He steals young Martin Chuzzlewit's grammar-school plan, making it his own by the ornamental addition of "four windows" (xxxv, 553). And he joins with Tigg Montague and Jonas Chuzzlewit in the Anglo-Bengalee plan for "building fortunes on the weaknesses of mankind" (xliv, 683). But for all of his plans for building upon the weaknesses of others, Mr. Pecksniff is exposed for the fraudulent architect that he is. Appropriately, he is exposed in conjunction with various architectural misadventures. At the beginning of the novel, for example, Mr. Pecksniff is knocked down and shut out by his own "front door" (ii, 9). Later, he is frightened by young Martin into tripping over a chair and falling "with his head in an acute angle of the wainscot" (xii, 210). Finally, at the end of the novel, he is struck down by old Martin and dragged up again by Mark Tapley so that he reclines "with his back against the opposite wall" (lii, 803). In the end, Mr. Pecksniff becomes a begging letter-writer who continually solicits money from Tom Pinch, claiming that he "built" Tom's fortunes better than he built his own (liv, 837). He remains to the end a false architect building mental and verbal structures which have no substance.

Tom Pinch, Mr. Pecksniff's protégé—a protégé who, according to Mr. Pecksniff, is lacking in any real architectural talent—finally sees through the Pecksniffian façade and makes his way to London. His joyous entry into London "down countless turnings, and through countless mazy ways," and his enthusiastic excursions "into the crowded carriage-ways at the peril of his life, to get the better view of church steeples, and other public buildings," suggest that Tom is more of an architect than Mr. Pecksniff supposes (xxxvi, 563; xxxix, 615). Mr. Fips' statement to John Westlock that "Mr. Thomas Pinch and his acquirements were as well known as the Church steeple, or the Blue Dragon" reinforces the idea of Tom's real architectural capabilities (xxxix, 607). As the result of Mr. Fips' inquiry on the behalf of old Martin, Tom is put to work in the Temple, working "with pens and ruler, and compasses" and "concentrating all the ingenious and laborious neatness he had ever expended on map or plan" for Mr. Pecksniff (l, 770-71). Thus, in spite of Mr. Pecksniff's selfish opinion to the contrary, Tom becomes, without knowing it, an architect. In the Temple, he creates for his unknown employer a "Home" (liv, 832). He, not Mr. Pecksniff, is the true architect, and his labor is the labor of love.

If Tom Pinch escapes Mr. Pecksniff's halls with little or no taint of the Chuzzlewitian curse of self-love, young Martin is not so fortunate. He sees through Mr. Pecksniff's architectural charlatanism but not through his own. He patronizes Tom Pinch by promising that when he becomes a famous architect, he will "build" Tom's fortune (xii, 191). He promises also that when he and Mary Graham are married and established in their new home, he will design and "build an architectural music-room" in which Tom may sit and entertain them with organ recitals (xii, 193). Although young Martin designs a grammar school, he is clearly in need, at this point, of schooling in the Chuzzlewitian curse of self-love. America, of course, epitomized by the nonexistent architectural city of Eden, is the "hard school" in which Martin must learn his lesson (xxxiii, 525).

When young Martin is driven out of the house of Chuzzlewit by old Martin for "any shelter he can find," he transports himself and his castle-building propensities from his shabby London hotel to America where people "are constantly changing their residences" and are in need, therefore, of "ornamental architecture applied to domestic purposes" (xiii, 230). This self-deceptive scheme entangles Martin in the architectural confusions and machinations of various American hypocrites. He is tutored by Mr. La Fayette Kettle and General Choke, who insist that Queen Victoria resides in the Tower of London which is "located in the immediate neighbourhood of your Parks, your Drives, your Triumphant Arches, your Opera, and your Royal Almacks" (xxi, 345-47). He is confused by the monumental Mr. "Elijahpogram" whose name, Martin thinks, is "all one word, and a building of some sort" (xxxiv, 532). He is duped by Mr. Scadder, the two-faced Eden land agent, whose hair hangs down "as straight as any plummet line" and whose contradictory eyes look out from under "arches" of brows (xxi, 353). And in Eden he and Mark are enlightened by the remarkable Hannibal Chollop who, as an American citizen, feels free "to convert another man's house into a spittoon" (xxxiii, 522).

In America, Martin finds that a man such as Hannibal Chollop is considered to be "a model of a man" and that America itself is considered to be "a model to the airth" (xxxiv, 534; xxxiii, 522). But this model America, as Mark Tapley notes, has few houses, and it has, as Martin notes, institutions which can only be designated "by the generic name of Old Bailey" (xxxiv, 535). Upon this model, the architecture of the world's nations is to be built. But the American architect-characters, like their English counterparts, construct only an elaborate façade of words, a windy rhetoric in which the model American wanders houseless amid "mineral Licks" and "boundless Perearers," seeking his "bright home . . . in the Settin Sun" (xxxiv, 534). Martin, however, having entered his American heart of darkness and died to self in the architectural city of Eden, is qualified to return home and to help lift the curse of self-love from the house of Chuzzlewit. He, unlike the model American, has a home to which he can return.

In addition to the architects who emanate from Mr. Pecksniff's halls, the house of Chuzzlewit includes a cousin, Chevy Slyme. His peculiar architectural talent is being "always waiting round the corner," a talent which allows him to take mortal offense at anyone whose talent might be of a more active and constructive nature (iv, 46). Thus, he rails at having to accept payment of his debts at the hands of Tom and Martin, "two architect's apprentices. Fellows who measure earth with iron chains, and build houses like bricklayers" (vii, 108). Slyme's agent on this side of the corner, Montague Tigg, is an intimate associate of the house of Chuzzlewit. Tigg, employing architectural metaphors, argues that for a man of Slyme's abilities to be detained for a bill demonstrates that "there is a screw . . . loose somewhere, that the whole framework of society is shaken" (vii, 103). Of course, Slyme finds his place in the framework of society by becoming a blackmailing and bribe-taking police officer, and Tigg finds his by becoming the grand architect of the Anglo-Bengalee Disinterested Loan and Life Assurance Company. Both of them build their fortunes on human weaknesses.

The most important branch of the house of Chuzzlewit, however, is the London firm of Anthony Chuzzlewit and Son. Jonas Chuzzlewit, along with Tigg and Pecksniff, is one of the three Anglo-Bengalee architects who build —or attempt to build—a fortune on human weaknesses. In fact, from childhood, he has been taught to build his fortune on the model of his father, a teaching which leads him to plan the murder of his father and to effect the murder of Tigg. Like most of the characters in the novel, Jonas is defined by architectural references. His hypocritical generosity is indicated by his showing Mercy and Charity "as many sights, in the way of bridges, churches, streets, outsides of theatres, and other free spectacles . . . as most people see in a twelvemonth" (xi, 175). His selfish lack of curiosity about other people is revealed by the fact that "he would as soon have thought of the cross upon the top of St. Paul's Cathedral taking note of what he did . . . as of Nadgett's being engaged in such an occupation" (xxxviii, 590). And his murderous schemes are objectified in his architectural dream of a "strange city," a city in which "the names of the streets were written on the walls in characters quite new to him" and where the "streets were very precipitous" and disappeared in "an interminable perspective" (xlvii, 721).

Jonas' architectural dream complements Tigg's dream of the horrible creature, identified by the initial *J.*, who breaks relentlessly through the door into his bedroom. This connection becomes clear when Jonas, on his way home from murdering Tigg, begins to worry about the inner and outer doors of his room:

> But he was thinking . . . of the closed-up room; of the possibility of their knocking at the door on some special occasion; of their being alarmed at receiving no answer; of their bursting it open; of their finding the room empty; of their fastening the door into the court, and rendering it impossible for him to get into the house. (xlvii, 726)

Jonas, like Tigg, fears that someone will burst through the door into his bedroom; but, as Tigg's dream foreshadowed, it is Jonas himself (he of the initial *J.*) who comes through the door. He is the creature who enters the room which is occupied, not by Tigg, but by his sleeping self. This entry, in the light of Tigg's dream, foreshadows Jonas' suicide. His self-murder at the end of the novel is, of course, the logical outcome of his murderous splitting of himself into two beings, one hidden inside the closed door, the other outside the closed door trying to get in.

After Jonas returns home, he remains watching "every avenue by which the discovery of his guilt might be approached" (li, 773). Appropriately, Jonas' discoverers come through a door, across the "ill-omened, blighted threshold, cursed by his father's footsteps in his dying hour, cursed by his young wife's sorrowing tread, cursed by the daily shadow of the old clerk's figure, cursed by the crossing of his murderer's feet" (li, 786). Jonas stands trapped in his house, watching the edifice of his schemes collapse inward upon him: "Inch by inch the ground beneath him was sliding from his feet; faster and faster the encircling ruin contracted and contracted towards himself, its wicked centre, until it should close in and crush him" (li, 782). Jonas is, in the end, the architect of his own destruction.

While Jonas builds the structure which falls in upon him, he is aided in the collapse of his schemes by several innocuous-seeming characters: Mr. Chuffey, Mrs. Gamp, and Mr. Nadgett. Mr. Chuffey, who is described as appearing as if "somebody had just found him in a lumber-closet" and as always receding "into a dark corner," is quite literally a part of the house of Anthony Chuzzlewit and Son (xi, 178, 182). He is sensate enough, however, to feel the evil that is destroying the house and to articulate the curse: "Oh! woe, woe, woe, upon this wicked house" (xxvi, 426). After the death of Anthony Chuzzlewit, Mr. Chuffey forces Jonas to attempt his removal from the house by repeatedly asking the ghostly architectural question: "Who's lying dead up-stairs?" (xlvi, 707). In response to Mr. Chuffey's haunting questions, Jonas requests the services of Mrs. Gamp—a request which leads John Westlock and the other agents of his exposure directly to him.

Mrs. Gamp, who makes her living—if not her fortune—by building upon human weaknesses—childbirth, sickness, and death—is a considerable artist and architect. Along with Mr. Mould, the coffin builder, corpse preparer, and funeral impresario, Mrs. Gamp works hard to hasten her fellow creatures through this mortal vale. So eager is she for Lewsome to die, for example, that she pins "his wandering arms against his sides, to see how he would look if laid out as a dead man; . . . her fingers itched to compose his limbs in that last marble attitude" (xxv, 412). She also creates, through the impression of her strong personality and intense physical presence upon her used mourning weeds, dead images of herself: "The very fetch and ghost of Mrs. Gamp, bonnet and all, might be seen hanging up, any hour of the day, in at least a dozen of the second-hand clothes shops about Holborn" (xix, 313). And in her own room, her gowns, shaped like herself, hang from her bedposts, creating the illusion that she has "hanged herself" (xlix, 748).

In addition to her professional creations, Mrs. Gamp creates, with great architectural specificity, a world of personal acquaintances. When she speaks of the deceased Mr. Gamp, she always provides him with an architectural ambience: he is laid out in "Guy's Hospital"; his wooden leg is always walking into "wine vaults"; and he is put to rest at last in "his long home" (xix, 313; xl, 625). Her own children, or so she tells Mrs. Harris, have "fallen out of three-pair backs, and had damp doorsteps settled on their lungs" (xl, 625). And, of course, Mrs. Harris, Mrs. Gamp's most wonderful creation, lives "through the square and up the steps a-turnin' round by the tobacker shop" (xl, 625). The directions to Mrs. Harris' lodgings seem very precise; yet, because they could apply to any architectural complex in the city, they are meaningless. Like all of Mrs. Gamp's lengthy and complicated retellings of conversations with Mrs. Harris, her directions to Mrs. Harris' lodgings are constructed as a labyrinth. Mrs. Gamp's monologues concerning her dialogues with Mrs. Harris could easily be visualized in the manner of a Saul Steinberg cartoon; that is, as labyrinthine speech-scrolls spiraling out of her mouth and looping around themselves and the listener in ever-expanding mazes of self-justification and obfuscation.[9]

Amid the architectural mazes of Mrs. Gamp's speech are found numerous important references to the destruction of the city by fire. When she goes to watch over Lewsome at the Bull in Holborn, she comments: "I'm glad to see a parapidge, in case of fire, and lots of roofs and chimley-pots to walk upon" (xxv, 411). And when Lewsome, wandering in the mazes of his delerium, cries out the name, "Chuzzlewit," Mrs. Gamp awakens terrified: "She expected to find the passage filled with people, come to tell her that the house in the City had taken fire" (xxv, 415). The fire, however, is in Lewsome's feverish brain from where it spreads, by way of Mrs. Gamp, to consume Jonas and his schemes. Mrs. Gamp's fears of fire are related in part to the irregular hours required by her professional services. As she tells Jonas, by way of a conversation with Mrs. Harris, "I've been knocked up at all hours of the night, and warned out by a many landlords, in consequence of being mistook for Fire" (xl, 631). Indeed, when Mrs. Gamp has her famous noisy falling out with Betsey Prig concerning the ontological status of Mrs. Harris, Poll Seedlepipe's pet bullfinch begins drawing so much water that "he must have thought it was Fire" (xlix, 757). The fire references surrounding Mrs. Gamp, along with the fire in Lewsome's brain and Mr. Pecksniff's fireworks diagrams and powder-magazine plans, suggest that some catastrophe is imminent, that some revelation is at hand. It is fitting that Bailey Jr. knock at Jonas Chuzzlewit's door with a knock "the like of which had probably not been heard in that quarter since the great fire of London" (xxviii, 456).

Ultimately, it is in the highly-wrought labyrinths of Mrs. Gamp's speech that the former architectural student, John Westlock, is able to discover an "outlet from this maze of difficulty" which surrounds the Tigg-Jonas-Lewsome relationship (xlviii, 744). In Mrs. Gamp's remarks about Mr. Chuffey and what he has said concerning the death of Anthony Chuzzlewit, John finds "a new way out, developed in a quarter until then overlooked" (xlviii, 745). As Jonas waits and watches for the avenue of discovery, John, Tom, and old Martin, with Mrs. Gamp as their snuffy Ariadne, find their way through the maze to the avenue leading to Jonas' door.

Mr. Nadgett, also one of the accusers of Jonas, is an architect of secrets, and his secrets in turn provide Tigg with the materials for the "construction" of a blackmail case against Jonas (xxxviii, 592). As a spy whose task it is to find out secrets while remaining secret himself, Mr. Nadgett's relationship to the architectural city is double. On the one hand, he is a product of it; he is of "a race peculiar to the City." (xxvii, 448). On the other hand, he exploits it, controls it, and even creates it. He opens doors "no wider than was sufficient for his passage out"; he always appears at Tigg's house in Pall Mall "as if he had that moment come up a trap"; and he is seen, always waiting for the man who never comes, on 'Change, at Garraway's, at the Bull in Holborn, in Kingsgate Street, in Cornhill, at the Mourning Coach Horse, and on London Bridge (xxvii, 448; xxxviii, 591). He pervades every part of the architectural city, calling our attention to these parts and relating them to each other. Not only does he construct the city as a coherent system of interrelationships by his presence in all of its parts, but he actually brings into existence certain architectural features by his mere presence in them or secret use of them—features such as the trap he comes up at Tigg's, the Mourning Coach Horse where he waits, and "that garret-window opposite" from which he spies on Jonas (li, 790).

Mr. Nadgett's garret-window, which is called into existence solely for the purpose of observing and trapping Jonas, is reminiscent of the window seen from the top of Todgers'. In the Todgers' view, the "man who was mending a pen at an upper window over the way" makes a disproportionate "blank" in the scene when he disappears from it (ix, 130). The window disappears with the man, leaving only a void in the nervous clutter of undifferentiated architectural features. Todgers' itself exists only to the extent that it is inhabited by Mrs. Todgers, the servants, and the "commercial gentlemen who helped to make up the sum and substance of that noun of multitude or signifying many, called Todgers's" (ix, 133). The damp side of the cistern which, according to Mrs. Todgers, "is Mr. Jinkins's" is a case in point (viii, 126). This damp side exists in the mind of the reader and in the minds of the characters only because Mr. Jinkins is relegated to it and is inseparable from it. Similarly, Bailey Jr. (named after the Old Bailey) pervades "all parts of the house," bringing them to existence in our consciousness, including a "garret window" from which he watches Jonas depart with the Pecksniff sisters (ix, 141; xi, 175). But Bailey's relationship to the Todgers' architecture is also reciprocal; he, like Mr. Nadgett, is a product of the architecture he pervades and shapes. For example, when he leaves Todgers' to take service with Tigg, he complains of the cockade on his new hat: "except that it don't turn round, it's like the wentilator that used to be in the kitchen winder at Todgers's" (xxvi, 420). He can not entirely escape

Todgers', but then the ventilator that used to be in the window of Todgers' kitchen has no existence apart from Bailey.

Mrs. Todgers, however, is the most influential architect of Todgers'. The house everywhere bears the shape of her commercial interests. It is, in fact, an extension or a projection of the inner construction of her heart: "But in some odd nook in Mrs. Todgers's breast, up a great many steps and in a corner easy to be overlooked, there was a secret door, with 'Woman' written on the spring" (xxxvii, 585). It is this labyrinthine architecture of the heart which ultimately is reflected in the world while remaining hidden from the world behind some hypocritical façade. As Mrs. Gamp puts it: "But we never knows wot's hidden in each other's hearts; and if we had glass winders there, we'd need keep the shetters up, some on us, I do assure you" (xxix, 464).

What is usually hidden in the architecture of the heart, although Mrs. Gamp would not admit it of herself, is the love of self. "At every turn," exclaims old Martin Chuzzlewit, is found "Self, self, self" (li, 788). The irony of this statement—which draws upon the labyrinth metaphor of the turn which is always the same—is, of course, that old Martin, the titular head of the house of Chuzzlewit, has initiated the selfish action in the novel. He drives young Martin from the house, accusing him of selfishness in his love for Mary Graham. While there is some truth to old Martin's accusation, the whole truth, as he admits at the end of the novel, is that the love between young Martin and Mary interfered with "the grace of his design"—his design that young Martin and Mary should fall in love by his direction and according to his plan (lii, 808). His own self-love has led him to attempt to be the architect of the young lovers' love. But the final irony at the expense of the old chief architect and head of the house of Chuzzlewit is that he, like King Lear, is houseless, an unaccommodated man. He tells Mr. Pecksniff, to whom he has flown for "refuge": "I have no fixed abode" (x, 157, 163). Houseless, he lives at various hotels in the city.

— 2 —

The architectural city, comprising the many houses of the house of Chuzzlewit, is a spatial construction. As such, it occupies and creates space: it defines the human community in spatial terms: void and mass, inner and outer, simple and complex, connected and disconnected. Urban space, or more exactly the lack of it, was largely responsible for the extent of the damage caused by the Great Fire. And space was the apparent concern of those architects who rebuilt the city. The Monument, for example, stands 202 feet high, the distance of its base from the baker's shop in Pudding Lane where the Great Fire broke out. It has on the south side of its base an inscription referring to the provisions of the Parliamentary Act for the rebuilding of the city: "the bridges, gates, and prisons should be new made, the sewers cleansed, the streets made straight and regular, such as were steep levelled, and those too narrow made wider, markets and shambles removed to separate places."[10] The Monument measures space, and the inscription on its base describes the more spacious rebuilding of the city.

But the view of the city from the top of Todgers', which is similar to the view from the top of the Monument, reveals only "steeples, towers, belfries, shining vanes, and masts of ships: a very forest. Gables, housetops, garret-windows, wilderness upon wilderness" (ix, 130). Because of selfish and hypocritical rebuilding and overcrowding, the view from the top conveys no clear definition of spatial (and hence human) relationships. The man-made architectural space takes on the random, chaotic qualities of a forest or wilderness, indicating a loss of human values in the city and anticipating the more literal wilderness city of Eden. Urban space is thus violated and exploited by selfish economic interests to the point of the almost total loss of meaningful human order and relationships. And this, ironically, is the new city memorialized in spatial terms by the Monument.

Upon closer examination at ground level, however, the city wilderness does reveal a structural pattern, or non-pattern, for which Dickens supplies the metaphor "labyrinth" or "maze" (ix, 127). According to Northrop Frye, a labyrinth is, in archetypal terms, "the image of lost direction"; according to Jorge Luis Borges, a labyrinth is, in architectural terms, "a structure compounded to confuse men; its architecture, rich in symmetries, is subordinated to that end."[11] The labyrinth of the architectural city in *Martin Chuzzlewit* is indeed an image of lost direction—direction lost through the inordinate love of self and the corollary exploitation of others. Dickens' urban labyrinth, through the endless repetition of its parts, is also an architectural construction contrived to baffle men, to frustrate relationships, and to discourage inquiry as to meanings and reasons. The architectural city is thus a vast spatial continuum of interlocking labyrinths, each of which is, with minor variations, like the other. And each of these interlocked labyrinths on the continuum represents a version of the house of Chuzzlewit.

So vast and all-inclusive is the labyrinth of the architectural city that it embraces every human habitation in the novel. It winds inward to embrace such Chuzzlewitian environments as Todgers', the warehouse of Anthony Chuzzlewit and Son, Mrs. Gamp's apartment in Kingsgate Street, Tigg's Anglo-Bengalee, and the Temple. It winds outward to include various far-flung Chuzzlewitian locations, such as Wiltshire, Liverpool, and the American Eden. It coils through Wiltshire, which is the architectural residence of Mr. Pecksniff, the site of Salisbury Cathedral which figures so prominently in Mr. Pecksniff's architectural exercises, and, ironically, the birthplace of Sir Christopher Wren.[12] It extends through Liverpool, which is the location of the eccentric tavern designed by a drunken architect, the site of the grammar school stolen from Martin by Mr. Pecksniff, and the point of arrival and departure between the Old and New Worlds. And finally, the labyrinth reaches into the depths of America: the home of Pawkins's board-inghouse, the site of the National Hotel, and the domain of the wilderness in which Martin, as Dickens before him, sails down the river (as Dickens writes in *American Notes*) past a "somber maze of boughs" and through "a labyrinth of floating logs" to the architectural city of Eden (xi, 161; xiv, 186). And here, in Eden, Martin, the outcast from the house of Chuzzlewit, comes to know the nature of himself and of the labyrinth—that Eden is, after all, another version of the cursed house of Chuzzlewit which is every-where self-love exists. He discovers, as Borges' Minotaur discovers of his labyrinth, that "all the parts of the house are repated many times, any place is another place. . . . The house is the same size as the world; or rather, it is the world."[13]

Within the labyrinth of the architectural city, each of the Chuzzlewitian habitations is hidden and can only be approached indirectly. Most famous-ly, Todgers' is located in "a labyrinth, whereof the mystery was known but to a chosen few" (ix, 127). The uninitiated stranger wanders "in and out and round about" and "back again," unable to reach his goal (ix, 127). The mazy difficulties encountered in trying to find or to approach Todgers' are recapitulated, with variations, in all the environments in the novel. Thus, the firm of Anthony Chuzzlewit and Son is located "in a very narrow street somewhere behind the Post Office" (xi, 175). Mr. Mould's establishment is buried "deep in the City . . . within the ward of Cheap," and his sitting room is located "at the back, over the little counting-house behind the shop; abutting on a churchyard small and shady" (xxv, 401). And Mrs. Gamp's apartment is located "at a bird-fancier's, next door but one to the cele-brated mutton-pie shop, and directly opposite to the original cat's-meat warehouse" (xix, 310). This indirection is everywhere repeated, even in America. In New York, which, as an American city, has straight streets, Colonel Diver leads Martin and Mark circuitously to the office of the Rowdy Journal: "Presently they turned up a narrow street, and presently into other narrow streets, until at last they stopped before a house" (xvi, 260).

Even the less sinister or less unpleasant environments in the city par-take of this mazy indirection. Tom and Ruth Pinch live in Islington in "a singular little old-fashioned house, up a blind street" (xxxvi, 576). Mr. Fips' ghostly office in Austin Friars is found "in a very dark passage on the first floor, oddly situated at the back of a house, across some leads" (xxxix, 609). And Tom Pinch's place of employment in the Temple can be found only by passing "through sundry lanes and courts, into one more quiet and more gloomy than the rest" (xxxix, 612). Even the Monument is hidden in such a maze:

> Mr. Pecksniff, with one of the young ladies under each arm, dived
> across the street, and then across other streets, and so up the

queerest courts, and down the strangest alleys and under the blind-
est archways, in a kind of frenzy . . . now thinking he had lost his
way, now thinking he had found it . . . until at length they stopped
in a kind of paved yard near the Monument. (viii, 122)

Ultimately, each of these hidden or difficult-to-find places is intercon-
nected by an infinity of "countless turnings, and . . . countless mazy ways"
(xxxvi, 563). Tom Pinch, for example, becomes lost in the connecting mazes
which lie between Islington and Furnival's Inn:

So on he went, looking up all the streets he came near, and going up
half of them; and thus, by dint of not being true to Goswell Street,
and filing off into Aldermanbury and bewildering himself in Barbi-
can, and being constant to the wrong point of the compass in London
Wall, and then getting himself crosswise into Thames Street . . . he
found himself . . . hard by the Monument. (xxxvii, 578)

The Man in the Monument, Tom thinks, ought to be able to direct him out
of these mazes to his destination in Furnival's Inn, for "if Truth didn't live
in the base of the Monument, notwithstanding Pope's couplet about the outside of it, where in London . . . was she likely to be found!" (xxxvii, 579).
But Tom is chagrined to find that the Man in the Monument is a cynic who
charges an entrance fee for the privilege of climbing the "long winding staircase" to the top while exclaiming: "They don't know what a many steps there
is! . . . It's worth twice the money to stop here" (xxxvii, 579).[14] The Monument, in other words, is a deceptive commercial enterprise. Its outward appearance belies the long spiral staircase—a vertical labyrinth—within. Truth
may not reside at the base of the Monument, but it may reside inside the
Monument on the spiral staircase leading to the top and the view from the
top. This view from the top, like the view from the top of Todgers', may reveal all too clearly the truth of disturbing discontinuities created by self-love
and hypocrisy. The viewer of the architectural city might be tempted to
come down "into the street by the shortest cut; that is to say, head-fore-
most" (ix, 131).[15]
      As a commercial structure which stands within a maze and which is it-
self internally organized as a maze, the Monument epitomizes the many
houses of Chuzzlewit which are also commercial and inwardly mazy. Todgers' commercial boardinghouse, for example, is not only located within a
maze, but is itself constructed internally as a maze. Internally, Todgers'
consists of "a maze of bedrooms," "remote back kitchens," a drawing-room
which would not have been taken for such "unless you were told so by somebody who was in the secret," "the oddest closets possible, with little case-
ments in them like eight-day clocks, lurking in the wainscot and taking the
shape of the stairs," and a cellarage which "had no connexion with the
house" (xi, 170; ix, 129, 141-43). Amid these complexities of inner struc-

ture are found numerous windows which provide little light or air, offer almost no outward views, and stare disturbingly inward at the inhabitants. For example, a skylight looks "distrustfully down at everything that passed below," the back parlor windows command "at a perspective of two feet, a brown wall with a black cistern on the top," and the drawing-room door has "two great glass eyes in its forehead, with an inquisitive green pupil in the middle of each" (viii, 124, 126; ix, 143). Such is the labyrinth of Todgers'.

This inward-looking, inward-turning architectural complexity is not merely a Dickensian exercise in oddity; it is an expression of the hypocritical dominance of commercial interests over personal and private needs. It is hypocritical because the uncomfortable commercial expediencies are continually disguised as personal, domestic comforts. Thus it is that Mrs. Todgers can boast that the back-parlor windows, which look out on the wall and cistern, have the "great advantage (in London) of not being overlooked" (viii, 126). Not only does she ignore the fact that the windows provide merely an unpleasant and claustrophobic view, but she forgets to mention that the window in the drawing room looks "point blank, without any compromise at all about it, into Jinkins's bedroom" (ix, 143). In sacrificing the human need both of privacy and community to the commercial exploitation of space, Todgers' is not a house at all; it is only a commercial labyrinth disguised as such.

Similarly, the house of Anthony Chuzzlewit and Son is literally a warehouse in which business shoulders "comfort out of doors" and crowds "domestic arrangements at every turn" (xi, 176). In the bedrooms, for example, the beds, washstands, and carpets are "huddled away into corners as objects of secondary consideration," leaving the offices available for sleeping-quarters (xi, 176). The office in which Jonas pretends to sleep the night before he murders Tigg had once "been a yard; and had been converted to its present purpose for use as an office. But the occasion for it died with the man who built it" (xlvi, 718). The open space of the back yard is absorbed by the useless commercial extension of the house. But this extension, which, like Todgers' cellarage, has little connection with the main house, does provide Jonas with access to "a door in the wall, opening into a narrow covered passage or blind-alley" which opens in turn into "a neighbouring street" (xlvi, 718). By means of such architectural ramifications, Jonas' room is connected both with the main house and with the larger labyrinths of the city.

In addition, the house of Anthony Chuzzlewit and Son is, like Todgers', constructed with a number of inward-looking windows. When Jonas reads his father's will inside the office with the glass partition, he looks up startled to see Mr. Pecksniff's face "on the other side of the glass partition looking curiously in" (xviii, 301). After his father's death, Jonas avoids "the reflection in the opposite windows of the light that burned above, as though it had been an angry eye" (xix, 319). On the evening before he murders

Tigg, he waits for nightfall in the unused back office under "a dirty skylight" —a skylight reminiscent of the dirty skylight which looks down into Todgers' (xlvi, 718). After he murders Tigg, Jonas, on the night of his exposure, looks out his window into a shop window where he sees some men reading a printed paper, and he sees, as in a mirror, the men act out "the blow he had struck in the wood" (li, 778). When his exposure does come, he finds that Nadgett has watched him from the opposite garret window; and when his fate is sealed, he bribes Slyme into allowing him five minutes in the glass-partitioned office while Slyme diverts the attention of his fellow officers down in the street by conversing with them from the window. Jonas is caught in the trap of his selfish schemes—a trap objectified in the many-windowed architectural labyrinth of his commercial house.

While the warehouse-home of Anthony and Jonas has few pretensions to domesticity or even to commercial impressiveness, it is suited to and expresses its inhabitants. It is, as Jonas jokingly remarks to the Pecksniff sisters, "Bachelor's Hall," and as such it is an extremely unpleasant and uncomfortable "home" to which Mercy Pecksniff is welcomed as Jonas' wife— a home justly suited (at least temporarily) for the chastisement of so mercenary an architect's daughter (xi, 177; xxvi, 426). Similarly, Mr. Mould's house, as J. Hillis Miller has discussed at length, is also suited to and an expression of him and his family.[16] The coffin shop and countinghouse below, the view of the graveyard outside, the press "whose mahogany maw was filled with shrouds, and winding-sheets, and other furniture of funerals" are all comfortable extensions of Mr. Mould and his business interests (xxv, 402). But to anyone not involved in the funeral industry, Mr. Mould's funeral house with all of its morbid ramifications could not help but be uncomfortable. In like manner, Mrs. Gamp's painfully cramped apartment, with its giant bedstead, treacherous chest of drawers, slippery chairs, tumbling wooden pippins, and hanging effigies of herself, is uncomfortable—if not dangerous—to the outsider. To Mrs. Gamp, however, it is a pleasant and "stately pile" (xlix, 747). While Mrs. Gamp's apartment reflects the deviousness and deadliness of her ways, it is only a part, like Todgers' cellarage and Jonas' room, of a larger complex of rooms in which vocation and avocation drive comfort out of doors. Poll Sweedlepipe's house in which Mrs. Gamp resides is, with the exception of her apartment and the staircase leading to it, a "great bird's nest" (xxvi, 418). The house which Tigg Montague converts into the Anglo-Bengalee, "resplendent in stucco and plate-glass," and the house which the brass and copper founder constructs as a "giant's castle" are further variations on those Chuzzlewitian labyrinths in which domesticity is sacrificed to commercial pursuits (xxvii, 432; ix, 134).

In the spatial continuum of the architectural city, however, the purest examples of comfort sacrificed to commerce are to be found in America. Since the Americans are more blatantly and less deviously hypocritical than the English, their habitations are more obviously commercial. New York, while it contains numerous turnings, is memorable in the novel primarily for its long rows "of staring red-brick storehouses and offices, ornamented with more black boards and white letters, and more white boards and black letters, than Martin had ever seen before" (xvi, 260). The Americans make the best possible use of architectural space, employing it only for storage, work, and advertising. Pawkins' boardinghouse, for example—an American version of Todgers'—reduces the business of boarding to the barest essentials. Pawkins' main room is "exquisitely uncomfortable: having nothing in it but the four cold white walls and ceiling, a mean carpet, a dreary waste of dining-table reaching from end to end, and a bewildering collection of cane-bottomed chairs" (xvi, 266). In contrast to this oppressive emptiness, Martin's bedroom at Pawkins' consists of "a very little narrow room, with half a window in it" (xvii, 295). Compared to the empty monotony and rigorous denial of human comforts found at Pawkins', Todgers', for all of its cramped angularity, seems almost cozy.

As Todgers' is repeated throughout England, Pawkins' is repeated throughout America. That "immense white edifice" known as the National Hotel is simply a larger version of Pawkins':

> There was a great bar-room in this hotel, and a great public room in which the general table was being set out for supper. There were interminable whitewashed staircases, long whitewashed galleries upstairs and down-stairs, scores of little whitewashed bedrooms, and a four-sided verandah to every story in the house, which formed a large brick square with an uncomfortable court-yard in the centre. (xxi, 350)

The National Hotel is oppressive not only because of its emptiness, coldness, and vastness, but because of its labyrinth effect of being everywhere and in all of its parts the same. As young Martin finds out, domestic architecture in America is almost nonexistent: Americans, as does old Martin Chuzzlewit, live in hotels. Dickens writes in *American Notes* that the saddest tomb he saw in the New York cemetery was "The Strangers' Grave. Dedicated to the different hotels in this city" (vi, 95).

The immense vacuity of the National Hotel is epitomized in Dickens' description in *American Notes* of the city of Washington. Washington, with its "spacious avenues, that begin in nothing, and lead nowhere," is, Dickens concludes, "a monument raised to a deceased project, with not even a legible inscription to record its departed greatness" (viii, 116-17). London and its Monument, for all of their architectural hypocrisies, are at least eloquent of the past, present, and future. American cities, Dickens seems to feel, are evocative of no such past and suggestive of no future. Even Philadelphia, which has some claim to historical and architectural interest, Dickens finds "distractingly regular," and he concludes: "After walking about it for an hour or two, I felt that I would have given the world for a crooked street" (vii, 98). The labyrinthine complexity of English cities is preferable to the commercial monotony of American cities. In *American Notes,* Dickens says farewell to his dreams of "cities growing up, like palaces in fairy tales, among the wilds and forests of the west" (viii, 127). And in so doing, he says farewell to Eden.

When Dickens returns home from America, he looks with relief, as he writes in *American Notes,* upon "the spires, and roofs, and smoke, of Liverpool" (xvi, 227). Similarly, when Martin and Mark view Liverpool after a year's absence, their hearts are gladdened at the sight of the old architectural jumble—"the old churches, roofs, and darkened chimney stacks of Home" (xxxv, 548). There is in such old labyrinthine cities—however steeped in centuries of selfishness and hypocrisy—a charming irregularity and smoky patina that are irresistible to Dickens and his characters. The Liverpool tavern room in which Martin and Mark relax after their arduous journey is totally non-American in its functionless oddity and angularity:

> It was one of those unaccountable little rooms which are never seen anywhere but in a tavern, and are supposed to have got into taverns by reason of the facilities afforded to the architect for getting drunk while engaged in their construction. It had more corners in it than the brain of an obstinate man; was full of mad closets, into which nothing could be put that was not specially invented and made for that purpose; had mysterious shelvings and bulkheads, and indications of staircases in the ceiling, and was elaborately provided with a bell that rung in the room itself, about two feet from the handle, and had no connexion whatever with any other part of the establishment. (xxxv, 549)

This crazily constructed tavern room is, of course, another version of Todgers'; and while, like Todgers', it contains many inconveniences and discontinuities, it is, unlike its American counterparts, interestingly irregular and thoroughly humanized. In this room, comfort is at least a possibility. And it is from the window of this room that Martin and Mark have the good fortune to observe Mr. Pecksniff pass by on his way to the dedication of the grammar school he has stolen from Martin. The Liverpool tavern room thus reaffirms the spatial continuum of the architectural city which stretches from London to Eden and back by way of Liverpool where, from the irregular tavern room, Martin and Mark are led to Mr. Pecksniff and the stolen grammar school.

As Dickens' treatment of the tavern room in Liverpool suggests, many of the English environments, in spite of their architectural irregularity, need not be uncomfortable or expressive only of selfish, commercial pursuits. Mrs. Lupin's Blue Dragon, for example, is an old and potentially uncomfortable commercial establishment. Yet, under the good auspices of the warm-hearted landlady, the Dragon provides a pleasant home for several characters in the novel. Old Martin's room, in spite of the "low roof and a sunken flooring, all down-hill from the door, and a descent of two steps on the inside so exquisitely unexpected," is a "good, dull, drowsy place, where every article of furniture reminded you that you came there to sleep, and that you were expected to go to sleep" (ii, 28).

Mrs. Lupin's soporific rooms at the Blue Dragon set the standard early in the novel for comfort. Her standards are duplicated in London and elsewhere. For example, John Westlock's bachelor's quarters in Furnival's Inn are quite pleasant compared to Jonas' bachelor's hall:

> There are snug chambers in those Inns where the bachelors live, and, for the desolate fellows they pretend to be, it is quite surprising how well they get on. John was very pathetic on the subject of his dreary life . . . but he really seemed to make himself pretty comfortable. His rooms were the perfection of neatness and convenience at any rate; and if he were anything but comfortable, the fault was certainly not theirs. (xlv, 691)

For all of John's mild hypocrisies to the contrary, his old inn lodgings are comfortable in themselves and made more so by his efforts. Ruth Pinch also is able to transform the room she and Tom rent in Islington into a charming habitation: "No doll's house ever yielded greater delight to its young mistress, than little Ruth derived from her glorious dominion over the triangular parlour and the two small bedrooms" (xxxix, 599). Even a three-sided parlor and small rooms rented from Mr. Nadgett can be made over into a cheerful and convenient home. And while Ruth transforms the Islington house into a home, Tom, employing his architectural skills, transforms the dusty old rooms in the Temple into a home for old Martin: "It looked a different place, it was so orderly and neat. Tom felt some pride in contemplating the change he had wrought, though there was no one to approve or disapprove of it" (l, 770). John, Ruth, and Tom are good architects who, through unselfish actions, transform their parts of the architectural city for the better.

Through the agency of honest and unselfish actions at least part of the architectural city can be transformed into a viable community: order can be created out of chaos, homes can be made out of commercial establishments, and the house of Chuzzlewit can be built anew. Even the Man in the Monument, cynic that he is, can transform his "stony and artificial" residence into a home sweet with country memories—"he liked plants, hung up bird-cages, was not wholly cut off from fresh groundsel, and kept young trees in tubs" (xxxvii, 579).

— 3 —

If the architectural city, comprising the houses of Chuzzlewit, is a spatial construction, it is also a temporal one. Cities, as Lewis Mumford says, "are a product of time": they are constructed in time, experienced in time, and ended in time.[17] Because a city is a continuum of past, present, and future spatial structures—an architectural space in process, created and known in time—it is a temporal as well as a spatial continuum. And in this continuum, spatial structures—because of their varying ages and functions —make time visible. Or, as Mumford states it: "In the city, time becomes visible: buildings and monuments and public ways . . . leave an imprint upon the minds even of the ignorant or the indifferent."[18]

While all of the structures in the architectural city of *Martin Chuzzlewit* exist in time and make time visible, it is the special function of the Monument to do so. Depicted among the various allegorical figures on the west base of the Monument is the figure of Time, winged and bald, helping to raise prostrate London from her ruins. On the north side of the base is recorded the date of the beginning of the Great Fire, 2 September 1666. Along with this date, there is an inscription warning that the Monument exists as a constant spatial reminder of that past time and as a reminder of that future time "of the final destruction of the world by fire."[19] Ultimately, the sculpted bowl of flames on the very top of the Monument is the most obvious reminder of the fire that is past and of the fire that is to come.

So visible is this pillar surmounted by its flames that in *David Copperfield,* for example, David, while waiting on London Bridge for the opening of the King's Bench prison, can watch the early morning sun "lighting up the golden flame on the top of the Monument" (xi, 167). In *Martin Chuzzlewit,* not only does the Monument stand visible above the city, horrified at its doings, but "the shadow of the Monument" falls on the "housetops, stretching far away, a long dark path," marking time as if it were the shadow cast by the gnomon of a gigantic sundial (ix, 130). The Monument then is a visible embodiment of London's past, present, and future: the Great Fire of 1666 and the rebuilding of the city, the duration of time marked by the Monument's shadow in the present, and the onrushing "Day of Judgment" when the architectural city and the house of Chuzzlewit will come to an end at the end of time (xxvii, 459).

As we are told at the beginning of the novel, the house of Chuzzlewit is an ancient house. It begins with Adam and Eve in Eden and extends down through Cain, the first murderer and city builder, through Guy Fawkes, the would-be destroyer of the Houses of Parliament, down to the present generation of Chuzzlewits. The present generation is atavistic, including, as it does, Jonas who, Cain-like, attempts to murder his father and succeeds in murdering his spiritual brother Tigg; Mr. Pecksniff who, Guy Fawkes-like, possesses plans for "Houses of Parliament" and for a "powder-magazine"; and young Martin who, Adam-like, is driven by his grandfather from the house of Chuzzlewit to seek his architectural way in the American Eden (ii, 14; v, 81).

Immediately after the conclusion of this mock genealogy of the ancient house of Chuzzlewit—a house which includes everyone—Dickens switches, in the second chapter, to the late autumn sun setting on the "vane upon the tapering spire of the old church" (ii, 7). The sun sets upon the spire and is extinguished by the "long dark lines of hill and cloud which piled up in the west an airy city" (ii, 8). This conjunction of spire and airy city anticipates by analogy not only the "constructing in the air a vast quantity of Castles, Houses of Parliament, and other Public Buildings" by the Chuzzlewitian architects, but also the Monument and the initial description of London as "a city in the clouds" (ii, 14; viii, 122). In addition, the Wiltshire spire casts "a long reflection on the grave-yard grass: as if it were a dial (alas, the truest in the world!) marking, whatever light shone out of Heaven, the flight of days and weeks and years, by some new shadow on that solemn ground" (v, 77).[20] In like manner, the Monument casts its shadow over the numerous little churchyards in the neighborhood, churchyards which bear "much the same analogy to green churchyards, as the pots of earth for mignonette and wall-flower in the windows overlooking them did to rustic gardens" (ix, 128). The Monument, like the Wiltshire spire, stands as a gigantic gnomon, casting its ever-moving shadow over the habitations of the living and the dead, over all the generations of the house of Chuzzlewit.

The Wiltshire sundial spire, which anticipates the sundial-Monument, is kept before the reader's eyes in the early parts of the novel by Dickens' several references to it and by Mr. Pecksniff's showing Martin the "room in which an idea for a steeple occured to me, that I may one day give to the world" (v, 81). It is recapitulated in the frequent early references to Salisbury Cathedral which boasts the grandest spire in England. Mr. Pecksniff shows Martin elevations of Salisbury Cathedral made from every point of the compass, and Tom Pinch, upon entering Salisbury, hears the cathedral's vesper bell ring and sees its towers rise before him (v, 72; xii, 197). These spires, towers, and the plans for them—along with Mr. Pecksniff's plans for Houses of Parliament, a powder magazine, and "a monument to a Lord Mayor of London"—prepare the reader for architectural London and the Monument near Todgers' (vi, 87).

London, in which Todgers' cellarage is reputed by some to be filled with gunpowder and over which the Monument casts its shadow, is redolent of the past, especially of those past architectural threats to the city—the Gunpowder Plot and the Great Fire. The architectural mazes which surround the Monument also bespeak the past. Amid the intertwining streets and alleys are found old "solitary pumps" and "fire-ladders," forgotten churches and overgrown churchyards, an occasional "ancient doorway" of a mansion converted into a warehouse, wine shops and wholesale grocers grown over the years into "little towns of their own," and "queer old taverns" ghostly with the memories of the "quaint old guests who frequented their dimly-lighted parlours" so many years ago (ix, 127-29). Here, too, is found Todgers', that ancient boardinghouse, hemmed in and crushed by the encroaching city, a "century's mud" layered on its single staircase window and a cellarage not connected to the house "within the memory of man" (ix, 129). Beneath these and other "familiar objects," Time, the ultimate architect and destroyer, burrows like a mole, marking his track "by throwing up another heap of earth," and constructing thereby that definitive architectural structure, the grave (xviii, 298; xix, 325).

While London and the Monument evoke the past and the dead citizens of the past, they exist in and are experienced in the present. In the present, all the characters in the novel move through London to keep their various appointments with each other. The Monument, as the most visible architectural expression of time in the city, provides, within the shadow of its gnomon, a significant place for keeping appointments—for making connections in the spatial and temporal continuum of the city. Thus, Mr. Pecksniff and his daughters, after many devious turns, end up "in a kind of paved yard near the Monument" to keep their early morning appointment at Todgers' (viii, 122). Shortly afterwards, old Martin Chuzzlewit arrives at the Monument to keep his appointment with Mr. Pecksniff; but before he enters Todgers', he loiters "in a gleam of sunlight, that brightened the little churchyard hard by" where "there may have been, in the presence of those idle heaps of dust among the busiest stir of life, something to increase his wavering" (x,155). The sundial-Monument and the nearby graves remind him of the final appointment he must keep. Several other characters also converge upon the Monument at different times. Jonas Chuzzlewit arrives at the Monument and Todgers' "at the jocund time of noon" (xi, 170). Mark and Martin, while in New York, make in effect a mental appointment "to see the Monument" and to "get to the top" (xvii, 296). Charity Pecksniff, after leaving her father's house, seeks refuge at her "peaceful home beneath the shadow of the Monument" (xxxii, 506). And Tom Pinch, in attempting to keep his appointment with John Westlock at Furnival's Inn, loses his way and finds himself "hard by the Monument" where he accidently encounters Charity Pecksniff (xxxvii, 578). Finally, on the fateful morning of Charity's wedding, many members of the house of Chuzzlewit converge upon the Monument and Todgers'. Mark and old Martin drive up in a carriage and stop near the Monument where shortly afterward Mark discovers the American neighbors from Eden and embraces them "over and over again, in Monument Yard" (liv, 827, 832). Of the Chuzzlewitian characters who are in one way or another associated with Todgers', only Mr. Moddle, Charity's groom, fails to keep his appointment near the Monument.

As a marker of time and coordinator of time and space for the keeping of appointments, the Monument is the center of a vast system of architecturally expressed time, a system of "steeples, towers, belfries, shining vanes . . . a very forest" (ix, 130). From the thirteenth century on, writes Mumford, "the bells of the clock tower almost defined urban existence."[21] In the

architectural city of *Martin Chuzzlewit,* human interactions are often so defined. Old Martin Chuzzlewit loiters near the Monument "until the church
clock, striking the quarters for the second time . . . roused him from his med-
itation" (x, 155). If old Martin is roused, young Martin, who has pawned
his watch in London, is not. Mark Tapley must repeatedly remind Martin,
during his clandestine and selfish meeting with Mary Graham in St. James'
Park, that "the clock at the Horse Guards was striking" (xiv, 241). Porten-
tiously, Martin and Mark depart for the New World with the "church-
towers humming with the faint vibration of their own tongues, but newly
resting from the ghostly preachment 'One' " (xv, 245). In America, they hear
the Watertoast Sympathizers cheer in defiance of England "such cheers . . .
as might have shaken the hands upon the Horse-Guards' clock, and changed
the very mean time of the day in England's capital" (xxi, 359). And in Eden,
Martin and Mark, through the agency of a near-fatal fever, wander outside
time and space to die to self—a necessary precondition of their rebirth and
reentry into the world. They must lose time in an almost-death in order to
gain time and learn how to live in it unselfishly and well.

While Martin and Mark journey outside of time and space, the Chuzzlewitian characters back in London go about their daily time routines, often to no very good purpose. For example, Mr. Nadgett, who is always
looking at the clock and keeping appointments with the man who never
comes, invariably appears at Tigg's in Pall Mall "when the clocks were
striking nine" (xxxviii, 591). Mrs. Gamp, too, is punctual. She arrives at
the Bull in Holborn to begin her nursing of Lewsome just "as the clocks
were striking eight" (xxv, 408). Such punctuality, of course, may represent
an abuse of time. Mrs. Gamp says that "all times of the day and night" are
"equally the same" to her, and when she attempts to prove the existence of
Mrs. Harris to John Westlock, she creates an imaginary appointment in the
city: "Don't I know as that dear woman is expecting of me at this minnit . . .
and is a-lookin' out of window down the street, with little Tommy Harris in
her arms" (xxix, 463; xlix, 759). In other words, Mrs. Gamp, like Nadgett
and so many others, distorts and exploits time as well as space.

Of such exploitation of time under the guise of punctuality and appointment keeping, Dickens has Tom Pinch say to the brass and copper founder
concerning the payment of Ruth's wages: "You may be punctual in that to
half a second on the clock, and yet be Bankrupt" (xxxvi, 571). Mr. Fips is
pleased with Tom's honest sense of time and makes his working hours at the
Temple flexible: "Let us say from half-past nine to four, or half-past four, or
thereabouts; one day, perhaps, a little earlier, another day, perhaps, a little later, according as you feel disposed, and as you arrange your work"
(xxxix, 613). Every day Tom faithfully does his work, adhering to this sched-
ule and expecting the appointment with his unknown benefactor that he
knows some time must come.

Tom's patient waiting for the appointment and the consequent revelation that must occur is part of the larger apocalyptic flow of time in the novel toward the future. As the Monument warns, some future revelation and judgment is to be expected. Early in the novel, Mr. Pecksniff, with unconscious irony, assures his daughters that they shall see London and everything else "All in good time. All in good time" (viii, 126). Later when young Martin is dismissed by Mr. Pecksniff, he prophesies to Tom and Mr. Pecksniff: "The day will come—he knows it . . . when even you will find him out, and will know him as I do, and as he knows I do" (xii, 211). Martin's prophecy comes true, but, before it does and before he finds out about himself, he answers Colonel Diver's dire predictions concerning the fate of England with the evasive and prophetic: "Time will show" (xvi, 258). Indeed, time will show many things concerning Martin and the house of Chuzzlewit. And as the criminal Chuzzlewitians—Tigg, Pecksniff, and Jonas —sink deeper into their fraudulent activities, the apocalyptic utterances increase in frequency and intensity. For, example, when Jonas mistreats Mercy after their marriage, the narrator exclaims in a biblical-apocalyptic apostrophe: "Oh woman, God beloved in old Jerusalem! The best among us need deal lightly with thy faults, if only for the punishment thy nature will endure, in bearing heavy evidence against us on the Day of Judgment" (xxviii, 459). Toward the end of the novel, when the trap begins to close about Jonas, John Westlock prophesies: "We shall gain our end in good time" (xlix, 761). And as old Martin prepares for the exposure of Mr. Pecksniff and the others, including himself, he says: "The time now drawing on . . . will make amends for all" (l, 772).

The most important and dramatic use of apocalyptic time, however, surrounds the character and career of Jonas Chuzzlewit. Jonas, who looks "a year or two" older than his father, is a deadly architect and surveyor who measures "every day and hour the lessening distance between his father and the grave, and cursed his tardy progress on that dismal road" (iv, 54; xxiv, 386). The shortening time is presented in terms of lessening spatial distance. Jonas' unnatural greed and hate speed up time. He not only grows to look older than his father, he succeeds—through his unsuccessful attempt to murder his father—in hastening his father's death. Thus, when Anthony has his fatal seizure, the noises he makes lead Jonas to conclude that there is "something wrong in the clock"; but as he later finds out, "another kind of time-piece was fast running down" (xviii, 306). Because of this and other violations of time, Jonas continually runs afoul of and is trapped in time. Although he is punctual in keeping his appointment at Tigg's "when the appointed hour arrived," he continually fails to notice that, wherever he goes in the city, Mr. Nadgett is keeping appointments with the man who never comes (xxviii, 449). Of course, Jonas is that man. Without knowing it, he always keeps his appointment with Mr. Nadgett. For example, when Jonas is foiled at the last moment in his attempt to escape on the Antwerp packet, he has unknowingly kept his appointment with Mr.

Nadgett who watches patiently from the parapet of London Bridge. In his rage at Tom Pinch for this frustration of his plans, Jonas becomes further a victim of time; he fails to give Tom time to explain about Mr. Nadgett—a failure about which the narrator intones: "If Jonas could have learned, as then he could and would have learned . . . what unsuspected spy there was upon him; he would have been saved from the commission of a Guilty Deed, then drawing on towards its black accomplishment" (xlvi, 713).

Jonas' violation of time and his fatal entanglements in it are particularly noticeable in his disturbed responses to its architectural expression in bell towers. He informs Tigg, for example, that he arises early in the mornings because "it's better to be up than lying awake, counting the dismal old church-clocks, in bed" (xxxviii, 595). Such is the measure of his restless guilt. Later, when he and Tigg journey into Wiltshire to keep their appointment with Mr. Pecksniff, flashes of lightning illuminate minutely "bells in steeples, with the rope and wheel that moved them" (xlii, 646). This strangely incandescent scene reveals Jonas' intention to murder Tigg, to shorten the time of another life. Bells which toll the passing hours and which are also potential alarm bells become increasingly distracting to Jonas in the midst of his murderous, time-violating plans. On the night of his planned departure from London to intercept Tigg and murder him after his appointment with Mr. Pecksniff, Jonas, while berating his wife, is interrupted by the sound of the striking clocks: "He started, stopped and listened: appearing to revert to some engagement . . . a secret within his own breast, recalled to him by this record of the progress of the hours" (xlvi, 714). He is so distracted that before retiring to his office bedroom, he must ask Mercy, "What's the time?" (xlvi, 714).

Inside his office bedroom, however, Jonas is tormented by bells: "The ringers were practicing in a neighbouring church, and the clashing of the bells was almost maddening" (xlvii, 718-19). The bells ringing out of time provide a perfect correlative to Jonas' murderous intentions to violate time. Ultimately, the bells find their way into his dream of a "strange city" in which precipitous streets are crossed by "ropes that moved deep bells, and swung and swayed as they were clung to" (xlvii, 721). The bell-hung dream city is not only an equivalent to London and its pealing bells and striking clocks but is the city of the apocalypse. Here, in this apocalyptic city, Jonas is told that, by virtue of his decision to murder Tigg, he has "appointed" that "wild hurrying to Judgment" that "Last Day for all the world" (xlvii, 721). In violating and exploiting time for his self-loving plans, Jonas disorganizes time (at least in himself) and brings about the end of time for Tigg, for himself, and for the entire bell-haunted city of his schemes.

At the "appointed time," Jonas is trapped, and his crimes are revealed (li, 775). As Mr. Nadgett says: "We chose our time"; and the revelation comes swiftly, joyfully:

> Hark! It came on, roaring like a sea! Hawkers burst into the street, crying it up and down; windows were thrown open that the inhabitants might hear it; people stopped to listen in the road and on the pavement; the bells, the same bells, began to ring: tumbling over one another in a dance of boisterous joy at the discovery. (li, 791,787)

The apocalyptic discovery is expressed in architectural terms: the door through which Jonas' accusers come, the window before which he is exposed, the windows of the other houses which are opened, the people yelling and listening in the streets, and, of course, the bells joyously ringing out the discovery. The architectural city responds to the discovery and amplifies it, signalling the end of time for Jonas. Although he bribes Chevy Slyme for five minutes in the glass-partitioned room, he, like Dostoevsky's Kirilov, needs even more time to kill himself, crying out to Slyme: "You're too soon. . . . I've not had time. I have not been able to do it. I—five minutes more—two minutes more!—Only one" (li, 794). For Jonas, the false architect who exploits and destroys time, there is no more time.

With the unmasking of Mr. Pecksniff (also at the appointed time) and with the confession by old Martin of his selfishness toward young Martin and Mary, the revelations are complete. The curse of self-love is lifted from the house of Chuzzlewit, or at least it is lifted from this main branch of the house. The family is reunited a different family in the Temple rooms which Tom Pinch has transformed into old Martin's home. London also is transformed. It is reconstructed in the eyes of the lovers, Ruth and John: "They went away, but not through London's streets! Through some enchanted city, where . . . everything was happy; where there was no distance, and no time" (liii, 817). For the little community of the unselfish, the architectural city is transformed for the better by love.

But for those who cannot transcend self, the city remains a confused and inhospitable labyrinth. The final convergence of the many Chuzzlewitian characters upon the Monument and the "commercial bowers" of Todgers' for Charity's wedding, and Charity's subsequent "overthrow" by Mr. Moddle before the strong-minded woman and the red-nosed daughters who "towered triumphant," represent a comic version of the earlier more serious defeats of selfishness and revelations of hypocrisy (liv, 826, 836). Charity is left with a "newly-furnished house," and Mr. Pecksniff is left houseless and unhoused, telling his tale of grievance against the "comfortably housed" Tom Pinch to the company of the alehouse (liv, 835, 837). The false architect becomes the houseless, unaccommodated man.

The novel ends (as Phiz's frontispiece illustrates so well) in a "darkening room"—perhaps the architectural music room which young Martin promised to build for Tom Pinch (liv, 817). Here, Tom, the first and best architect of the house of Chuzzlewit, sits at his organ and contrives in the soaring architectonics of his well-beloved music the final happy vision of what is past, passing, and to come. And, as Ruth, "bestrewn with flowers by children's hands," enters from the garden to sit by Tom as he plays, it becomes clear in this final architectonic vision that Eden, the once and future city, is within (liv, 817).

The architectural city, comprising the many houses of Chuzzlewit, is a larger, more complex, and more coherent city than any Dickens had previously created. It is the first city in his novels to express a theme; and in so doing, it prepares for those more organic and thematic cities of *Dombey and Son, Bleak House, Little Dorrit, Our Mutual Friend,* and all the great novels to follow.

Harland S. Nelson

STAGGS'S GARDENS

The Railway Through Dickens' World

AS A city man, Dickens was used to change; his essays early and late in his career deal with it, the late ones more soberly than the early ones; but on the whole he took change as a regular thing in life. In some matters he did more than accept change: he desired and campaigned for it—change in government, in welfare systems, in law, in the living conditions of the poor. One kind of change in the city, however, seems to have caused him a buried uneasiness, and in his writings he regularly connected that kind with the railroad. Both in his novels and in his essays he was talking about physical changes in places. But this kind of change means something important too in the symbolic dimension that the city has in Dickens.

I say his uneasiness is "buried" because it is not usually explicit, and it sometimes appears off to one side of his focus, as in the essay "Railway Dreaming," where Dickens' whimsy is to talk of the Paris he is coming away from as the moon. What puts him in that fancy is the railroad trip:

> I am never sure of time or place upon a Railroad. I can't read, I can't think, I can't sleep—I can only dream. Rattling along in this railway carriage in a state of luxurious confusion, I take it for granted I am coming from somewhere, and going somewhere else. I seek to know no more. Why things come into my head and fly out again, whence they come and why they come, where they go and why they go, I am incapable of considering.[1]

Mr. Dombey's manager Carker has the same trouble (though the consequences are more serious) during his flight after his plot breaks down. At the remote country place where he ends up the waiter must correct him about the day of the week—"Wednesday, Sir? No, Sir. Thursday, Sir"— and tell him the time:

> "Wants a few minutes of five o'clock, Sir. Been travelling a long time, Sir, perhaps?"

[41]

"Yes."
"By rail, Sir?"
"Yes."
"Very confusing, Sir."[2]

The main interest here is that Carker is coming apart; the main interest of
"Railway Dreaming" is Parisian places and people. But central to both
pieces is a kind of disorientation, and travel by railroad produces it. Dickens
comes near being explicit about this in a *Household Words* article, "An
Unsettled Neighbourhood" (11 November 1854). Having set down a considerable list of these changes, Dickens (in the person of the narrator, of
course) denies that he is complaining about any of them:

> But what I do complain of, and what I am distressed at, is, the state
> of mind—the moral condition—into which the neighbourhood has
> got. It is unsettled, dissipated, wandering (I believe nomadic is the
> crack word for that sort of thing just at present), and don't know its
> own mind for an hour.

The tone is humorous, but the point is there: the railroad unsettles the
mind.

Another way the uneasiness about railroads comes out is in the disrup-
tion and the mighty upheaval of things that their coming causes. The specific parallels Dickens makes between the railroad train and Death (in the
often-quoted passage from chapter xx of *Dombey and Son,* and the one less
often quoted from Book IV, chapter xi, of *Our Mutual Friend*) are based on
that; in both passages the narrative argues for the parallel by describing the
train's hurtling progress through every kind of human scene and activity.
But the clearest example is another often-quoted passage from *Dombey
and Son* describing how the neighborhood around Staggs's Gardens is being
devastated to make room for the right of way.

> The first shock of a great earthquake had, just at that period,
> rent the whole neighbourhood to its centre. Traces of its course were
> visible on every side. Houses were knocked down; streets broken
> through and stopped; deep pits and trenches dug in the ground;
> enormous heaps of earth and clay thrown up; buildings that were
> undermined and shaking, propped by great beams of wood. Here, a
> chaos of carts, overthrown and jumbled together, lay topsy-turvy at
> the bottom of a steep unnatural hill; there, confused treasures of
> iron soaked and rusted in something that had accidentally become
> a pond. Everywhere were bridges that led nowhere; thoroughfares
> that were wholly impassable; Babel towers of chimneys, wanting half
> their height; temporary wooden houses and enclosures, in the most
> unlikely situations; carcases of ragged tenements, and fragments of
> unfinished walls and arches, and piles of scaffolding, and wilder-

nesses of bricks, and giant forms of cranes, and tripods straddling above nothing. There were a hundred thousand shapes and sub- stances of incompleteness, wildly mingled out of their places, upside down, burrowing in the earth, aspiring in the air, mouldering in the water, and unintelligible as any dream. Hot springs and fiery erup- tions, the usual attendants upon earthquakes, lent their contribu- tions of confusion to the scene. Boiling water hissed and heaved with- in dilapidated walls; whence, also, the glare and roar of flames came issuing forth; and mounds of ashes blocked up rights of way, and wholly changed the law and custom of the neighbourhood.

In short, the yet unfinished and unopened Railroad was in progress; and, from the very core of all this dire disorder, trailed smoothly away, upon its mighty course of civilisation and improve- ment. (vi)

The tone here is not exactly apprehensive; it sounds more like awe. And of course later this chaos is entirely subdued by a bustling new order (xv). That new order, though—like the new order brought about by the railroad in "An Unsettled Neighbourhood"—is not entirely reassuring; it is possible too that even in this passage the "mighty course of civilisation and improve- ment," rising from such a hellish core, is not only iron but ironic.[3]

What was it about railroads that unsettled Dickens? The disorder they caused? He was obsessively neat by temperament, to the point of requiring Catherine by letter, when he was traveling in Italy, to "keep things in their places. I can't bear to picture them otherwise"; and at Gadshill running up- stairs for his hairbrush if the wind mussed his hair, and conducting daily inspections of his children's bureau drawers, leaving notes pointing out any disorder he found.[4] But that concern was personal and familial, surely not to be identified with unease about disorder on the public scale, especially dis- order that was not mere chaos but the necessary clearing away of the old and outworn so that new order might appear. Dickens was always ready to root out the obsolete growths of the past, whether the glacial bureaucracy of a Circumlocution Office or a legal labyrinth like Chancery; and the dreadful London slums that he called Jacob's Island in *Oliver Twist* and Tom-All- Alone's in *Bleak House* certainly would have been pulled down if Dickens had had his way.

All this is true. But at the same time it must be significant that when Dickens thinks of railroads, before anything else he sees smashed houses and blocked streets, and feels time and place swirl. The railroad unsettles the mind; so it threatens one's sense of order and place. That is clearly not good. It also destroys existing entities like Staggs's Gardens. That may be good or not, depending on what Staggs's Gardens is like.

It was a little row of houses, with little squalid patches of ground before them, fenced off with old doors, barrel staves, scraps of tarpaulin, and dead bushes; with bottomless tin kettles and exhausted iron fenders, thrust into the gaps. Here, the Staggs's Gardeners trained scarlet beans, kept fowls and rabbits, erected rotten summer-houses (one was an old boat), dried clothes, and smoked pipes. Some were of opinion that Staggs's Gardens derived its name from a deceased capitalist, one Mr. Staggs, who had built it for his delectation. Others, who had a natural taste for the country, held that it dated from those rural times when the antlered herd, under the familiar denominations of Staggses, had resorted to its shady precincts. Be this as it may, Staggs's Gardens was regarded by its population as a sacred grove not to be withered by railroads: and so confident were they generally of its long outliving any such ridiculous inventions, that the master chimney-sweeper at the corner, who was understood to take the lead in the local politics of the Gardens, had publicly declared that on the occasion of the Railroad opening, if ever it did open, two of his boys should ascend the flues of his dwelling, with instructions to hail the failure with derisive jeers from the chimney-pots. *(Dombey and Son,* vi)

Not a very prepossessing spot, though I think I hear a note of affection for the Gardeners, out of date and shortsighted as they are. In the former respect they suit their neighborhood, for Staggs's Gardens appears possibly to be quite old; it goes back at least to the days of that dead capitalist, and perhaps to "rural times"—in either case, beyond its inhabitants' memories. If Staggs's Gardens is old, Dickens' affection is accounted for; he has, Angus Wilson says, "a certain vague attachment to 'old things' and 'old buildings.' "[5] Not all old buildings, surely: not Tom-All-Alone's. But generally speaking, Wilson is right. Good places in Dickens are often old—Agnes Wickfield's home in *David Copperfield,* for example, is very old.

Age itself, though, is not what these places are valuable for. Wilson goes on to say Dickens always suspected "reverence for the past," and he is right about that, too. "There are hundreds of parrots," Dickens wrote from Italy in 1844, "who will declaim to you in speech and print, by the hour together, on the degeneracy of the times in which a railroad is building across the water at Venice; instead of going down on their knees, the drivellers, and thanking Heaven that they live in a time when iron makes roads, instead of prison bars and engines for driving screws into the skulls of innocent men."[6] There are also those dummy volumes in his library with individual titles like *Superstition* and *The Rack* under the general title *The Wisdom of Our Ancestors*[7]; and there are his descriptions of eighteenth-century London in *Barnaby Rudge* (xvi) and *A Tale of Two Cities* (I, i), and his scorn for the Pre-Raphaelites.[8]

But if Dickens does not value these good places merely for being old, he does value them for something that old places have. Being old, these places are "old-fashioned"; that is the point, as Esther Summerson shows by her delight with the furniture at Bleak House, which is "old-fashioned rather than old, like the house" (vi). "Old-fashioned" means something special to Dickens. For one thing, it means plenitude and variety; there is no barrenness or monotony in it.

> All the movables [in Esther's apartment], from the wardrobes to the chairs and tables, hangings, glasses, even to the pincushions and scent-bottles on the dressing-tables, displayed the same quaint variety. They agreed in nothing but their perfect neatness, their display of the whitest linen, and their storing-up, wheresoever the existence of a drawer, small or large, rendered it possible, of quantities of rose-leaves and sweet lavender. *(Bleak House, vi)*

> [The Wickfield drawing room] seemed to be all old nooks and corners; and in every nook and corner there was some queer little table, or cupboard, or bookcase, or seat, or something or other, that made me think there was not such another good corner in the room; until I looked at the next one, and found it equal to it, if not better. *(David Copperfield, xv)*

Another feature of the old fashion is a pleasing irregularity. The outside of the Wickfield house is all "angles and corners, and carvings and mouldings, and quaint little panes of glass, and quainter little windows." Another of these old-fashioned places is the house of Gabriel Varden, the master locksmith in *Barnaby Rudge;* "it was not planned with a dull and wearisome regard to regularity, for no one window matched the other, or seemed to have the slightest reference to anything besides itself" (iv); as in Bleak House, one goes up and down steps to get from one room to the next. Bleak House, however, is the best example. The description is much too long to quote in full, but Esther makes a great deal of how rambling and "delightfully irregular" the place is: one of those houses "where you go up and down steps out of one room into another, and where you come upon more rooms when you think you have seen all there are, and where there is a bountiful provision of little halls and passages, and where you find still older cottage-rooms in unexpected places, with lattice windows and green growth pressing through them" (vi). Not surprisingly, Bleak House is also the place where Dickens draws the line most clearly between value and mere age. It "seemed to be an old-*fashioned* house" to Esther when she first saw it, and so it proved to be, "old-*fashioned* rather than old" (italics mine).

Plenitude, variety, unpredictable and delightful irregularity: Dickens wants to keep them in the world, and anything that threatens them is the enemy. The place where they are most directly threatened is Coketown, and the main villain is Gradgrind, or rather, the Hard Fact philosophy by which Gradgrind orders life. If Bleak House and Gabriel Varden's home and

Agnes Wickfield's show what the old fashion is, Thomas Gradgrind's Stone
Lodge shows the new:

> A very regular feature on the face of the country, Stone Lodge was.
> Not the least disguise toned down or shaded off that uncompromis-
> ing fact in the landscape. A great square house, with a heavy porti-
> co darkening the principal windows, as its master's heavy brows
> overshadowed his eyes. A calculated, cast up, balanced, and proved
> house. Six windows on this side of the door, six on that side; a total
> of twelve in this wing, a total of twelve in the other wing; four-and-
> twenty carried over to the back wings. A lawn and garden and an in-
> fant avenue, all ruled straight like a botanical account-book. Gas
> and ventilation, drainage and water-service, all of the primest qual-
> ity. Iron clamps and girders, fireproof from top to bottom; mechani-
> cal lifts for the housemaids, with all their brushes and brooms;
> everything that heart could desire.[9]

Order alone is plainly not what Dickens wants; the kind of order matters,
too. Staggs's Gardens is a scruffy corner of the city, but it has things Dickens
values just the same, and it is certainly preferable to Coketown and Fact.
Old-fashioned irregularity and variety make life interesting, the machinelike
order of Stone Lodge makes for intolerable dullness. Gradgrind's children
complain of that; it is why their father catches them peering through the
fence at the forbidden circus.

Coketown is a long way from Staggs's Gardens in the Dickens world, and
it may seem an even longer way in my argument. I began by suggesting
that Dickens' "vague attachment to 'old things' " is to be seen in his description of Staggs's Gardens; went on to the "old-fashioned," which is what
appeals to Dickens in old things; and then went to Coketown to show the
antithesis of the old fashion. Does the old-fashioned itself exist in *Hard
Times?* It does, in a human being, where Dickens is most concerned to find
it. In the human world of Coketown, the old fashion stands over against the
"calculated, cast up, balanced, and proved" view of life. It appears in Sissy
Jupe, the girl from Sleary's horse-riding (the circus), who finds the curricu-
lum so indigestible at M'Choakumchild's hard-fact school. Her place in the
schoolroom and her appearance emphasize her contrast with the boy Bitzer
in whom the system (as is later proved to Gradgrind's sorrow) succeeds completely. She sits at the end of a row diagonally across the room from Bitzer,
and further back, so that she is also higher up than he is, and the sunbeam
that strikes her ends at him: "But, whereas the girl was so dark-eyed and
dark-haired, that she seemed to receive a deeper and more lustrous colour
from the sun, when it shone upon her, the boy was so light-eyed and light-
haired that the self-same rays appeared to draw out of him what little colour
he ever possessed" (I, ii). Sissy is far from Bitzer in the schoolroom, and in
every other way too: higher up and nearer the natural light (and by the

same token farther from the factual lectern) which confirms her fullness of being as it reveals Bitzer's deficiency.

Sissy's rich coloring suggests richness and warmth of spirit, which events prove that she does indeed have. So far my authority for calling Sissy "old-fashioned," however, rests on her total inability to take in the hard facts, which symbolized in Stone Lodge are so unlike the kind of facts embodied in, say, Bleak House. But there is a parallel in Sissy with something in *Dombey and Son* which also justifies calling her "old-fashioned," and which will get us back to Staggs's Gardens. Sissy's loving and gentle nature is like Paul Dombey's, and Paul is called "old-fashioned" for that by Miss Blimber at Dr. Blimber's school for young gentlemen,

> a great hot-house, in which there was a forcing apparatus incessantly at work. All the boys blew before their time. . . . No matter what a young gentleman was intended to bear, Doctor Blimber made him bear to pattern, somehow or other. . . . Under the forcing system, a young gentleman usually took leave of his spirits in three weeks, . . . and at the end of the first twelvemonth had arrived at the conclusion, from which he never afterwards departed, that all the fancies of the poets, and lessons of the sages, were a mere collection of words and grammar, and had no other meaning in the world. (xi)

Paul's spirits do not depart in this way, but, like Sissy at M'Choakumchild's, he does not flourish on the Blimber plan. Miss Blimber does not mean to compliment him: as she explains in her written report to his father, to be "old-fashioned" is to be "singular in his character and conduct, and . . . without presenting anything in either which distinctly calls for reprobation, he is often very unlike other young gentlemen of his age and social position" (xiv). On this account, she tells the boy, the Blimbers naturally can't like him as well as they could wish. "Little thinking that in this, he only showed again the difference between himself and his compeers," Paul begs her "to have the goodness to try and like him"; he repeats the plea later to Mrs. Blimber, adding how fond he himself is of them all (which is true). Not so fond, of course, as of his sister Florence, he adds "with a mixture of timidity and perfect frankness, which was one of the most peculiar and most engaging qualities of the child"; but of course Mrs. Blimber wouldn't expect that, would she? " 'Oh! the old-fashioned little soul!' cried Mrs. Blimber, in a whisper." What such characters take as a term of reproach we may safely take otherwise: to be old-fashioned, in *Dombey and Son,* is to be fully and authentically human, particularly in the department of the affections, like Sissy in *Hard Times,* and the good Dickens people everywhere in his novels.

But with Paul Dombey we have returned to Staggs's Gardens. For that is where Mrs. Toodle lives, who is a well of simple good sense and love and human fellow feeling, and who nursed Paul after his mother died. Paul's life, in a sense, comes from Staggs's Gardens. It cannot be chance, then, that in chapter xiv Paul's health fails, in chapter xv we learn that the completed railroad has worked a transformation which has entirely wiped out the old Staggs's Gardens, and in chapter xvi Paul dies.

Dickens is working here by suggestive parallels in the action; the passing of Staggs's Gardens is in some way the same thing as the death of Paul. It is time to look at the passage describing what has replaced Staggs's Gardens.

There was no such place as Staggs's Gardens. It had vanished from the earth. Where the old rotten summer-houses once had stood, palaces now reared their heads, and granite columns of gigantic girth opened a vista to the railway world beyond. The miserable waste ground, where the refuse matter had been heaped of yore, was swallowed up and gone; and in its frowsy stead were tiers of warehouses, crammed with rich goods and costly merchandise. The old by-streets now swarmed with passengers and vehicles of every kind: the new streets that had stopped disheartened in the mud and waggon-ruts, formed towns within themselves, originating wholesome comforts and conveniences belonging to themselves, and never tried nor thought of until they sprung into existence. Bridges that had led to nothing, led to villas, gardens, churches, healthy public walks. The carcasses of houses, and beginnings of new thoroughfares, had started off upon the line at steam's own speed, and shot away into the country in a monster train.

As to the neighbourhood which had hesitated to acknowledge the railroad in its straggling days, that had grown wise and penitent, as any Christian might in such a case, and now boasted of its powful and prosperous relation. There were railway patterns in its drapers' shops, and railway journals in the windows of its newsmen. There were railway hotels, office-houses, lodging-houses, boarding-houses; railway plans, maps, views, wrappers, bottles, sandwich-boxes, and time-tables; railway hackney-coach and cabstands; railway omibuses, railway streets and buildings, railway hangers-on and parasites, and flatterers out of all calculation. There was even railway time observed in clocks, as if the sun itself had given in. Among the vanquished was the master chimney-sweeper, whilom incredulous at Staggs's Gardens, who now lived in a stuccoed house three stories high, and gave himself out, with golden flourishes upon a varnished board, as contractor for the cleansing of railway chimneys by machinery.

To and from the heart of this great change, all day and night, throbbing currents rushed and returned incessantly like its life's blood. Crowds of people and mountains of goods, departing and arriving scores upon scores of times in every four-and-twenty hours, produced a fermentation in the place that was always in action. The very houses seemed disposed to pack up and take trips. Wonderful

> Members of Parliament, who, little more than twenty years before, had made themselves merry with the wild railroad theories of engineers, and given them the liveliest rubs in cross-examination, went down into the north with their watches in their hands, and sent on messages before by the electric telegraph, to say that they were coming. (xv)

What was a seedy suburb is now a busy commercial center. But this does not mean merely new "tiers of warehouses"; when Dickens says Staggs's Gardens has vanished from the earth, he does not mean it has been entirely demolished. Much has survived. But it is all changed: Staggs's Gardens has been commercialized, and everyone is running an enterprise geared to the railroad (as "any Christian might in such a case, [the neighborhood] now boasted of its powerful and prosperous relation"). This is the same thing that happens in "An Unsettled Neighbourhood": house fronts have "broken out into shops, and particularly into Railway Dining Rooms, . . . [and] three eight-roomed houses out of every four . . . set up as Private Hotels, . . . [and] all the boys who are left in the neighbourhood, tout to carry carpet-bags," and much more.

Even more noticeable is the rush and hurry, a continual "fermentation" of crowds and goods coming and going. This too is the case in "An Unsettled Neighbourhood"; in fact, there it is the chief complaint of the narrator: the railroad "has put the neighbourhood off its head, and wrought it to that feverish pitch that it has ever since been unable to settle down to any one thing, and will never settle down again. . . . Everybody wants to be off somewhere. Everybody does everything in a hurry." The account of this flurry in Staggs's Gardens is mildly whimsical, and more deliberately humorous in "An Unsettled Neighbourhood." But a rush like that, in Dickens, can be anything but funny. The people who work in the mills in Coketown, at "the crashing, smashing, tearing" looms *(Hard Times,* I, xi), live crammed together in a "labyrinth of narrow courts upon courts, and close streets upon streets, which had come into existence piecemeal, every piece in a violent hurry for some one man's purpose, and the whole an unnatural family, shouldering, and trampling, and pressing one another to death" (I, x). Ruined, Carker races with less and less rational purpose to his last morning and death beneath an express train, realizing in that moment "that the rush was come" *(Dombey and Son,* lv). As he lies dying, Paul fancies that there is a great rushing river, and he is on it, and it is carrying him away (xvi). And it is the rush and the power of the train carrying the bereaved Mr. Dombey to Leamington that makes him take it as "a type of the triumphant monster, Death" (xx).

The center of interest at this point in *Dombey and Son* is the death of Paul, and the ruin of Mr. Dombey's hopes that the name "Dombey and Son" will once more mean exactly what it says. But, as many critics have seen, this is the novel in which Dickens first makes everything relate to everything else; and Paul's death, as I have already noted, is connected by the narrative order to the swallowing up of Staggs's Gardens by the commercial life that attends the railroad's coming. Paul himself is a victim of the commercial spirit, since Mr. Dombey sent him to Dr. Blimber's fatal school to prepare him for his place in the Dombey mercantile dynasty. That decision led to the death of the "old-fashioned" boy, with his gentleness and loving kindness, "so very unlike other young gentlemen of his age and social position." So the transformation of Staggs's Gardens, though the magnitude of it excites wonder, and though it has its happy aspects ("villas, gardens, churches, healthy public walks"), is a change for the worse, to be seen as the death of something, not as a birth.

What happens to Staggs's Gardens, then, must mean something like the dehumanization of that neighborhood. The life here is not healthy life; in Dickens the image of well-being is tranquillity and stable order, in out-of-the-way private places, not public ones. Those good places I mentioned earlier are all out of the rush of affairs; Gabriel Varden's house is on a quiet shady street in Clerkenwell, a suburb then, Dickens says, where the open country was still close by. (Angus Wilson says that the country for Dickens was always "a conventional but adequate symbol . . . for the innocent happiness of life."[10]) Agnes Wickfield's home is in Canterbury, a quiet country town not at all like London; Bleak House is actually in the country. The change of a peaceful (even though seedy) suburb, then, into a humming commercial center looks like the loss of private well-being, of individuality, whatever the material gains. This is not what Stephen Marcus says; he sees Dickens as "[affirming] the life that emerges from all this upheaval."[11] But my interpretation is supported, it seems to me, by ominous undertones in the last sentence of the passage in which Dickens describes the transformation of Staggs's Gardens—a sentence that I do not remember seeing discussed before, though the rest of the passage has been examined often enough:

> Night and day the conquering engines rumbled at their distant work, or, advancing smoothly to their journey's end, and gliding like tame dragons into the allotted corners grooved out to the inch for their reception, stood bubbling and trembling there, making the walls quake, as if they were dilating with the secret knowledge of great powers yet unsuspected in them, and strong purposes not yet achieved.[12]

These are not monsters to be at ease with even if they are tame at present. Disquieting as their work has already been, they will do much more than they have done yet. They will make Coketown.

Marcus says the railroad in *Dombey and Son* is "the great symbol of social transformation." He goes on to explain why this was a happy choice: the railroad was "perhaps the single most revolutionary social development

of the nineteenth century: it was the modern world's first giant step in alter-
ing its means of locomotion, and it led to further alterations so far-reaching
that the railroad can be said to have literally changed the nature of human
life." Citing statistics from J. H. Clapham's essay "Work and Wages" in
G. M. Young's *Early Victorian England,* Marcus points out that Dickens
was writing *Dombey and Son* at the height of the British railway-building
boom.

> A railway *system* had sprung into existence and had imposed itself
> on the life of society. Under its impact, England was being trans-
> formed: the face of the country, the nature of cities, their relation to
> each other and to the countryside—all this was being altered. Not
> only were the conditions of travel changing, but so was the very idea
> of a journey. . . . Finally, it transformed humanity's ideas of speed
> and motion; it changed the very rhythm by which men live; it de-
> stroyed traditional notions of space and time and created new ones
> in their place. In short, the railway altered the nature of reality.[13]

Everything Marcus says here helps explain why Dickens wrote as he
did about the railroads and the changes they made. But there is reason to
say that Dickens saw something else, too, in the railroad. Social transformation is what he saw, with great accuracy, as something that came with the
railroad, a *result* of the railroad. I do not seriously quarrel with Marcus for
identifying railroad and social transformation in *Dombey and Son* as symbol
and referent, rather than as cause and effect, but in doing so he is using a
rhetorical device rather than describing exactly what Dickens is doing.

I think it would be more exact to call Dickens' railroad, in *Dombey and
Son* and elsewhere, a symbol of the Industrial Revolution. Of course that
had been going on all through the nineteenth century, but the railroad
made it all suddenly much more visible. And of course there was Coketown,
too, before Dickens put it in a novel; and as House says, the Dombey sort of
commercialism is that of the eighteenth-century merchant, not the new industrial sort.[14] But the mercantile spirit, like the poor, we have always with
us; what makes the difference in its power is the tools it has to work with.
The effect of the railroad that Dickens always emphasizes is *speed:* the
speed of its going, the rush of the life that it organizes. That is exactly what
made the Industrial Revolution a revolution: the speed with which things
could be done, and the vast increase, as a result, of the numbers of things
that could be turned out. Railroad building was itself a crucial part of the Industrial Revolution; men saw that those mountains of goods needed to be
distributed at a pace commensurate with the pace of their production. It was
not for making the beauties of the Lake country and Scotland available to
the toilers and spinners that rails were laid. It was to move goods. The resi-
dents of that unsettled neighborhood who seem after the coming of the railroad to think that their main business is "to go 'down the line' " are quite

right. Keeping moving, in order to keep things moving, *has* become their business.

The artist is not an economic historian, and he may perceive more than he can explain. I do not think Dickens knew exactly what he was capturing. I think he was recording what he saw, which was the railroad invading a neighborhood, people changing their livelihoods, and a general unsettled atmosphere of hurry; and what he felt about what he saw, which was a disquiet that he could not put a name to. But, looking at the various writings I have been dealing with, looking at the qualities he is concerned for as well as at the narrative events, and allowing for the differences of emphasis that follow from different plots and situations, we see in *Hard Times* a city where life is entirely organized by manufacturing, with no room for human sympathy and feeling; and we see in *Dombey and Son* that kind of full humanity extinguished by the mercantile spirit, both in an individual human life, and in the life of a community; and the instrument of that mercantile spirit is a great force that turns everything upside down in its passing. The transformation to the rushing life devoted to profit making is caused by the railroad, and Coketown is where the change tends: the triumph of calculating, dehumanizing industry, a sorry end for the greatest technological changes in history.

Coketown and what was Staggs's Gardens are places, but they are also images of human society, as are all cities in Dickens. If my reading is true, Dickens feared that the human city had been fundamentally changed, and changed for the worse. Marcus thinks that Dickens affirmed the new life and activity where Staggs's Gardens used to be, implying that by the time he wrote *Dombey and Son* he had changed his mind about "the personal as a necessary mode of existence."[15] I think Marcus misses the ambiguity of the passage describing what Staggs's Gardens has become. As between the past and the present, of course, there is no doubt which Dickens would choose. But he certainly had strong reservations about the form the new industrial civilization and culture was taking. Angus Wilson says that monument to the new age, the Great Exhibition of 1851, "received little notice in *Household Words*"; and Wilson quotes Dickens' remark in a letter to his assistant editor Wills: "I have always had an instinctive feeling against the Exhibition, of a faint, inexplicable sort."[16] Dickens' phrasing there suggests exactly the kind of intuition that I see him struggling in these novels to express. Thus the ambiguity of tone about Staggs's Gardens, the effect of something unsaid in spite of the teeming detail. In some places Dickens' "instinctive feeling" breaks through: one is the sentence about "the neighbourhood which had hesitated to acknowledge the railroad in its straggling days, [but which] had grown wise and penitent, as any Christian might in such a case, and now boasted of its powerful and prosperous relation." Surely that would be a thrust to any reader who remembered St. Paul's injunction "Be not conformed to this world" (Romans 12:2). I see a hint too of fatal pride in one sentence—"There was even railway time observed in clocks, as if the sun itself had given in"—a hint which is echoed in the passage about railroad building in *Bleak House* (see note 3). Most important, and more generally, Dickens continued to affirm "the personal as a necessary mode of existence" in the novels after *Dombey and Son*, even though he saw in the proliferating industrial society less and less place for privacy, for individuality, and for the graces.[17]

I do not know whether it is a hopeful note, indicating a possible way out in the future, or a despairing one, showing why opportunities before the human race never come to what they should; but I think I see something more than satiric humor in what Dickens says about the people in Staggs's Gardens, and the "wonderful Members of Parliament," too, who had such fun at the expense of the engineers' fantastic plans twenty years ago. They were all so sure that the railroad would never come. Is that why, when it came, it made their lives and their civilization over? If they had been able to conceive a new thing before it was upon them, might they have prepared for it, and put it to their service, instead of becoming slaves themselves?

They did not, at any rate. So the city of *Pickwick Papers, Oliver Twist,* and *Martin Chuzzlewit,* a place one sees as a setting for human exuberance and variety, becomes the city of *Bleak House, Hard Times, Little Dorrit,* and *Our Mutual Friend,* where increasingly for Dickens' people life is a struggle to shield from the roaring streets some small preserve of private happiness.

R. Rupert Roopnaraine

TIME AND THE CIRCLE IN *LITTLE DORRIT*

> When we accept the burden of our past, we also accept our future.
> They have the same face, the same being, the same time. This time
> of absolute responsibility, like that of radical irresponsibility, is
> circular. In neither case can one escape the motion of the wheel.
> —Georges Poulet, *Studies in Human Time*

IT NO longer seems necessary to preface an essay which makes high claims for the alertness of Dickens' prose and the complexity of his poetic art with combative assertions regarding his aesthetic and/or moral seriousness. The critical achievements of the last twenty years should by now have rendered obsolete the need for apologetics. A great deal of recent American criticism, with its concentrated focus on symbolic and rhetorical devices, on architectonics and techniques of narration, has discovered in Dickens an inventive strategist of the novel. F. R. and Q. D. Leavis, though seething with predictable hostility against the whole trend of American criticism of Dickens "from Edmund Wilson onwards,"[1] have recently elevated Dickens to their own exclusive pantheon of master-novelists. In this preoccupation with Dickens as poet, recent criticism, whether "wrong-headedly" American or stringently English, has come a long way since George Henry Lewes' 1872 judgment that "the world of thought and passion lay beyond his horizon,"[2] or George Santayana's magisterial dismissal in his 1921 essay: "It is remarkable, in spite of his ardent simplicity and openness of heart, how insensible Dickens was to the greater themes of the human imagination—religion, science, politics, art."[3] Examples of this kind of attitude are all too easy to find in the Dickens criticism that preceded the fifties. Our concern here, however, is with the Dickens who has engrossed the critical imagination of the past two decades—the subtly intelligent artist whose mature works provide powerful illustrations of theme, language, and structure wholly in the service of the moral vision.

This paper sets out to explore the implications of a single metaphor: the metaphor of circularity. Taking as my point of departure the recurrence of the metaphor at several crucial points in *Little Dorrit*, I hope to demonstrate that this metaphor functions at the philosophic no less than at the stylistic and structural levels. Rooted in the controlling vision of the work, it often rises to the surface of the text, forcing us continually to move inward from the periphery to the deep center.

[54]

Dickens is explicit in his use of the metaphor. It occurs, for instance, at the beginning of book II, chapter xxvii, "The Pupil of the Marshalsea." Clennam, a late convert to Merdleism, has just felt the devastation to property and to self that has followed in the wake of the crash. He has at long last succeeded in disposing of his wealth. Consumed as he always has been by guilt and remorse, his decision to invest in Merdle's enterprises seems almost like an act of unconscious volition, almost as though he has willed his own perdition. Ironically, he has also involved the guileless and innocent Doyce in his self-immolation. So, even if Clennam's original guilt has been atoned, a fresh source of remorse has arisen out of its ashes to gnaw at his soul. In a spirit of moral scruple and renewed atonement, he demands to be taken to the Marshalsea. We find him there, brooding and sliding imperceptibly into that seductive "unnatural peace," where the will, already benumbed in Clennam, is lulled into a deep coma, and jail rot sets in. Listless and brooding over the events that have brought him to the Marshalsea, he is struck by the fact that Little Dorrit occupies a central place in his recent life. It begins to dawn on him that "the youthful figure with tender feet going almost bare on the damp ground" embodies all that has been noble and principled, and that his present plight is the "inevitable reward of having wandered away from her." All things considered, it is not particularly surprising that, in reviewing the recent events of his life, all his thoughts should lead back to Little Dorrit. However, he does find it remarkable, "not because of the fact itself; but because of the reminder it brought with it, how much the dear little creature had influenced his better resolutions."[4] And then Dickens, as ever unwilling to resist the final twist of the screw, apostrophises: "None of us clearly know to whom or to what we are indebted in this wise, until some marked stop in *the whirling wheel of life* brings the right perception with it" (720; italics mine).

To the modern Judaeo-Christian imagination, nurtured as it is on the concept of linear time, this notion of circularity is a deeply disquieting one. The "whirling wheel of life," with its implications of a detached, cynical fate and of a mechanical rotation of life's events and experiences, becomes the symbol of utter, irreversible futility. Human lives, trapped on a great cosmic roulette wheel spun by a wanton fate, fall victim to fortuitousness and contingency. It is an even bleaker vision than that of the fashionable jeremiahs of an absurd universe, where the contingency of phenomena becomes the index of a complete lack of harmony and purpose. At least *they* leave man his will, indomitable and self-sufficient, through which he can impose order on a chaotic universe and thereby transcend contingency. The world of *Little Dorrit* offers no such solace. There is nowhere to turn. Dickens warns us at the beginning of the novel that it would be futile to look to human capacity for comfort. After Clennam has wistfully confided to Mr. Meagles that he is adrift, at the mercy of the current, he adds with deepening resignation and passivity: "I have no will. That is to say, . . . next to none that I can put in action now. Trained by main force; broken, not bent" (20). Thus, man's last refuge from a chaotic, disruptive universe turns out to be a mirage. Hillis Miller puts the question: "Is there nothing to do but suffer passively through life, subject in one way or another to the illusions and injustices of the prison of the lower world, and waiting only for the escape at death into the morning without night?"[5] In *Little Dorrit* we are closer to the tragic vision of the Greeks, where man is the plaything of the gods, a cipher to be juggled with and disposed of according to the caprice of some malevolent deity.[6]

This notion of circularity is central to the total vision of the novel, so central indeed that the overall structural movement of the book follows a circular pattern. Old Dorrit's final relapse into his Marshalsea identity at Mrs. Merdle's dinner party marks the closing of a thematic circle. His final address to the guests has often been cited as further proof that the prison in which we are immured is deep within us, that there can be no escape. It is also the supreme instance where the irreducible reality of the Marshalsea rises up to assert itself over the ephemeral reality which the old man has been trying to construct since his release. As such its obvious metaphoric correlative is the castle which Dorrit builds in his fancy and which obsesses him more and more as he draws closer and closer to death. The scene is justly famous. The whole situation is doubly ironic since the collegiates whom he addresses, being Merdle's acolytes, are in fact criminals. The scene is thus poetically integrated. Its purely thematic ironies are, moreover, tremendously enhanced by its structural appropriateness. We are, in an imaginative if not in a factual sense, back at the Marshalsea. Dorrit has come full circle on the "whirling wheel of life" and has arrived at the "marked stop." Perhaps the bitterest irony of all is the fact that even after all the suffering and the waste, Old Dorrit dies without ever arriving at the "right perception." The impression of the closed circle is reinforced by the description of his face at death. Having completed life's futile circle, his features soften into what they were when he was a child. Riveted at the dying man's bedside, the ill-used daughter watches as his face "quietly, quietly, . . . subsided into a far younger likeness of her own than she had ever seen under the grey hair, and sank to rest" (650).

This metamorphosis at death ironically fulfills one of his fondest hopes. We recall how, in a bout of self-pity and remorse, he had regretted that his children would never know him as he really was, before the prison taint had blighted his soul, "unless my face, when I am dead, subsides into the long departed look" (227). Miller cites this as an instance of the reassertion of "the purity of childhood, . . . this nucleus, miraculously preserved in the depths of the human spirit, untouched throughout all the vicissitudes and delusions of life, which returns to the surface at the last moment and displaces the shams and weaknesses which have made the face a distorted mask."[7] He prefaces this remark with a seemingly innocent sentence: "To die is to return momentarily to the self one was as a child, and to reveal the fact that the innocence of childhood is the one stage of life which escapes from the shadow of the prison." While this may hold true as a comment on the Dickens "world," it is grossly misleading when applied to *Little Dorrit*. The "momentary return to the self one was as a child," far from holding out a promise of an innocent prelapsarian world, has, within the context of this particular novel, horrifying implications. We have no evidence to suppose that the newborn innocent child would escape the soilure of the world. All the evidence in *Little Dorrit* points to the contrary. We have, for example, no reason to assume Dorrit's previous innocence. The novel is strewn with people whose minds, in childhood, have been smashed and twisted out of shape: Maggy, Tattycoram, Miss Wade, Clennam, even the good Amy to some extent. The only child who seems to have escaped "the vicissitudes and delusions of life" is the dead Meagles twin, and even she does not altogether escape. She is kept alive by Ma and Pa Meagles and becomes the focus of their own peculiar sickness. In the real sense suggested by the novel, the womb was the first prison, a place of confinement and protection, only a point on the continuous circle which includes life and death.

This circular movement is repeated time and time again in the course of the novel. After a week of harrowing despair in the Marshalsea, Clennam has begun to arrive at a truer assessment of his feelings for Amy. He nobly rejects her offer to settle his debts: "Liberty and hope would be so dear, bought at such a price, that I could never support their weight, never bear the reproach of possessing them" (760). It is Clennam's finest hour. Trying to spare her any further contact with the "tainted place," he tells her: "I am disgraced enough, my Little Dorrit. I must not descend so low as that, and carry you—so dear, so generous, so good—down with me. GOD bless you, GOD reward you! It is past" (760). Then in a sentence rich in ironic and poetic resonances, Dickens adds: "He took her in his arms, as if she had been his daughter." Again he sums up in a single phrase one of the fundamental themes of the novel: the theme of the parent-child relationship, what Miller calls the theme of "the tragedy of childhood distorted, betrayed, forgotten." Moreover, we glimpse the essence of Clennam's former illusions about his relationship with Amy. Not least of all, we are encouraged to speculate, as John Wain suggests, on Amy's own "permanently disabled psychological state in which the relationship of father and daughter is the only one she can think of as real."[8] But here again, it is the structural appropriateness of the situation which compels attention. In an ironic way Clennam's clasping Amy in his arms "as if she had been his daughter" closes the circle of Amy's life. The exemplary daughter is at last enfolded in a disinterested paternal embrace.

The sense of a completed circle is reinforced strikingly on the occasion of Amy's wedding. She is back at the place of her christening, the place of refuge from the cold hostile night of her long vigil with Maggy. Among those present "was Little Dorrit's old friend who had given her the Burial Register for a pillow: full of admiration that she should come back to them to be married, after all" (825).

This circular pattern is repeated with variations in several key chapters of the novel: book I, chapters i, iii, xi, xxi; book II, xiii, xvi, xx, xxviii. To illustrate this pattern I shall confine my analysis to chapter i, in so many ways a perfect microcosm of the entire novel, both thematically and structurally. It introduces the motifs which will be repeated and elaborated throughout the novel: there is the obvious prison cell, with its "prison taint on everything," and the harsh contrast between the prison and the outside world (ironically the prison and the outside world will, as the novel progresses, turn out to have a great deal in common). The gaoler's gentle daughter who feeds the "birds" prefigures the redemptive role Amy is to play later in the Marshalsea: "The fair little face, touched with divine compassion, as it peeped shrinkingly through the grate, was like an angel's in the prison" (5). Her reaction to Rigaud-Blandois, the instinctive recoil of innocence from contact with evil, is a preparation for Amy's similar recoil later in the novel. Blandois' patronizing of Cavaletto foreshadows Old Dorrit's subsequent patronage of the collegiates, thus serving to underline the warped personal relationships induced by the prison. To vary his diet, the resourceful Cavaletto has recourse to fantasy: "I can cut my bread so—like a melon. Or so—like an omelette. Or so—like a fried fish. Or so—like a Lyons sausage" (7). In his own comical way, he announces one of the major themes of the work: the counterplay between reality and illusion. The chapter establishes the key contrast between sun and shadow, a dialectical pattern which will be underlined and elaborated in several variants throughout the novel: poverty and wealth, reality and illusion, permanence and transitoriness. The intrigue of wills and codices which plays a large part in the dynamics of the plot is announced in Blandois' own account of his problems with his wife's will and property.

Technically it is one of those cinematic passages which led Eisenstein to cite Dickens as an early master of montage and parallel cutting, techniques which are at the root of all filmic method.[9] The chapter is in three movements: a long atmospheric introduction, the prison cell, and a closing paragraph which returns us to the panoramic point of view established in the introduction. The chapter opens in long-shot, a slow static take of Marseilles "burning in the sun." It cuts, in medium-shot, to the people "being stared out of countenance by staring white houses," and then, drawing hypnotically closer to the objects, it focuses in close-up on the "vines drooping under their load of grapes." It then cuts to the harbor and in a long, slow pan dwells on the "boats and ships blistered at their moorings," ending with a shot of the "distant line of the Italian coast." The eye comes to rest on the misty horizon. Then follows another cut, in long-shot, to the faraway "staring roads." We track in to the "horses with drowsy bells," and then, in a brilliant series of sharp, short cuts, we are confronted with close-ups of the "lizard passing swiftly over rough stone walls" and the "cicala, chirping his dry hot chirp, like a rattle." After another pan, increasing in speed and tension, of the houses and the churches, we are drawn back to the vantage point of the opening establishing shot. We next cut to the prison, to the interior of the cell which we never leave again until the end of the sequence. The interior of the cell and its inhabitants are described in minute detail. In the description of Blandois and Cavaletto, we are at once warned of the terrifyingly deterministic way in which the environment creates and controls its inhabitants. David Gervais draws attention to "the matter-of-fact way the men are introduced as one feature, not even the most noticeable one, of the general scene."[10] The aching sense of physical and spiritual claustrophobia is unrelieved. The light and sounds of the outside world barely reach the cell: "Even the echoes were the weaker for imprisonment, and seemed to lag" (7). After this prolonged, unrelieved sequence in the cell, we at last move to the outside world again, only to find ourselves in the larger prison of Marseilles. And we again take up exactly the same visual stance as that of the opening shot: "The wide stare stared itself out for one while; the sun went down in a red, green, golden glory." (14). We have, in terms of viewpoint, come full circle. This circular movement of the individual chapters cited and of the novel as a whole is the structural manifestation of the metaphor of circularity which is deeply rooted in the directing vision of the work.

The metaphor recurs at several crucial points throughout the book, sometimes as a variation on the central conception of life as a "whirling wheel," sometimes as a poetic extension of it. Describing the slow, insidious degradation produced by the prison, and comparing the beginning of Dorrit's decline to Doctor Haggage's achieved state of decrepitude and squalor, Dickens again has recourse to the image of the circle: "Now, the debtor was a very different man from the doctor, but he had already begun to travel, by his opposite segment of the circle, to the same point" (63).

The circle has its physical correlative in the spinning wheel of the little woman in the fairy story which Amy tells to Maggy. Here the spinning wheel becomes the symbol of life's activity, a source of consolation, the circumscribed symmetry of habit: "When the Princess made enquiries why the wheel had stopped, and where the tiny woman was, she was informed that the wheel had stopped because there was nobody to turn it, the tiny woman being dead" (294). The cessation of the wheel's spinning marks the cessation of life with its unfathomable secrets and its griefs.

The metaphor of the circle becomes on occasion the condensed expression of the very essence of futility. The *circulus vitiosus* is transposed from the realm of logic to the plane of living experience, itself ironically seen as the very acme of non-logic, of absurdity. Lord Decimus Tite Barnacle is described, on the occasion of Pet's wedding, as the Grand Master of the "Art of How Not To Do It." The description concludes: "The discovery of this

Behoving Machine was the discovery of the political perpetual motion. It
never wore out, though it was always going round and round in all the State
Departments" (405). Earlier, in the brutal exposition of "the whole science
of government," the Circumlocution Office has been described as going on
"mechanically, every day, keeping this wonderful, all-sufficient wheel of
statesmanship, How not to do it, in motion" (105). The twin principles of
waste and futility on which the Circumlocution Office has been founded have
their parallels in the social world. The High Priestess of this world of varnish and "genteel mystifications," Mrs. General, is described in much the
same way: "Mrs. General had no opinions. Her way of forming a mind was
to prevent it from forming opinions. She had a little circular set of mental
grooves or rails on which she started little trains of other people's opinions,
which never overtook one another, and never got anywhere" (450).

Immediately after witnessing the transactions between Miss Wade and
Blandois, Clennam, who has been disturbed by the implications of his
mother's connection with the ominous, swaggering foreigner, decides to follow Miss Wade and Tattycoram. He is astonished to see them enter Casby's
house. Clennam, hot in pursuit of the key that will unlock his own private
prison, follows them. After being harassed by the sybilline utterances of Mr.
F.'s Aunt, Clennam is shown into the Patriarch's room. He tries to prize information out of Casby concerning Miss Wade's whereabouts. But the Patriarch, an accomplished master in the art of evasion and euphemism, surren-
ders nothing. The discouraged Clennam recognizes the futility of any further
attempts to wheedle anything out of Casby. At this point our attention is
drawn to Casby's particular little mannerism, his habit of twirling his
thumbs around and around: "His turning of his smooth thumbs over one another as he sat there, was so typical to Clennam of the way in which he
would make the subject revolve if it were pursued, never showing any new
part of it nor allowing it to make the smallest advance, that it did much to
help to convince him of his labour having been in vain" (539). This particular mannerism of Casby's is what no doubt prompted the rebellious Pancks,
in his fiery revolutionary harangue to the inmates of Bleeding Heart Yard,
to describe Casby as a "slow-going benevolent Humming-Top, . . . smoothly
spinning through the yard" (801).

At times the wheel becomes the wheel of Ixion, with connotations not
primarily of recurrence and futility but of anguish and human ruin. It is also
in this sense that the Circumlocution Office is described as a wheel. Clennam, who has gone there to pursue Doyce's case and already shaken the
Barnacles with his mild but persistent "I want to know," is described as
spending a great deal of time "with various troublesome Convicts who were
under sentence to be broken alive on that wheel" (542). As David Gervais
points out, Clennam's ominous "I want to know" is invested with a significance deeper than that of merely emphasizing the frustrations produced by
a bumbling civil service: "It reminds us of the weight oppressing his life; the

feeling that not just a specific social institution but life itself is futile and meaningless."[11] Again, this is the sense in which Pancks speaks of the wheel in the seditious address to Bleeding Heart Yard. Exposing the patriarch as the real source of their grief, he describes his own subsidiary function as his agent: "What has my life been? Fag and grind, fag and grind, turn the wheel, turn the wheel!" (802).

A further enrichment of the theme of the futility and determinism of circular motion comes from Mr. Plornish when he goes to visit Clennam in the Marshalsea. It is characteristic of Dickens that he should use one of the minor comic figures to voice one of the most somber themes of the novel. Mr. Plornish, "in his philosophical but not lucid manner," is consoling Clennam on his misfortune: "He had heerd it given for a truth that accordin' as the world went round, which round it did rewolve undoubted, even the best of gentlemen must take his turn of standing with his ed upside down and all his air a flying the wrong way into what you might call Space" (731). And thus, in a single sentence, the philosophical Mr. Plornish focuses our attention on the tragic absurdity of the upsidedown world of *Little Dorrit,* a world where nothing is what it seems, where the illusions have more substance than the realities, where gentlemen are criminals, where fathers are not really fathers, and daughters turn out to be mothers. The inhabitants of this world have as much chance of escaping the vicious circle of life as do the travellers at the Great St. Bernard Inn of eluding the sinister "lasso" which Blandois, "with a long, lean flourish" throws around their names.

How do the people of this world, trapped on the "whirling wheel of life," react to their bitter lot? What are their strategies of escape, of transcendence? Is it a question of making the best of it until the wheel stops spinning, like the tiny woman of Amy's fairy story? Or is it rather, as Mr. Plornish muses, a question of passively waiting until the world spins around again so that things will be righted, even if only for a short while before it "rewolves" yet again, returning them to the same point as before? We can gauge the responses of the characters to the "whirling wheel" by examining their own attitudes toward time, and more specifically toward time past. Most of the major characters of the novel and several of the minor ones have very specific attitudes toward time past. These attitudes are not always as explicitly stated as those of Clennam, his mother, and Flora, but are obliquely reflected, like those of Little Dorrit and her father, in their responses to present experience.

"The time-sense of the Victorians was, of course, the linear one, which for twentieth-century man, so accustomed to the idea of 'recurrence,' seems to be almost equivalent to having no time-sense at all." This is one of the rather bland conclusions reached by John Henry Raleigh in his essay on the three kinds of time in the English novel.[12] Using as a model Nicholas Berdyaev's three basic categories of time-history—cosmic, historical, existential—Raleigh sets out to trace the development of the time-sense in the

major English novelists. For Berdyaev cosmic time was symbolized by a
circle and referred to "the endless recurrence of things, . . . the circular character of human and natural experience."[13] This particular notion of time,
Raleigh assures us, is the monopoly of the post-Victorian novelist and an essential ingredient of the modern angst. He cites Hardy and James as pre-
cursors, and Joyce (particularly in *Finnegans Wake*) as the consummate
prophet of circular time. ("Hardy's sense of the past is, partially anyway, a
metaphorical expression of cosmic time, whose essence is the endless recurrence of things."[14]) Raleigh sees the Victorian novelists as innocently committed to the notion of linear time, that is, Berdyaev's historical time, symbolized by a horizontal line. "What is absent in the Victorians," Raleigh
contends, "is that more profound sense of the past, . . . the obsession of
modern man that the past is continually impinging on the present and as-
suming the proportions of a nightmare."[15]

In *Little Dorrit,* however, we are much closer to Joyce's "millwheeling
vicociclometer" than Raleigh would have us believe. It is very much a novel
of memory, of time past, and of inexorable recurrence. K. J. Fielding has
found it "as saturated with a sense of past time as *David Copperfield.*"[16]
Far from being "uninterested in such matters," Dickens has given us novels
shot through with speculations on time. While these speculations may not
assume the proportions of that metaphysical concern with time which we associate with Proust, Joyce, and Mann, they nevertheless indicate a more
than casual and "signally unintellectual" interest in man's relation to the
temporal. In matters concerning time, Raleigh attributes to Hardy the maturity and seriousness he strenuously denies the "liberalist" Dickens and the
flippant Trollope. Ironically, what he has to say about Hardy applies with
peculiar force to the world of *Little Dorrit:* "In Hardy too [as well as in
James] time is taken seriously and becomes, in fact, dramatized as a malignant Fate, lying ominously in the future, waiting to strike down humans."[17]
It is precisely this time-sense, circular and tragic, which underlies *Little
Dorrit* and accounts in large part for its grim, brooding tone.

Nowhere is the metaphor of circularity more tragic in its implications of
life-destroying tedium and waste than in the description of the Clennam
house with its dark secrets, its crutches, and its symbolically crippled mistress who, in the words of Flora, "sits glowering like fate in a go-cart":

> The house in the city preserved its heavy dulness through all these
> transactions, and the invalid within it turned the same unvarying
> round of life. Morning, noon, and night, morning, noon, and night,
> each recurring with its accompanying monotony, always the same
> reluctant return of the same sequences of machinery, like a dragging
> piece of clockwork. (339)

Clennam and Little Dorrit are the only major characters whose actions in the present are determined by their heightened consciousness of an affective past. The result is that they are the characters who suffer most intensely in the present. Indeed, the intensity of their suffering stands in direct proportion to the degree of affectiveness of their past. Of all the characters in the novel, Clennam is the only one who consciously orients his life backward into the past. On his first visit to the old house, a place from which every attempt has been made to exclude time forcibly, he goes to his childhood room in the garret and the past comes flooding back to him: "He leaned upon the sill of the long low window, and looking out upon the blackened forest of chimneys again, began to dream. For, it had been the uniform tendency of this man's life—so much was wanting in it to think about, so much that might have been better directed and happier to speculate upon—to make him a dreamer, after all" (40). The grown man, disillusioned, gnawed by ennui, returns to the Bachelardian attic, a place where "the airy folly of a boy's love had found its way." The *paysage intérieur* is distinguished by the "blackened forest of chimneys." It is here that his recent interest in Pet Meagles has been born. We know it is doomed to come to nothing because it is rooted in a boy's "airy folly." Her face has had "a tender hold upon him, because of some resemblance, real or imagined, to this first face that had soared out of his gloomy life into the bright glories of fancy" (40).

A sense of guilt is the overpowering motive force which directs Clennam's actions in the present. Of all motivations, guilt is the one which is most powerfully rooted in the past. It is the grimness of the past which, throughout the novel, threatens not so much to suffuse Clennam's present as to obfuscate it entirely. After his first meeting with Flora, who has been until then the source of the only tender memories of his past, Clennam returns to his room, a disabused man:

> When he got to his lodging, he sat down before the dying fire, as he had stood at the window of his old room looking out upon the blackened forest of chimneys, and turned his gaze back upon the gloomy vista by which he had come to that stage in his existence. So long, so bare, so blank. No childhood; no youth, except for one remembrance; that one remembrance proved, only that day, to be a piece of folly.
>
> It was a misfortune to him, trifle as it might have been to another. For, while all that was hard and stern in his recollection, remained Reality on being proved—was obdurate to the sight and touch, and relaxed nothing of its old indomitable grimness—the one tender recollection of his experience would not bear the same test, and melted away. (164)

We have been well prepared for Clennam's disillusionment. Previously, in a marvellously condensed sentence Dickens had captured the bittersweet essence of disillusionment, fixing the awful moment in which the awareness dawned on Clennam that the soft fragrances of the past have faded and grown musty with the passing of the years. As Clennam entered the airless Casby house, "the smell of its old rose-leaves and lavender, . . . those faded scents in truth saluted him like wintry breath that had a faint remembrance in it of the bygone spring" (145). All that remains truly affective in Clennam's past is its grimness. Even before this final disenchantment, the changing of "the lily into a peony," we have been made aware of the difference between the truly affective and the static in Clennam's memory. Flora and all she once stood for, unlike his mother, has occupied a fixed place in Clennam's past. None of the tenderness of that time has reached down to Clennam's present: "Ever since that memorable time, though he had, until the night of his arrival, as completely dismissed her from any association with his Present or Future as if she had been dead (which she might easily have been for anything he knew), he had kept the old fancy of the Past unchanged, in its old sacred place" (150). So it becomes more than merely comic when Flora, the "moral mermaid," urges Clennam to detach himself from the past, that is, *their* past, and to be happy: ". . . but that is past and was not to be, dear Mr. Clennam you no longer wear a golden chain you are free I trust you may be happy" (155). The words gain their peculiar poignancy from the fact that we are aware that the past to which Clennam is chained is of an altogether different nature.

We know the extent to which the grim realities of Clennam's past force themselves onto his present. In the first powerful and phantasmagoric evocation of the London Sunday, the ringing of the bell that "shook every house in the neighbourhood for three hundred seconds, with one dismal swing per second, as a groan of despair," triggers a train of vivid recollections in which Clennam relives the Sundays of his childhood and sees them, "all days of unserviceable bitterness and mortification, slowly passing before him" (30). He undergoes a similar experience of the obfuscation of the present by the past later in the same chapter, when he goes to visit his mother. After her rusks and wine, she takes up the book and starts to read, "sternly, fiercely, wrathfully. . . . As she read on, years seemed to fall away from her son like the imaginings of a dream, and all the old dark horrors of his usual preparation for the sleep of an innocent child to overshadow him" (35-36). It is precisely this obfuscation of the present by the past that renders Clennam so peculiarly inadequate to the experiences of the present. This is the source of the paralysis of Clennam's will. His conception of his relationship with Little Dorrit is distorted by the inability to live in the present without reference to the past and to the preconception at some past time of what his future reactions ought to be. As he comes to realize later in the novel, he never thought of himself as old until "the night that the roses floated away."

After Mr. and Mrs. Meagles have left for Italy to comfort Pet and have urged Clennam to come down to Twickenham while they are away so that "the Babies on the wall" would have "a kind eye upon them sometimes," he returns one day to discover that Mrs. Tickit has seen Tattycoram looking in at the garden gate. Mrs. Tickit is in the process of describing the experience to an impatient Clennam. In the course of her tortuous account she ironically provides a critique of the Clennams of this world who cannot dissociate the past from the present:

> "As I was saying, I was thinking of one thing and thinking of another, and thinking very much of the family. Not of the family in the present times only, but in the past times too. For when a person does begin thinking of one thing and thinking of another, in that manner as it's getting dark, what I say is, that all times seem to be present, and a person must get out of that state and consider before they can say which is which." (529)

It is this inability to "say which is which," in psychological terms, that determines the sterility of Clennam's response to living experience in the present.

The river flowing past Twickenham is less the river of life or death for Clennam and more "the river of sweet forgetfulness," Lethe. What it promises is a life outside of time, unharassed by the anguish of the temporal world. On his first visit to Twickenham we see him in his characteristic posture of vacillation, weighing the pros and cons of falling in love with Pet. The chapter closes with Clennam in his dreaming stance, the one we saw him in previously in his old room in London:

> He softly opened his window, and looked out upon the serene river. Year after year so much allowance for the drifting of the ferry-boat, so many miles an hour the flowing of the stream, here the rushes, there the lilies, nothing uncertain or unquiet.
> . . . And he thought—who has not thought for a moment, sometimes?—that it might be better to flow away monotonously, like the river, and to compound for its insensibility to happiness with its insensibility to pain. (200)

It is only with this particular vision of the river still fresh in our minds that Clennam's committing Pet's roses to it gains its full poignancy. What in fact Clennam seems to be doing is severing a part of himself, his emotional life, from any possible projection into the future. The "night of the roses" is to become that moment in the past where Clennam's emotions have ebbed away. It is Clennam himself who deliberately establishes the river as symbol: "While the flowers, pale and unreal in the moonlight, floated away upon the river; and thus do greater things that once were in our breasts, and near our hearts, flow from us to the eternal seas" (338).

Little Dorrit's past, her experiences as the "child of the Marshalsea," is altogether different from Clennam's in the extent and results of its affectiveness. Far from obfuscating her present, it illuminates it. Like Maggie Tulliver, for whom the past is the only effective moral agent, Amy gathers strength from her memories. As a result of the undiminished force of her memories, she is able to discern the real that lies beneath the varnish of the illusory. We come to rely on her perceptions in this shifting world of uncertain phenomena. It is primarily through her reactions to experience that we gauge the quality and extent of its illusoriness. For her, Venice is unreal, a city whose "streets are paved with water." Thus we are warned of the inauthenticity and factitiousness of the world which her father tries to fabricate after leaving the Marshalsea. After Old Dorrit has returned to London to see Fanny and Sparkler settled and to consult with the mighty Merdle, Little Dorrit is left in Rome at the mercy of the Varnisher. Previously, she has been acutely aware of the reality of her recent past which has been threatening to surge through to the present. As she contemplates the old Amphitheatre, the worlds of past and present are fused:

> The ruins of the vast old Amphitheatre, of the Old Temples, of the old commemorative Arches, of the old trodden highways, of the old tombs, besides being what they were, to her, were ruins of the old Marshalsea—ruins of her own old life—ruins of the faces and forms that of old peopled it—ruins of its loves, hopes, cares, and joys. Two ruined spheres of action and suffering were before the solitary girl often sitting on some broken fragment; and in the lonely places, under the blue sky, she saw them both together. (612)

It is she alone who intuits the correspondence between the "two ruined spheres of action and suffering." The others, "tongue-tied and blindfolded moderns," are dead to the vital experience of the past. Intent on obliterating the past, they devote their efforts to the elaboration of an illusory present. In sharpest contrast to Little Dorrit is Mrs. General whose only concession to the past consists in "scratching up the driest little bones of antiquity, and bolting them whole without any human visitings—like a Ghoule in gloves" (612).

But it is this living reality of the past which, by contrast, points up the illusoriness of the present, its false pursuits, its counterfeit values, its general air of varnish. Thus, Little Dorrit becomes a fixture in Venice, the unreal city, leaning over her balcony, "the little figure of the English girl who was always alone." The sight of the gondolas taking people to "music and dancing" throws her back to the time of her own "party," the night she had spent with Maggy outside the old Marshalsea gate:

> She would think of that old gate, and of herself sitting at it in the dead of the night, pillowing Maggy's head; and of other places and of other scenes associated with those different times. And then she would lean upon her balcony, and look over at the water, as though

they all lay underneath it. When she got to that, she would musing-
ly watch its running, as if, in the general vision, it might run dry,
and show her the prison again, and herself, and the old room, and
the old inmates, and the old visitors: all lasting realities that had
never changed. (467)

She urges Clennam to remember her as she was, the "shabby girl in the
threadbare dress," that is, in her moments of greatest authenticity. When
she comes to him at the end of the novel it is as the child of the Marshalsea,
firmly rooted in reality. For Little Dorrit it is the reality of the past which
illuminates the present, showing it up for what it really is: a castle conjured
up in an old man's sick fancy. She has quiet but strong reservations about
her new life: "All that she saw was new and wonderful, but it was not real; it
seemed to her as if those visions of mountains and picturesque countries
might melt away at any moment, and the carriage, turning some abrupt corner, bring up with a jolt at the old Marshalsea gate" (463).

Flora, whom Trilling calls Dickens' "monument to the discovered discontinuity between youth and middle age, . . . the nonsensical spirit of the
anti-climax of the years,"[18] is, in this context of the novel, a parody of the
affective memory. Flora's free-wheeling associations and her never-ending
allusions to "the times forever fled" are no more than the conscious exploitation of reminiscence, points of contact with happier days. There is not, in
Flora's case, any Proustian suffusion of the present by the past. Memory for
Flora is not that magical chemistry which dissolves the space between past
and present. The past remains out there, a fixed set of frozen experiences,
powerless to transform and suffuse Flora's equally static present. She describes this period of her life to Little Dorrit, whom she has engaged as her
needlewoman, more in an effort to entangle herself in Clennam's present life
than out of an impulse of disinterested generosity: "We were all in all to one
another it was the morning of life it was bliss it was frenzy it was everything
else of that sort in the highest degree, when rent asunder we turned to stone
in which capacity Arthur went to China and I became the statue bride of the
late Mr. F." (284-85). It is proof of the extent to which we ourselves have
participated in Clennam's disillusionment that the very thought of Flora
and the young Clennam swooning in ecstasy over *Paul et Virginie* boggles
the mind. But, as she herself says to Clennam when he comes to announce
the news of Little Dorrit's great fortune, "still 'tis distance lends enchant-
ment to the view."

At times, Flora takes leave of the present entirely and, shedding com-
mas like superfluous ballast, floats out into the past. Highly discomfitted
after their first meeting, Clennam "tried at parting to give his hand in frankness to the existing Flora—not the vanished Flora, or the Mermaid—but
Flora wouldn't have it, couldn't have it, was wholly destitute of the power of
separating herself and him from their bygone characters" (159). Flora, it

seems, has found a part in which to cast herself and exploits the past. It is her refuge, not unlike Maggy's "ev'nly place" or Mrs. Plornish's "little fiction." Her present is a burlesque of the affective memory. Clennam, not surprisingly, is appalled and strangely moved by this grotesque performance. As "the relict of the late Mr. F." performed her antics, Clennam became "more and more lightheaded every minute." He watched her "going through all the old performances—now, when the stage was dusty, when the scenery was faded, when the youthful actors were dead, when the orchestra was empty, when the lights were out" (155).

The pathos of Flora's situation is enhanced even further by the fact that she is the only record of change in the ticking house. All too conscious of the thickening effects of middle age, she complains feelingly to Clennam: "But if we talk of not having changed, look at Papa, is not Papa precisely what he was when you went away, isn't it cruel and unnatural of Papa to be such a reproach to his own child, if we go on in this way much longer people who don't know us will begin to suppose that I am Papa's Mama!" (151). It is a richly ironic passage. It not only serves to emphasize Casby's mysterious immunity to the passing of the years, but it underlines one of the great themes of the novel, Amy's own mothering of *her* father with all its implications.

For Casby is indeed outside the reach of time, or so it seems for a while. He turns this immunity into a ruse; it allows him to turn to the world a profitable façade of innocence and serenity. He is "as unchanged in twenty years and upward, as his own solid furniture—as little touched by the influence of the varying seasons, as the old rose-leaves and old lavender in his porcelain jars." Casby's house is a kind of timeless vacuum, a "sober, silent, air-tight house," where the door seems to "shut out sound and motion" (145). But ironically, as the door shuts out the sounds and motion of the outside world, the resulting hush only serves to emphasize the ticking away of time. Nothing changes, but the entire house ticks:

> There was a grave clock, ticking somewhere up the staircase; and there was a songless bird in the same direction, pecking at his cage, as if he were ticking too. The parlour-fire ticked in the grate. There was only one person on the parlour-hearth, and the loud watch in his pocket ticked audibly. (145)

It looks for a while as though Casby is to escape unscathed. It seems as though he will go on resembling his picture as a boy, "the Seraphic creature with the haymaking rake." Unlike Dorian Gray's, it reveals no sign of the corruption of the grown man's soul. It is not until Pancks "defathers"[19] Casby in Bleeding Heart Yard that time revenges itself on the Patriarch. It is one of the many ironies of this timeless house that Mr. F.'s Aunt "measures time by the acuteness of her sensations and not by the clock."

There are those characters in the novel for whom time has stopped completely, who remain locked in a frozen past. Both Mrs. Clennam and the pathetic Maggy fall into this category. The first time we are introduced into Mrs. Clennam's room, we are struck by its atmosphere of death and mummification, its "black, bier-like sofa . . . propped up behind with one great angular black bolster like the block at a state execution." To reach her room, Clennam had to go up the staircase "which was paralleled off into spaces like so many mourning tablets." The fact that time has stopped, that every vigorous attempt has been made to exclude the living present, is emphasized over and over again:

> There was a fire in the grate, as there had been night and day for fifteen years. There was a kettle on the hob, as there had been night and day for fifteen years. There was a little mound of damped ashes on the top of the fire, and another little mound swept together under the grate, as there had been night and day for fifteen years. There was a smell of black dye in the airless room, which the fire had been drawing out of the crape and stuff of the widow's dress for fifteen months, and out of the bier-like sofa for fifteen years. (33)

It is the dirge that marks the death of time. The incantatory rhythms, the regular recurrence of the key phrase "for fifteen years," the mounds of ashes, the smell of black dye, all point to the death and ritual burial of time.

Together with the impression of a place in which time has stopped, where reality has been frozen at a particular point in the past, goes the impression of contracted space. In a frequently quoted sentence, the implications of which reverberate throughout the novel, Mrs. Clennam tells Arthur "the world has narrowed to these dimensions." Mrs. Clennam, with her twisted, life-negating Calvinism, is so cut off from life and the present that, when the reality of the world intrudes, she finally freezes into a statue and the old house collapses. She prides herself on the fact that her seclusion has kept her free from the temptation "to set her heart on the hollow vanities of the world." But Mrs. Clennam does not escape her own particular brand of jail rot. The corruption of the world is within the walls of the house. Frozen into a distorted attitude of vengeance and holy wrath, Mrs. Clennam is beyond change. She boasts grimly to Arthur: "All seasons are alike to me. I know nothing of summer and winter, shut up here. The Lord has been pleased to put me beyond all that" (34). Preparing us for her ultimate petrification, Dickens comments: "With her cold grey eyes and her cold grey hair, and her immovable face, as stiff as the folds of her stony headdress,— her being beyond the reach of the seasons, seemed but a fit sequence to her being beyond the reach of all changing emotions" (34).

This seclusion brings with it a peculiar distortion of reality. The prisoner can do no more than imagine the changing world of life and action from a frozen perspective. But things are no longer as they used to be. Like

Miss Havisham's decaying wedding cake, the old house is slowly crumbling. It is "full of noises," haunted by the eerie rustlings of the past. Reality is pounding at the doors in the shape of a cloaked and sinister criminal. Mrs. Affery may wear her apron over her head, but there can be no escaping the intrusion of reality. One can, like Mrs. Clennam, simply refuse to acknowledge its existence. Looking forward to the stopped clocks of Satis House and its time-defying mistress, Dickens presents us with a character who, through sheer force of will, would resist the passing of time. But while this strategy may keep reality at bay for a while, it produces its own "mental unhealthiness":

> To stop the clock of busy existence, at the hour when we were personally sequestered from it; to suppose mankind stricken motionless, when we were brought to a standstill; to be unable to measure the changes beyond our view, by any larger standard than the shrunken one of our own uniform and contracted existence; is the infirmity of many invalids, and the mental unhealthiness of almost all recluses. (339)

In Maggy's case we find a variation on the same theme. For Maggy time has also stopped. After a brutal childhood she had been put into hospital. There she found a haven of security and happiness, an "ev'nly place" which she has refused to leave. Maggy functions in the present, but she found her "marked stop" when she was ten years old and has stayed there ever since.

To seek refuge from the harsh realities of the present both Mrs. Plornish and young John Chivery have recourse to the same strategy. For them, the escape from the anguish of the temporal world takes the form of pastoral illusion. Bleeding Heart Yard, like the Marshalsea, is a place of "blighted fruits": "Blossom what would, its bricks and bars bore uniformly the same dead crop."

In keeping with the fundamental paradox of the novel, the Plornishes are at once the most economically deprived and the most harmonious of the families portrayed. After their rise in the world, Mrs. Plornish has the shop-parlor decorated. Pressed on all sides by the severe realities of Bleeding Heart Yard, she constructs her "little fiction," her place apart. The Happy Cottage becomes their *locus amoenus,* a resting place from the business and harassment of the world. Complete with its painted dog and "circular pigeon-house, enveloped in a cloud of pigeons," it becomes in reality the resting place of several of the novel's travelers, footsore from "the pilgrimage of life":

> To Mrs. Plornish, it was still a most beautiful cottage, a most wonderful deception; and it made no difference that Mr. Plornish's eye was some inches above the level of the gable bed-room in the thatch.

> To come out into the shop after it was shut, and hear her father sing
> a song inside this cottage, was a perfect Pastoral to Mrs. Plornish,
> the Golden Age revived. (574)

Early in the novel, the child Amy, sitting in the lodge with her godfather Bob the turnkey, asks about the fields which lay beyond the walls of
the Marshalsea. After reassuring her that they were not locked, Bob describes them to her as "lovely. Full of flowers. There's buttercups, and
there's daisies and there's—there's dandelions, and all manner of games"
(69). Afterward he falls into the habit of taking her into the country for walks
and there she would pick "grass and flowers to bring home." Thus, it comes
as no surprise to us when young John, fantasizing about his projected marriage to Amy, transforms her chamber into "a very Arbour . . . with a trellis-
work of scarlet beans and a canary or so." He dreams of marriage to Amy
and in his fancy "they would glide down the stream of time, in pastoral domestic happiness." But all his fancies, nurtured in the shadow of the Marshalsea wall, come to grief on the Iron Bridge. After Amy has rejected him,
young John erects one of his tombstones in St. George's Churchyard. Like
so many of the dreamers in the novel, he becomes the victim of his own illusions. His disenchantment is, Dickens grimly reminds us, the "affecting
illustration of the fallacy of human projects." After this, Young John, nursing his grief, takes refuge in a pastoral grove, a sanctuary outside of time,
sheltered from the hard realities of the present. Metamorphosing the linen
hung up to dry into shady trees, he would sit there for hours, "disconsolate
in the tuneless groves." When the ubiquitous Pancks, hot on the trail of the
Dorrit fortune, goes to enlist Young John, he must "lure that pining shep-
herd forth from the groves."

Consistent with the dialectical patterning of the novel, this romanti-
cism, innocent and somehow pathetic in Mrs. Plornish and Young John, finds
its antithesis in Mrs. Merdle's "affectation of pastoral primitivism."[20]
Echoing that earlier grotesque—the caked and painted Cleopatra of *Dombey
and Son*—Mrs. Merdle too is a nature lover. But alas, she must submerge
these delicate inclinations. All her pastoral yearnings must be sacrificed if
she is to survive in the jungle of banquets and marriage registers. Acknowl-
edging this fearsome power of Society to Mrs. Gowan, who has come to play
out her own little farce of offended gentility, the redoubtable Bosom ratio-
nalizes her own and the world's corruption: "If we were in a more primitive
state, if we lived under roofs of leaves, and kept cows and sheep and creatures, instead of banker's accounts (which would be delicious; my dear, I am
pastoral to a degree, by nature), well and good. But we don't live under
leaves, and keep cows and sheep and creatures" (391). She had previously
made the same point to Fanny when there seemed to be a very real danger
of Sparkler falling into the latter's net. Perhaps in some "Millennium,"
some idyllic wonderland, such a union would be countenanced. Speaking for

herself, "a more primitive state of society" would be "delicious." She recalls a poem she had once read, "something about Lo the poor Indian whose
something mind! If a few thousand persons moving in Society, could only go
and be Indians, I would put my name down directly; but as, moving in Society, we can't be Indians, unfortunately—Good morning!" (242). Whereas
Little Dorrit draws her unique moral strength from an uncompromising
sense of the real, Mrs. Merdle, parroting a respect for the social realities,
outlines a rationale for flagrant opportunism.

The story of Old Dorrit is the story of the triumph of the past. Nowhere does the past reassert itself more brutally than in the final days of
the old man. After leaving the prison a destitute orphan, the Father of the
Marshalsea sets about converting his former shabby gentility into something
altogether more grand, more brilliant. His obsession is to be accepted as a
full-fledged member of Society, *le beau monde* of the Merdles and the Barnacles. The fortune which has miraculously devolved upon him enables him
to realize his deepest fantasy, already nurtured in the shadow of Marshalsea
wall. And so Old Dorrit, moving from illusion to deepening illusion, builds
away at the castle which is the stuff of his fancy. We see him in the coach
traveling back from England where he has just added some more varnish to
the family name. He has been hailed and deferred to as Merdle's friend. He
has seen Fanny ensconced in the golden cage, more brilliant than the Bosom
itself. And, as he rides back to Rome fondling the great jewels intended for
the wooing of Mrs. General, we find him "building on, building on, busily,
busily, from morning to night. Falling asleep, and leaving great blocks of
building materials dangling in the air; waking again, to resume work and
get them into their places" (636).

In his new role as the rich gentleman with connections, surrounded by
servants and valets, he finds Little Dorrit a source of constant embarrass-
ment. Her great unforgivable sin has been to acknowledge the reality of
the Marshalsea past, and in so doing, to threaten the fragile structure of his
castle. He consults with Mrs. General and between them, the castle-builder
and the "eminent varnisher," they come up with the remedy for Little
Dorritt: what she needs is the "formation of a surface, . . . that graceful
equanimity of surface which is so expressive of good breeding." They
summon the delinquent Amy and prescribe the cure. And now, for the first
time since their rise in the world, she feels a deep misgiving, a growing suspicion that she has lost her father, that she "could never see him as he used
to be before the prison days." But she makes excuses for him, as she has always done: "She felt that, in what he had just now said to her, and in his
whole bearing towards her, there was the well-known shadow of the Marshalsea wall. It took a new shape, but it was the old sad shadow. She began with sorrowful unwillingness to acknowledge to herself, that she was
not strong enough to keep off the fear that no space in the life of man could
overcome that quarter of a century behind the prison bars" (478). And so

she absolves him of all blame. Instead of reproach, she finds "no emotions in her faithful heart but great compassion and unbounded tenderness." But Old Dorrit now slips into his role of injured parent, one for which he had had much practice. In this grotesque playing out of another of her father's fantasies, Amy is cast as the ungrateful, unfeeling daughter. Old Dorrit urges her to eradicate the past, to blot out the Marshalsea experience:

> "I have suffered. Probably I know how much I have suffered, better than any one—ha—I say than any one! If *I* can put that aside, if *I* can eradicate the marks of what I have endured, and can emerge before the world a—ha—gentleman unspoiled, unspotted—is it a great deal to expect—I say again, is it a great deal to expect—that my children should—hum—do the same, and sweep that accursed experience off the face of the earth?" (479)

Seeing Amy constantly humiliated before him, even the broken, resigned, and unprotesting Frederick explodes. It is his one act of energy throughout the novel. The breakfast topic has been whether or not Mr. and Mrs. Gowan were "desirable acquaintances," people proper enough for a gentleman's daughter to consort with. At first it seems as if they are to be blackballed. What operates against them is their former connection with "an obtrusive person of the name of Clennam." This connection, however tenuous, with a past which he is determined to eradicate, damns them in Old Dorrit's eyes. But then he discovers, via Edward Dorrit, Esquire (formerly Tip), that the Gowans are on intimate terms with *the* Merdle. This, of course, decides the matter. Amy will visit the Gowans. After bestowing his "magnificent accordance," Old Dorrit settles down to his figs and French newspaper. It is at this point, after the patronized and humiliated Amy has left the table and Old Dorrit is luxuriating in the self-satisfaction of having magnificently attended to the niceties of life, that Frederick erupts: "His eyes became bright, his grey hair rose on his head, markings of purpose on his brow and face which had faded from them for five-and-twenty years, started out again, and there was an energy in his hand that made its action nervous once more" (485). And he challenges them, the castle-building father, the varnished sister, and the vain, fatuous brother: "Have you no memory?" And of course he is right. Old Dorrit is aiming at nothing less than the eradication of memory. This is what will motivate his monstrous treatment of young John Chivery in the London hotel. The cigars will become, ironically, true testimonials, but testifying to a past which must at all cost be denied, swept away.

But the past takes its revenge on Old Dorrit. As he moves closer and closer to death, the past reasserts itself more and more powerfully on his dissolving consciousness. The final scene at Mrs. Merdle's dinner party is merely the culmination of a process which had begun on the drive back from London. We see him on his return to Rome, an exhausted old man, climb-

ing the stairs, looking for his daughter. He arrives to find Amy and Uncle
Frederick sitting peacefully in front of the fire. For a moment time stands
still. Dickens now has recourse to the same brilliant device of *dédoublement*
which he had exploited to dramatize Dombey's splintered consciousness just
prior to the suicide which Florence averts. The subject watches itself become object:

> It was a curtained nook, like a tent, within two other rooms;
> and it looked warm and bright in colour, as he approached it
> through the dark avenue they made.
>   There was a draped doorway, but no door; and as he stopped
> here, looking in unseen, he felt a pang. Surely not like jealousy?
> For why like jealousy? There were only his daughter and his brother
> there: he, with his chair drawn to the hearth, enjoying the
> warmth of the evening wood fire; she seated at a little table, busied
> with some embroidery work. Allowing for the great difference in the
> still-life of the picture, the figures were much the same as of old;
> his brother being sufficiently like himself to represent himself, for a
> moment, in the composition. So had he sat many a night, over a
> coal fire far away; so had she sat, devoted to him. Yet surely there
> was nothing to be jealous of in the old miserable poverty. Whence,
> then, the pang in his heart? (638-39)

From this point onward, the past, having gained a foothold in Old Dorrit's
consciousness, becomes more and more insistent. As he sits at dinner, he is
powerfully reminded of the old room in the Marshalsea. Little Dorrit notices him looking around, distracted, "as if the association were so strong
that he needed assurance from his sense of sight that they were not in the
old prison-room" (642). As the past advances, the need for reassurance
grows stronger. "He put his hand to his head as if he missed his old black
cap." At this point Old Dorrit's consciousness is utterly at the mercy of
the implacably advancing past. It finally overwhelms him at the dinner
party. The Marshalsea, the irreducible reality of the novel, rises up to confront its erstwhile father. The welcoming address to the new collegiates by
the Father of the Marshalsea, now serene in his well-accustomed role, is a
tour de force of irony and pathos. So total is the invasion of the past that
Old Dorrit loses all sense of the present. The evolution is complete. He has
moved from evasion to illusion to the last stages of mythomania with the
concomitant loss of hold on reality. The circle of his life is closed:

> The broad stairs of his Roman palace were contracted in his failing
> sight to the narrow stairs of his London prison; . . . And from that
> hour his poor maimed spirit, only remembering the place where it
> had broken its wings, cancelled the dream through which it had since
> groped, and knew of nothing beyond the Marshalsea. (649)

It is the final triumph of circularity. There would be some consolation if we felt that, in the end, "ripeness is all." But in this vision of the world as a "whirling wheel of life" there is nothing which we can call truly redemptive. Old Dorrit passes his last days with no greater awareness of Little Dorrit's self-effacement and sacrifice. He dies as he lived, absorbing her goodness, accepting her sacrifice, as things due to him: "He loved her in his old way. They were in the jail again, and she tended him, and he had constant need of her, and could not turn without her; and he even told her, sometimes, that he was content to have undergone a great deal for her sake" (649). We are not encouraged to believe that Old Dorrit has learned the lessons of the past. We can, without too much ingenuity, interpret his final desire to divest himself of his watch and his trinkets and his clothes, to send them "piece by piece, to an imaginary pawnbroker's," as a subconscious impulse to strip himself of the layers of factitious selves which hide his soul from God. He becomes a Lear aspiring to the vulnerable nakedness of poor shivering Tom. But at best it remains a subconscious impulse, denying us the consolation we may have derived from a consciously motivated gesture toward innocence and moral restitution. The gesture is a distorted echo, an ironic recurrence of an earlier denouement. We recall the occasion of Amy's birth, many dreams ago, a time when the newly arrived debtor was just beginning to slide downward, to "travel by his own segment of the circle" to Dr. Haggage's "point." On that occasion, to find the money to pay the worthy Haggage, he had to resort to the pawnbroker: "the rings had begun to fall from the debtor's irresolute hands, like leaves from a wintry tree."

To clinch his argument that the Victorians were committed to a concept of time as linear, Raleigh takes as his cue the ending of the novel, which he finds "a specific and concrete manifestation of the general sense of time-history underlying the novel as a whole."[21] He goes on to argue that the conventional happy ending of a Dickens novel "does make sense if it be regarded as a literary convention metaphorically expressing the Victorian time-sense: i.e., man projected into an imprecise but, nevertheless, happy future. . . . The assumption about futurity here is that these happy few will continuously but mistily compound their happiness, piling cheer on cheer, for the rest of their mortality."

It seems superfluous to point out how far removed we are, at the conclusion of *Little Dorrit*, from the kind of nebulous and gratuitous optimism which Raleigh sees as being characteristically Dickensian. Consistent with the bleak vision that informs the entire work, the ending is achingly devoid of optimism, of anything that is even potentially redemptive. The final sentence, with its slow, measured cadence, cheats us of those feelings of relief and elation which the happy ending should generate: "They went quietly down into the roaring streets, inseparable and blessed; and as they passed along in sunshine and shade, the noisy and the eager, and the arrogant and the froward and the vain, fretted, and chafed, and made their usual uproar" (826). What we are left with are the echoes of the "usual uproar" of the bustling London streets. We catch a last glimpse of our hero and heroine before they are swallowed up by the jostling crowds. So little has changed. We are left with the empty feeling that out of the wreckage of so many dreams and the waste of so many lives, this is all we can salvage—"a modest life of usefulness and happiness." Another "marked stop" has been reached, but it is no more than a momentary respite from the relentless motion of the whirling wheel.

Angus Easson

MARSHALSEA PRISONERS

Mr. Dorrit and Mr. Hemens

JOHN DICKENS' imprisonment in the Marshalsea Debtors' Prison is well known. Charles Dickens drew on his experience of the prison during his father's confinement for both *Pickwick Papers* and *David Copperfield* (where the prisons are the Fleet and the King's Bench respectively), and in *Little Dorrit* the Marshalsea itself is a prominent physical object, moving into increasing symbolic significance as the novel proceeds. Dickens' memories of the prison are remarkably accurate and the telling use of detail has been discussed—the "gulf" between Dorrit and Old Nandy, for instance, when the pensioner is entertained to tea (I, xxxi, 372-73).[1] To trace the topography of the prison as it appears in *Little Dorrit* alongside an account like that of James Neild in the *State of Prisons in England and Wales* (1812) is to discover the vividness and accuracy of Dickens' recall. The buildings are an integral part of the novel; at no time can Dorrit's confinement be lost sight of as it is acted out in his physical environment. In this setting William Dorrit lives out the rôle of Father of the Marshalsea, in a society of which his family is the aristocracy.

Yet here the point begins to shift, from physical detail, the accuracy of which can be checked and the use easily appreciated, to the far more intangible qualities of atmosphere and tone. Could a man like Dorrit exist in the Marshalsea, be accepted as a kind of aristocrat? or—perhaps a more proper artistic question—is Dickens' presentation of the atmosphere or tone of the prison based on his childhood observation, or is it created by him for the purposes of the fiction? It is difficult, of course, to offer conclusive evidence in such a delicate area of artistic presentation, but it is possible to offer, by way of illustrative contrast, the situation of a prisoner in the Marshalsea, four years before John Dickens was imprisoned there. Dickens is hardly likely to have known of this case, so any similarities between Giles Hemens and the character of William Dorrit (Hemens' aloofness, for instance, and his contempt for the lower orders) is coincidental. The interest lies in its evidence of the atmosphere in the prison, of the social interrelationship of the debtors, and of the prisoners' sharply different responses to the man apart. Its evidence of what things *were* like allows a fuller consideration of what Dickens can do in the way of creative projection of character and situation.

The case of Giles Hemens, preserved amongst the Marshalsea papers at the Public Record Office,[2] offers a fascinating view of conditions and personalities. The enquiry into his affairs led to the dismissal of the Keeper of the prison, but there is no reason to suppose that there were radical changes in conditions or the behavior of the prisoners as a result.

Giles Hemens, of 5 Denmark Street, Soho, a broker, aged between fifty-six and sixty, was brought to the prison on 18 February 1820. He was extremely poor (though he insisted upon remaining on the socially superior Master's side of the prison) and relied upon the assistance of his friends to keep going at all. Shortly after his arrival in the Marshalsea, Hemens sent to a particular friend, asking him to come on a visit, "to which, he sent me word he was desirous to do, and fully meant it, but having a debtor here of the name of Dolman, he was afraid to come." Hemens seems to have been a man who concerned himself with other people's business (there is, for instance, a letter written by him on behalf of a certain Singler Shrubsole, who had not yet been discharged, though entitled to be so); and it happened that a few days after his friend's refusal to come, Hemens "promiscuously met the said Dolman on the parade of this place." After talking with him, and agreeing that he had been hard done by, Hemens took it upon himself to write to his friend, Dolman's creditor, "being," as he rather naïvely observed later, "desirous of my friend's call when it suited him." These proceedings highly annoyed Dolman, who asked Hemens up to his room to meet a third man, and a little dramatic episode was laid on for Hemens' benefit. "Mr. Dolman, on my entering the room, laid his head on the table in a posture of listening or of sleep, [and] his friend began as follows. . . ." He rated Hemens for writing to the plaintiff, for "the consequences is you have wrote to the man's injury; you have prevented his settling with his plaintiff, and 'tis a pity people here had no means to stop such proceedings." Hemens tried to leave, and Dolman, to conclude the melodramatic scene, "in haste and a rage got from his listening posture [and] calling me a damned rascal, took his stick with intent to strike me, but I left the room."

About four or five weeks later, on 18 May, when Hemens was in the snuggery with some friends and other prisoners, a certain McMoles entered. McMoles came over to Hemens "in a very blustering manner and swore that Hemens had been the ruin of Mr. Dolman," whereupon Hemens went to his room, but later, while saying goodnight to friends, McMoles appeared again. He "swore in the most vehement manner and I was immediately surrounded by a number of the lower order of prisoners, most of whom [says Hemens] I know not by name, not being in the habit of associating with them." Turning to go upstairs to his room, Hemens was seized by Mc-

Moles about the leg and dragged along, while a filthy sack used as a door-mat was thrown over his head, and so he was brought to the pump, where "I was pumped on as long as they thought proper," his clothing being badly damaged.

Hemens sent for his wife immediately next morning, telling her what had happened. But about eleven o'clock, two of the prisoners who acted as constables to the Prisoners' Committee, came with their constables' staves in their hands to conduct Hemens before the Committee. Here he had to answer the charge of interfering in Dolman's business: the Committee was unsatisfied by his defense, "and they said they would consult to what I should be subject." Despite Hemens' protest that he had already suffered enough, "the sentence was that I should be sent to Coventry for one month." Leaving the room, Hemens saw he was to be attacked again, but when he turned to ask the Committee's help, they had already broken up, "and I conceived some of them was well acquainted with what was going on." A claim for protection made to the turnkey proving futile, "I summed up my courage and went towards my room; on turning the corner I saw a number of the blackguard part. The hint was given and out came from a window above a pail of slush all over me," and three more bucketfuls followed before he reached his room, and his greatcoat was torn.

It was in this state that his wife found Hemens when she arrived about 12:30, he having taken to his bed. She tried to see the Keeper of the prison, John Cruchley, but was turned away, the eventual answer being that Hemens might, if he wished, be locked in the strong part of the prison belonging to the Admiralty. Hemens was disgusted and considered "that 'twas a place of solitary confinement calculated for the worst order of prisoners and not for debtors, and that my friends could not comfortably come there to see me." So he stayed close in his room for three successive weeks, and his wife had to give him close attention, "doing which, in going to the shop for necessary articles, to the Tap for beer, to the cistern for water, and other places for decency sake, I was always insulted with the foulest language and vilest oaths, and other expressions as I consider it not proper here to name."

On Wednesday, 7 June, the climax came. At a quarter past eleven at night, when Hemens and his roommate were both in bed, there came a knock at the door. No answer was given when they asked who it was, except for a second knock. Again no answer to an enquiry, and after more knocks and thumping, Hemens "got out of bed with fear and trembling," the door was broken open, and an unknown number of people came in, one of whom was apparently the ringleader, Mortimer Madden, who "is a dreadful bad character," along with McMoles, Hill, and Marshall. They dragged Hemens down two flight of stairs, intending as one said, "to have let me down the privy," but "some few having collected at the bottom of the stairs, they beat me about the head." Hemens was thrown under the stairs, he was given a second beating by someone, and his shirt was torn off his back.

Eventually the watchmen came and called the turnkeys, who persuaded Hemens to go to the Admiralty prison. There were conflicting reports about his
injuries, but there had been sufficient disturbance for an investigation to
take place, conducted by the titular head of the prison, the Knight Marshal,
and by the chief administrative official, the Deputy Prothonotary. In the
prison these two found "certain inscriptions on the walls of the prison in 3
several parts, the letters of which were upwards of a foot long, the word[s],
I believe, were *Hemens sent to Coventry,*" and the Knight Marshal gave
orders "to have the inscriptions immediately erased and . . . they were
erased or nearly so before we quitted the prison." The Keeper, John Cruchley, attempted to justify himself, blaming Hemens for his interference in
other people's affairs, but he was dismissed. Hemens obviously was not
blameless: Cruchley's reason for the prisoners' dislike of him sounds convincing; but the behavior of the turnkeys, the watchmen, and "the lower order of prisoners" shows a lack of discipline and the rule of the mob.

By the time John Dickens was imprisoned, four years later, things
may have changed. I do not see Giles Hemens as William Dorrit, any more
than I see John Dickens in that role. But at least Hemens' case provides
some kind of evidence—very much colored by most of the affair being preserved in the words of Hemens and his wife, but evidence nonetheless.

The impression given by an historical account like this of the prison is
of a mean, vicious, crowded, noisy, squalid jail, very much like the report
Dickens gives in the Fleet scenes of *Pickwick Papers*. That word "report" is
of course, deliberately loaded; Dickens in the 1830s drew heavily on personal
experience, but by the 1850s he was not artistically content with how things
were. Hemens' case is interesting evidence on conditions; interesting, also,
because it shows a man who set himself apart from the other prisoners. But
instead of becoming a respected (or, at least, tolerated) figure, as William
Dorrit strives to be, he was derided and persecuted by his fellows, and driven
for refuge into an Admiralty cell, a place he felt incompatible with his position and dignity. It is imperative to notice, though, that even given this general distinction between Hemens and Dorrit, the contrast is not a simple
one, least of all simple in the complexity of Dickens' art. This complexity
lies in our awareness that aspects of the prison are figments of Dorrit's
imagination; the contrast of appearance and reality, one of the basic concerns of the novel, is subtly conveyed. Yet, while Dickens does not deny the
prison's discomforts and inconvenience, its filth and miseries, these are subordinated, and what does emerge is important for Dorrit's progress. When
his wife is giving birth to Amy, Dorrit is offered this advice by the doctor
who attends the confinement:

> "A little more elbow-room is all we want here. . . . Elsewhere,
> people are restless, worried, hurried about, anxious respecting one
> thing, anxious respecting another. Nothing of the kind here, sir.

We have done all that—we know the worst of it; we have got to the
bottom, we can't fall, and what have we found? Peace. That's the
word for it. Peace." (I, vi, 63)

Dorrit's acceptance of the doctor's position enforces an essential paradox of
the novel (one of many), that what in fact is imprisonment should be regarded as liberty; that absence should be felt as positive good rather than
the simple lack of bad. If imprisonment is liberty, then the necessity for action is removed and the individual is free from responsibilities. The point,
made with Dorrit, is echoed throughout the novel: for Dickens has provided a series of mirrors in which we see reflected the same concerns, though
the situations that frame them vary.

One thing which was clear about the Fleet prison in *Pickwick Papers* is
that there was very little peace. But in the Marshalsea, by a careful use of
detail, Dickens gives the impression of a kind of rest, close to inertia. The
stress he lays on the squalor, though, should give us pause before it is
termed *peace*. The reader is aware of a dichotomy between what Dorrit
chooses to believe and matters as they really are. The prison is a place
where Dorrit can fix on a belief in it as a refuge, but its reality is present, for
otherwise Dorrit's self-deception loses its force.

Few of the other characters see the Marshalsea as a refuge. John Chivery, in love with Amy, does, it is true: "With the world shut out . . . they
would glide down the stream of time, in pastoral domestic happiness" (I,
xviii, 212). But Chivery's visions of happiness are mere fantasies, part of an
illusion akin to Mr. Dorrit's. Again, when the Dorrits, traveling abroad after their release from the Marshalsea, come to the monastery of the Great
Saint Bernard, the place is both refuge and prison, according to whose vision
it is seen through. It is a refuge in the flood of night, which "at last rose to
the walls of the convent . . . as if that weather-beaten structure were another Ark, and floated on the shadowy waves" (II, i, 432). But the Saint
Bernard actually fulfills this function of a refuge, since it aids travelers and
the monks choose their way of life. For William Dorrit, it serves as another image of the prison from which he can never escape. In an ironical
passage, Dorrit questions a young monk and shows amazement that anyone could accept imprisonment voluntarily on such terms, the very kind of
terms Dorrit has accepted for twenty years. Dickens subtly shows Dorrit's
own dual position, aware of and yet outwardly oblivious to his situation,
when the conversation is hastily ended after the monk has insinuated that
"Monsieur could not realize, perhaps, how the mind accommodated itself in
such things to the force of necessity" (II, i, 441). Dorrit has contrived a necessity which in the end proves stronger than himself.

Dickens is concerned to keep Dorrit's pretensions and illusions distinct
from the actualities of the world. The idea of commotion and activity in the
prison is always present for the reader. It is an idea enforced by the very end

of the novel, which does not promise that Amy Dorrit and Arthur Clennam shall live simply, happily ever after. There is no escape from the road we must take, except that which leads to Dorrit's moral and physical collapse. The Marshalsea is the chief image mirrored in the surrounding interests of the novel: it exists as an image of the great world of Society, for the world itself is a prison: at evening, "aslant across the city, over its jumbled roofs, and through the open tracery of its church towers, struck the long bright rays, bars of the prison of this lower world" (II, xxx, 763). And just as Society has its pretensions, so has the Marshalsea. The Dorrits are the aristocracy of the prison, they have "blood"; the Chiverys have authority and wealth. There is a correspondence between this Marshalsea society and Fanny Dorrit's marriage into the governing aristocracy: between this and Henry Gowan's marriage with the Meagles' money, where the blood is bad and the money useless. Society as a prison is enforced by prison as Society. The prisoners themselves have a social organization, dignifying themselves under the title of Collegians—again, an example of Dickens utilizing what was a fact of prison life. The symbolic treatment of the prison is pursued through Amy's attitude toward it. She sees the prison as it actually is, with "a pitiful and plaintive look for the high blank walls; for the faded crowd they shut in; for the games of the prison children as they whooped and cried, and played at hide-and-seek, and made the iron bars of the inner gateway 'Home' " (I, vii, 69). There is none of Dorrit's self-deception, as when he tells newcomers of the advantages of the Marshalsea: "It looked small at first, but there was very good company there—among a mixture— necessarily a mixture—and a very good air" (I, vi, 65). Amy is aware of the shadow of the prison, a shadow both literal and figurative. High walls and narrow space make shadow prominent, but the shadow of the narrow prison becomes a trench or grave. For Amy the sun rises everywhere on freedom save in the Marshalsea, where it comes on "the living grave . . . with her father in it" (I, xix, 231). At night, it "fell dark there sooner than else- where, and going into it . . . was like going into a deep trench. The shadow of the wall was on every object" (I, xx, 245). The historical prison becomes a threat, an encroachment on the individual, as Dickens extends it into an imaginative realm. Whatever darkness we feel in Mortimer Madden or Mc- Moles when they attacked Giles Hemens, we remain aware that for Hemens there was nothing beyond the facts of the assault. For Dorrit there is death in his acceptance of a self-created reality.

Both Dorrit and Amy, aware of a reality in the prison, treat the nature of that reality quite differently, and this difference is plain in their reactions when, released from the Marshalsea, they travel in Italy. Dorrit knows what the world might think of the Marshalsea and attempts to deny it ut- terly, until reclaimed by what he has created. Amy, however, so far accepts the reality of the prison that their release, actuated as it is by a fairy-tale event, cannot convince her of the reality of their new life. Venice, paved with

water, is no more than a dream, while the Marshalsea without her father is
so unthinkable that she imagines it in ruins:

> The ruins of the vast old Amphitheatre, of the old Temples, were
> ruins of the old Marshalsea—ruins of her own old life. . . . Two
> ruined spheres of action and suffering were before the solitary girl
> often sitting on some broken fragment; and in lonely places, under
> the blue sky, she saw them both together. (II, xv, 612)

Amy recognizes reality, but Dorrit cannot escape it. The Marshalsea is one
reality of the book, firmly rooted in its realistic presentation. The physical
details of the prison are established and used, but, as I have tried to suggest
by the example of Giles Hemens, the tone of the prison was rather different
from that established by Dickens in the novel. The purpose of his presentation of the Marshalsea is to relate the prison to the whole atmosphere of the
novel, to the themes of debt and gentility, and more particularly to present
the character of William Dorrit.

Dorrit begins to build a world of deception around himself from his first
entry into the prison. The difference between a criminal and a debtors'
prison adds immeasurably to the force of Dickens' metaphor. The people
who enter the Marshalsea are not initially corrupt, as may be presumed of
those in a criminal prison like Newgate. A criminal faces a fixed penalty but
the debtor must pay "in life and money both" (I, xxxv, 422). Once in the
Marshalsea, however, Dorrit's sense of moral bankruptcy is soon established. The ceremonial and artificial nature of Dorrit's position as the Father
of the Marshalsea is underlined when Frederick Dorrit proudly recalls forty
or fifty new prisoners introduced in a day to his brother, and William agrees
that on "a fine Sunday in term time, it is quite a Levee" (I, viii, 83). When
Dorrit comes into his fortune, he is very close to acting the King or Pope,
for

> taking Clennam and his daughter for supporters, [Dorrit] ap-
> peared at the window leaning on an arm of each. The Collegians
> cheered him very heartily, and he kissed his hand to them with great
> urbanity and protection. When he withdrew into the room again, he
> said "Poor creatures!" in a tone of much pity for their miserable
> condition. (I, xxxv, 421)

Dorrit hedges himself about with forms and ceremonies. All new prisoners
are introduced to him in his room, since he "disliked an introduction in
the mere yard, as informal—a thing that might happen to anybody" (I, vi,
65).

The terrifying point that Dickens is at pains to make is that Dorrit is
always aware of himself within the figure of the Father of the Marshalsea.
The figure may deceive or entertain others, but Dorrit does not deceive him-

self[3] until, at the moment of his triumph, he breaks down at the Roman
dinner and becomes in real earnest what he has acted out. The mask and the
face only become one when the integration is least wanted. By hysterical
outbursts he shows the difficulty of concealing from others what he knows
of himself: after an attempt to force his daughter into an association with
John Chivery, Dorrit breaks down and "both the private father, and the Father of the Marshalsea were strong within him then" (I, xix, 230); and earlier in the same scene he claims that, unless "my face, when I am dead, subsides into the long departed look . . . my children will have never seen me"
(I, xix, 227). Even this is deception and an ironical comment, for his children have seen Dorrit as he more truly is than ever they could in earlier
life. The cry—"my children will have never seen me"—represents a pressing human desire to have the exterior he is presenting accepted as part of
his real self. When Dorrit hears of his inheritance, the truth comes upon
him for a moment, as he "looked steadfastly at Clennam, and, so looking at
him, seemed to change into a very old haggard man" (I, xxxv, 418). This
revelation of fortune may be seen as a high point of Dorrit's consciousness,
for his whole system of subterfuge is revealed as he lays it by to summon his
family from their jobs. Dickens makes the point explicit: "This was the first
intimation he had ever given, that he was privy to the fact that they did
something for a livelihood" (I, xxxv, 420). At few points in the book does
Dorrit so much have the appearance of a vicious man. Entering into a deception by which he was not deceived, he has chosen that Amy should play
it out for half her lifetime.

The status the Dorrits pretend to in the prison is as absurd as the pretensions of people in the other prison, that of Society. The correspondencies
between Society and the Marshalsea are pursued, for instance, in the world
of the Gowans. Henry Gowan, who presses his claims to gentility and is an
amateur artist, proves as bankrupt artistically as Dorrit is spiritually, and
the link is well made between them when Dorrit determines to commission
his portrait. He speaks of his wish "to present a gentleman so connected,
with some—ha—Testimonial of my desire to further his interests" (II, vi,
561)—some *Testimonial:* this has been the cant term used for the money
given by outgoing prisoners to Dorrit. The testimonials have been Dorrit's
shame, though he never admitted their necessity, and he attempts to bind
Gowan in the same degradation. His final justification of them is similar to
Gowan's justification of his way of life: "In the acceptance of these—ha—
voluntary recognitions of my humble endeavours to—hum—to uphold a
Tone here—a Tone—I beg to be understood that I do not consider myself
compromised" (II, xix, 648). It is a debt due to him from Society, he implies,
just as Gowan feels that Society owes him a living. Dorrit's main aim is to
preserve "the genteel fiction that they were all idle beggars together" (I,
vii, 73-74).

Dorrit fails to deceive himself, and it is doubtful whether he deceives many other people. His shabby gentility fits well into the background of the Marshalsea, but the only person who wholeheartedly believes in Dorrit is Amy. Even in her belief, Amy does not harbor illusions about her father. Dorrit's is an empty title, a hollow product of inertia in remaining imprisoned, and even in this empty fiction, a "disposition began to be perceived . . . to exaggerate the number of years he had been there; . . . he was vain, the fleeting generations of debtors said" (I, vi, 65). The testimonials are given, it is true, but not always in a spirit of reverence. Departing Collegians originally presented these testimonials wrapped in paper and slipped under Dorrit's door, signing themselves with facetious names (I, vi, 65). Dorrit indeed declares that the possession of moral qualities is essential for a man who would maintain a position in the Marshalsea (I, xix, 224-25), but afterward the Collegians are described as "laughing in their rooms over his late address in the Lodge" (I, xix, 229). They laugh at him though; they do not dispute his right to title or testimonials.

The two important points in the creation of William Dorrit within the context of the Marshalsea are Dorrit's insistence on gentility and the prisoners' tolerance (and even acceptance) of him largely on his own terms. Giles Hemens did not find himself even tolerated. The historical impression is that a person like Dorrit would certainly have been ignored in the Marshalsea, if not actually set upon by the prisoners. Without the tone of gentility within the prison itself (however far qualified), the pretensions of Dorrit could not have taken root. Given the ironic function of Dorrit, questioning the basis of the social pretensions of the Gowans, Barnacles, Stiltstalkings, and even the Merdles, there was the need to create the background which allows him to exist. As Dickens had declared to John Forster, "The exact truth must be there; but the merit or art in the narrator, is the manner of stating the truth."[4] Dickens chose to create the tone of the prison because the character of Dorrit was more important for the novel than a description of the historical prison. The Marshalsea functions throughout the novel—an obvious example of its integrity to the whole structure is its influence once Dorrit has escaped its physical boundaries. He moves into polite Society, where he mirrors the prisonerlike state of the people he meets. To act the man of wealth and position is easy for Dorrit, once out of prison, since he has played the part for twenty years. Yet when he has built castles in the air and is at dinner in Roman Society, the final integration of prison and Society is made, as Dickens overlays one idea by another. So closely are the Marshalsea and Dorrit linked that a very early claim of Dorrit's is fulfilled. In a maudlin outburst, he had insisted: "Go out and ask what funeral here [in the Marshalsea] (it must be here, I know it can be nowhere else) will make more talk, and perhaps more grief, than any that have ever gone out at the gate. They'll say your father's" (I, xix, 228). Dorrit's fortune and release should mean the end of this idea, but Dorrit is indeed doomed to die in the Marshalsea. What is only a dream of his daughter's becomes reality for him. Amy tells how "I have over and over again dreamed of taking my place at dinner at Venice when we have had a large company, in the mourning for my poor mother which I wore when I was eight years old" (II, xi, 554). The struggle to refute what has so effectively moulded him proves too much for Dorrit, and at dinner he reverts to the shadow of the Marshalsea:

> [Amy] was gently trying to get him away; but he resisted, and would not go.
> "I tell you, child," he said petulantly, "I can't be got up the narrow stairs without Bob. Ha. Send for Bob. Hum. Send for Bob —best of all the turnkeys—send for Bob!"
> He looked confusedly about him, and, becoming conscious of the number of faces by which he was surrounded, addressed them:
> "Ladies and gentlemen, the duty—ha—devolves upon me of— hum—welcoming you to the Marshalsea. Welcome to the Marshalsea! The space is—ha—limited—limited—the parade might be wider. . . . I am accustomed to be complimented by strangers as the —ha—Father of the Marshalsea. Certainly, if years of residence may establish a claim to so—ha—honourable a title, I may accept the—hum—conferred distinction. My child, ladies and gentlemen. My daughter. Born here!" (II, xix, 646-48)

Dorrit does not desire to return physically to his prison; the prison is even stronger, for he carries it with him, like an Old Man of the Sea. The mirror and the image have become one. The people of Society are welcomed as debtors into a prison which for one man at least is the only world. Dickens' exploration of the bonds of Society (bonds which are both links and manacles) has been achieved by the creation of image to convey what he means; facts are not enough in themselves, for the implications of what he has to say demand the act of creation.

Stanley Tick

THE SAD END OF MR. MEAGLES

IN THE penultimate chapter of *Little Dorrit,* Mr. Meagles is shown lead-ing Little Dorrit from the Marshalsea, where she had been visiting Clen-nam. Meagles guides the young woman into her coach and places the pre-cious papers beside her, thus completing his great good deed of recovering the stolen Clennam documents. The following words conclude the chapter:

> In her joy and gratitude she kissed his hand.
> "I don't like that, my dear," said Mr. Meagles. "It goes against my feeling of what's right, that *you* should do homage to *me*—at the Marshalsea Gate."
> She bent forward, and kissed his cheek.
> "You remind me of the days," said Mr. Meagles, suddenly drooping—"but she's very fond of him, and hides his faults, and thinks that no one sees them—and he certainly is well connected, and of a very good family!"
> It was the only comfort he had in the loss of his daughter, and he made the most of it, who could blame him?[1]

Asked as it is, at the conclusion of the novel, the narrator's question should be only rhetorical; after all, it had not been Dickens' practice to write eight hundred pages without informing his readers whether a character's joys or disappointments were deserved or not. We do, of course, feel a bit sorry for the final plight of characters like Mercy Pecksniff and Edith Granger (but not for Stephen Blackpool any more than Little Nell, both of whom shall surely be rewarded in Heaven); and we may be elated at Dom-bey's rather unexpected happiness in old age. Yet until we reach the trou-bling ("dark") complexities of the very late studies—those of Pip, Wrayburn, Headstone, and presumably of John Jasper—we are invariably reassured at watching the wheel of fortune go its sensible ways through Dickens' plots. And this is pretty much as true for *Little Dorrit* as it is for *Oliver Twist* —save for the case of Mr. Meagles.

[87]

I am confident that the narrator's question about Meagles *is* meant to be rhetorical, not enigmatic, its implied answer being "no one" or "nobody." That is to say, Meagles' appeal from sorrow cannot be gainsaid. Yet such a conclusion implies that *Little Dorrit* is either more incoherent or more problematic than it is commonly thought to be. Let me begin my argument by making as strong a defence of Mr. Meagles as Dickens himself allows us to, thereby revealing the deep and disturbing pathos of his sad end.

However ill-assorted, the major characters in *Little Dorrit* are generally understood to be representatives in some grim, grey allegory about the effects of repression and restriction. Hence our widespread critical agreement about reading this novel in terms of its "pervasive prison" imagery. The forces operating against the human grain are shown to be omnipresent, including, as they do, psychological, social, and economic determinants: the walls of prisons and bureaucracies, matched by the barriers of class and environment, are structures which threaten and restrict the limits of human development. But Mr. Meagles doesn't fit anywhere into the allegory. He is not an example or victim of repressive forces, and he is neither suffering under nor contending against his present or past circumstances. On the contrary, Meagles is the one important character in the novel who is not anxiety-ridden, ambitious, or at cross-purposes with his environment (the saintly Little Dorrit always and necessarily excepted).

In the very best Dickensian sense of the word, Mr. Meagles is content with his lot. So that we may be in no doubt about this character's virtue, Dickens assigns to Meagles two unmistakable rewards: a loving and respectful family, and a habitation which is a pastoral paradise (in a novel otherwise set amidst urban horrors). It is my contention that Meagles' behavior is without exception exemplary; moreover, the various inferences by which critics have endeavored to find this character deserving of his sad end are, when studied, so unconvincing as to demonstrate their opposite. Certainly Meagles is quaint and amusing as well as thoroughly virtuous, and he commands our affection in addition to our esteem. But we must recognize that throughout the novel he is to be the chief agent for doing good deeds (in the Clennam/Dorrit story particularly), all his efforts instances of unabashed benevolence.

Alone among the good people, however, Meagles is left sad at the novel's end. His pathos is, I think, reminiscent of that of certain other of Dickens' aggrieved parents or guardians; I have in mind Daniel Peggotty and Thomas Gradgrind especially. Yet the latter, we know, is largely to blame for his daughter's awful marriage, and so deserves his fate. The Peggotty example is much nearer, except that there is no audience in *Little Dorrit* for Meagles' sad exit. By which I mean that the Peggotty-'Em'ly strand in *David Copperfield* is an integral part of the theme of David's growing up, and in particular it reflects on the narrator's own child-parent and then suitor-husband experiences. By contrast, the Meagles-Pet theme has no clear ethical or structural role to play in this novel; indeed, the presence and purpose of the Meagles family deserves more critical consideration than it has so far received.[2]

Four specific failings have been charged against Meagles by various critics, but before I consider any of these, let us review the presumably all-important first appearance of the character: a reader's initial response is almost invariably conditioned by Dickens to be reliable. In the case of Meagles, then, our response is one of unqualified affection: the man seems jovial, honest, polite, thoroughly likeable. The documentation is all offered in the second chapter.[3] Here are the opening lines of description: "The speaker, with a whimsical good humour on him all the time, looked over the parapet-wall with the greatest disparagement of Marseilles; and taking up a determined position by putting his hands in his pockets, and rattling his money at it, apostrophised it with a short laugh" (15). The dialogue with Clennam, who is as yet unnamed, then continues until "a cheerful feminine voice" interrupts, whereupon the narrator offers a few more lines of description: "Mr. Meagles . . . appeared (though without any ill-nature) to be in that peculiar state of mind in which the last word spoken by anybody else is a new injury" (16). At this point, we are given several richly descriptive lines: "It was Mrs. Meagles who had spoken to Mr. Meagles; and Mrs. Meagles was, like Mr. Meagles, comely and healthy, with a pleasant English face which had been looking at homely things for five-and-fifty years or more, and shone with a bright reflection of them"[4] (16).

Pet Meagles is now brought forward, and she is described in a manner which, once again, no Dickens reader could misinterpret: she is drawn altogether lovely and fine. (The staid but reliable Clennam is made to indicate his unconditional approval of the girl.) Along with Pet, Tattycoram is mentioned, and by way of explaining that peculiar name, Meagles says to Clennam: "Why, the fact is, Mrs. Meagles and myself are, you see, practical people" (17). Thereafter, Meagles refers to himself and to Mrs. Meagles as "practical people" seven times in the next few pages. The reader recognizes that a Dickensian pedal point is henceforth in operation, a device Dickens uses often, generally for its comic effects. There can be no question how this verbal eccentricity functions here: it is a euphemistic index to a charming modesty.

> "Well! One day when we took Pet to church there [at the London Foundling Hospital] to hear the music—because, as practical people, it is the business of our lives to show her everything that we think can please her—Mother . . . began to cry so, that it was necessary to take her out. 'What's the matter, Mother?' said I. . . . 'You are frightening Pet, my dear.' 'Yes, I know that, Father,' says Mother, 'but I think it's through my loving her so much, that it ever came into my head.' 'That ever what came into your head, Mother?' 'O dear, dear!' cried Mother . . . 'when I saw all those

children ranged tier above tier, and appealing from the father none of them has ever known on earth, to the great Father of us all in Heaven, I thought, does any wretched mother ever come here, and look among these young faces, wondering which is the poor child she brought into this forlorn world, never through all its life to know her love, her kiss, her face, her voice, even her name!' Now that was practical in Mother, and I told her so. I said, 'Mother, that's what I call practical in you, my dear.' " . . .

"So I said next day: Now, Mother, I have a proposition to make that I think you'll approve of. Let us take one of those same children to be a little maid to Pet. We are practical people. So if we should find her temper a little defective, or any of her ways a little wide of ours, we shall know what we have to take into account. We shall know what an immense deduction must be made from all the influences and experiences that have formed us—no parents, no child-brother or sister, no individuality of home, no Glass Slipper, or Fairy Godmother. And that's the way we came by Tattycoram." (17-18)

Being practical people, the Meagles changed the foundling's arbitrarily given name of Harriet Beadle because they hoped that "a playful name [Tatty] might be a new thing to her, and might have a softening and affectionate kind of effect." "Beadle" they objected to with all the indignation of Charles Dickens writing the opening chapters of *Oliver Twist*. They chose "Coram" because it was the name of "the blessed creature" who built the foundling home. We do not have to be widely read in Dickens to know how we should regard a couple who adopts an orphan out of compassion and charity—and who thereupon gloss over this act (resorting to euphemism) rather than call attention to it.[5]

As well as earning our affection and applause, the eccentric use of *practical* cues in Meagles' claim to our strong admiration. He is, as I have said, a good man as well as a lovable one. The sense of respect I have in mind here, also provided for us in this first meeting with Meagles, derives from Clennam's unintentional reference to Meagles' dead child. This girl, Pet's twin, died in early childhood, and when Clennam realizes that his question touches on that misfortune, he endeavors to apologize:

"I am afraid I have inadvertently touched upon a tender theme."

"Never mind," said Mr. Meagles. "If I am grave about it, I am not at all sorrowful. It quiets me for a moment, but does not make me unhappy. Pet had a twin sister who died when we could just see her eyes—exactly like Pet's—above the table, as she stood on tiptoe holding by it." . . .

"Yes, and being practical people, a result has gradually sprung up in the minds of Mrs. Meagles and myself which perhaps you may

—or perhaps you may not—understand. Pet and her baby sister were so exactly alike, and so completely one, that in our thoughts we have never been able to separate them since. It would be of no use to tell us that our dead child was a mere infant. We have changed that child according to the changes in the child spared to us, and always with us. As Pet has grown, that child has grown; as Pet has become more sensible and womanly, her sister has become more sensible and womanly, by just the same degrees. It would be as hard to convince me that if I was to pass into the other world tomorrow, I should not, through the mercy of God, be received there by a daughter, just like Pet, as to persuade me that Pet herself is not a reality at my side." (19)

It seems to me incontestable that these are the sentiments of a Dickensian moral hero.[6] We are meant to be deeply impressed by the speaker's artless eloquence, and by his ability to communicate this most intensely felt of experiences. Meagles' account of grief is perfectly modulated, betrayed neither by sentimentality nor false heroics. Furthermore, in speaking of this distressing and awkward subject, Meagles reveals no affectation; he maintains at a high level both his own dignity and due consideration for his listener.

Despite this undeniably sympathetic appearance—in deeds, words, and circumstance—Mr. Meagles' fate in the novel will contradict the expected reward for true virtue. Pet's bad marriage promises to haunt the Meagles' peace. (Unlike Little 'Em'ly, Pet cannot be sent to the other end of the earth, or ultimately from the earth.) Thus, despite his goodness and his efforts on behalf of Doyce, Clennam, and Little Dorrit, Mr. Meagles ends by suffering a sharp diminution of what we have been conditioned (by all Dickens' previous novels, as well as by the ethos of *Little Dorrit* itself) to believe is earned contentment. He becomes an unfathomable contrast to both Clennam and Little Dorrit, who, if they are also shown to suffer undeservedly, are entirely repaid with mutual happiness and prospects of a joyful future. All of this being so, we are forced to ask what Dickens is trying to express through the Meagles story; how, if at all, does it correlate to the novel's accepted allegorical sense?

Before I attempt to answer, I want to establish Meagles' innocence as well as his goodness, for the narrator's rhetorical question about Meagles ("who could blame him"?) is generally either overlooked or wrongly answered. The misreading (by answering, "we can") is certainly understandable, for it is that reading—and only that reading—which allows a determined critic to preserve some consistent sense of this novel's thematic and ethical unity. Those critics, then, who set out to justify Meagles' punishment charge him with at least one of several sins: spoiling his daughter, Pet; treating Tattycoram insensitively; showing indiscriminate awe for highborn families; and/or condescending to Daniel Doyce.[7] None of these charges stands up well to scrutiny, and even their combined weight does not provide much more than a stitch or two for the wide mourning-dress Meagles is forced to wear at the conclusion. Yet each of these charges is worth considering, for the means of refutation serve to confirm Meagles' goodness as well as his innocence.

The notion that Pet has been spoilt, it turns out, is revealing not for the sense it makes about Pet or Mr. Meagles but for the hint it contains about "Nobody's Fault" (see my second note). The Pet Meagles who is characterized in *Little Dorrit* is in no sense spoilt, though the basis for such a charge is none other than the narrator himself. As we shall see, the accusation is not found in the draft. By studying the manuscript of *Little Dorrit,* I have discovered the cause of this confusion, though not the nature of Dickens' apparent reconsiderations about the character.

The truly spoilt young women in Dickens' works, from Fanny Squeers to Bella Wilfer, are identifiable as such with all their failings shown.[8] But Pet Meagles neither behaves nor speaks at all out of turn; she is never pert, willful, or in any need of correction. On the contrary, she is shown to be both sensible and sensitive, most acutely aware of other people's feelings.

We first see Pet as she approaches the friendless and haughty Miss Wade; the ship's passengers are at this moment dispersing.

> "Are you"—she turned her eyes, and Pet faltered—"expecting anyone to meet you here, Miss Wade?"
> "I? No."
> "Father is sending to the Poste Restante. Shall he have the pleasure of directing the messenger to ask if there are any letters for you?"
> "I thank him, but I know there can be none."
> "We are afraid," said Pet, sitting down beside her, shyly and half tenderly, "that you will feel quite deserted when we are all gone."
> "Indeed!"
> "Not," said Pet, apologetically and embarrassed by her eyes, "not, of course, that we are any company to you, or that we have been able to be so, or that we thought you wished it."
> "I have not intended to make it understood that I did wish it."
> "No. Of course. But—in short," said Pet, timidly touching her hand as it lay impassive on the sofa between them, "will you not allow Father to render you any slight assistance or service? He will be very glad." (24)

This, it seems to me, is a performance of someone very nearly the opposite of spoilt. All the more odd, then, that only thirty or so lines beneath this we come across a reference to Pet being spoilt; she is said "to shrink childishly in her spoilt way, a little closer to Mr. Meagles."

The word simply does not fit any of the girl's actions. Pet demonstrates outstanding sensitivity throughout the novel, several times in highly trying moments: when she must tell Arthur Clennam about her engagement to Gowan; when she tries to reassure her father about her hopes for a happy marriage. In her troubled life after that marriage, Pet shows nothing but high discretion and quiet courage. Her weakness, to state it simply, is the warmly human one of a romantic vision. Although Pet is quite indifferent to the Gowan name and lineage, she is attracted to Henry by full romantic inclination. As events prove, she would have been incomparably better off had she chosen Clennam's torpid virtues—if ever he worked up sufficient spirit to offer his hand.

In this novel of false patriarchs and generally indifferent parents, Mr. and Mrs. Meagles demonstrate a mature responsibility toward their daughter; their behavior commands our respect. That Pet enters into an extremely unhappy marriage with Gowan is far less a matter for guilt-finding than it is for pity. Mr. Meagles is to be commended for his discretion and wisdom insofar as he permits his daughter to choose for herself the man she most desires—though her choice of Gowan is decidedly not to Meagles' liking. It is worth emphasizing how much Meagles is disinclined toward Gowan, and how deep are his misgivings about Pet's decision to marry the man. Meagles does all that he, in honor, can do to dissuade Pet from her choice. Surely, then, it is to his credit that Meagles will neither bully the girl nor take away from her (temporary) joy by enlarging on his own suspicions.

There are three parallel cases in the novel of innocently misplaced affection: John Chivery's love for Little Dorrit, Flora's love for Arthur Clennam, and Little Dorrit's dedication to her indifferent father and family. Perhaps Clennam's love for Pet ought to be mentioned as well. In each of these cases, just as in Pet's, the sadness brought by unreciprocated affection is not in any way deserved. And certainly there is no ironic salute being offered either to folly or vice.

Rather than consider the story, those commentators who would argue that Meagles' final punishment is caused by the crime of spoiling Pet cite the three passages in the novel where the narrator himself uses the term *spoilt* (16, 25, and 198), especially the first of these, in which the narrator observes that Pet is "round and fresh and dimpled and spoilt." Neither this nor the second ascription of *spoilt* (25), appears in the manuscript. Instead, "timid" is used several times to describe "Baby" Meagles, as she is there called. "Timid" was evidently altered to "spoilt" in proof, but Baby's behavior remains unchanged. In chapter xvi of the manuscript, "spoilt" does appear; "Baby" is then changed to "Pet." Save for the name change, however, Dickens' second thoughts about this character were simply not carried out.

Probably the majority of commentators who seek to understand Meagles' fate in the otherwise unexceptional scheme of *Little Dorrit* fix on his treatment of Tattycoram; "indifferent parents to Tattycoram" is the way in which Lionel Trilling expresses his case against Meagles.[9] The charge seems to me entirely unjust, and anyone who endorses it finds himself having to accept Miss Wade's point of view as opposed to that of someone like Clennam. That aside, in a novel where "natural" parents are represented by the likes of Mr. Dorrit, Mrs. Gowan, Mrs. Clennam, and the Merdles, the behavior of the Meagles to this adopted child must be considered nothing but commendable.

Tattycoram, we are told straight off, is "a sullen, passionate girl" (25). In her first appearance, she is shown to be tempestuous and unreliable. No sooner does she express her furious discontent to Miss Wade than she recants:

> "When my temper comes upon me, I am mad. I know I might keep it off if I only tried hard enough, and sometimes I do try hard enough, and at other times I don't and won't. What have I said! I knew when I said it, it was all lies. They think I am being taken care of somewhere, and have all I want. They are nothing but good to me. I love them dearly; no people could ever be kinder to a thankless creature than they always are to me." (27)

And on Meagles' side, there is much to praise. When, for example, he explains to Clennam the circumstances of Tattycoram's running off, Meagles makes no attempt even to soften the girl's harsh accusations against himself, though these accusations are unjust. The narrator reveals that Meagles "was far more intent on softening her case than the family's" (322).

In this matter of Tattycoram's accusations, we are given what seems to be a problem in tonality. To some extent, the charges are openly debated in the novel, and it is partly from the debate that the reader arrives at a judgment. Miss Wade is allowed to articulate Tattycoram's resentment. She charges Meagles with gross hypocrisy and cruelty in his attitude toward and treatment of Harriet:

> "Here is your patron, your master. He is willing to take you back, my dear, if you are sensible of the favour and choose to go. You can be, again, a foil to his pretty daughter, a slave to her pleasant willfulness, and a toy in the house showing the goodness of the family. You can have your droll name again, playfully pointing you out and setting you apart, as it is right you should be pointed out and set apart. (Your birth, you know; you must not forget your birth.) You can again be shown to this gentleman's daughter, Harriet, and kept before her, as a living reminder of her own superiority and her gracious condescension." (328)

To this, the narrator merely reports of "poor Mr. Meagles' inexpressible consternation in hearing his motives and actions so perverted." Clennam comes to the support of Meagles, but the discussion is broken off by Miss

Wade's appeal to the gentlemen's compunction. And there the issue stands, if issue it is, until the conclusion of the novel, when Tattycoram returns to the Meagles.

> "Dear Master, dear Mistress, take me back again, and give me back the dear old name! . . ."
>
> Father and Mother Meagles never deserved their names better, than when they took the headstrong foundling-girl into their protection again.
>
> "Oh! I have been so wretched," cried Tattycoram. . . . "always so unhappy, and so repentant! . . . I knew she had got a power over me, through understanding what was bad in me, so well. It was a madness in me, and she could raise it whenever she liked. I used to think, when I got into that state, that people were all against me because of my first beginning; and the kinder they were to me, the worse fault I found in them. I made it out that they triumphed above me, and that they wanted to make me envy them, when I know—when I even knew then, if I would—that they never thought of such a thing. . . . I have had Miss Wade before me all this time, as if it was my own self grown ripe—turning everything the wrong way, and twisting all good into evil." (811)

Undeniably, our twentieth-century sensibilities respond to the social implications of Tattycoram's inferiority complex, but the girl's confused anger cannot—except in paradox—justifiably be ascribed to the benevolence of Mr. Meagles. Between the two, the patron and the foundling, at the very least a reasonable balance is struck.

If one had really to excuse Meagles for what Dickens in his letters called "tuft-hunting," that is, respecting class more than character, an apologist could point out that Meagles after all had come from a poor man's home. But no such excuse is necessary, for despite his willingness to think well of "society," Meagles' judgments about people remain sound and unaffected throughout the novel. Somewhat similar to the narrator's references to Pet as someone spoilt, Meagles' several apparent bows to upper-class unworthies simply do not influence his behavior. (Perhaps this too was part of an undeveloped theme in "Nobody's Fault.")

On more than one occasion, we should note, Meagles is the author of slighting or equivocal references to the well-born, references which clearly reveal his basically good judgment about people, regardless of their class. At Pet's wedding, for example, where so much seems to be made of the assorted Barnacles present, Meagles is shown to be more concerned about Clennam's turning up than about "the most elevated Barnacle expected" (400). If a single line, however, is wanted to acquit Meagles of this charge, we should quote his mocking reference to Mrs. Gowan, as "that elegant connection of ours" and "that ornament of society" (526). If we recall how in my opening quotation (the lines concluding the novel's penultimate chapter) "the only comfort" said to be left to Meagles is the idea of "that very good family" from which his son-in-law comes, then the pathetic ring to "who could blame him" deepens considerably; the claims of the high birth are here steeped in irony. (One might also keep in mind that Meagles never lets up in his battle against the Circumlocution Office despite the fact that it is run by assorted Barnacles.)

Finally, to read Meagles' attitude toward Doyce as one of guilty condescension is to show little appreciation of Dickens' sense of whimsicality. Paternalism can be humorous as well as reprehensible, and such is the case with Meagles overseeing Daniel Doyce. Apart from that, Meagles is—as Doyce himself acknowledges—"a sagacious man in business"; events show that neither Clennam nor Doyce is at all so.

The most negative comment on Meagles' attitude toward Doyce is not the narrator's but Clennam's, he who is neither practical nor creative:

> Clennam could not help speculating . . . whether there might be in the breast of this honest, affectionate, and cordial Mr. Meagles, any microscopic portion of the mustard-seed that had sprung up into the great tree of the Circumlocution Office. His curious sense of a general superiority to Daniel Doyce, which seemed to be founded, not so much upon anything in Doyce's personal character, as on the mere fact of his being an originator and a man out of the beaten track of other men, suggested the idea. (194)

To which one can say very little more than "perhaps": the span from the "microscopic portion of a mustard-seed" to the full-grown tree is hardly assignable to Meagles as we see him. That is to say, as the novel itself is given to us, such a conjecture can have no significant place in accounting for Meagles' final sorrow—and it is this issue I am concerned about.

If any of these four allegations carried weight, if indeed Meagles were in any way or sense guilty of a misdeed for which punishment were in order, then surely he would be cast out of his symbolic Eden—into the gloom and chill and closeness of urban London. But not so. We are assured at the novel's end that Mr. and Mrs. Meagles (with Tattycoram) will continue to occupy their idyllic cottage in the countryside. Nothing of any charge against Meagles can contradict this continuing testimony to virtue, his association with the cottage at Twickenham.

> It was a charming place (none the worse for being a little eccentric), on the road by the river, and just what the residence of the Meagles family ought to be. It stood in a garden, no doubt as fresh and beautiful in the May of the Year, as Pet now was in the May of her life; and it was defended by a goodly show of handsome trees and spreading evergreens. (191)

Even at the risk of redundancy, Dickens works at identifying the cottage with its inhabitants. We are told that when the family traveled it was one of Mr. Meagles' whims to have the cottage kept always "as if they were always coming back the day after tomorrow" (192). At all times, then, despite their periods of foreign residence and travel, this home is to be identified with the Meagles: the pastoral virtues of the place are made to inhere in its owners.

At several points in the novel, Dickens describes in leisurely and luxuriant detail both the setting and the cottage (see particularly chapter xxviii). The pastoral paradise motif is clearly being celebrated once again in Dickens: the goodness, health, and restorative vitality of Nature. Thus, the setting, the cottage, and, by implication which Dickens has made unavoidable, the inhabitants are representative of the virtue and value of natural phenomena. In this manifestation, the early and late Dickens are hardly distinguishable in their subscription to the romantic myth, *Our Mutual Friend* being as convincing as was *David Copperfield*.

Although the restorative role of pastoral goodness is not given a large direct emphasis in *Little Dorrit,* it is continually and powerfully implied by the presentation of London in the most somber, even ominous shades. Each of the three principal sites described in London is made "home" for at least one major character or family: I refer to the Marshalsea prison, Bleeding Heart Yard, and the Clennam residence. All three, of course, contrast particularly with the beauty and healthfulness of Meagles' environment. Consider, for example, just these few lines describing the Clennam house (they occur in chapter iii, "Home"):

> An old brick house, so dingy as to be all but black, standing by itself within a gateway. Before it, a square courtyard where a shrub or two and a patch of grass were as rank (which is saying much) as the iron railings enclosing them were rusty: behind it, a jumble of roots. (31)

The sunshine, the clear air and blue heavens, all the Arcadian virtues are associated with Meagles. Yet even their mythic powers cannot save him from his sorrowful fate.

In both his action and his attitudes, Mr. Meagles is a wholly benevolent force. He is presented as a man who, despite his lowly origins, has decently earned sufficient money so that he can retire and enjoy his plenitude. Of obscure birth, Meagles has won—and deservedly so—a good name. In the course of the novel's adventure, Meagles is the chief agent for working good deeds: he searches for and is able to recover the stolen Clennam papers; he fetches Doyce back from the Middle East so that Arthur Clennam can be released from debt and restored to the business partnership in good standing (and it was Meagles who helped the hapless Clennam to the position in the first place). Meagles alone is clever enough to avoid investing in the Merdle speculation, though all the others, including the "shrewd" Pancks, take a plunge. On the other hand, Meagles is generous enough to go on paying Henry Gowan's ill-gained debts.[10] And finally, Meagles is immensely tactful: he remains completely calm and dignified while the (upper-class) harridan Mrs. Gowan behaves abominably to him; and he retains his poise in the face of Miss Wade's haughty and insolent provocation on behalf of Tattycoram.

In a novel overfull with inept parents, with men who have not good names—or who are undeserving of the respect they receive; in this study of fathers who lose their incomes, or who are unable to provide adequately for their families; in contrast to all these, Meagles is not only blameless, but of exemplary virtue. Yet his ways, like his fate, seem not to illuminate any important sense of *Little Dorrit*. In a novel whose characters either serve or suffer the forces of human repressiveness, Meagles' benign existence seems a meaningless contrast. Put another way, in this novel of commercial interests, Meagles is an irrelevant Christian.

When, quite early in the novel, Miss Wade treats Meagles to one of her cynical observations, she is deflected by his courteous invitation for assent: "Well, well. But it's not natural to bear malice, I hope?" (23). Meagles' use of *natural* strongly suggests the Christian quality of the man's openness, which in the case of Miss Wade and Tattycoram alike amounts to nothing else than quite genuine forgiveness. That Meagles is a pious man is undeniable, I think, once we read his expression of grief over the loss of his child, spoken in the second chapter (see also his reference to Lillie on pp. 193-94). It is made perfectly clear from this initial portrait of Meagles that he is one of Dickens' upstanding men who is able to invoke God's name with commendable humility. He is one of God's good people whose belief is made explicit and shown to be honest and appropriate. One could say that he deserves the cottage at Twickenham.

At the conclusion of the story, Mr. and Mrs. Meagles choose not to be present at the celebration of Clennam's marriage to Little Dorrit. It is only his unfailing tact which attributes their absence to Mrs. Meagles' distress alone. For it no doubt would be supremely painful for them to witness so great a happiness and thereby be reminded of their own loss. The Meagles in fact have no place at that celebration, for the question posed by their undeserved sorrow is not answered by the conventional pieties of *Little Dorrit*.

It requires only a few words now to conclude my argument, for only two surmises are possible. The first is that *Little Dorrit*, as no less than John Forster was the first to observe, fails to reward us insofar as it is incoherent both in characterization and narrative. That being so, we might regard Little Dorrit and Mr. Meagles as totally unrelated *exempla*, their separate and contradictory fates being in fact incomparable. But I hesitate to make this my conclusion, if only because of the external evidence, from *Dombey and Son* on, of Dickens' concern to unify his plots. For Dickens to have developed both the Meagles and the Clennam/Dorrit stories as he did, all the while allowing them to stand in no relationship to one another, strikes me as much less likely than this second thesis: that the intended relationship is there but ambiguous—perhaps made deliberately so.

The two stories, as I have argued, do not freely comment on each other; but they certainly can be made to do so, and with a quite devastating result. For if we choose to read these nearly contradictory *exempla* as windows onto one and the same world, then we must acknowledge a dreadfully dark cloud hovering over Little Dorrit's Christian landscape (we note the "sunshine and shade" allusion in the novel's last line: Meagles' fate provides the shade). To change the image, the voice of Job is once again to be heard in the land. Little Dorrit, our "good angel," has been known to us all along; but who is the devil successfully maltreating the Meagles? Dickens does not force this contrast to our attention; nevertheless, he allows it to be drawn by failing—I must, at this point, add, deliberately—to account for the pathos of Meagles' exit. If we are more disturbed than edified by our study of Mr. Meagles, perhaps that is what Dickens intended all along—even from that early, quizzical title of "Nobody's Fault."

Chesterton, we recollect, felt *Little Dorrit* to be the saddest of all Dickens' novels, but he does not spell out the reasons; he makes no mention of Meagles. Yet it is Meagles' fate which casts an especially unsettling gloom over the end of the story. We have now to reflect on the amiable, jolly Pickwickian traveler who is treated roughly by events, and condemned without cause to perpetual unhappiness. The novel is sad indeed.

Anthony Winner

CHARACTER AND KNOWLEDGE IN DICKENS

The Enigma of Jaggers

> But the strangest, most enigmatic figure in the book, perhaps in
> all Dickens' work, is Jaggers. Who is he, this Prospero, this
> manipulator, agent and source of Pip's and Estella's fortunes? Is
> he good and benevolent as he sometimes seems? Or cynical and
> malign as he appears at other times? It is almost impossible to
> pin him down. Yet around him undoubtedly hangs the guilt—
> social and personal—that is the pervading theme of the book.—
> Angus Wilson, Afterword to *Great Expectations*

THE ENIGMA of Jaggers is that of the difficult relations between social
and individual life: of the different types of knowledge and response each involves. Standing at the crossroads of several of Dickens' most complexly
weighted concerns, Jaggers represents and incarnates the dilemma of his author's attitudes toward society. He is not a caricature, not an instance of that
twisting of energy and interplay of fancy and observation which animate
Dickens' marvelous humor figures. Unlike, for example, the grim antics of
the Smallweed family in *Bleak House,* the attorney's attributes—huge fore-
finger, recurrent handkerchief, compulsive handwashing—elicit not delighted
comprehension but the need to comprehend, to "pin down."

Jaggers is Dickens' fullest yet also most ambiguous response to the
questions of knowledge and authority, of force and evil, which perplex the
novels from the Fleet Prison scenes in *Pickwick Papers* onward. In their
broadest, if most abstract and un-Dickensian, implications, the questions
that intersect in Jaggers involve the difficulties of novelistic omniscience in a
post-Providential world. A convinced if nondoctrinal Christian, Dickens accepts the premise that an extensive fictional realm must be ordered by principles of knowledge and value that borrow their force and truth from God:
that the ultimate meaning of a novelistic action imitates the Providence
which, apportioning destinies and deserts, makes sense of the seeming ambiguities and injustices that bewilder mundane existence. At the same time,
however, Dickens mirrors an age in which direct recourse to Providential in-

terpretation has become problematic, in which the center of graspable meaning has shifted from God to earthbound man and particularly to that creation of earthbound men, society. Dickens believes both in Providential order and in a loose variant of Comte's dictum that "Society is the only Divinity."[1] For the creator of the benevolent and malign Jaggers, as earlier for the creator of the Rousseauistic arch-criminal Vautrin, the social has become a dimension rather than a circumstance of the individual self. To act with mature force, the individual must come to terms both with the inner dimension and the outer fact of society: must *know* socially as well as personally. Goodness without knowledge is weak, but knowledge, as Jaggers exemplifies, is borne at the expense of decent selfhood.

For Dickens, knowledge of society, and especially of its institutions, corrupts. His characteristic response to a tainted and tainting world is to take upon himself as narrator the burden of knowing. Protecting the innocence that is crucial to goodness from the experience that corrodes goodness, his narrative omniscience tends to transform the Providential into the paternal. And paternal omniscience, while diminishing neither Dickens' novelistic energy and breadth nor the resonant density of his plots, does often have the effect of insulating decent characters from the traumas and possibilities for growth contained in the social realities the narrative presents. Because they are so often exempted from social demands and actualities, good characters frequently remain passive and childlike; rarely are they vibrantly or dramatically commensurate to the public world surrounding them. Though a major part of Dickens' achievement renders the criterion of rounded character beside the point, one senses that, at least from *Dombey and Son* on, it is not beside the point to Dickens. If paternal omniscience works against the creation of forceful multidimensional protagonists, the desire to create a character combining the narrator's grim knowledge with dramatically plausible decency is equally evident. The hope for such a character is implicit in the repeated pleas for social awareness and responsibility.

The novels of the fifties are attempts both to portray and to bridge the type of separation notable in the split narration of *Bleak House*. Dickens insists upon the dangers of innocent feeling deprived of experiential backbone. In *Hard Times* and *A Tale of Two Cities,* the compartmentalization of destructive social processes on the one hand and personal values and culture on the other comes to predict with increasing directness the threat of engulfing anarchy or revolt. The unusually complex portrait of Arthur Clennam in *Little Dorrit* is an effort to dramatize a resilient decency tempered to survive and counterweight social corrosion. The protective conclusion to these novels is ever more muted, but since the actualities treated are ever more darkly pressing, the happy endings appear sentimental fiats. The last-minute rescues performed by the plots seem to derive more from a stubborn and beleaguered sense of the justice of happy endings than from the enriching fairy-tale structure of *Oliver Twist* or *The Old Curiosity Shop*. Artistically,

the strain of defensive separation between innocence and experience manifests itself in a growing disjunction between comic gifts and darkening realities.

The drama of what J. Hillis Miller calls Pip's "self-creation" responds
to the challenge of separation.[2] Abjuring paternal omniscience, Dickens
allows Pip to confront and to learn to bear what the narrator previously has
borne. Dickens returns to the autobiographical impulse of the opening sections of *David Copperfield,* expanding the meaning of private education to
an exemplary social significance. The largest intention of the process of education and maturation upon which *Great Expectations* rests is the creation
of a selfhood able to function plausibly and decently in hard times and a bad
society. The figures Pip encounters refract his own possibilities, suggest a
possible direction for his selfdom. Each is, in a sense, father to the mature
Pip, and the novel is as memorable for its empathy with the complexities of
filial roles as it is for its insights into childhood generally. Of the figures that
impose themselves on Pip, Jaggers is the most difficult to comprehend. Rep-
resenting the unsavory facts of social experience and the dismal necessities of
social authority, the attorney stands at the far end of a spectrum extending
from the gentle and wholly personal Joe. Other Dickensian characters proceeding as Pip does from "restless aspiring discontented" (xiv)[3] youth to
adulthood are either rescued for decency by sentimental fiat or doomed to
moral or literal destruction. Pip belongs in neither group. Crossing the
dangerous bridge Jaggers provides, he proceeds to the humane coherence,
control, and earned wisdom that mark his restrospective narrative of self-
creation.

— *1* —

The achievement of selfhood demands comprehension of "the identity
of things" (i), a knowledge which, reaching and resonating beyond innocence, involves contact with a world shrouded in what Jaggers calls an "atmosphere of evil" (li). Beginning with *Oliver Twist,* Dickens' depiction of
this realm combines, as John Bayley comments, "the genre of Gothic nightmare with that of social denunciation, so that each enhances the other."[4]
The novels from *Dombey and Son* to *Our Mutual Friend* combine variations on the libertarian motif of society as a criminal conspiracy to defraud
man of his natural estate with elements from the Gothic plot of omnipresent
mystery, persecution, and depredation. The shrouded society at large becomes a Gothic institution, blocking and terrifying because its motives are
inscrutable, its depersonalizing power channeled into mysterious labyrinthine ways. The individual must exercise all his strength and knowledge to
extricate himself; innocence must be bracketed defensively into what Wemmick terms the "private and personal" life. To defend this life becomes one of
the central tasks of Dickens' narrative personae. More vital than the gen-

eralizing satiric anatomy which often recalls Carlyle is the role of keeping alive the light of genuine feeling, of extricating this light from the inhuman opaqueness of social abstraction. Indeed, satire finally serves less as a means of denouncing society than as a buffer walling off the good characters from too immediate an involvement with society.

An index to Dickens' developing conviction of the grim hopelessness of the public world and to the impossibility of useful contact with it is the distance between Oliver Twist's simple demand for a second helping and Arthur Clennam's impossible plea, "I want to know," with which he tries to pry information out of the Circumlocution Office. Knowledge and reason, though less crucial than Dickens' primary requirements of heart, feeling, and compassion, are demanded if a character is to achieve completeness. The whole man must possess the force of tried and tempered understanding. Lacking this, he will resemble John Jarndyce, who in other respects approximates the ideal, in being withdrawn from the pulse of experience. Sentiment by itself is unreliable: it leaves Jarndyce open to the insidious behavior of people such as Skimpole, that parody of the man of feeling. The hardness of facts must not tempt one into mere fancy or unworldly emotion. Yet, from *David Copperfield* to *Great Expectations,* decent sentiment appears the only recourse to the world as found. Social processes and realities (usually a pejorative in Dickens' vocabulary) are so hard, so cruel or criminal, that there can arise no protagonist who might believably reduce them to understanding.

Dickens' nearest approach is with Clennam:

> all that was hard and stern in his recollection, remained Reality on being proved—was obdurate to the sight and touch, and relaxed nothing of its old indomitable grimness. . . .
>
> He was a dreamer . . . because he was a man who had, deep-rooted in his nature, a belief in all the gentle and good things his life had been without. Bred in meanness and hard dealing, this had rescued him to be a man of honourable mind and open hand. Bred in coldness and severity, this had rescued him to have a warm and sympathetic heart. . . .
>
> And this saved him still from the whimpering weakness and cruel selfishness of holding that because such a happiness or such a virtue had not come into his little path, or worked well for him, therefore it was not in the great scheme, but was reducible, when found in appearance, to the basest elements. A disappointed mind he had, but a mind too firm and healthy for such unwholesome air. (I, xiii)

Clennam must be "rescued" by innate and unalterable good nature both from "Reality" and from the erosion of dreams central to realistic fiction. Despite his immersion in grim life, despite his involvement in the Merdle speculation, he remains heroically exempt from the probable effects and moral diminution of the general unwholesomeness. His innocent dreams are rewarded by the love and hand of Little Dorrit, who embodies the "active resignation, goodness, and noble service" (II, xxxiii) which are for Dickens the essence of Christian behavior. But the meanness, hard dealing, and indomitable blocking of dreams shown in the novel are so striking that Clennam's exemption and the concluding union of his goodness with Amy's Providential promise are hardly believable counterweights. Such happiness as exists is, as usual in the fiction before *Great Expectations,* discontinuous with social or public actuality. The discontinuity renders the happiness as abstract as the "roaring streets" (II, xxxiv) which the "blessed" couple enter at the very end of the novel. Integration or wholeness of character would involve accepted and concrete knowledge of, and action directed toward, the mystery that is social reality. But barely concealed behind the façade of society's secrets lurks a power that can annihilate character.

— 2 —

The intricacies of society and the network of crimes that often underlies them constitute the great secret. Nadgett, the private investigator in *Martin Chuzzlewit,*

> was the man at a pound a week who made the inquiries. It was no virtue or merit in Nadgett that he transacted all his . . . business secretly and in the closest confidence; for he was born to be a secret. He was a short, dried-up, withered old man, who seemed to have secreted his very blood. . . . How he lived was a secret; where he lived was a secret; and even what he was, was a secret. . . . He carried contradictory cards, in some of which he called himself a coal-merchant, in others a wine-merchant, in others a commission-agent . . . as if he really didn't know the secret himself. . . . Some people said he had been a bankrupt, others that he had gone an infant into an ancient Chancery suit which was still depending, but it was all a secret. He carried bits of sealing-wax and a hieroglyphical old copper seal in his pocket, and often secretly indited letters. . . . He belonged to a class; a race peculiar to the City; who are secrets as profound to one another, as they are to the rest of mankind. (xxvii)[5]

While Nadgett is a comic conceit rather than a threat, the themes of which he is a carrier are increasingly viewed as virulent in the later fiction. Opacity and inscrutability become peculiar, dismal determinants of the official, social world. In the darkness of secrecy, impervious to knowledge, breed miasmal threats to individuals and their rightful dreams. In *Little Dorrit,* the whole of London becomes to Clennam's imagination "wrathful, mysterious, and sad":

> the dim streets by which he went, seemed all depositories of oppres-

sive secrets. The deserted counting-houses, with their secrets of books and papers; . . . the banking-houses, with their secrets of strong rooms and wells, the keys of which were in a very few secret pockets and a very few secret breasts; the secrets of all the dispersed grinders in the vast mill, . . . he could have fancied that these things, in hiding, imparted a heaviness to the air. . . . He thought of the secrets of the lonely church-vaults, where the people who had hoarded and secreted in iron coffers were in their turn similarly hoarded, not yet at rest from doing harm; and then of the secrets of the river, as it rolled . . . between two frowning wildernesses of secrets, extending, thick and dense, for many miles, and warding off the free air and the free country swept by winds and wings of birds. (II, x)

Until the mid-fifties Dickens usually implies that, if compassionate responsibility can illuminate and civilize the wilderness of secrets, then the badness and criminality nurtured in these dark places will be purged by the influx of free air. Fundamental human evil—a definitive bad nature, often a compound of murderous envy and a lust for overlordship—does at times occur, but even figures such as Sikes and Fagin are presented as being somehow contiguous products of an irresponsible or oppressive society. After *Hard Times,* however, Dickens insists more and more frequently upon the existence of innate, unregenerate evil. "There are people," proclaims the French landlady in *Little Dorrit,* "who have no good in them—none. [I tell you that] there are people whom it is necessary to detest without compromise. That there are people who must be dealt with as enemies of the human race, . . . people who have no human heart, and who must be crushed like savage beasts and cleared out of the way. They are but few, I hope; but I have seen . . . that there are such people" (I, xi). Rigaud, the landlady's subject, Orlick, and Riderhood in *Our Mutual Friend,* belong to this accursed breed. Their melodramatically vile natures are identifiable at once by the instinctive aversion they inspire in decent people. What is appalling about these avatars of Satan is less their intrinsic evil than the intertwining of this evil with the entire warp of social existence. As Pip recognizes, Orlick is an obvious descendant of Cain (xv). But Orlick also embodies a diabolic force which, making use of the organic secrecy of society as a resource and refuge, spreads out through Compeyson to Magwitch and thence to Pip. Rigaud, the savage beast and enemy of the human race, readily adapts the protective coloration of a corrupt social world and can plausibly mouth to his evil purposes the old libertarian dictum that the criminality of society forces individuals to become criminal in their turn. "I sell anything that commands a price. How do your lawyers live, your politicians, your intriguers, your men of the Exchange! . . . Society sells itself and sells me: and I sell Society" (II, xxviii).

Since evil, absorbed into the secret plots of public life, frustrates direct

challenge and insidiously defies comprehension, it can apparently be avoided
only by eschewing the public in favor of the private. But such avoidance is
rarely possible and always for Dickens is tinged with irresponsibility. Insofar as society incorporates evil, social experience, even knowledge, is corrupting. Yet without such experience, innocence is either vulnerable and
unavailing or abstract and sentimental. The secret matrix of bad nature,
crime, and evil jeopardizes the ideal of the free life of mutual good will. The
organizing secret, which will become a pivot of much popular fiction in the
sixties,[6] is for Dickens not a device but a defining aspect of the society.
And the definition calls forth a growing conservatism. Because evil and crime
exist with ubiquitous ramifications, society must exist as a defense, a necessary bulwark to innocence.

— 3 —

Contrapuntal to the generally acknowledged pessimism of Dickens' portrait of society, one finds a pervasive consideration of the protective function society should exercise. Society remains a dismal hole-and-corner affair; the protection it offers is as often as not a mockery. Dickens' distaste
for social knowledge and experience is ever present; such protection as there
is partakes of the unpleasant nature of its source—a point that militates
against sentimentality. In *Bleak House,* Inspector Bucket, Dickens' first extensive treatment of a socially omniscient guardian and his prefiguration of
the complexity and ambivalence later fulfilled in Jaggers, is tainted by professional opacity, secrecy, and disguises. He is the opposite of the moral
transparency Dickens cherishes. Bucket "knows" people and he "knows"
the world, but he himself is largely unknown. An almost hypnotic expertness
—perhaps the public counterpart to sentimental intuition—underwrites his
uncanny comprehension of social events and processes. Entering the third-
person narrative in Tulkinghorn's chambers, he informs Snagsby: "You're a
man of the world, you know, and a man of business, and a man of sense.
That's what *you* are!" (xxii). Snagsby, of course, is no such man; Bucket's
rhetoric is a form of coercion. Yet the inspector's standing off from the par-
ticularities of individual cases is made necessary by his professional function. If Snagsby, who in private life is coweringly uxorious, does not conform to Bucket's official description, he must be made to do so, to accept his
public duties. Bucket's omniscience is social, not personal, and is inevitably
prescriptive about the responsibilities of social existence. He parallels the
third-person narrator in being a dramatic stage manager of the plague-
connected outer world which stretches from Tom-All-Alone's to Chesney
Wold.[7] His knowledge, clearly, works for the good, but is contaminated by
the materialism and shabbiness of motive characteristic of all public involvement. Arresting George, he comments: "There's a reward out. . . . You and
me have always been pleasant together; but I have got a duty to discharge;

and if that hundred guineas is to be made, it may as well be made by me as any other man" (xlix). Duty and law exact the sacrifice of pleasantness; it is unsentimentally fair that Bucket at least be paid for the guardianship that renders him, apparently against his innate good nature, shady, ambiguous, and mysterious.

Bucket is benign, aware of the fragile decencies he must often override. His counterpart, Tulkinghorn, is just the opposite. The wholly negative aspects of Dickens' idea of official society are siphoned off from the inspector to the malignant attorney. In a characteristic procedure, the duality of a theme is conveyed through doubling: the villainously mysterious man of secrets and the protectively mysterious man of knowledge are sides of the same coin. The darkly enigmatic Tulkinghorn becomes a manifestation of Dickens' extreme discomfort with the idea that society is both a congeries of threatening secrets and also a system of protection.

> [Tulkinghorn] wears his usual expressionless mask—if it be a mask—and carries family secrets in every limb of his body, and every crease of his dress. Whether his whole soul is devoted to the great, or whether he yields them nothing beyond the services he sells, is his personal secret. He keeps it, as he keeps the secrets of his clients; he is his own client in that matter, and will never betray himself. (xii)

> Whether he be cold and cruel, whether immovable in what he has made his duty, whether absorbed in love of power, whether determined to have nothing hidden from him in ground where he has burrowed among secrets all his life, whether he in his heart despises the splendour of which he is a distant beam, whether he is always treasuring up slights and offenses, . . . whether he be any of this, or all of this, it may be that my Lady had better have five thousand pairs of fashionable eyes upon her, in distrustful vigilance, than the two eyes of this rusty lawyer. (xxix)

Tulkinghorn's private motive and personal feeling, whatever they may be, are buried in "his calling. His calling is the acquisition of secrets, and the holding possession of such power as they give him" (xxxvi). Both the narrative tone and the association of the lawyer with attributes Dickens detests indicate that a form of evil lies behind these series of conditional conjectures.

This evil, however, is not inborn or personal but of the same kind as that contained in the secret social processes which provoke Dickens' divided reactions. Direct statement and explicit condemnation would be reductive. For while Tulkinghorn's malignancy extends the motif of a criminal and inhuman public world, his mystery belongs to the thematic continuum that includes the protector Bucket: an opacity made necessary by the nature of society, a mask behind which knowledge, whatever its purpose, is compelled

to function. By leaving the lawyer's motives for pursuing Lady Dedlock un-
clear, Dickens allows him to act as the nemesis brought into being by her
crime: a social justice, devoid of mercy or compassion, that is analogous to
the laws that condemn Magwitch to death. Moreover, Tulkinghorn's professions of duty and service to Sir Leicester are treated with sufficient ambiguity
to mitigate somewhat the impression that his secrecy is wholly malicious
and to reinforce the idea that his actions are necessary to the social bulwark.
Indeed, there is an obvious parallel between these professions and Bucket's
frequently expressed sense of duty and respect toward the baronet.

Ultimately, Dickens' presentation of the single essence of society in its
dual aspects of Bucket and Tulkinghorn lends itself to a misleading sense of
the theme. Tulkinghorn is so shrouded in secrecy and damning associations
that he verges on a Gothic gimmick; the relation between Bucket's personal
decency and his official mystery is only tenuously established. The separation between the components and implications of the essential theme befogs
Dickens' complex conception.

— 4 —

In *Bleak House* Dickens' treatment of the intertwining of society's dread
secrecy and its protective function is inchoate. In *Great Expectations* Pip's
coming to consciousness involves from the beginning the mystery that entangles public and private. Plot, theme, and character all depend upon a
process of unraveling, of knowing. Growing and maturing in interaction with
the fallen world beyond the "sanctified" forge, Pip achieves the sober, balanced control and somewhat Wordsworthian wisdom that mark his narration and attest the integration of decent sentiment with dismal knowledge.
More nearly than any other character in Dickens, Pip is permitted the experience of rescuing himself. And this rescue is signaled by his exemption
from the disjunctive separation between personal and social being that elsewhere results in compartmentalized themes and characters.

Compartmentalization is a shaping, consciously controlled motif in
the novel. The terms of the divided life are parodied, albeit with warm sympathy, in Wemmick, who is both a preface and a parallel to Jaggers. For
Wemmick, "the office is one thing, and private life another" (xxv). The Little Britain Wemmick, Jaggers' dessicated "subordinate," the petty tyrant
with his regalia of "remembrances of departed [executed] friends," has
"such a post-office of a mouth that he had a mechanical appearance of smiling, . . . [but] it was merely a mechanical appearance" (xxi). When Pip,
in the office, asks how to invest money for Herbert, Wemmick replies that it
would be better simply to pitch the money off a Thames bridge.

> "—Invest portable property in a friend? . . . Certainly [one]
> should not. Unless he wants to get rid of the friend. . . ."

"And that . . . is your deliberate opinion, Mr. Wemmick?"

"That . . . is my deliberate opinion in this office. . . . Walworth is one place, and this office is another. Much as the Aged is one person, and Mr. Jaggers is another. They must not be confounded together. My Walworth sentiments must be taken at Walworth; none but my official sentiments can be taken in this office. . . . You will be welcome [at Walworth], in a private and personal capacity." (xxxvi)

The Wemmick Pip finds at Walworth appears to be one of the few contented and fulfilled figures in the novel, a man who smiles "with relish, and not merely mechanically" (xxv). Wemmick's "Castle" contains the features Dickens associates with the good, decent life: it is neat, clean, and warm, boasting both loyal family love and responsible sentimental love (Miss Skiffins). The tone of the hearth and home scenes, indeed, is so sentimental as to suggest a conscious exaggeration, even parody, of the Dingley Dell type of contentment and innocence in Dickens' fiction. As far from the office as the near vicinity of the City will permit, the "Castle" lies beyond a miniature moat and drawbridge; garden and livestock are kept out of sight, "so as not to impede the idea of fortifications" created by the painted-on battlements. " 'So, sir,' said Wemmick, smiling again, but seriously, too, as he shook his head, 'if you can suppose the little place besieged, it would hold out a devil of a time in point of provisions' " (xxv). And not only in point of provisions, for Wemmick is a fanciful Crusoe: "I am my own engineer, and my own carpenter, and my own gardener, and my own Jack of all Trades. . . . Well, it's a good thing, you know. It brushes the Newgate cobwebs away, and pleases the Aged" (xxv). Private and personal values are besieged by corrosive social forces; to survive, they must be defended by the strategies the "Castle" stands for.

Walworth feelings and expectations are ever under threat. When Wemmick invites Pip to his wedding, the entire expedition consists of defensive feints and blinds to its joyous meaning—a meaning darkened in any case by the fact that the episode occurs as a digression from the account of Magwitch's recapture and final illness. Wemmick, taking up a fishing-rod, pretends they are just going for a walk. Each stage of the proceedings is calculatedly fortuitous. "Halloa! Here's a church! . . . Let's go in! . . . Here's a couple of pairs of gloves! Let's put them on! . . . Here's Miss Skiffins! Let's have a wedding." " '*Now*, Mr. Pip,' said Wemmick, triumphantly shouldering the fishing-rod as we came out, 'let me ask you whether anybody would suppose this to be a wedding-party!' " As the scene concludes, Wemmick's expression of affection for his wife and her abilities is "altogether a Walworth sentiment. . . . Mr. Jaggers may as well not know of it. He might think my brain was softening, or something of the kind" (lv). In Grahame Smith's words, Wemmick can maintain his Walworth self "only at the expense of spiritual fragmentation."[8]

Smith argues that Wemmick forms "a subsidiary, and reinforcing, expression of the book's organizing principle, the corrupting power of money."[9] The "Castle" is stocked with much "portable property"—the almost extorted gifts of condemned criminals and Dickens' convincingly gruesome symbol for materialism; Wemmick's reaction to the news of Magwitch's death is a crudely inhuman regret at "the sacrifice of so much portable property" (lv). Yet to view Wemmick on this evidence as a figure of fundamental corruption is surely to ignore the evidence of tone throughout. The radical sentimentality of the Walworth scenes may be self-parody on Dickens' part—a comment on the excesses of sentiment uncontrolled by interaction with dismal reality—but these scenes clearly rest on warm allegiance. Wemmick's "portable property" bears much the same meaning as Bucket's willingness to accept the reward money. The contagion of materialism binds together home and office, Wemmick and Jaggers, strongly implying that compartmentalization cannot be absolute. Walworth is financed by the dubious wages earned by service to a tainted society. The Castle and the City cannot be, ultimately must not be, wholly separated: for in the world portrayed in *Great Expectations* both are necessary.

At Walworth, Wemmick tells Pip in an "extra-official" conversation of the dangers Magwitch is running; since the information was garnered at Newgate, the clerk is "restrained by fealty to Little Britain from saying as much as he could" (xlv). Nonetheless, the professional facts and advice, however hedged in the circumlocutions of officialese, are elicited by private sentiment for Pip. And though Wemmick feels and acts for Pip alone, considering Magwitch no more than another criminal in possession of goods, his Walworth sentiment for the former is strong enough to override "official responsibilities" in abetting the latter's escape. To help Pip, Wemmick integrates, albeit awkwardly and briefly, the two sides of his split existence: office knowledge provides crucial information about Magwitch and Molly; private feeling places the knowledge at Pip's service. If fealty to Little Britain compromises sentimental innocence at Walworth, it must still be remembered that fealty in Dickens is a positive trait. The professionalism of law and office would be exiguous, indeed inhuman, without the compassionate humanity of home, but compassion would be unavailing without official experience. The several parallels between law and home, as well as the frequent and ambiguous pairing of Jaggers and the Aged, suggest the need for the climactic confounding of the two realms that occurs in chapter li. Wemmick, whose divided self warns of the necessity for such confounding, is a subordinate to the major meaning which is dramatized in Jaggers, his "principle."

— 5 —

Jaggers is the pivot of Dickens' shaping conception, the guide who instructs Pip in the infernal world that lies spread before him once he leaves

the village. The attorney contorts, even martyrs, his individuality into a
wholly official self so that others may be defended against a ravaging public
reality. He embodies both law and the human cost of law. As Dorothy van
Ghent remarks:

> In this book, whose subject is the etiology of guilt and of atonement,
> Jaggers is the representative not only of civil law but of universal
> Law, which is profoundly mysterious in a world of dissociated and
> apparently lawless fragments; and his huge forefinger, into which he
> is virtually transformed and which seems to act like an "it" in its
> own right rather than like a member of a man, is the Law's mystery
> in all its fearful impersonality.[10]

Jaggers' mystery and force are related to the functioning of some absolute in
a fragmented world, yet "universal Law" does not account satisfactorily for
the attorney's enigmatic behavior. The same evidence can be interpreted in
several ways. Angus Calder comments that, in the province of crime,

> Jaggers is the tribal deity. . . . He is credited with the power of
> life and death. . . . His trade is the perversion of justice. His tools are
> bullying and deception. . . . Yet, though Pip finds him poor com-
> pany, it is never asserted that he is a bad man.
>   For the society where he makes the rules—"Little Britain"—
> is, like Greater Britain, a society without plausible standards by
> which his conduct may be judged. His clients are guilty, but their
> poverty nearly eradicates their guilt.[11]

Calder goes on to compare Jaggers to Raymond Chandler's corrupt police-
man in *The Big Sleep,* who is "as honest as you could expect a man to be in
a world where it's out of style."

Dickens is hardly so permissively relativistic. Neither in Magwitch's
case nor in any other is it suggested that poverty nearly erases guilt. A different kind of relativism, however, does shed light on the enigma of Jaggers.
Civil and universal, or divine, law are fundamentally different: the former is
relative, often a perversion of the latter. Jaggers as a sub-deity spawned by
and representative of a perverse society is distinctly unappealing, and most
of Dickens' references cast him in this role: an embodiment of the manifold
injustices of civil law. What confuses interpretation, and what keeps Pip
from asserting Jaggers' badness, is that the attorney does also and contra-
dictorily represent universal law: a version, however fallen its mundane practice, of "the greater Judgment that knoweth all things and cannot err" (lvi)
which Pip believes awaits Magwitch. Jaggers is the closest approximation to
a Providential figure—a Mr. Brownlow or a John Jarndyce—in the public
plot of the novel. An attorney for the defense, his dispositions often seem the
awkward imitation of Providential order in a bad world. His actions at their

best bear the meaning he offers to Pip when explaining why he placed Estella with Miss Havisham.

> "Put the case that he [Jaggers] lived in an atmosphere of evil,
> and that all he saw of children was, their being generated in great
> numbers for certain destruction. Put the case that he often saw chil-
> dren solemnly tried at a criminal bar. . . . Put the case that he habit-
> ually knew of their being imprisoned, whipped, transported, ne-
> glected, cast out, qualified in all ways for the hangman, and growing
> up to be hanged. Put the case that pretty nigh all the children he saw
> in his daily business life, he had reason to look upon as so much
> spawn, to develop into the fish that were to come to his net—to be
> prosecuted, defended, forsworn, made orphans, bedevilled somehow.
> . . . Put the case, Pip, that here was one pretty little child out of the
> heap who could be saved." (li)

Jaggers' view is supported by all the details of the society Dickens presents,
specifically by Magwitch's story of his life. In such a society, Providential
dispositions may have to emulate, or appear to emulate, Satan's strategies;
or, in a frequent romantic motif to which Jaggers' practice conforms, perversion of truth and justice in a perverted world may be the only way to
rescue the real thing. As a fallen figure of true law, Jaggers' type of power
and knowledge works as nearly for the good as a bad actuality will allow.
Recalling Comte's idea that "Society is the only Divinity," we may see the
attorney as anticipating the ambiguous priestly function later to be assigned
lawyers and detectives.

Jaggers brings together the roles of Tulkinghorn, the power-driven
emanation of society's evil secrets, and of Bucket, the all-knowing detective-
guardian. Like these two, he belongs to the social world; his comprehension
is directed mainly to that part of human behavior which is of public or official note. "The bad side of human nature," unlike the good, is generalizable
and predictable. Meeting Pip at Satis House, the attorney warns: "Behave
yourself. I have a pretty large experience of boys, and you're a bad set of
fellows" (xi). During the first stage of Pip's expectations, Jaggers often appears the objective spokesman for the intuitions of guilt and crime the boy
associates with his own nature. As Pip's snobbishness, falsity, and ingratitude come to approach Jaggers' general rule of badness, the attorney's share
of the narrative increases. Pip's case, of course, is relatively innocuous, but
his flaws parallel the evil criminality of Orlick and Compeyson, whose vi-
ciousness is Jaggers' domain.

After Wopsle's reading at Pumblechook's (xv), Pip feels himself an unnatural murderer, a George Barnwell. Given Jaggers' association with mur-
derousness, it is not surprising that his next appearance should be in the
scene—thematically a continuation of the reading—where Wopsle pontif-
icates upon a newspaper account of "a highly popular murder" at the

Three Jolly Bargemen. When Jaggers interrupts "coldly and sarcastically," "everybody started and looked up, as if it were the murderer." "I do say Guilty," Wopsle insists.

> "I know you do," said the stranger; "I knew you would. I told you so. But now I'll ask you a question. Do you know, or do you not know, that the law of England supposes every man to be innocent, until he is proved—proved—to be guilty?" (xviii)

Much in the fashion of Bucket, Jaggers' cross-examination reiterates and varies the issue of knowing.

The reference to legal supposition suggests the parodoxes of Jaggers' profession. In point of fact, the law rarely supposes innocence: Magwitch is prejudged guilty repeatedly. Jaggers himself seems to assume the guilt or complicity of all men. Pip describes him as "the strange gentleman, with an air of authority not to be disputed, and with a manner expressive of knowing something secret about every one of us that would effectually do for each individual if he chose to disclose it" (xviii). Later in the chapter, during the interview with Joe and Pip, Jaggers "threw his finger at me . . . to express that he knew all kinds of things to my disparagement, if he only chose to mention them." Wemmick follows his master in having the "same air of knowing something to everybody else's disadvantage" (xx). So extensive and authoritative a knowledge of guilt approximates divine omniscience. Universally shared guilt verges on an innocence analogous to that postulated by the theology of the Fall. Legally, Jaggers' omniscience is a perversion of justice; universally, it is part parody, part imitation, of Providence.

Pip tells Wemmick that he does not know what to make of the attorney.

> "Tell him that, and he'll take it as a compliment. . . . He don't mean that you *should* know what to make of it [his manner]. —Oh!" for I looked surprised, "it's not personal; it's professional: only professional. . . .
>
> "Always seems to me," said Wemmick, "as if he had set a man-trap and was watching it. Suddenly—click—you're caught!"
>
> Without remarking that man-traps were not among the amenities of life, I said I supposed he was very skilful?
>
> "Deep," said Wemmick, "as Australia." (xxiv)

Reaching as far as Magwitch in Australia, Jaggers' professional knowledge binds together the public plot of the novel, which rests upon the secrecies and determinations of badness in society. Jaggers' mysteriousness cloaks the authority that holds the criminality of the public world at bay. Pip's reservation about mantraps, however, indicates the unpleasant and misguided emphasis, the false construction, characteristic of Jaggers' omniscience. Learning from the attorney, Pip must be able to use professional knowledge on behalf of humane amenities rather than of the jungle code.

Jaggers, being his own "Castle," seems at first to have no personal life within his battlements. Unlike Wemmick, he "seemed to bring the office home." Meals at Walworth are warm and joyous; Jaggers presides over his dinner as a sardonic deity. He guides conversation so as to wrench "the weakest part of our dispositions out of us." He is much taken with "the blotchy, sprawly, sulky fellow," Drummle, whom he dubs "the Spider" and who, he tells Pip, "is one of the true sort" (xxvi). Drummle's bad nature and its potential affiliation with the "atmosphere of evil" explain the attorney's interest. Moreover, the attraction Drummle holds sheds light on the grounds for Jaggers' professional interest in Pip, which is stimulated by the dark auspices of crime and guilt born in the young boy's original encounter with Magwitch. Jaggers is often associated in Pip's mind with this encounter; the "disadvantage" he labors under during his coming-of-age interview with the attorney reminds him of that "old time when I had been put upon a tombstone" (xxxvi).

The dismal impersonality surrounding Jaggers is an epitome of the world he represents. Pip, during his birthday dinner,

> could not help wishing more than once . . . that Mr. Jaggers had had an Aged in Gerrard-street, or a Stinger, or a Something, or a Somebody, to unbend his brows a little. It was an uncomfortable consideration on a twenty-first birthday, that coming of age at all seemed hardly worth while in such a guarded and suspicious world as he made of it. (xxxvi)

This world, however, is not of Jaggers' making. And Pip is soon forced to admit its realities into his private and personal concerns. After Magwitch's return, Pip risks losing those very amenities which Jaggers lacks. All circumstances begin to appear suspicious, to have "an ugly look to one as prone to distrust and fear as the changes of a few hours had made me" (xl).

Truly to come of age, Pip must come to terms with these changes, must "rescue" compassion and sentiment from distrust and fear. Jaggers can contribute to the rescue precisely because his own sentiment, as Dickens is at pains to stress, is not wholly secreted and forgotten. Jaggers is no Tulkinghorn, not in some mysterious way an author of the dismal reality for which he so often speaks. As Pip's perceptions of things become clearer, the personal warmth behind the attorney's mask enters more clearly into evidence. During the first stage of his expectations, a period of essential innocence, Pip had felt the free-floating and undeserved guilt that is Dickens' major contribution to the portrait of childhood. The second stage begins in Jaggers' Little Britain office, a point of intersection for real evils. The attorney remarks darkly and professionally: "Of course you'll go wrong somehow, but that's no fault of mine" (xx). Yet at the dinner gathering Jaggers warns

Pip, "don't have too much to do with" Drummle, "keep as clear of him as you can" (xxvi). Throughout the second stage there are hints of a personal and paternal protectiveness on Jaggers' part. Indeed, the juxtaposition of the attorney and the Aged insinuates that the former may occupy in his professional sphere something of the position of the latter. Jaggers' knowledge becomes in regard to Pip a joint testing and guarding. Where Miss Havisham and Magwitch selfishly and vengefully manipulate destinies, Jaggers' rescue of Molly and Estella and his rather distant overseeing of Pip appear tempered versions of sentimental benevolence. Manipulation, after all, can be a good, as Pip's endowing of Herbert indicates. Of course, one is more apt to remember the attorney's ruthless exhibiting of Molly's hands and his manhandling of evidence than his disinterested shielding of the vulnerable. But, as the third stage makes clear, Jaggers can imitate Providence only within the unpleasant and defensive possibilities of a world largely hostaged to Fortune. His guarded and suspicious benevolence is the obverse of the malign, institutional inscrutability of society.

For the mature Pip, and obviously for Dickens, a benevolence thus defined is profoundly equivocal and uncomfortable. The price Jaggers embodies is too high. In the third stage Pip begins to demand that Jaggers' omniscience and the professionalism cloaking it be rendered personal, transformed into compassionate comprehension. Pip is "glad for once to get the better of him in cross-examination" (xlviii). In chapter li, the climax of this strand of the narrative, Pip's pressing demands force Jaggers' own sentiments into the open, confounding personal and official and laying bare the underlying thematic connections among the attorney, Wemmick, and the young man. Pip invades Jaggers' omniscient realm. "Perhaps I know more of Estella's history than even you do. . . . I know her father, too" (li). Jaggers is brought to "an indefinably attentive stop."[12] When Pip states that Magwitch neither knows of nor claims his paternity, "for once, the powerful pocket-handkerchief failed. My reply was so unexpected that Mr. Jaggers put the handkerchief back into his pocket without completing the usual performance." Pip's next sentence contains four "I knew's."

Taylor Stoehr comments that in this confrontation with Jaggers Pip does not know why he "was hot on tracing out and proving Estella's parentage" and that "after all the 'feverish' effort 'to hunt the matter down,' Pip drops the subject without a word." "The clue to the meaning of the discovery is not in either of Pip's hypotheses, but rather in the very ambiguity which he feels in his motives."[13] Such a reading, however, overlooks the pervasive resonance of "the identity of things" theme as well as the meaning and tone of Pip's mastery of the occasion. Here at last Pip has the advantage in knowing, and puts it to use on behalf of personal values. Jaggers tries to evade the subject.

But I could not submit to be thrown off in that way, and I made a

passionate, almost an indignant appeal to him to be more frank and
manly with me. I reminded him of the false hopes into which I had
lapsed, the length of time they had lasted, and the discovery I had
made: and I hinted at the danger that weighed upon my spirits. I
represented myself as being surely worthy of some little confidence
from him, in return for the confidence I had just now imparted. I
said that I did not blame him, or suspect him, or mistrust him, but I
wanted assurance of the truth from him. And if he asked me why I
wanted it and why I thought I had any right to it, I would tell him,
little as he cared for such poor dreams, that I loved Estella dearly
and long. . . . And seeing that Mr. Jaggers stood quite still and
silent, and apparently quite obdurate, under this appeal, I turned to
Wemmick, and said, "Wemmick, I know you to be a man with a
gentle heart. I have seen your pleasant home, and your old father,
and all the innocent cheerful playful ways with which you refresh
your business life. And I entreat you to say a word for me to Mr.
Jaggers, and to represent to him that . . . he ought to be more open
with me!"

Pip asserts the "right" of feeling, of his passionate dream and its bereaving
loss, against Jaggers' silence, suspicion, and mistrust. Two modes of being,
two expectations about reality, stand opposed.

But the opposition is not, as in the series of analogous earlier scenes
culminating in Clennam's futile challenge to the Circumlocution Office, absolute. Jaggers' knowledge is incomplete without Pip's. And what is true of
knowledge is true of character as well: the official guardian would be incomplete—would, indeed, be a villain—without a private soul. Not only are
the Little Britain and Walworth Wemmick confounded in the scene of revelation and integration Pip precipitates, but a similar split and a similar
impetus to integration are revealed in Jaggers.

"*You* with a pleasant home?" said Mr. Jaggers.
"Since it don't interfere with business," returned Wemmick,
"let it be so. Now, I look at you, sir, I shouldn't wonder if *you* might
be planning and contriving to have a pleasant home of your own,
one of these days, when you're tired of all this work."
Mr. Jaggers nodded his head retrospectively two or three times,
and actually drew a sigh. "Pip," said he, "we won't talk about 'poor
dreams'; you know more about such things than I, having much
fresher experience of that kind."

Behind the professional there flickers a man who may, like Wemmick, have
a "gentle heart"—the central compassionate value of the novel and the
keynote of Dickens' idealized portrait of Joe, whom Pip blesses as "this
gentle Christian man" (lvii). Decent feelings and their dreams are not Pip's
alone; his experience is merely "fresher." Jaggers' experience is retrospec-

tive and rusty, but it clearly underlies the case he puts about Molly: "that when she was set at liberty, she was scared out of the ways of the world and went to him [me] to be sheltered." The shelter is minimal, but none the less better than the heap. Jaggers' home is really an embattled castle, just as Wemmick's "Castle" conceals a true home. Any shelter in a world whose ways are so often evil is covered by the sentiment of home. But sentiment requires the radical defense of tainted knowledge. Jaggers explains to Pip why the secrecy surrounding Estella's parentage should not be cleared up:

> "But, add the case that you had loved her, Pip, and had made her the subject of those 'poor dreams' which have, at one time or another, been in the heads of more men than you think likely, then I tell you that you had better—and would much sooner when you had thought well of it—chop off that bandaged left hand of yours with your bandaged right hand, and then pass the chopper on to Wemmick there, to cut *that* off too."

To function at all, official guardianship must adapt the crude and often cruel terms of society to its purposes. And such adaptation, Dickens suggests, involves an irreducible measure of adoption. Because Jaggers' motive is at least in part one of feeling, he and the law he represents are rescued for the comprehension, even the rueful acceptance, of those subscribing to the values Pip here appeals to. The force of this appeal hectors the attorney not only into a recognition of the right of sentiment, but also into a personal association with such sentiment. At the same time, however, Jaggers' statement of the realities persuades Pip to acquiesce in the need for secrecy. Pip begins by demanding that the attorney be less secretive, "more open," more "frank and manly." After heeding Jaggers' case, he does drop the subject immediately. His so doing may indicate the ambiguity and confusion of his own motives, but it is also a vital acknowledgement that, in the world he has come to know, "such things" require the shelter of opacity. The acknowledgement anticipates in a small way Conrad's major theme of the reliance of civilization upon the protective lie or concealment. The presence of something like this meaning helps explain the absence of any definitive judgment upon Wemmick and Jaggers. Both the divided life and the professional suppression of all that Dickens holds dear are too serious and complex, in an unhappy sense too serviceable, to receive easy moral pigeon-holing.

Pip's narration of the conclusion to the scene rests upon his compassionate understanding of why Jaggers and Wemmick, having shown themselves in "a weak and unprofessional light," must unite in closing the breach. The two are "happily relieved by the opportune appearance" of the tearful Mike, who relates that his "eldest daughter was taken up on suspicion of shop-lifting." Mike blubbers that "a man can't help his feelings." Jaggers responds: "I'll have no feelings here. Get out." "And Mr. Jaggers and Wemmick appeared to have reestablished their good understanding, and went to work again with an air of refreshment upon them as if they had just had lunch." The mild irony of Pip's tone does not detract from his essential acceptance of this brutal dismissal. Mike, we learn, is a repetitious customer, who "either in his own person or in that of some member of his family, seemed to be always in trouble (which in that place meant Newgate)." The rejection of feelings accentuates their presence and pertinence earlier in the scene. Mike's conformity to the rule of the heap underscores the accuracy of Jaggers' official knowledge and advice.

— 6 —

The theme of *Great Expectations* is not guilt per se but the entanglement of guilt, crime, law, and selfhood: the bafflingly confounded nucleus of personal motive, social dimension, and the demands of civilization. Pip's story is a *Bildungsroman* describing the cultivation of civilization on the part of an individual. The narrative bridges what Barbara Hardy, speaking of the earlier novels, sees as the "frequent gap between the story of an individual's history and moral *Bildung,* on the one hand and the portrait of a society, on the other."[14] Pip's three stages are innocence, experience, and understanding—the latter meaning much what it means in Wordsworth. In the last two, Jaggers and Wemmick act both as influences on and indexes of Pip's movement from childish innocence and its proneness to guilt to a matured comprehension of the problematic identity of persons and things. Dickens insists through his career that no man is an island, but nowhere does he come so near to dramatizing the belief as a lesson of character as with Pip.

During the illness after Magwitch's death, Pip "confounded impossible existences with [his] own identity" (lvii). His feverish hallucinations all involve his being dangerously but inextricably a part of some larger whole: a brick in a house wall set in a "giddy place," "a steel beam of a vast engine, clashing and whirling over a gulf." The qualities of people blur into a confusion of good and evil: "I sometimes struggled with real people, in the belief that they were murderers, and . . . would all at once comprehend that they meant to do me good." The images resolve into Joe, who relates the concluding information about many of the characters—a device which has the effect of distancing destinies, implying that they are no longer possible identities for Pip, who has his own. Here too echoes of themes blur together. Joe's comment on Orlick's robbery of Pumblechook recalls the Walworth motif: "Still, a Englishman's ouse is his Castle, and castles must not be busted 'cept when done in war time." These comments pick up most of the strands of experience, but Joe's essential innocence shrinks from the East Wind of their darker resonance. His abrupt departure—and later the fact that he, not Pip, wins Biddy—hints at Pip's exclusion from simple inno-

cence. The ending of the original conclusion, and the only line from it repeated in the rewritten version, contains the phrase that suffering has
taught Estella "to understand what [my] heart used to be" (lix). The past
tense points to unalterable change: to the sobriety of lost or radically reduced possibility.

The meaning of this rather grey tone and its sources in Pip's experience suggest a different interpretation from that J. Hillis Miller presents in
his remarks on the sunlight which breaks into the courtroom during Magwitch's trial.

> The light is God's judgment before which earthly judge and earthly
> judged, gentleman and common thief, are equal. But the meaning of
> the passage is as much social as religious. It is a final dramatization
> of the fact that social eminence such as Pip had sought and social
> judgments such as have hounded Magwitch all his life are alto-
> gether unimportant as sources of selfhood. At the center of Dickens'
> novels is a recognition of the bankruptcy of the relation of the indi-
> vidual to society as it now exists, the objective structure of given in-
> stitutions and values. Only what an individual makes of himself, in
> charitable relations to others, counts. And this self-creation tends to
> require open revolt against the pressures of society. Human beings
> are themselves the source of the transcendence of their isolation.[15]

While one can certainly agree that the limitations and contortions of selfhood so frequent in the novel stem from a general bankruptcy, Pip himself
neither revolts from society nor is allowed to create a self wholly apart from
it. The wound or fall Dickens associates with social existence marks him, but
does not destroy him. Rather, from the brilliant periodic sentence at the beginning, in which Pip, "the small bundle of shivers growing afraid of it all,"
presents himself as the issue of the entire landscape and reality of the village, to the somber, understanding heart of the ending, the story of self includes the facts of the world. Though as Barbara Hardy reminds us, Pip's
complexity relies "very largely on narration rather than drama,"[16] the
narration is the drama of self-creation.

Insofar as Pip's education is an attempt to relate "moral *Bildung*" to
the facts of society, it may be contrasted usefully with Balzac's portrait of
Rastignac in *Père Goriot,* a novel Dickens may well have read.[17] In a celebrated passage, Balzac comments that his protagonist

> had seen the three attitudes of men toward the world: obedience,
> struggle, and revolt; the family, society, and Vautrin. He dared not
> choose among them. Obedience was dull, revolt impossible, struggle
> uncertain. . . . He remembered the pure emotions of [his family's]
> quiet life, the days he had passed among those who loved him. Those
> dear creatures found a full, continuous, unclouded happiness in
> obeying the simple laws of the domestic hearth. But despite these

exemplary thoughts, Eugene did not feel brave enough to go and preach the doctrine of simple faith to Delphine [his socially ambitious mistress].[18]

"Active resignation," not challenge, is Pip's lesson. Yet despite this and other fundamental differences, Pip is Dickens' only protagonist to fall within the sense of the Balzacian conception of man as inextricably involved in social processes. The endemic fascination of society lures Pip from pastoral values as it does Rastignac; neither can go home again. In Balzac's novel, only a revolt such as Vautrin's commanding and archetypal crime can extricate one from the labyrinth of social life. Dickens believes revolt to be a mean, loathsome criminality of spirit. Pip's mentor in the ways of the world is a protector speaking for the necessity of impurity. But the protector, the third component in Dickens' equivalent to Balzac's triad, is quite as difficult as Vautrin to pin down: he would have to bear a name rather than a description, Jaggers. No less than Balzac's Janus-figure—the archcriminal who later becomes the master detective—Jaggers knows the network of secret and villainies constituting the "objective structure" of social reality. The pressures and actualities of "society as it now exists" are the ground of Jaggers' uncertain struggle rather than Pip's. Accepting the meaning and value of the struggle, Pip is freed to choose simple faith.

The choice, however, involves acknowledgment not only of social evils but also of his own proneness to personal versions of these evils. To mature, Pip must reject his share in the false expectations fostered by society; to survive, he must turn to Jaggers for a degree of protection against institutionalized evil. Should the guarded but also guardian society be bankrupt, the individual would be utterly vulnerable. Even private "charitable relations," such as Pip's to Herbert, require the legalities that are the positive expression of society—the different, colder, institutionalized charitable relation epitomized in Jaggers' protection of Pip. Jaggers stands for the hedged but nonetheless vital good purposes of a structured society. Symptomatically, Little Britain and the public world of *Great Expectations* contain nothing so absolutely impervious to individual fulfilment as the Circumlocution Office or the Gothic villainy of French society in *A Tale of Two Cities*. Legality is astigmatic but not wholly blind. Despite the invidiously different sentences originally accorded common thief and apparent gentleman, the sentence ultimately passed on Magwitch is, Dickens implies, as just as a fallen world will permit. Magwitch's crimes are facts; they can be forgiven only by divine mercy. Here below, one must not attempt "to bend the past out of its eternal shape" (lvi).

Dealing in facts and realities, Jaggers cannot be an appealing figure. His foreclosed poor dreams, mentioned only glancingly, may guarantee comprehension of his role but they do not invite affection. He is, after all, a fallen Providence. He tampers with evidence, will not listen publicly to the voice of feeling, tyrannizes over the poor and weak, hoards portable property. Even were the case less prejudicial, Dickens' obvious standing off from the attorney would preclude a realized, human character. Jaggers is an enigma with which Dickens cannot come to terms: the enigmatic function, at once defensive and offensive, of society. If realism is the limitation and deflation of dream by factual probabilities, then Jaggers is Dickens' most complexly articulated case on the nature of realism: the attorney is the ambiguous restriction inherent in great expectations in their widest sense.

Initially, Jaggers appears to be the antithesis of Arthur Clennam, the gentle dreamer whose innate decency rescues him from meanness and hard dealing, coldness and severity, to be "a man of honourable mind and open hand," "to have a warm and sympathetic heart." The attorney seems characterized by the pejoratives. But the gap, the discontinuity between warm individual qualities and meanly frigid social processes, no longer prevails in *Great Expectations* as an absolute division. Jaggers is the pivot of Dickens' effort to dramatize, in however minimal, dismal, and enigmatic a fashion, both the need for and the possibility of the very relation J. Hillis Miller finds completely bankrupt. Jaggers' official existence permits Pip's personal amenity of self-creation. Like a grimly reversed Sancho Panza and Don Quixote, each has by the end taken over something of the quality of the other: Jaggers acknowledges the ghost of poor dreams; Pip, the necessity for secrecy. Through the interchange, Pip's narration borrows Jaggers' fallen omniscience and thereby achieves an authority in regard to realities that no other of Dickens' novels attains.

Henri Talon

SPACE, TIME, AND MEMORY IN *GREAT EXPECTATIONS*

BECAUSE *Great Expectations* is supposed to be an autobiography, it necessarily conveys both a strong sense of the narrator's personality and of time as experienced by him. From the past that he conjures up he recovers what was once the suffering or joy of the present, the longing for the future —in short, all that gives intensity to time whose characteristics, even futurity, are stimulated in the very process of remembrance. But the impact of his evocation upon us also depends on the scope of intelligence and largeness of heart he evinces at the time he is writing; in other words, on the wealth of his present as an autobiographer.

This present, as he lives it with pen in hand, is primarily an endeavor *to understand.* He experiences what Kierkegaard made clear long ago,[1] that life which is lived forward can only be understood backward, so that an appropriate motto for all great autobiographies and autobiographical novels would be Nietzsche's remark: "Perhaps the long sentence of my life ought to be read backward. Before, when I read it normally, it did not make sense."[2]

Since Pip's scrupulous conscience has been the cause of his constant uneasiness, he tends, as he reviews his past, if not to exaggerate his weaknesses and faults, at least to underline them in order the better to recapture the movement of his life punctuated by various mistakes. He always brings out that deficiency of the self which—according to a Victorian philosopher—[3] is man's lot in life but not in the novel which "represents him as being what he vainly tries to be: adequate to himself." But Pip is always so fully aware of not being what he ought to be that, on reading him, we understand why anxiety has been said to be the source of human time. True, he also mentions things that give joy to remember, but we feel that the fountainhead of his retrospect is to be found in the question: "Why, on this or that occasion, did I behave so ill?" As De Quincey remarks: "The dread book of account, which the Scriptures speak of, is, in fact, the mind itself of each individual."[4] Indeed, it is moral concern that has made a writer of this unassuming "partner in the House of Clariker and Co."

He relates his life so earnestly that time as experienced appears to be essentially self-questioning. He is not content to recall striking events but mentions also minor incidents that reveal something of himself. "I have," he says, "forgotten nothing in my life that ever had a foremost place there, and little that ever had any place there" (lix). To find his identity he must embrace his whole career, totalize and interpret all that is significant. Remembering is not merely the resurrection of past occurrences, but a new approach to them. He can now account for what eluded him once, and brief comments naturally stem from his narrative. "I told poor Biddy everything. Why it came natural for me to do so, and why Biddy had a deep concern in everything I told her, I did not know then, though I think I know now" (xii). The boy who was ashamed of the commonness of his brother-in-law could not possibly realize how deeply he was influenced by him, but the narrator knows "right well that any good that intermixed itself with my apprenticeship came of plain contented Joe" (xiv).

Implicitly or explicitly he passes judgment on the various Pips who emerge from his childhood and adolescence; and the distance between self and self—what Saint Augustine calls *distensio animae*—[5] as it reveals whatever wisdom and moral worth he has now achieved also shows the creativeness of time between the living experience and its meditative evocation. Indeed, there is a kind of finality in his statements, as if he believed that, whatever his remaining span of life might be, he will change no longer since, on finding Estella again, he has fulfilled his destiny. And we may remark that in his life as he chooses to tell it almost everything is linked with the story of his love which provides the central line every good autobiography demands. As Bachelard has said: "You can only revive the past by linking it to a necessarily present emotional theme."[6]

Pip's memory is primarily what might be called the memory of the heart, and this is why all the chronological landmarks of *Great Expectations* are so vague. The only calendar that really matters to him is the calendar of feelings. The trifling remarks that suggest the date of the action[7] are mere allusions, brief descriptive features of the setting or of the times, mentioned quite casually. Such hints would have meant more to contemporary readers than to us, yet I am inclined to believe that they felt as we do, that in this respect, precision is a matter of indifference to the narrator.

He is lavish of details about the milieus in which he grew up, and it is obvious that he finds the truly significant moments of his life in those meetings with other people without which an individual would have no history. But who are these people? Miss Havisham lives outside time and all the others outside the currents of national history. Thus Pip's autobiography is about the private relations that have oriented and stimulated his own development, nourished his inner life. To almanacs, which are common property, he makes no reference. The only chronological indications he gives are the landmarks of his personal experience of time—a few milestones on his own path. Thus: "At the appointed time I returned to Miss Havisham's" (xi), "Here am I getting on in the first year of my time" (xiv), and so forth.

Naturally, there stand out striking events like his first encounter with Magwitch, his early acquaintance with Miss Havisham and Estella, his meeting with Jaggers, the bearer of momentous news, and so on. Without such memorable occurrences life would be mere duration. In Pip's autobiography all that proved important in his career is shown firmly rooted in stirring moments. In these is to be found the principle of individuation. As for the intervals between these strong beats of existence, he may sum them up rapidly, for they are the mere constitutive elements of dull continuance, the crumbs or the dust of all-but-forgotten happenings—seemingly useless time as opposed to formative time. Thus we read: "I now fell into a regular routine of apprenticeship life, which was varied, beyond the limits of the village and the marshes, by no more remarkable circumstances than the arrival of my birthday and my paying another visit to Miss Havisham" (xvii). Before Jaggers' coming to the village, there elapse four years that are summarized in ten pages or so. Later we find, "As I am now generalizing a period of my life with the object of clearing my way before me, I can scarcely do so better than by at once completing the description of our usual manners and customs at Barnard's Inn" (xxxiv).

When a period, without being punctuated by remarkable occurrences, has yet been lived in depth, he briefly attempts to re-create that which alone matters to him: its emotional climate. "I am now going to sum up a period of at least eight or ten months," he says (xii), and then he mentions the behavior of Estella, alternately cold, condescending, or familiar, then Miss Havisham's possessive, frightening love for her, partly conveyed through telling gustative images. For instance, when Pip said that Estella was growing prettier, Miss Havisham "would seem to enjoy it greedily," and when they played cards, she looked at the girl "with a miserly relish." He conjures up their strange trio, walking round and round the room, crooning "Old Clem" so softly "that it made less noise in the grim old house than the slightest breath of wind." He also tells about his trust in Biddy, her concern for him, the wild speculations of Pumblechook and his sister about his future. In the small world he describes, to speak of others is another way of speaking of himself. Everything he says about them refers us back to him and sometimes brings him to resume his self-questioning: "What would I become with these surroundings? How could my character fail to be influenced by them?"

Why should he bother to date facts, then, since his emotional and mental growth was determined by relationships whose first impact can never be ascertained with any precision. His narrative conveys the impression that time for him, born from involvement with others, is essentially the movement and meaning of his inner life, something all his own.

Equally personal is his sense of space. To begin with, a landscape is for him, in Amiel's words, *"un état d'âme."* He says to Estella: "You have been in every prospect I have ever seen, . . . on the river, on the sails of the ships, on the marshes, in the clouds, in the light, in the darkness, in the wind, in the woods, in the sea, in the streets" (xliv). Space associated with his childhood lives in his memory. It is his "root of piety," and this is why it need not be named or defined in recognized geographical terms. When speaking of his village and the surrounding country, the narrator uses a possessive adjective or pronoun and not the names by which they would be known to everybody: "our village," "ours is the marsh country" (i); "a wooden house, as many of the dwellings in our country were" (ii). A neighboring city is localized by reference to the village; it is simply "the nearest town" (iv). Long before phenomenologists and other philosophers and psychologists began to speak of *der gelebte Raum, l'espace vécu,* "existential space,"[8] Dickens had experienced that a few privileged places are part and parcel of oneself. And no one conveys this experience better than his Pip whose marsh country is *his* because there he first became aware of the identity of things.

He *feels* the distinctive features and atmosphere of places, and of none better than the marshes. He *feels* their varying moods according to the season and time of night or day. And the conflict which developed early in his soul between social ambition and loyalty to Joe has a spatial correlative and polarity—Satis House and the Forge—which heralds Proust's own sense of the connection between the individuality of places and the diversity of his frames of mind.[9]

Satis House does more than give birth to love and social ambition; it ensures the triumph of a fairylike vision over the arithmetical conception of existence that Pumblechook and Mrs. Joe stand for. For years Pip will be unable fully to understand that reality can never yield to fairy tales, and for years he will look upon that mansion as the place where the "thick curtain" that shut him out of romance and indeed out of everything "save dull endurance" (xiv) will be removed forever. He looked forward to the day when he was "to admit the sunshine into the dark rooms, set the clocks a-going and the cold hearths a-blazing, tear down the cobwebs, destroy the vermin—in short do all the shining deeds of the young Knight of romance and marry the Princess" (xxix).

As for home and the Forge of which he was so long miserably ashamed, it nonetheless preserved in his heart the "sanctity" which Joe had imparted to it (xiv). It lived in his memory, and since what a man does and thinks in solitude gives such an insight into his character, it is good to hear that "many a time of an evening when I sat alone looking at the fire, I thought, after all, there was no fire like the forge fire and the kitchen fire at home" (xxxiv). Satis House and the Forge belong to Pip's personal mythology, and on reading *Great Expectations* I have often thought of what G. van der Leeuw has said about space and time: "We can live with clocks, angles, and square feet. And all these are assuredly necessary. Except that we cannot actually live by them. When one says space and time, one means one's own life. That is, one means not empty surface, not a chronometer, but myth."[10]

In those lonely London nights he feels very near his village, and then, as at various other times, how well he conveys the impression that sentimental nearness or remoteness has nothing to do with physical distance. His rooms and occupations are in London, but the landscape that dwells in his memory is his marsh country, his village and its neighboring town. On the contrary, his first week in London after he left Joe and Biddy was so crowded with new impressions that he felt as if many months had elapsed and "the space interposed between myself and them partook of that expansion, and our marshes were any distance off. That I could have been at our old church . . . on the very last Sunday that ever was, seemed a combination of impossibilities, geographical and social" (xxii).

But of all places, that which he experienced most intensely is probably the ruined garden whose "green and yellow paths" he and Estella trod in childhood. Years later he walked one night in this garden "with a depressed heart" (xxxviii), but on a previous occasion, in Estella's company, he had seen it bathed in the light of hope. "It was all in bloom for me. If the green and yellow growth of weed in the chinks of the old wall had been the most precious flower that ever blew, it could not have been more cherished in my remembrance" (xxix). This is Pip's "lived space," space which flows along a man's dreams, space which time, as Minkowski puts it, *"porte en lui en le vivifiant."*[11]

Pip's final return to the village after eleven years' absence is certainly the expression of his love for Joe and Biddy but also of other profound pieties: faithfulness to all the places where his sensitiveness as a child—the birthright of a man's being as Wordsworth reminds us—[12] was awakened, and where he first experienced the yearnings of love and its pains.

He has his roots both in the village and in what he calls "the old spot" (with the garden wall still standing) which Estella herself has come to regard as the most precious reminder of the past. "Everything else has gone from me little by little," she says, "but I have kept this" (lix). On finding again that spot of earth pregnant with so many common memories, they discovered mutual ties of unsuspected strength. Those places, which seem to hold within themselves so much of a man's and a woman's personal history, can well reveal each to each as no previous experience ever did. Thus Pip's autobiography ends in the very land where it began, and its circularity answers the demands of truth and satisfies our aesthetic sense.

This constant association of time and space is indeed inevitable[13] in either genuine or supposedly autobiographical writing. To remember is to put back into a definite place, at a certain time, an image that has just risen in one's mind. The past becomes a fragment of space now present in you. And memory, as the conjunction of one particular moment and one particular spot, is often emphasized in *Great Expectations.* For instance, whenever

Pip thinks of the death sentence passed on Magwitch, "the whole scene starts out again in the vivid colours of the moment, down to the drops of April rain on the windows of the court glittering in the rays of April sun" (lvi).

Past emotion is not always gradually recollected in tranquillity but may surge forth all of a sudden with the remembrance of one particular occurrence and its setting. In the course of a talk with Herbert in their London rooms, Pip had to turn his "head aside," for, says he, "with a rush and a sweep, a feeling like that which had subdued me on the morning when I left the forge . . . smote upon my heart again" (xxx). And as sensuous memory is as retentive as the memory of the heart, the recurrence of a sensation may cause the resurgence of past feelings and of the whole atmosphere of one hour. Thus, because during a tense conversation Biddy had plucked a black-currant leaf which she "rubbed . . . to pieces between her hands, . . . the smell of a black-currant bush has ever since recalled to me that evening in the little garden by the side of the lane" (xix).

Pip's narrative of recurrent attitudes enables the reader to form a good idea of his character. From childhood, imagination, senitiveness, and conscience have been the ruling forces of his being. He has lived time (indeed as we all do) as expectation, desire, and moral exigency. It is this last aspect that I wish to emphasize: present and future as the confluence—whether liked or disliked, conducive to harmony or conflict—of "can" and "ought to." Pip experienced this early. His behavior toward Magwitch as a child heralds his future reactions to promptings of the heart and to his sense of obligation. It is true that his help to the convict manifests primarily the compulsion of fear but also the incentive of pity, as Magwitch felt at once and acknowledged years later: "You acted nobly, my Boy" (xxxix). Indeed, pity made the fearful child bold enough to say to the starving man bolting down his food: "I am glad you enjoy it" (iii).

This definite statement of fact we can accept as true, although the middle-aged narrator tends to exaggerate the child's sensitiveness to distress. He credits him with reflections that are really the afterthoughts of the autobiographer who, having learned that suffering brings about understanding, likes to imagine that even seven-year-old Pip resented other people's blindness and lack of charity in terms of irony. Who can believe that the little brat whose naïvety was revealed so amusingly in the village churchyard could say to himself, on watching Mrs. Joe's Christmas guests enjoying themselves: "What terrible good sauce for a dinner my fugitive friend on the marshes was"? (v).

But the narrator is a moralist and his discourse[14] shows that, having come to regard time as what a philosopher would name an ethical category, he can emphasize the call of conscience and his feeling of guilt to the point of distortion. The man casts his shadow on the boy who appears older than his years. Of this inaccuracy he seems to be unconscious. He realized, as I have shown, that to remember is to make a selection from the past, but he imagined that an honest man's memories are what they are inalterably. Thus, speaking of his conversations with Magwitch in prison, he can say that the dying man never "tried to bend the past out of its eternal shape" (lvi). However, the reader always welcomes the slight twist that the would-be sincere autobiographer gives to his past unawares, for it helps reveal his present spiritual position and thereby conveys that sense of time as moral development and human enrichment which is the ultimate truth of his self-portrait.

However, constantly recurrent attitudes bear their own truths within themselves and make it clear that all his life Pip has experienced unfaithfulness to others as a self-betrayal that brings about remorse and unhappiness. Even as a young boy he felt that loyalty is a moral imperative. During the convict hunt he was grieved to think that the poor wretch he had fed might imagine that he had brought the soldiers there. "Would he believe that I was both imp and hound in treacherous earnest, and had betrayed him?" (v). Years later, when Orlick prepared to murder him, it was not so much death he feared as a possible misinterpretation of his conduct. "Estella's father would believe I had deserted him; . . . Joe and Biddy would never know how sorry I had been that night, none would ever know . . . how true I had meant to be" (liii). The adult reacts as the child had done, but what used to be a sort of moral instinct has grown into the certitude that man reaches self-fulfillment through faithfulness to those he loves. Now loyalty appears to him not only as a principle that should guide a man in his lifetime, but also as that which ensures the survival of his true self in the memory of others. "The death close before me was terrible," he says, "but far more terrible than death was the dread of being misinterpreted after death." Obedience to the dictates of conscience, which had recently given meaning to his life, could also secure that triumph over death which a loving heart yearns for: his friends' remembrance.

A man's fate is largely the result of his attitude toward the future. Pip's early love for Estella awakened in him social ambition and a wish to acquire knowledge. He looked forward to the future with determination because he had set himself a goal: to become a gentleman. His will to reach it made his present very full: he worked hard and economized in order to buy books (xvii). Difficulty acted as a stimulant. But his "great expectations," his certainty that he would come into a handsome property, changed his way of life. He no longer bent his efforts toward a hard victory but indulged in the vague hope of receiving new favors. Miss Havisham, he thought, "had adopted Estella, she had as good as adopted me, and it could not fail to be her intention to bring us together" (xxix). The future had become not so much something aimed at as something waited for; not a history one has to write but a fairy tale written by somebody else. "She reserved it for me to re-store the desolate house, admit the sunshine into the dark rooms, . . . in short, do all the shining deeds of the young Knight of romance and marry the princess" (xxix). He failed to understand that dreams do not come true unless one transmutes them into definite plans, a line of action to be pursued. Instead of facing the fact that Estella treated him as a mere boy and did not show him that respect which is the true foundation of love, he indulged in a fallacy to account for her behavior: she was haughty simply because she resented his "being so set apart for her and assigned to her" (xxix).

From his way of considering the future there resulted the vacuity of his present. He spent money lavishly, had a servant, joined a gentlemen's club, went to the theatre, and yet time hung heavy on his hands. Today hardly seemed to be his because he had not looked forward to it earnestly on the day before. It is anticipation that gives plenitude to the present, not so-called enjoyment, as the narrator confesses: "There was a gay fiction among us that we were constantly enjoying ourselves, and a skeleton truth that we never did" (xxxiv). When he went out with Estella her indifference to him made him feel the inanity of his life the more keenly. "There were picnics, fête days, . . . all sorts of pleasures, . . . and they were all miseries to me" (xxxviii).

These London years were years of escapism, passivity, and boredom, all the heavier because he was a *déraciné*. He could have no access to any active, recognized social group. The Finches of the Grove were idle, pretentious nobodies. And thus he experienced—no doubt without being clearly aware of it—a certain social frustration which added to the emotional frustration of which he was only too conscious. His present was dull, miserable, and inevitably devoid of *élan* because he looked to the future as to a vague promise instead of living it as a firmly willed project.

These years were also darkened by his recurrent feeling of guilt. To begin with, he had an inkling of the disturbing truth—so obvious to the narrator that he seems to credit his younger self with the same clarity of thought —that "hankerings after money and gentility" were wretched (xxix). For years he had reproached himself for his neglect of home and "lived in a state of chronic uneasiness" (xxxiv). Joe, of whom he was ashamed, he also admired. In his eyes, the simple-hearted, simple-minded blacksmith stood for the Christian virtues of meekness and charity. To remember Joe was to preserve a sense of value. And, confusedly, in his own mistaken way, Pip had always aspired to live by values. Even his wish to become a gentleman was more than mere social ambition. It was also a yearning for knowledge, refinement, urbanity, in short, greater human worth. But in a society that idolizes money the degradation of values is inevitable. (In this respect it is significant that only two persons, Joe and Biddy, are looked upon by Pip as referential models.) The Finches of the Grove were caricatures of true gentlemanliness as defined, say, by Thomas Browne or Richard Steele, and still upheld by a few men like Newman and Ruskin. Led astray by Mrs. Joe,

Pumblechook, and Estella, tainted by his London environment, Pip could not but go wrong in his unsteady, groping quest for personal improvement. And, brooding over his "worthless conduct" to Biddy and his brother-in-law, he said to himself in despair that he "could never, never, never, undo what [he] had done" (xxxix).

Pip was wrong. Because time is irreversible, it does not follow that the meaning of the past is settled forever. As he himself was about to demonstrate, the meaning of the past lies in the inspiration a man draws from it to shape his present and future. Therefore it is always changing.

On Magwitch's return all his dreams collapsed, but a personal setback brought about a new moral life. Because he was forced to face ugly facts he ceased to behave as an overgrown child. His long-ineffectual sense of duty and fidelity asserted itself in response to reluctant but compelling pity for the often ill-advised but always generous convict. For the first time in his life Pip at once recognized the claims of the past upon the present, looked to the future with a sense of urgency, and therefore ceased to experience the present as vacuity and boredom. For the first time in his life he achieved that balance between past, present and future which Karl Jaspers calls the "cipher" (*Chiffre*) of Time.[15]

The virtue of fidelity, which he revered in Joe, was the first feature of Magwitch's personality that struck him and helped him to overcome his instinctive repulsion. On the spur of the moment he had said to the convict: "If you come here to thank me, it was not necessary," but a few minutes later, prompted by awakening compassion and greater understanding, he added: "I am glad that, thinking I deserve to be thanked, you have come to thank me" (xxxix). And on seeing that his visitor's eyes were full of tears he apologized for his first harsh words and wished him well. Of course, he still felt dread and abhorrence. He experienced that what is received may bind painfully, that gratitude may be an unwelcome yet imperative duty. He wholly agreed with Herbert: "You must get him out of England before you stir a finger to extricate yourself" (xli).

Magwitch's narrative of his own life showed Pip that fidelity is creative when it leads to a hard work that redeems the past. Magwitch provided him with a norm by which to judge himself. "I only saw him as a much better man than I had been to Joe" (liv). Very soon his sense of responsibility toward his convict was transmuted into affection, probably the only genuine— because unresented—form of gratitude. Duty ceased to be felt as an injunction and became the answer of himself to himself. When he had to leave Magwitch, his heart was unexpectedly heavy (xlvi). His mind "was wholly set on Provis' safety" (liv) and therefore his unabated love for Estella nonetheless ceased to be the morbid obsession with, and cultivation of the self through suffering that it had been for years. His last meeting with her at Satis House sets off the fact that she had always been to him an object to dream of rather than a person to fight for and live with. "You have been in every line I have ever read, . . . in every prospect I have ever seen" (xliv). And if, now, we are more sensible than before of the core of egoism in Pip's love for her, it is because of the contrasting effect resulting from his attitude toward Magwitch, the first person for whose safety and well-being he forgets himself entirely. At last Pip had achieved existential transcendence.

In the story of his life, Pip has succeeded in doing what Rousseau meant to do in his: *"pouvoir en quelque façon rendre mon âme transparente aux yeux du lecteur."*[16] But whereas Rousseau was conscious that he had failed to make himself altogether transparent to himself *("Mais moi, . . . que suis-je moi-même?"*[17] he asked several years after the *Confessions),* our fictional autobiographer seems to have entertained no such doubt. And yet he gives us the impression that he cannot always see through the young boy he was, nor fully understand—as I shall try to show—the significance of his own life.

His decision to do all in his power—even risk his own life—in order to help Magwitch is a fine assertion of free will in the face of necessity. From the time of the convict's return to his death, Pip lived intensely and dangerously. Through his action he made himself grow and indeed be. But the ontological role of time is clear to the reader, not to him. The middle-aged autobiographer believes that a man's life is determined once for all, on some memorable occasion like his own first visit to Satis House. From then on, it will be "a long chain of iron or gold" (ix) says he, forgetting that his own is rather a strand of both metals twisted together. He is seemingly unaware that through his forgiveness of Miss Havisham, his devotion to Magwitch, his return to Joe and Biddy, his eleven years' work abroad, he has achieved the *Glückswürdigkeit* which was finally realized when he and Estella were united.

In the framework of this essay, mentioning Pip's forgiveness of Miss Havisham leads one to study not the part she plays in his life, but her significance as regards time and memory in man's life. Having been forsaken by her fiancé on the day set for the wedding, Miss Havisham has refused to forget the collapse of her great expectations, and, by stopping the clocks, forbidding all allusions to the calendar, shutting out the light of day, she has tried to stay the very course of time. But, ironically, everything in her rooms testifies to its irresistible flow. Around her all is decay, rot, and ruin. Space always bears the marks of time, and in Satis House time has recorded its passing as it always does when people cease to use it creatively: it destroys. Miss Havisham herself, a mere bag of bones in her yellowed, torn wedding dress, a prematurely old woman in a youthful garment, a derisive caricature of what she was once, bears witness to the inescapable sway of time over things and people.

Allowing the past to usurp a place it should not have, ever harping on the injustice of her lot, walking round her apartment mechanically, she has no present to speak of. Her life is the negation of the creativeness of time as the instrument of freedom. Like a cracked gramophone record that keeps on playing the same few bars, she goes on cursing men. In her diseased mind, time is out of joint. Neurosis causes "dyschrony." The cancerlike past which smothers the present also warps her vision of the future which she conceives, not as progress and betterment, but as the repetition of past cruelty. Because her lover jilted her, Estella must break the heart of her admirers. The future, which ought to be a prospect of hope, has become that of despair.

In several respects, Miss Havisham's behavior contrasts with Pip's and, as we shall see later, Magwitch's. She never forgave Compeyson and was haunted by his memory. On the contrary, Pip forgives Miss Havisham readily and thereby refuses to let the past embitter his life. He transcends resentment; and he transcends guilt, too, by helping Magwitch as a son would a father, and begging Joe's forgiveness also as does a long-ungrateful son on returning home. Thus Dickens shows both hatred and remorse as two antithetical yet equally abnormal ways of magnifying the past. Resentment and ingratitude twist both the moral and psychological life of man and distort his sense of time. In both cases forgiveness alone can restore health and normalcy. This is why forgiveness looms large in *Great Expectations*.

Miss Havisham never gave a thought to Estella's happiness. She never envisaged that her daughter's future should be her own. She allowed her past to weigh heavily on the young girl's life. She is responsible for Estella's self-alienation. "You speak of yourself," Pip says to her, "as if you were some one else" (xxxiii). Estella cannot live either the present or the future with emotional plenitude. "There are sentiments, fancies—I don't know what to call them—which I am not able to comprehend. When you say you love me, I know what you mean, as a form of words, but nothing more" (xlv).

On the contrary, Magwitch wished Pip to become a man entirely different from himself: well-informed, polished, happy. The convict's past—that of a wretch seemingly forgotten by God and cast off by society—awakened his desire to see his "son" shape his own existence freely. He certainly harmed Pip unawares by fostering his escapism and having him live in enervating idleness, but he atoned for all this on his return since Pip, seeing in the convict's life a model of admirable faithfulness, took the decision that made a man of him.

For years, Magwitch lived a personal myth that illumined his solitary, hard-working existence. His immediate gratitude for the child's kindness and innocence grew into a reverence and love that redeemed his past and ennobled the egoism inherent in his very generosity. Perhaps people cannot live without a private mythology. Miss Havisham had hers, and so had Pip, but Magwitch's alone was almost always inspiring because it was entirely founded on respect for moral value as he thought he could see it in another human being. Then time as myth is truly creative.

In the *Physics* Aristotle wondered whether there would be any time (in this case mathematical time) if there were no such thing as a soul.[18] On reading *Great Expectations* we might well ask the same question with reference to "lived time," which expresses the character, the moral and psychological balance or imbalance of Pip and others.

Although this supposedly autobiographical story testifies to a certain trust in time, since it tells of a man's growth and ultimate self-realization, yet it mainly conveys a sense of time in its minor key: the time of trial, suffering, and guilt. It has been said truly that one of Dickens' subjects is the moment missed.[19] To this one might add, in telling Jaspersian language,[20] that in Pip's case, "to miss the moment" is "to miss oneself." Because of his blindness, passivity, and indecision, he long remained a rather colorless, insignificant character. Only when he made up his mind to do his duty at whatever risk, and to live up to his principle of integrity at whatever cost, did he "reach himself." There remained for him to work hard for years, as Magwitch had done, in order to strengthen his inner poise, enable himself to assume new responsibilities and find happiness on returning home. Thus a man does not live fully unless he associates work and love. Hard-working but loveless Jaggers merely survives, he does not live. And it is not paradoxical to say that Miss Havisham is as much a victim of her idleness—required by class prejudice and made possible by money—as of Compeyson. Because "lived time" is the expression of the soul, only through inner equilibrium (to which work contributes so much) can one achieve the right balance of the three characteristics of temporality.

Deborah Allen Thomas

THE EQUIVOCAL EXPLANATION OF DICKENS' GEORGE SILVERMAN

GEORGE SILVERMAN'S EXPLANATION is a remarkable and perplexing work. This tightly constructed and pessimistic piece of short fiction, which first appeared in the *Atlantic Monthly* in 1868 near the end of Dickens' career, differs strikingly from the loosely knit, happily ended novels like *Pickwick Papers* and *Oliver Twist* with which Dickens achieved his early reputation. Its neurotically insecure first-person narrator seems less like Esther Summerson, Pip, and David Copperfield than like Dostoevsky's underground man and Eliot's J. Alfred Prufrock. Nevertheless, "George Silverman's Explanation" has only recently begun to receive the attention which it deserves. George Saintsbury dismissed it as "almost worthless,"[1] while, in his introduction to the volume of Dickens' works in which this piece appears, Andrew Lang sweepingly declared, "there is nothing of interest to be said about George Silverman."[2] Subsequent scholarship nearly always seems to have followed Lang's suggestion. Many notable studies of Dickens' fiction, including those by Edmund Wilson, J. Hillis Miller, and Taylor Stoehr, say nothing about "George Silverman's Explanation"; other studies, such as those by Sylvère Monod and K. J. Fielding, mention it only in passing.[3]

Against the background of this widespread neglect, a few recent critics have offered thought-provoking analyses. Harry Stone considers "George Silverman's Explanation" to be Dickens' "most unequivocal and uncompromising picture of frail humanity engulfed in a tragic universe."[4] Barry Bart sees it as "Dickens' deepest examination of the consequences of the ethic [of] renunciation"[5] implicit in the conclusions reached by Pip in *Great Expectations*, Arthur Clennam in *Little Dorrit*, and Eugene Wrayburn in *Our Mutual Friend*. Dudley Flamm, who basically agrees with Stone and Bart, contends that through the narrative technique of this work "Dickens . . . reveals his bleakest view regarding self-extrication from guilt, because he seems to say that once the prosecutor has moved wholly within the accused's mind, there may be no possible extrication."[6] However,

Stone, Bart, and, to a large extent, Flamm view "George Silverman's Explanation" primarily in the context of Dickens' novels;[7] in this context, they see Silverman's dilemma as that of a basically innocent man who has been victimized by his surroundings.[8] When "George Silverman's Explanation" is examined in connection with some of Dickens' other experiments in short fiction, its equivocal nature becomes more apparent and the issue of Silverman's innocence becomes more difficult to resolve.

Prior to the publication of "George Silverman's Explanation," Dickens had produced a number of other brief prose works narrated in the first person by their central characters. Some of these works, such as "A Madman's Manuscript" in *Pickwick Papers* or "A Confession Found in a Prison in the Time of Charles the Second" in *Master Humphrey's Clock,* are early ones which merely present sensational situations; their narrative technique serves little function beyond that of lending a contrived illusion of authenticity to the material which they contain. Later, however, Dickens used the confessional or self-explanatory mode for several short pieces whose narrative method focuses attention upon the peculiar personalities of their speakers. Two of these later works are particularly relevant to "George Silverman's Explanation."

The more familiar of the two is "The History of a Self Tormentor," Miss Wade's manuscript of self-justification in *Little Dorrit.* As her words reveal, Miss Wade's vision of the world is jaundiced. She begins with the assumption that she can cut through disguising appearances to underlying "truth," and she assimilates all of her experience to this overruling impression. She asserts at the beginning of her manuscript: "I have the misfortune of not being a fool. . . . If I could have been habitually imposed upon, instead of habitually discerning the truth, I might have lived as smoothly as most fools do" (663).[9] This impression is like a colored glass through which she persistently looks at life. As a child, she misinterprets the kindness of the girls with whom she is raised, and, like Browning's Duke who executes his Duchess for smiling indiscriminately, Miss Wade interprets any kindness shown to others by her "chosen friend" as an act of disloyalty to herself:

> "One of them was my chosen friend. I loved that stupid mite in a passionate way that she could no more deserve, than I can remember without feeling ashamed of, though I was but a child. She had what they called an amiable temper, an affectionate temper. She could distribute, and did distribute, pretty looks and smiles to every one among them. I believe there was not a soul in the place, except myself, who knew that she did it purposely to wound and gall me!" (663)

As she grows older, her actions are no less biased by her peculiar impression of what is truth. She loathes the good-natured nurse of the family in which she first serves as a governess, and she quarrels with the mistress of the household who tries to make her position easy. In another family, again as a governess, she becomes engaged to her employers' nephew, but she scorns his open admiration of her, concludes that his attachment makes her appear ridiculous, favors another man, quarrels with her fiancé's aunt, and angrily departs. The events which she describes are clearly open to more interpretations than the one she puts upon them. Her fierce attachment to her childhood friend and her identification with the girl whom she later takes to live with her seem at least implicitly lesbian, and such details combine to suggest that her particular "truth" is a delusion. Nonetheless, her *idée fixe* is a powerful one; it governs her behavior and distorts her life.

At the same time that a reader recognizes Miss Wade's delusion, he becomes aware of the sources of her personal torment. Lionel Trilling remarks that it is impossible "to read Miss Wade's account of her life . . . without an understanding that amounts to sympathy."[10] As her self-history demonstrates, several important reasons for her bitterness lie wholly or largely beyond her control. She is apparently illegitimate, and much of her misery as a child and as a woman stems from the accident of her birth. In her girlhood, she is innocently deceived by the woman who pretends to be her grandmother. In later years, she is cynically deceived by the man who encourages her to break her engagement and then abandons her in order to court another woman. In the rest of *Little Dorrit,* Miss Wade is a mysterious but clearly unpleasant person; Pancks, a character who has a slight business connection with her, remarks that "a woman more angry, passionate, reckless, and revengeful never lived" (540). Miss Wade's manuscript provides a different perspective upon her personality. It not only displays her faults but it arouses sympathy for her suffering, and the resulting conflict between compassion and condemnation produced by her explanation resembles "the tension between sympathy and moral judgment" which Robert Langbaum has termed the hallmark of the dramatic monologue.[11] In her manuscript, Miss Wade reveals that her view of herself is seriously distorted, but she presents her case in such a fashion that it cannot be automatically assessed.

"The History of a Self Tormentor" is not an isolated example of Dickens' experimentation with this kind of fictional disequilibrium. A relatively obscure short work entitled "Holiday Romance"[12] focuses even more directly on this split between a reader's knowledge and that of the characters involved. As Dickens conceived it, this piece was designed as a joke[13] whose humor was to come from the clash between adult wisdom and childish naïveté. Three of the four "romances" which it contains are third-person fantasies, pictures of the world as children presumably would like it to be, while the "Introductory Romance from the Pen of William Tinkling, Esq." is a first-person monologue whose eight-year-old narrator, like the speakers in some of Browning's best monologues, is supremely unconscious of the limitations of his point of view. Throughout most of his monologue, he expresses himself in what is supposedly a childish prattle. His style combines simple sentences with ornate expressions apparently borrowed from unspecified books. His description of his make-believe marriage illustrates these qualities as well as his characteristically juvenile emphasis on details like toys and spending money:

> Nettie Ashford is my bride. We were married in the right-hand closet in the corner of the dancing-school, where first we met, with a ring (a green one) from Wilkingwater's toy-shop. *I* owed for it out of my pocket-money. When the rapturous ceremony was over, we all four went up the lane and let off a cannon (brought loaded in Bob Redforth's waistcoat-pocket) to announce our nuptials. It flew right up when it went off, and turned over. (691)[14]

"Holiday Romance" is far from being one of Dickens' most successful works. A reader of Tinkling's section cannot escape the sensation that the youthful narrator is being manipulated: he is given a designedly cute name and forced to say the kind of banalities that entertain doting grandparents. Tinkling's monologue is not a genuine treatment of the problem of a child in an adult world like that presented in *David Copperfield* or Joyce's "Araby." It is rather an adult's semiserious creation of what childhood might resemble, and its resulting tone is uncomfortably coy. Dickens' humorous intention seems to have led him into overemphasizing the conflict between speaker and reader inherent in this work; the split between different degrees of knowledge, which was so effective in Miss Wade's monologue, here becomes simply strained. However, the very fact that this type of conflict is used to excess in Tinkling's remarks indicates Dickens' willingness to experiment with the technique of contrasting attitudes within a first-person narrative.

Thus Flamm's comment about "George Silverman's Explanation" that "no other Dickens story told in the first person derives so much of its effect from the difference between what the reader is aware of and what the character-narrator is aware of"[15] is perceptive but incorrect. The discrepancy between different levels of awareness is crucially important in the monologues of Miss Wade and William Tinkling, and both of these pieces are closely related to "George Silverman's Explanation." Like Miss Wade, George Silverman believes that he has been misunderstood by the world, although Miss Wade is far more bitter than Silverman about this misunderstanding; and, in a manner resembling that of his female predecessor, he gives vent to his feelings in a manuscript designed as an explanation of himself. Like "Holiday Romance," "George Silverman's Explanation" was produced shortly before Dickens' second visit to America;[16] the "queer combination of a child's mind with a grownup joke,"[17] implicit in the one work and manifested in Tinkling's monologue, was undoubtedly in his thoughts as he composed the other. In the context of these relationships,

George Silverman's narrative deserves careful reconsideration.

As in the monologues of Miss Wade and William Tinkling, the focus of "George Silverman's Explanation" lies on the personality of its narrator. Like these pieces, it exploits a duality implicit in its speaker's words. Edgar Johnson's passing comment calls attention to this double effect:

> The narrator of the story, rescued from a slum childhood and brought up as a clergyman, seems to himself always to be acting with the most nobly disinterested of motives, but is constantly striking others as selfish and disingenuous. . . . Believing himself cruelly misjudged, Silverman at the same time has a lurking suspicion of his own guilt. What sort of man is he, really? These ambiguities, in fact, represent the very point of the story, and one feels as if it were haunted by Dickens' troubled consciousness of ambiguities within himself. But he could not grapple successfully with the theme; it wavers half-heartedly between apologia and accusation, an unresolved conflict.[18]

To a certain extent, this conflict is indeed unresolved. Unlike William Tinkling's romance, "George Silverman's Explanation" ends with no suggestion that the speaker will outgrow his present attitude. Unlike Miss Wade, the narrator does not invite condemnation upon himself by luring another person to share his unhappy life. However, the essential ambiguity of "George Silverman's Explanation" is not necessarily a flaw, and it can be understood without recourse to Dickens' personal state of mind. It is, I believe, the consequence of Dickens' success in sustaining two contrasting attitudes throughout a first-person monologue.

George Silverman receives his impressions through the haze of his own personality. His abortive opening chapters reveal his insecurity:

FIRST CHAPTER

It happened in this wise—

But, sitting with my pen in my hand looking at those words again, without descrying any hint in them of the words that should follow, it comes into my mind that they have an abrupt appearance. They may serve, however, if I let them remain, to suggest how very difficult I find it to begin to explain my explanation. An uncouth phrase: and yet I do not see my way to a better.

SECOND CHAPTER

It happened in *this* wise—

But, looking at those words, and comparing them with my former opening, I find they are the self-same words repeated. This is the more surprising to me, because I employ them in quite a new connexion. For indeed I declare that my intention was to discard

the commencement I first had in my thoughts, and to give the pref-
erence to another of an entirely different nature, dating my explanation from an anterior period of my life. I will make a third trial,
without erasing this second failure, protesting that it is not my design to conceal any of my infirmities, whether they be of head or
heart. (729)

Not until the third chapter does he "begin to explain . . . [his] explanation," and he achieves his goal only by approaching it from an oblique direction: "Not as yet directly aiming at how it came to pass, I will come upon
it by degrees" (730). The words with which he ends the piece make clear
that this "explanation" arises only from an overpowering urge to give expression to his confusion: "I pen it for the relief of my own mind, not fore-
seeing whether or no it will ever have a reader" (756). As this tortuous
beginning and diffident conclusion indicate, his angle of vision is a peculiar
one. In his manner, he resembles a person like the humble Mr. Smith, from
"Thoughts about People" in *Sketches by Boz,* given the opportunity to attempt to justify himself.

When he is a child in a Preston cellar, Silverman's impoverished
mother calls him "a worldly little devil" (730), and the sting of this rebuke
haunts him as he greedily yearns for shelter, clothing, and food. In reaction,
after his parents die of fever and he has been rescued from the family lair, he
becomes shyly altruistic—the attitude which dominates the backward perspective of his monologue. While staying at an old farmhouse in order to
recover from possible contamination, Silverman asks himself, "How not to
be this worldly little devil?" (736), and the remainder of his piece recounts
his efforts to avoid any possible imputation of worldly aspiration. His dilemma, as Johnson observes in the passage which I quoted earlier, lies in
the fact that he "is constantly striking others as selfish and disingenuous."
Subsequent events show, on an ever-increasing scale, the conflict between
his efforts to be unworldly and the assumption of the world that he is very
worldly indeed. At the farmhouse, when he avoids the girl to whom he is attracted for fear that he may spread contamination, her family accuses him of
moroseness and a lack of sociability. Later, when he has won a fellowship to
Cambridge, he suspects that Verity Hawkyard, the religious hypocrite who
first sent him to school, has suppressed an inheritance due to him from his
grandfather. Instead of demanding his property in a worldly fashion, however, he effectively relinquishes all claim to it in a voluntary letter of gratitude
for Hawkyard's charity to him. In return, Hawkyard and his congrega-
tion rant through a service for the benefit of "our poor, sinful, worldly-
minded brother here present" whose "now-opening career . . . might lead
to his becoming a minister of what was called 'the church.' . . . Not the
chapel, Lord. The church" (744). In due time, Silverman does become a minister of the Church. The mother of a former pupil presents him a modest

living and persuades him to serve, without additional payment, as her private secretary and as her daughter's tutor. Once again, the fear of worldliness infects Silverman's peace of mind. In a grand gesture of self-effacement, when he discovers that he and his lady's daughter mutually love one another, he quietly transfers the affection of his beloved Adelina to another pupil whom he views as a worthier man. He marries the couple and breaks the news to Adelina's mother, who promptly accuses him of worldliness and of having arranged the marriage for financial gain. She forces him to resign the living, stains his reputation, and hounds him into seclusion. Only through the efforts of the few people who stand by him does he finally receive "a college-living in a sequestered place," and from this place, he explains, "I now pen my explanation" (756). Silverman's remarks are dominated by the distorting influences of his childhood and the peculiar bent of his gradually emerging personality. His overriding desire to appear unworldly lies at the center of his impressions.

In the context of his monologue, however, this overriding desire appears to be an obsession, and it soon becomes clear that George Silverman's behavior is confined by neuroses as restrictive as those which form the prison of Miss Wade. From his own prevailing point of view, he is a well-intentioned and much-maligned individual. Nevertheless, the framework of good intentions which he constructs for himself rests on several questionable assumptions. M. K. Bradby contends that an important motive behind Silverman's supposedly self-effacing actions is egotism:

> The first factor which troubles George Silverman is a subtle pervading egotism in his attitude towards other people. At each crisis in his life, what concerns him most is that he, George Silverman, shall do the lofty-minded thing. Compared with this it is a small matter that the little girl at the farm should feel snubbed, or her father led to judge unjustly; or that Brother Hawkyard should succeed in his fraud; or even that the adored Adelina should suffer the pangs of a first love unrequited. He cannot put himself into other people's places and realise that their feelings are as poignant as his own.[19]

This comment is, I believe, a perceptive one. As his dealings with Adelina, Brother Hawkyard, and the family at the farmhouse demonstrate, Silverman is less concerned with love, justice, and friendship than with living up to his own exalted standards. Like the bashful narrator in Dickens' framework for *The Holly-Tree Inn* (the Christmas number for 1855), Silverman cannot commune with his fellow human beings. Unlike this earlier Christmas speaker, however, he does not fully recognize his own limitations. Although he can refer to his abnormal sensitivity toward the idea of being considered worldly as "the delicate, perhaps the diseased, corner of my mind" (744), he does not fully realize that he, as much as the wretched hermit in *Tom Tiddler's Ground* (the Christmas number for 1861), has a responsibility toward society. Despite his claim that he has chosen a religious career because he considers himself "qualified to do my duty in a moderate, though earnest way, if I could obtain some small preferment in the Church" (746), Silverman gives no evidence of enthusiasm for ministering to someone else's day-to-day human problems. His professional efforts at helping others appear confined primarily to a small number of pupils, and he tells us more about Hawkyard's religious activity, which he despises, than his own. At the end of his monologue, he has retreated to the kind of isolation which his predecessor in *The Holly-Tree Inn* contemplated but did not carry out. In other words, while consciously calling attention to his generosity, George Silverman unconsciously reveals that he has created a private and self-centered world for himself.

Any final assessment of this speaker must take both elements of his personality into consideration. George Silverman should be understood not only as the shy and much-maligned altruist that he presents himself as being, but as the unsocial and neurotically self-centered individual that his remarks and behavior show him to be. As in the case of Browning's Andrea del Sarto, we see both what he believes and what he demonstrates about himself. Indeed, both of these figures self-deludingly attribute their problems to a combination of their own loving sacrifice and the failure of others to understand them. Just as Andrea del Sarto blames his personal failure to achieve artistic greatness on his passion for his wife and comforts himself with the conviction that "I am something underrated here," so George Silverman excuses his withdrawal from society on the basis of his unworldly desire not to take advantage of anyone and explains that he possesses "a timidly silent character under misconstruction" (738). Silverman's description of himself at the farmhouse near the ruined Hoghton Towers, watching the birthday celebration which he has refused to attend, provides a striking illustration of the two components of his character:

> Ah! if they could have seen me next day, in the ruin, watching for the arrival of the cart full of merry young guests; if they could have seen me at night, gliding out from behind the ghostly statue, listening to the music and the fall of dancing feet, and watching the lighted farm-house windows from the quadrangle when all the ruin was dark; if they could have read my heart, as I crept up to bed by the back way, comforting myself with the reflection, "They will take no hurt from me,"—they would not have thought mine a morose or an unsocial nature. (737-38)

On the surface, this passage merely demonstrates Silverman's growing diffidence and his willingness to sacrifice his own happiness to protect those for whom he cares. Nevertheless, the words which he chooses for this description contain disturbing connotations. The young girl whom Silverman admires would hardly have felt easy if she could have seen him "gliding out from behind the ghostly statue," peeping at her birthday festivities from the darkened ruin, and secretively creeping up the stairs to his bed. Had the farmer who scolds him for not being sociable actually been able to read George Silverman's heart, he undoubtedly would have wondered why the boy did not discuss his fear of contamination openly or at least find a better alternative to the party than Hoghton Towers after dark. Silverman himself considers this episode a significant one, and he uses it as an analogy for the life which he remembers at college:

> I can see others in the sunlight; I can see our boats' crews and our athletic young men on the glistening water, or speckled with the moving lights of sunlit leaves; but I myself am always in the shadow looking on. Not unsympathetically,—God forbid!—but looking on alone, much as I looked at Sylvia from the shadows of the ruined house, or looked at the red gleam shining through the farmer's windows, and listened to the fall of dancing feet, when all the ruin was dark that night in the quadrangle. (746)

Once again, Silverman peers out of darkness at the activities of others. The sense of himself as "always in the shadow looking on" indicates the angle from which he forever gathers his impressions of life. Although he claims that his attitude is sympathetic, the basis of his claim and even the validity of his wish to interact with people only as a sympathetic observer remain dubious. Like a voyeur, he shrinks from involvement while he maintains that his intentions are harmless. His mental position is pathetic, but it is not entirely free from blame.

The ambiguities of Silverman's attitude result from the fact that he is his own advocate. In a letter to Wills, the subeditor of *All the Year Round,* Dickens commented about his fascination with the narrative technique of his monologue at the same time that he called attention to the seminal importance of the scene in Hoghton Towers which I have just discussed:

> Upon myself, it has made the strangest impression of reality and originality!! And I feel as if I had read something (by somebody else) which I should never get out of my head!! The main idea of the narrator's position towards the other people, was the idea I *had* for my next novel in A. Y. R. But it is very curious that I did not in the least see how to begin his state of mind, until I walked into Hoghton Towers one bright April day with Dolby.[20]

In the context of this letter, it is significant that George Silverman remembers himself in this location not on a "bright . . . day," but in the dark. This small change emphasizes the peculiarity of "the narrator's position towards the other people." Despite his diffidence, George Silverman is intelligent. Once he has conquered his initial problem of beginning his explanation, he presents his view of his life persuasively, and a reader's final judgment remains in doubt. It is never completely clear what part of his disinterestedness is genuine selflessness and what part is the rationalization of an abnormally introverted man.

Consequently, I believe that the case for Silverman as the innocent victim of injustice cannot be made as convincingly as may at first appear. Indeed, Dickens' original idea of saving Silverman's "position towards" others for his "next novel" in *All the Year Round* links this ambiguous speaker with the openly reputable and secretly murderous Jasper, whose divided personality is apparently the crux of the following, uncompleted *Mystery of Edwin Drood*.[21] It is far too easy for a literary critic to assume that Dickens' sympathy for the dilemma of this quiet, university-educated scholar is unqualified and to forget, as Philip Collins correctly observes, that "few of his characters are intellectuals, and most of those who are he presents as ludicrous or detestable."[22] Even Pip and David Copperfield do not receive a university education although, as Collins notes, "both can command in their later boyhood sufficient funds to get as good an education as Dickens cares to give them."[23] Such evidence, in conjunction with his practice in the monologues of William Tinkling and Miss Wade, suggests that Dickens intended a reader to see through at least part of Silverman's explanation and to recognize not only the extent to which this narrator has been victimized by society but the astigmatism inherent in his point of view.

In Silverman's monologue, however, neither judgment nor sympathy ultimately predominates. A reader's awareness of Silverman's limitations is balanced by compassion for his problems. In this work, Dickens has presented one of his favorite situations—that of self-sacrificing renunciation[24]— but he has intentionally complicated the reader's understanding of this situation through his chosen narrative technique. Like Conrad's Jim, Dickens' Silverman seems designed to remain forever enigmatic. The equivocal nature of his explanation reflects the ambiguity of human life.

John Greaves

GOING ASTRAY

ON 13 August 1853 Dickens printed in *Household Words* an article of his own entitled "Gone Astray." In it he described the adventures of "a very small boy," himself, lost in London and wandering through the City. It may be of interest to glance briefly at the history of the places he saw, to trace his footsteps as far as possible, and to see what remains today.

He begins by saying that he was taken by "Somebody" (identity unknown), as an immense treat, to be shown the outside of Saint Giles' Church. St. Giles in the Fields, as it was and is still known, now stands at the top of Shaftesbury Avenue, but is no longer adjacent to the dreadful district of those days known as the Rookeries of St. Giles. Dickens refers to the denizens of this district in "Gone Astray": "I had romantic ideas in connection with that religious edifice, firmly believing that all the beggars who pretended through the week to be blind, lame, one-armed, deaf and dumb, and otherwise physically afflicted, laid aside their pretences every Sunday, dressed themselves in holiday clothes, and attended divine service in the temple of their patron saint." By the time Dickens wrote this paper much rebuilding had taken place; by 1846 only ninety-five houses of the infamous Rookery remained. In these houses 2,850 people were still crammed in a plot of ground covering less than an acre and a quarter. It is amazing that, in spite of all the filth, with fifty people sometimes sleeping in one room at a charge of threepence per head for a night's shelter, the inhabitants usually enjoyed excellent health. When disease did strike, however, it was naturally very severe, and in 1843 a fever epidemic broke out in St. Giles. In 1665 the Great Plague of London had its origin in this parish; in only one month, July, 1,391 persons were buried in the churchyard. Dickens' fascination for the district, besides the rather morbid one, was for the costermongers' stalls containing vegetables and flowers which decorated the narrow streets. In one street was a large water tank erected when water in this densely populated district was almost as scarce as in the desert.

The present church, once a lazar house founded by Matilda, the Queen

St. Giles in the Fields
(All illustrations reproduced by courtesy of the
Trustees of The Dickens House)

of Henry I, is the third on this site. The present building was designed by
Flitcroft in 1731-33. The churchyard was closed in 1853, at the time Dickens
was writing "Gone Astray," as it was by that time overfull. At this moment
the churchyard is a children's playground. Most of the gravestones ranged
along the wall or alongside the church have lost their inscriptions. Many

famous names appear in the registers: Mary Milton, daughter of John Milton; the two children of Shelley; the daughter of Lord Byron; Colley Cibber, the actor-manager—all were baptized here. In the marriage register are such names as Adrian Scroope, one of the signatories on the death warrant of Charles II; several theatrical personalities—David Garrick, Frances Kemble, John Philip Kemble; and Douglas Jerrold, author and friend of Dickens. Mrs. Siddons, the actress, signed as witness at the marriage of Frances Kemble. The burial register includes the names of Richard Pendrell, preserver of Charles I at Boscobel; Sir Godfrey Kneller, painter; and Luke Hansard, printer to the House of Commons. Many criminals executed at Tyburn are buried in this churchyard, including Claude Duval, the highwayman, recorded under his proper name of Peter du Val. After the highwayman was executed he was apparently "lying in state" in the Tangier Tavern, in nearby Dyott Street. There appears to be no foundation for one authority's statement that Duval was buried under the center aisle of St. Paul's Church, Covent Garden: St Paul's has no records of such a burial, whereas I have seen the name of Peter du Val in the burial register at St. Giles on the date after his death. The Tangier Tavern is gone, but Dyott Street is still there east of the church. Queen Matilda, who founded St. Giles Hospital for lepers, provided 27s. for "one Pitance and a Cup of Charity." This took the form of a bowl of ale given to condemned criminals on their way to execution. The gallows were first sited at Smithfield, where many were burned. Later the place of execution was moved to the present site of St. Giles Circus, where Oxford Street and Tottenham Court Road meet, and later still to Tyburn at Marble Arch. St. Giles stood on the main road from Newgate Prison to the place of execution, hence the bestowal of a cup of ale there. After execution many of the bodies were returned to St. Giles for burial, and I was assured by the verger that he had counted as many as 162 names in the burial register with (Executed) against them. Besides being administered at the Great Gate of the Leper Hospital, the cup was later given at a nearby tavern, The Bowl, now demolished, and at The Angel, an inn which still stands (rebuilt) beside the churchyard. The cup of ale was undoubtedly more welcome to the condemned wretches than the nosegay traditionally bestowed on them at St. Sepulchre's Church, soon after they left Newgate on their last journey.

In his *Life of Dickens* John Forster says that as a young lad Dickens "had a profound attraction of repulsion to St. Giles." This is quite evident as, apart from the novelist's reference to this district in "Gone Astray," he returned to it again and again, especially in his earlier writings. In *Nicholas Nickleby* it is in a cellar in "the labyrinth of streets which lies between Seven Dials and Soho" that Kate and Nicholas discover Mantalini turning a mangle. Again, "two wretched people were more than once observed to crawl at dusk from the inmost recesses of St Giles"—the fate doled out to Sampson and Sally Brass in the tidying-up at the end of *The Old Curiosity*

The Rookery, St. Giles

Shop. In *Barnaby Rudge* Dennis and Hugh go by St. Giles to Tottenham Court Road and Green Lanes where they meet Gashford, the secretary of Lord George Gordon. Most of the article entitled "On Duty with Inspector Field," originally appearing in *Household Words* on 14 June 1851 and now included in *Reprinted Pieces,* is concerned with St. Giles, begins with "How goes the night? St. Giles' clock is striking nine," and describes Dickens' descent into a thieves' cellar called Rat's Castle. In "Shy Neighbour-hoods" Dickens mentions a whole street of British birds for sale, who had got into bad company in St. Giles. *Sketches by Boz* contains at least two references to St. Giles, one in a piece called "Seven Dials," where the brick-layer's laborer's only recreation was leaning against posts in that district of an evening, and the other in "Gin Shops," where some of the handsomest in London were said to be in St. Giles. And in *Pictures from Italy* Dickens compares the filth of Genoa with that of St. Giles and remarks on the un-fairness of looking upon poverty in Naples, "a pair of naked legs and a red scarf," as being attractive, whereas poverty in St. Giles was considered repulsive.

The next place visited in "Gone Astray" was Northumberland House. As Shaftesbury Avenue does not appear on the maps of those days, Dick-ens possibly went along the High Street into one of the streets running into Seven Dials—St. Andrew Street or Monmouth Street—and so into St. Mar-tin's Lane, which would have led him past St. Martin's Church to Charing Cross. Trafalgar Square was not there at that time, only the Golden Cross Hotel of *Pickwick* fame. Just here, opposite the Golden Cross, Dickens would have come upon Northumberland House at the corner of the Strand.

It was while viewing the lion on top of Northumberland House that young Charles lost "Somebody" who accompanied him. This lion was an object of special interest in those days. My mother used to tell me that when a girl she was taken by her father to see this animal; that must have been in the early 1870s. It was the Percy lion with outstretched tail belonging to the Northumberland family. The tale told to my mother was the familiar one extant at the time that when the lion heard one o'clock strike on the neigh-boring clocks, it would wag its tail—it is possible that Dickens was told the same story and presumably his companion slipped away while he was star-ing at the lion. The lion can now be seen on top of Syon House, residence of the Dukes of Northumberland at Islesworth.

Another legend regarding this lion was that it was first placed with its head toward Carlton House and St. James' Palace. Following a slight from royalty received by the Duke of Northumberland, the lion was turned with its back to St. James' Palace and its face to the City of London. The quarrel was made up after the accession of George IV and the lion was restored to its original position—with considerable difficulty, as it is twelve feet long and cast in lead!

The lion is mentioned by Dickens in two of the *Sketches by Boz*. In "Horatio Sparkins" he rather ungallantly says that Miss Teresa Malder-ton was as well known as the lion atop of Northumberland House with an equal chance of "going off," referring of course to her chance of getting mar-ried. In describing Scotland Yard in a paper bearing that name, he says it was "a very small tract of land bounded on one side by the river Thames, on the other by the gardens of Northumberland House."

Northumberland House was built in 1605 for Henry Howard, Earl of Northampton, who died there in 1614; at that time the building was known as Northampton House. The mansion was bequeathed to his nephew, Thomas Howard, Earl of Suffolk, and renamed Suffolk House. After the marriage of Elizabeth, daughter of the second Earl of Suffolk, to Algernon Percy, the tenth Earl of Northumberland, in 1642, it was renamed Northumberland House. In 1766 a great part of the northern front was rebuilt. By 1867, little of the great mansion remained: not much more than the stone

Northumberland House

gateway facing the Strand and surmounted by the lion survived. The house was finally sold and demolished in 1874 for the building of Northumberland Avenue, connecting Charing Cross with the Victoria Embankment. During its later years it was a famous place for sightseeing, practically the last relic of the days when the Strand led from the City to Westminster and was lined by great houses occupied by noble families, with gardens stretching down to the river. Northumberland House was thrown open to the public in 1851, the year of the Great Exhibition. Many alterations were carried out during its history: in fact it was said to have been commenced by a Howard, continued by a Percy, and completed by a Seymour.

Dickens' distress at being lost led him into a court where he sat on a step. Which court that was there are no means of knowing, but he soon decided to go and see the Giants at Guildhall and seek his fortune. This would have led him along the Strand and past St. Mary's Church where his father and mother were married, and Somerset House where his father worked. St. Mary le Strand was built in 1714, on the site of a huge maypole which was pulled down by the Puritans and which had been replaced on the Restoration by an even taller one, one hundred and thirty-four feet high. Dickens does not mention either of these places in "Gone Astray." Soon he came to Temple Bar, now replaced by the griffin on a pillar to mark its site, and the City boundary. The Law Courts which today are first passed on the north of the Strand were not built at that time, and indeed the site was not cleared of its numerous courts and alleyways until 1866-68.

Temple Bar, designed by Sir Christopher Wren in 1670, was for some time in its history decorated with the heads of traitors who had been executed. It was often looked on as an obstruction to traffic, and in *Bleak House* Dickens refers to it as "that leaden-headed old obstruction, appropriate ornament for the threshold of a leaden-headed old corporation." In *Barnaby Rudge* the Prentice Knights took an oath not on any account to damage or in any way disfigure Temple Bar, which was strictly constitutional and always to be approached with reserve. Temple Bar was "headless and forlorn" when Mr. Dorrit passed under it, and David Copperfield and Dan'l Peggotty both came through the gateway into the City. Tom Pinch in *Martin Chuzzlewit* stopped beneath it to laugh to himself over the beefsteak pudding made by his sister Ruth. Beside it, at No. 1 Fleet Street, was the bank said to be Tellson's in *A Tale of Two Cities,* outside which Jerry Cruncher sat on a stool chewing a straw. Child's Bank, which was demolished in 1879 and rebuilt a few feet back from its old frontage, had accounts for Oliver Cromwell, Nell Gwyn, and William III, and rented rooms over Temple Bar from the City Corporation for its records. The Bank is still there beside The Griffin. The old gateway also featured in *Our Mutual Friend* and *Master Humphrey's Clock.* In "Gone Astray" Dickens says "it took me half an hour to stare at it, and I left it unfinished even then. I had read about heads being exposed on the top of Temple Bar, and it seemed a wretched old place, albeit a noble monument of architecture and a paragon of utility." In 1888 Temple Bar was moved to Theobald's Park, Waltham Cross, some twelve or thirteen miles north of London, and later replaced by the present Griffin memorial on its site. Vandals, apparently much less well behaved and responsible than the old Prentice Knights, have sadly disfigured Temple Bar with their scribblings. Numerous schemes to have Temple Bar returned to the City have all failed.

Soon after passing the alleyway on the left leading to the site of Clif-
ford's Inn, which is featured in *Pickwick Papers, Little Dorrit, Bleak House,*
and *Our Mutual Friend,* and where claims for losses in the Great Fire of
London were assessed, is the Church of St. Dunstan in the West. The original church was probably built in the early part of the eleventh century; the
old building with its three chapels was restored in 1613 and again in 1701,
when a flat roof replaced the arched one. A row of shops was attached to the
church. The building just escaped destruction in the Great Fire of 1666,

Fleet Street, showing St. Dunstan in the West with clock and Temple Bar,
as seen by Dickens when he was lost

which stopped only three doors away, and again escaped when threatened by
fire in 1730.

John Donne, poet and Dean of St. Paul's, was vicar here from 1624 to
1631; Izaac Walton of *The Compleat Angler* fame, who lived for some
years at the nearby corner of Chancery Lane and Fleet Street, was vestry-
man from 1629 to 1644. There is a tablet outside the church and a window
inside to his memory. The figure of Queen Elizabeth standing over the ves-

try door in the courtyard stood originally on Lud Gate, one of the City
gates, demolished in 1760. Beneath the statue of the Queen appear the figures of King Lud and his two sons which also came from the old gateway.

The church was rebuilt in 1831-33, when the present great tower was
erected. The previous building, then, must have been the one seen by young
Dickens and to which he referred in "Gone Astray." In 1831 the line of
the building was put back from its original site, projecting into Fleet Street,
and an octagonal church was built behind the tower, over the old churchyard. The chimes in the tower were those referred to in Dickens' second

St. Dunstan in the West in 1814,
as seen by Dickens when he was lost

Christmas Story: "High up in the steeple of an old church, far above the
light and murmur of the town and far below the flying clouds . . . dwelt
the Chimes." No longer, however, could Trotty Veck hear the whispered
"Haunt and hunt him," nor the words "Break his slumber," nor the lusty
voice of the bells joining with the music of the band to mark the end of his

St. Dunstan in the West in 1832,
as it appeared when referred to in "The Chimes"

dream—if dream it was. The chimes no longer dwell in the steeple; having
fallen into disrepair, they were broken up some years ago and only one solitary bell remains. But the handsome tower illustrated in *The Chimes* is still

there to remind us of Trotty Veck on his "breezy, goose-skinned, blue-nosed, red-eyed, stony-toed, tooth-chattering" post outside the church door.

The clock was originally supplied by Thomas Harrys of Water Lane in 1671, to commemorate the escape of the church five years earlier. The figures of the savages or Hercules used to strike the hours and quarters and turn their heads. The clock was the first in London to have a minute hand. When the church was rebuilt in 1831, the clock and figures were sold and later adorned the Marquis of Hertford's villa in Regent's Park. During the First World War, this house became St. Dunstan's Lodge, connected with the work of blind people. In 1935 the clock and figures were restored to the church, where they can now be seen. The figures have been "civilized" and gilded smartly to celebrate their three hundredth anniversary. There are many literary references to these figures: in *Tom Brown's Schooldays,* Scott's *The Fortunes of Nigel,* Dickens' *David Copperfield* and *Barnaby Rudge.*

When Dickens wrote "Gone Astray" the clock and figures were no longer at St. Dunstan in the West, but they were of course when he was a boy. They were not in fact at Trotty Veck's church in 1844, hence no doubt their omission in *The Chimes.* In "Gone Astray" Dickens says, "Who could see these obliging monsters strike upon the bells and go?" The toyshop, "an enchanted spot," as Dickens describes it, and which took an hour or more to escape from, is no longer there. The original pork-pie shop which was a door or two away from the church may have been there when Dickens wrote "Gone Astray." This shop probably inspired the famous legend of Sweeney Todd, the Demon Barber of Fleet Street, and may also have inspired Dickens to allow Sam Weller to relate the story of the Pork Pie Shop and Sausage Factory in *Pickwick Papers.*

Before arriving at his next place of call Dickens would have passed Bouverie Street on the right, where he was to found *The Daily News,* and also the "dark court" on the left where he placed "with fear and trembling into a dark letter-box" his first literary effort, "A Dinner at Poplar Walk." He could not have known then that this dark turning would be so important to him, but he did of course know by the time he wrote "Gone Astray." Further along on the same side of Fleet Street is the famous tavern, The Cheshire Cheese, thought to have been where Sydney Carton and Charles Darnay celebrated the latter's acquital at the spy trial in *A Tale of Two Cities.*

At the top of Ludgate Hill is St. Paul's Cathedral, from whose dome and cross of gold the boy found it so difficult to take his eyes. As he satisfied himself with a long look at the exterior on his way to the Guildhall, it is not necessary to devote any space here to its long history, beyond saying that this great building was to feature in at least fourteen of his books and writings; possibly only in *Hard Times* and *Drood* is it not mentioned.

From here Dickens would have gone into Cheapside, along Wood Street

where the coaches arrived from Rochester and Chatham, and along Cat-
eaton Street, now Gresham Street, to the Guildhall, where he at last discovered the Giants, Gog and Magog. Both inside and outside the Guildhall
appeared rather different to Dickens as a boy than it does today. The wing
on the left as one faces the Guildhall, where the Bardell vs. Pickwick case
was heard, has been demolished, and soon the right-hand wing containing
the picture gallery will go as well, so that a less impeded view of the Guildhall itself will be obtained from the courtyard. For many years after its partial destruction in the Great Fire of London, when the original oak roof was
burnt, the Guildhall had an ugly flat roof. This was the one that Dickens
would have seen above the Great Hall, as it was not replaced until 1865.
This in turn was destroyed in the Blitz in 1940. The giants were also burnt
at the same time, so that those we see now are not those known to Dickens
either as a boy or later in life. The original ones as Dickens knew them were
described in *Master Humphrey's Clock* by Jo Toddyhigh who says those
"still older and more barbarous figures which succeeded those destroyed in
the Great Fire were about fourteen feet in height." In "Gone Astray" the
boy considered their pedestals to be about forty feet high, but he was no
doubt exaggerating. He found them better-tempered and altogether more
shiny-faced than he had expected. He got into a corner and fell asleep under Magog. In being replaced, the giants have been reversed for some reason or other; Magog is now on the south and opposite side. The figures are
now nine feet three inches tall. On awakening Dickens heard the City roaring, which he would certainly do now—more so, in fact. At a baker's shop
nearby he bought a penny German sausage ("highly peppered horse")
and took it into the Guildhall to eat, a proceeding which would certainly
now be frowned on by the commissionaire in charge. It was interesting during the Dickens Fellowship Centenary Dinner in the Guildhall in June 1970
to remember the young boy eating his frugal meal below the giants. Here
Dickens encountered the black dog with a bit of white over his eye, which he
called Merrychance. Merrychance eventually was unable to resist the temptation of the sausage, which he grabbed and ran away with, leaving the
poor boy with only his loaf of bread, which he washed down with a penny-
worth of milk bought from a milkwoman outside the Guildhall.

From the Guildhall he would have gone along Throgmorton Street, into
which Lothbury now leads. "Up courts and down courts—in and out of
yards and little squares—peeping into country-house passages and running
away—poorly feeding the echoes in the court of South Sea House." Most
of such courts and squares around Threadneedle Street and Old Broad
Street have gone; so has South Sea House, although the site is occupied by
a more modern building bearing that name and now housing a bank. There
is still a gateway leading to a courtyard, and a second gateway leading out of
the court into Old Broad Street bears the date 1833. The original building,
erected between 1720 and 1727, was approached by a gateway leading into

a court. It was built to house the South Sea Company, incorporated in 1710, to pay ten million pounds to seamen engaged in the wars. After the scandal of the South Sea Bubble, the affairs of the company dwindled and the site of the House disposed of in 1854, a year after the writing of "Gone Astray." Previously, in 1826, part of the building fronting Broad Street had been destroyed by fire.

From South Sea House Dickens went on to the Royal Exchange, which is still there but rebuilt. At the back of this building was once Freeman's Court, where Dodson and Fogg, the rascally solicitors, had their office. The

South Sea House, 1830

first Royal Exchange building was destroyed in the Great Fire of London. The second building opened in 1669, included a stone tower in the Italian style, and was destroyed by fire on 10 January 1838. It is said that when the fire was at its height, the tower chimes began to play their popular tune "There's nae luck about the house." This must have been the building seen by Dickens and referred to in "Gone Astray": "When I found myself on 'Change, and saw shabby people sitting under the placards about ships, I settled that they were misers, who had embarked all their wealth to go and buy gold-dust or something of the sort, and were waiting for their respective captains to come and tell them that they were ready to set sail. I observed that they all munched dry biscuits, and I thought it was to keep off seasickness." Dickens and his illustrator, Hablot K. Browne, went to see the ruins of the Royal Exchange the day after the fire. The Royal Exchange was to feature many times in Dickens: Pip saw fluey men there, and Herbert Pocket went on 'Change at busy times to walk in and out and to look about; Quilp had appointments there every day; Flintwinch went on 'Change, and so did Scrooge in his dream and no doubt out of it as well; Mr. Toots, when overcome by the thought of Walter marrying Florence, went there to see the time; and shabby-genteel men were often seen on 'Change in *Sketches by Boz*.

From the Royal Exchange it was a natural move to look at the Mansion House, which features in two stories apart from "Gone Astray": in *Barnaby Rudge* Mr. Haredale tries in vain to enlist the Lord Mayor's help in locking up the murderer Rudge, whom he has captured; and in *A Christmas Carol* the Lord Mayor gives orders to his fifty cooks and butlers to keep Christmas as a Lord Mayor's household should. At first sight the Mansion House appears today as Dickens saw it in the adventures described in "Gone Astray," when a dinner was being prepared there, but there have been alterations of quite a substantial nature. The stone balustrade which protruded into the street was removed in 1840 and the superstructure on the roof—two stories containing servants' quarters and known as the Mare's Nest—was also removed at the same time, leaving the building as it is now. The grated kitchen window through which the boy peeped at the cooks is still as it was with its semicircular iron grill. "Cut along, you, sir!" said the cook whose black whiskers frightened him. Dickens obeyed, no doubt never sparing a glance at the building on the roof or bothering about the stone balustrade lining the street. It is likely that he "cut away" down Cornhill. This would have taken him past St. Michael's, the church of *A Christmas Carol;* the alleyway leading to the George and Vulture, where Mr. Pickwick was "suspended"; St. Peter's Alley leading to the raised churchyard where Bradley Headstone had his stormy interview with Lizzie Hexam; Leadenhall Market where Captain Cuttle bought the chicken for Florence's dinner; and The Blue Boar, where Sam Weller wrote his famous valentine.

Finally he would have wandered into Leadenhall Street, where he found his next building to wonder at, India House. East India House, erected in 1800 on the corner of Leadenhall Street and Lime Street, was a grand building containing a concert hall, paintings, marble statuary, and many Indian and oriental exhibits. Among its curiosities was Tippoo's organ, designed in 1790 for the amusement of the Sultan of Mysore. It depicts an East India Company officer being mauled by a tiger; when played it produces shrieks and, after every fourth shriek, a growl from the tiger. This can now be seen at the Victoria and Albert Museum, Kensington. The Charter of the East India Company was transferred to the Crown in 1858, and four years later the building was demolished. Of this great house Dickens says in "Gone Astray": "Sir James Hogg himself [chairman of the East India Company] might have been satisfied with the veneration in which I held India House. . . . I have no doubt of its being the most wonderful, the most magnanimous, the most incorruptible, the most practically disinterested, the most in all respects outstanding establishment on the face of the earth." The site is now occupied by a large building containing banks, shipping of-

Mansion House Kitchen Window

fices, etc., once known as Royal Mail House.

    After gazing into various shops and running away from a sweep, Dickens was chased by some boys down turnings and into doorways. One wrote what was supposed to be his mother's name and address on his white hat with a stump of black-lead pencil: "Mrs. Blores, Wooden Leg Walk, Tobacco-stopper Row, Wapping"—needless to say, no such address exists or ever did. After a rest in a churchyard, quite impossible to identify, a nap, a pump (perhaps Aldgate Pump), and a bun, he found himself in Goodman's Fields or thereabouts looking at a theatrical poster. The poster represented a scene in a play then being performed at a theatre in that neighborhood which Dickens says "is no longer in existence." One can neither wander into Goodman's Fields nor see any trace of the theatre; indeed one cannot identify the theatre he referred to with any certainty. But there is still a Goodman Street and a Goodman's Yard in the district. Goodman's Fields occupied the site of the streets south of Aldgate East Station, those between

East India House

Mansell Street and Leman Street. Petticoat Lane (now Middlesex Street) would have led into what is now Mansell Street, and Goodman's Fields was south of the present Alie Street. None of the two or three theatres in Goodman's Fields qualify as they ceased to operate in the eighteenth century. The theatre answering closest to the description was the Royalty Theatre opened in 1787, but this was in Well Street, Wellclose Square, a little distance from Goodman's Fields. Dickens did of course say "thereabouts," so maybe this was the theatre to which he referred. It was possibly to Wellclose Square that Dickens was taken at the end of "Gone Astray," because here was one of the old watchhouses. The Royalty Theatre was under the management of John Palmer, an actor from Drury Lane, who opened his theatre with a production of *As You Like It*. Having no license, Palmer was arrested and the theatre was reopened with burlesque and pantomime. Macready, Dickens' friend, tried to make a success here. The name was changed to the East London. It burned down in 1826 and was rebuilt in 1828 as the Royal Brunswick Theatre, but was so poorly constructed that it collapsed three days after its reopening while a company was rehearsing *Guy Mannering,* killing fifteen and injuring twenty. By the time Dickens wrote "Gone Astray," therefore, it would have been no longer in existence. He could have known it before it was burnt in 1826, when plays with music were being produced to conform with the provisions of the Licensing Act of 1737. No theatres except Drury Lane and Covent Garden were allowed to produce plays without music; hence Dickens' humorous description of the dramatic shipwreck followed by a fiddler rendering a comic song and the donkey offered as a prize in a lottery. Young Dickens held programme number 47, and was in terror lest he win the donkey and be forced to take it home.

It may be interesting at this point to refer briefly to the theatres there had been in Goodman's Fields and thereabouts, although none of them was the theatre referred to in "Gone Astray." There were two or three theatres bearing the name Goodman's Fields at various times. One was a shop in Leman Street converted into a theatre by Thomas Odell in 1729; Fielding's second play, *The Temple Beau,* was first produced here. Another theatre was built in Ayliffe Street in 1733 by Gifford, who had been stage manager at the theatre in Leman Street. Frightened by the implications of a play submitted to him called *The Golden Rump,* abusing the King and his ministers, he sent it to Robert Walpole, which led to the passing of the Licensing Act of 1737. Gifford was given £1,000 for his trouble, but under the Act he was unable to produce plays in his theatre. To get around the prohibition he issued tickets for a concert at the theatre in Ayliffe Street and between the two halves of the concert produced *The Winter's Tale,* its first performance for a hundred years. It was in this theatre that David Garrick deputized for Yates and made his professional debut as Richard III on 9 October 1741. The theatre closed at the end of the 1742 season. Meanwhile, Odell's theatre in Leman Street, which had been used for exhibitions of rope-walking and acrobatics, became a theatre again, but it closed in 1741. It became a warehouse and burnt down in 1802. Yet another and older theatre was recorded by a periodical called *The Observator,* which stated that in 1703 there was a performance in Goodman's Fields in the passage by the Ship Tavern, between Prescot Street and Chamber Street. Both these streets still exist, and, although none of these old theatres could have been the one attended by Dickens, we have discovered that the district was given to theatres.

On emerging from the theatre Dickens abandoned the idea in his mind of going into the army, and ran about saying that he was lost, until he found a watchman in his box. These old fellows were the butts of young bloods in those days and earlier, and were frequently turned upside-down in their boxes. The watchman took the boy to the nearest watchhouse, presumably in Wellclose Square. In 1932 the site of this old watchhouse could still be traced on the south side of this square, but it has now vanished. Most of the surrounding buildings—warehouses, a few private houses and shops—are windowless and in course of demolition. Some parts of the square are completely cleared. In the center of the square remains a school for seamen's children, built in 1869, so that it would not have been there when Dickens was lost.

It is still possible to wander in Dickens' footsteps and to see much of interest, but with a very different view from that seen by him as a boy. In preparing this article I checked over the route several times, and although I did it in sections, I concluded my research with a very healthy respect for the energy displayed by the young legs of Dickens, an energy he was later to put to good use in his twenty-mile walks when engaged in writing his books. It must be remembered too that much of his younger walking about the streets of London would have been over the very unfriendly surface of cobblestones, which now exist only here and there. Although today it is a trifle easier and much of the surroundings are changed, the spirit of that tiny boy in the white top hat still seems to precede one in trying to follow his footsteps.

And there are hosts of other figures equally vivid and real who stream out of the many places one passes, creations of the boy in later life, who swarm round regardless of the modern life filling these streets. With such companions and such memories one is never alone or dull in "going astray."

BOOKS CONSULTED:

Clunn, Harold P. *The Face of London.* London: Phoenix House, Ltd., 1951.
Dexter, Walter. *The London of Dickens.* London: Cecil Palmer, 1930.
The Dickensian (1941).
Hartnoll, Phyllis, ed. *Oxford Companion of the Theatre.* London: Oxford University Press, 1967.
London Transport (Dickens Fellowship). *The London of Dickens.* 1970.
Piper, David. *The Companion Guide to London.* London: Collins, 1964.
Timbs, John. *Curiosities of London.* London: Virtue & Co., 1867.
———. *Romance of London.* London: Chandos Library, 1869.
Walford, Edward. *Old and New London.* London: Cassell, Retter, Galpin & Co., 1973, vol. III.

PART TWO

Edmonton Centennial Conference Papers

Ian Watt

ORAL DICKENS

IN *A Room of One's Own,* Virginia Woolf asserts that "it is part of the novelist's convention not to mention soup and salmon and ducklings" when he describes luncheon parties; the novelists "seldom spare a word for what was eaten."[1]

One knows what she means, but she's wrong. Actually, there are two kinds of novelists: those that do and those that don't. Among the moderns, Joyce, Hemingway, Thomas Wolfe, and Scott Fitzgerald, not to mention Philip Roth, typically activate our tastebuds, while Conrad and Lawrence[2] and Henry James[3] don't, although people occasionally pass the port, meet in the Café Royal, or pour cups of tea. Earlier, there's very little about food and drink in Melville, but lots in the English novelists of the nineteenth century—in Mrs. Gaskell and Meredith as well as in Surtees and Trollope. In the richness and variety of his treatment of food and drink Dickens is the indisputable master among the Victorian novelists; as, equally indisputably, he is both the heir of the tradition of Fielding and Smollett, and profoundly original.

— 1 —

Dickens' first published work, "Mr. Minns and his Cousin" (1832), was originally entitled "A Dinner at Poplar Walk." Though minimally gastronomic, it does contain, besides the large dinner at the cousin's, a very decent breakfast and an evening brandy-and-soda.[4] Dickens' first published volumes—*Sketches by Boz* in 1836 and *The Pickwick Papers* in 1837—are rich with eating and drinking. Statistically, *Pickwick Papers* probably has the densest alimentary concentration in all Dickens' novels: there are apparently thirty-five breakfasts, thirty-two dinners, ten luncheons, ten teas, eight suppers, while drink is mentioned 249 times.[5] One goes through the book with envy, not only at the quality and quantity of the supplies, but at the way that they visit upon gross overindulgence—on that of Messrs. Pickwick, Winkle, Snodgrass, and Tupman, for instance—no worse retributions than permanent obesity, temporary inebriation, or occasional bouts of narcolepsy: those stern natural laws whose mildest sanctions in the real world are dyspepsia and hepatitis surrender to the Napoleonic unreality of Dickensian comedy.

The first gastric phase in Dickens lasts for something like a decade. Accounts of eating and drinking diminish very little, but, although they are normally of a relatively straightforward kind, Dickens also begins to use them to show larger moral and social conflicts. Thus *Oliver Twist* (1838) and *Nicholas Nickleby* (1839) make much of the contrast between grownup overeating and youthful starvation. The two are memorably juxtaposed in such famous scenes as Oliver Twist in the workhouse asking for more, or Nicholas Nickleby hungering at Dotheboys Hall: in each case, Dickens, by insisting on the choice fare on the tables of the elders, dramatizes the naked intergenerational power play.

The climax of this first phase is presumably *A Christmas Carol* in 1843. As with the charmed immunity to gastritis enjoyed by the gormandizers of *The Pickwick Papers,* it illustrates the extent to which Dickens' attitude toward food can bend not only normal reality but even his own apparent narrative purpose. Thus, in the vision summoned by the Ghost of Christmas Present, Scrooge's utilitarian parsimony would surely best be underlined by making us see how his fifteen-shilling-a-week clerk had a miserable Christmas dinner; but Dickens' own involvement in the happy satisfaction of appetite said no, and consequently both the antiutilitarian economic theme and Scrooge's dramatic change of heart (represented by his later gift of an enormous turkey) are largely undercut when we are invited to observe how the normal Cratchit Christmas fare would in any case have been a splendid triumph over narrow circumstances: "There never was such a goose," and "Oh, a wonderful pudding!"[6]

For Dickens, essential human values are at issue here. The Cratchits cannot really afford their festivities; and if they try it is simply because good people characteristically place a high value on the good things of existence: conviviality, generosity, the quality of human life, even the truths of religion find their focus in a shared appreciation of the bounty on the festive board. Scrooge, of course, represents the opposite forces of existence—the calculating, the selfish, the isolated, the unspiritual: to him Christmas humbug is an offensive violation of the whole economic code, and of the social and moral attitudes which it dictates. These conflicting attitudes had been given a peculiar importance in the Victorian world by the triumph of industrial capitalism. The most obvious way to accumulate capital is, in general, to spend as little as possible; and so the conflict between the wish to consume and the need to conserve faced Dickens with a real and perpetual political dilemma. Prophetically, he gave literary expression to the only viable solution which Victorian society as a whole was to adopt—the Christmas feast, a temporary moratorium from the Protestant ethic, a few days when, as Claude Levi-Strauss has pointed out, a burst of ritualized giving matches the wasteful extravagances of the potlatch among primitive people, and momentarily restores the principle of reciprocity in social life.[7]

Quite early, then, Dickens expanded the role of food and drink so that they played a vital part both in the plot structure and in the moral significance of his novels. In the second phase, in the novels which follow *The Christmas Carol,* those from *Martin Chuzzlewit* (1844) and *Dombey and Son* (1848) to *Hard Times* (1854) and *Little Dorrit* (1857), these characteristics continue; there is still a great deal of eating and drinking, but in keeping with Dickens' new fictional directions, there is less simple celebration of the pleasures of the table, while the appetites are presented in a much larger psychological and social perspective.

In *Martin Chuzzlewit,* as is usual in the later Dickens, the attitude of the characters toward eating and drinking is deeply diagnostic. Thus the genteel female indifference affected by Mercy and Charity Pecksniff (shown in their disgust, for instance, at John Westlock whose clothes smelled "oh it's impossible to say how strong . . . of smoke and punch") is contrasted with the proper feminine concern for the creature comforts of their males shown by Mrs. Lupin and especially by Ruth Pinch, with her fully described, and eventually triumphant, production of a beefsteak pudding. The good and generous characters—Tom Pinch, that apologetically "great eater," John Westlock, and Mark Tapley—all have robust appetites; but their appetite is of a very different kind from the greed of such people as the inmates of Major Pawkins' boardinghouse in New York, where "everybody seemed to eat his utmost in self-defence" (16, 21, 270). As befits its traditional comic nature, the structure of *Martin Chuzzlewit* is very largely organized through scenes of eating and drinking. The novel begins with supper at the Pecksniffs', which itself follows the farewell feast of John Westlock offstage, and is succeeded by the installation banquet for the new aspirant to architecture, young Martin Chuzzlewit. When the novel moves to London the great contrasts of theme and character are made through the dinner at Todgers', the hollow splendor of the entertainment at the Anglo-Bengalee Disinterested Loan and Life Assurance Company, and the various marvellous scenes with Sairey Gamp. The conclusion is heralded by the breakfast at old Mr. Chuzzlewit's, then by the dinner celebrating the nuptials of Ruth Pinch and John Westlock, and finally by the appropriately aborted wedding breakfast at Todgers' for Cherry Pecksniff and her Augustus.

Martin Chuzzlewit anticipates much of the darker side of the later novels, and in so doing reveals an important advance in Dickens' presentation of the varied pathologies of oral appetite. There are, for instance, the boarders at Major Pawkins': "Dyspeptic individuals bolted their food in wedges; feeding, not themselves, but broods of nightmares" (271); and much the same could be said of Jonas Chuzzlewit's hectic and joyless drunkenness. At the same time the basic theme of the predatory relatives fighting among themselves for old Chuzzlewit's fortune is consistently presented in terms of vampirism, scavenging, and cannibalism. Dickens' comic aim, though, mitigates the consequences of these individual and social perversions of appetite. Dickens cannot save Jonas from death, because he has murdered; but he completely relieves our gloomy foreboding of what sort of fare could be expected at Todgers'. The late Sunday dinner to honor the Pecksniffs is not at all what we might expect from that establishment's seedy environment or from Mrs. Todgers' lifelong mortification at the insatiable appetites of her lodgers for gravy; the meal is princely in substance and genuinely festive in its ceremony: "Oh, Todgers's could do it when it chose! Mind that" (146).

The carnival spirit, in fact, can even humanize hypocrisy and cruelty. When first seen eating, Pecksniff conceals his greed with evangelical rhetoric; but in the dinner scene at Todgers', by the time Pecksniff has risen in drunken muddlement thirty times from his bed in an attempt to rejoin the company, we can no longer take his villainy seriously; and he becomes almost lovable when he courts Mrs. Todgers, and defying current linguistic prudery, pronounces: "The legs of the human subject, my friends, are a beautiful production." There follows his climactic proposal, whose phallic substitution is child's play to a normally contaminated mind: "I should very much like to see Mrs. Todgers's notion of a wooden leg, if perfectly agreeable to herself!" (152-53). The ancient traditions of feasting and comedy have outwitted Victorian sexual taboos.

Later, Pecksniff, together with that other great, greedy and heartless hypocrite, Sairy Gamp, combine to snap their fingers even at death. For seven nights the corpse of old Anthony Chuzzlewit lies above stairs, and, although its presence haunts his guilty son Jonas, Mrs. Gamp and Mr. Pecksniff, to say nothing of the undertakers, jovially reprove mortality by ordering and devouring whatever their delicate fancies and Jonas' captive purse can provide.

Mrs. Gamp and Mr. Pecksniff are complusively oral in another sense. They exemplify Dickens' characteristic tendency to make greedy people eloquent—Mr. Chadband in *Bleak House* is another obvious example. Even when old Martin Chuzzlewit finally unmasks Gamp and Pecksniff, their oratorical genius rises to the occasion; and we are surely justified in concluding that the perfunctory nature of their come-uppance in the story suggests Dickens' sympathetic understanding of how an anxious and hypocritical preoccupation with food and drink can be the result of the same loneliness that underlies the individual's basic drive to create an ideal image of himself through words and to impose this image on others.

In the later novels Dickens becomes less comic and less forgiving: witness his relentless treatment of the plethoric and revengeful cruelty of Major Bagstock in *Dombey and Son* (1848), and of the obscure psychological compensations which lead Mrs. Clennam, in *Little Dorrit* (1857), to alleviate her bedridden isolation by secretly indulging in partridges and punch, at the cost of compromising her ostentatious puritanism. On the other hand, Dickens makes no condemnation of the love of food and drink, even for women; here again he understands very well how it can become an obsessional compensation for personal sorrow and frustration: witness the genuine sympathy in his treatment of Flora Finching, whose frequent recourse to the consolation of brandy in her tea is the present manifestation of her now permanently frustrated "past appetite for romantic love" (158).

In *Dombey and Son* the class contrasts in eating, earlier used in *Chuzzlewit*, function in a much more insistent way. None of the rich enjoy their plenty, and all their reunions are the reverse of festive. In the "cold collation" for Paul Dombey's christening, "there was a toothache in everything"; and the nuptial breakfast for Mr. Dombey's second wedding freezes the blood. The would-be rich, meanwhile, try to maintain their status by keeping what they have to themselves; Mrs. Pipchin, for instance, consumes hot mutton chops to strengthen her constitution from the former ravages of Peruvian mines, while her defenceless little boarders get dinner "chiefly of the farinaceous and vegetable kind" (57, 101).

But the household servants over whom the rich and the would-be rich tyrannize contrive to have their appropriate revenges. Below stairs, special hot suppers and accompanying beverages, we notice, celebrate Paul's death, the flight of Edith and Florence, and the final crash when Dombey's mansion is put up for sale. There is no community of feeling among social classes even within the same household, at least until the last chapter when the broken father joins his daughter, her husband, and Captain Cuttle to open Sol Gills' long-promised bottle of ancient Madeira.

David Copperfield (1850) does not add much that is new to the fictional role of eating and drinking; but Dickens' vivid recall of how the world looks to the hungry child produces several memorable scenes. I still remember my own agonized incredulity as a boy at the way my parents were heartless enough to laugh at the harrowing scene where young David, on his way to Salem House school, is cheated out of his chops, his ale, his potatoes, and even his batter-pudding, by William the waiter. And it was when the well-upholstered and amply-provisioned passengers in the coach mocked David Copperfield, even calling him a "boa-constrictor," for his allegedly preternatural gulosity (70) that I first became conscious of what still seems to me the most enduring truth about human affairs: that all power relations, whether between nations, or classes, or age groups, are most directly and yet most hypocritically expressed in the distribution of food and drink.

Many aspects of these relations are illustrated in the novel, from Steerforth's first act in "taking care of" David's seven shillings to purchase "a royal spread," and the conflicts between David and Dora over the grocery bills when they have set up house, to the various ways in which food, more specifically the withholding of food, was used as the major instrument of Victorian paternal tyranny. The most imaginative instance, perhaps, occurs when Mr. Murdstone first baffles David with the dizzy arithmetic of calculating the cost of "five thousand double-Gloucester cheeses at fourpence-halfpenny each, present payment" (84-85, 54-55), and then punishes him by sending him to bed in disgrace with a dry slice of bread for dinner. The fantasies of parental sadism could hardly go further in elaborate refinement.

In Dickens' last phase—that succeeding *Little Dorrit* in 1857—one can detect some interesting developments in Dickens' own views of food and drink, as well as in the way he uses these concerns in his fiction.

The Uncommercial Traveller (1861) may be regarded as a biographical summing up of the period of the dark novels, as they have come to be called. In vivid contrast to *Sketches by Boz*, two essays, ironically entitled "Refreshments for Travellers" and "A Little Dinner in an Hour," attack the inhospitality, the slowness, and the total culinary bankruptcy of English country inns and railway hotels; Dickens is here, alas! much closer to my own cheerless frequentations than to the jovial gormandizing celebrated in *Boz* and *Pickwick*. Two other essays, "The Boiled Beef of New England" and "A Plea for Total Abstinence" (again, the title is ironical), take up two of the ways in which the less well-to-do are oppressed: by the usually miserable character of the public eating places for the poor, and by the blind punitive rancor of the temperance movement.

Dickens' last completed novel, *Our Mutual Friend* (1865), is not so much concerned with eating and drinking as most of the earlier novels, but it summarizes Dickens' basic moral and social attitudes. Dickens had rarely achieved anything as brilliantly outrageous as the ceremonial dinners at the Veneerings, fashionable, competitive, wholly unconcerned either with the pleasures of the table or with any adequate human feeling—neither of which would be possible in any case under the frigid tyranny of a butler called the Analytical Chemist. Nor, on the other hand, had Dickens earlier presented anything so close to the hidden yearnings of the human appetite as the total generosity and openness of Mr. Boffin's Bower: a reception room combining the advantages of a larder and tap room, where the ungrateful Silas Wegg, from the comfort of the settle, is permanently offered his choice of fare from the inviting case bottles and pies, cold joints, and other solids drawn up on the shelf in open view.

If *Our Mutual Friend* offers a climactic simplification of one side of Dickens views on hospitality, *Great Expectations* (1861) offers perhaps the supreme example in Dickens of a comprehensive integration of eating and drinking into every aspect of the novel. Most obviously, food and drink are mentioned hundreds of times; and the attitude of almost every character toward the subject is presented, not only in itself, but as diagnostic of his moral essence and his social role. The rather few characters whom we can think of as good—notably Pip, Joe, Wemmick, Herbert Pocket, Abel Magwitch —are all fond of good food and drink; and in their various ways they express their love and consideration for others through the giving of food. How they do it is the subject of Barbara Hardy's "Food and Ceremony in *Great Expectations,*" the only serious study I know of attitudes to food in Dickens' novels. Her theme, briefly, is that, in *Great Expectations* as in *Bleak House,* "the same moral values are attached to meals—to the giving, receiving, eating, and serving of food. These values might be summed up as good appetite without greed, hospitality without show, and ceremony without pride or condescension."[8]

The novel begins with Magwitch terrifying Pip: "You know what wittles is. . . . You get me wittles." Next morning Pip raids the Christmas larder and smuggles out his haul. When he sees Magwitch wolfing down mincemeat and pork pie and cheese with terrifying animality, Pip's sympathy finally gets the better of his terror and disgust: "Pitying his desolation . . . I made bold to say, 'I am glad you enjoy it.' " At first Magwitch doesn't hear him, but when Pip repeats his civility, Magwitch answers, "Thankee, my boy, I do" (3, 16). "The rudest meal in the novel," Barbara Hardy comments, is thereby turned "into an introductory model of ceremony."[9]

This early reciprocity of compassion and gratitude is immediately rewarded. Magwitch, soon captured, protects Pip by concealing his theft of the food; and Joe easily forgives the theft itself when, in answer to Magwitch's apology, he answers, "God knows you're welcome to it." Later, Magwitch, no longer threatening to eat Pip's "fat cheeks," determines to provide Pip with his great expectations; in his convict exile, he often imagined: "Here's the boy again, a looking at me whiles I eats and drinks!" (36, 2, 304). But by the time Magwitch returns to England, snobbery has inhibited Pip's natural humanity; when Magwitch visits him in his Temple chambers, Pip at first intends to remain standing and let his guest drink his hot rum-and-water alone; he only changes his mind when, to his uncomprehending amazement, he notices that there are tears in Magwitch's eyes.

In this scene with Magwitch Pip is in a sense only repeating the way Mrs. Joe used to stand over Pip and Joe while she fed them, and the even more contemptuous rejection of Pip by Estella, when she first brought him beer and bread and meat at Satis House, "without looking at me, as insolently as if I were a dog in disgrace." The human importance of these reciprocities, or their damning absence, is expanded in two other episodes of the novel. First, the scene when Joe comes up to London and has breakfast with Pip and Herbert Pocket; Pip, ashamed of Joe's rough country manners, allows the reunion to become painfully embarrassing. He later blames himself: "I had neither the good sense nor the good feeling to know that this was all my fault." His own memory should really have afforded him a corrective parallel, for when, a country bumpkin himself and also just arrived in London, Pip had dinner with Herbert Pocket, his host so kindly

corrected his table manners that "we both laughed and I scarcely
blushed." "In London," says Pocket, "it is not the custom to put the knife
in the mouth—for fear of accidents—and . . . while the fork is reserved for
that use, it is not put further in than necessary" (57, 210, 169).

Magwitch himself, of course, had originally become a criminal out of
hunger; he first came to consciousness "down in Essex, a thieving turnips
for my living." So Compeyson only had to tempt him: "What can you do?"
he asked, and Magwitch replied, "Eat, drink . . . if you'll find the materials." Magwitch remains, in his own words, "a heavy grubber" (328, 329,
312), and for the same psychological reasons, no doubt, a heavy smoker; but
we are obviously meant to see him as a victim of a sick society, not as psy-
chologically maimed himself, as so many of the other characters in *Great
Expectations* are.

Outside this quartet of benevolent eaters, Pip, Joe, Magwitch, and
Herbert Pocket (and perhaps some of their echoes, like Clara, Wemmick
and his Aged Parent), attitudes to food in *Great Expectations* are diagnostic in quite a different way. Most obviously there is the petty egotistical
tyranny of Pumblechook, bringing his Christmas offering of port and sherry
to Mrs. Joe, but then dispensing hospitality with it to the sergeant of the
search party and claiming all the credit; or Wopsle with his Christmas sermon on the gluttony of swine—the memory haunts Pip, and is only exer-
cised when he later toasts a sausage made from Wemmick's pig. Mr. Jaggers
is tyrannical in a different way: he "cross-examined his very wine," and
"seemed to bully his very sandwich as he ate it." Then there is the way that
social pressure dictates the mode of eating: Wemmick is a vastly congenial
table companion at his Walworth home; but in the official world of Little
Britain, he merely "put[s] fish into the post-office" of his mouth. The implication of this gastric mutation is extended when Wemmick and Jaggers,
united as proper unfeeling citizens of Little Britain, bully their poor client
Mike for insulting them with his tears: "Get out of this office. I'll have no
feelings here. Get out," says Jaggers; Mike does, and the two then go back
"to work again with an air of refreshment upon them as if they had just had
lunch" (229, 159, 396, 394).

As is usual in Dickens, it is the women characters who present the
strongest examples of individual and social pathology, and almost without
exception their symptoms are manifested through their attitudes to food.
Mrs. Joe Gargery, who had married beneath her, even takes out her revenge
on the bread and butter; she holds the bread against her "square impregna-
ble bib . . . stuck full of pins and needles," and slaps the butter on "as if she
were making a plaister." The vultures around Miss Havisham are all car-
rion-hungry, waiting until they can "come to feast upon her"; there is Camilla, who claims, "If I could be less affectionate and sensitive, I should
have a better digestion and an iron set of nerves"; Georgiana, "an indiges-
tive single woman, who called her rigidity religion and her liver love"; and

Miss Sarah Pocket, who, Joe reports, on Miss Havisham's death is left "twenty-five pound per-annium fur to buy pills, on account of being bilious" (6, 8, 82, 193, 441).

Satis House is itself an ironically named symbol of unsatisfied appetite. Once the home of a wealthy brewer who married his cook, it is now the mausoleum of love, betrayed twenty-five years ago and now turned into hatred of others and the self. Miss Havisham lives on, waiting to replace the decaying bride cake on the great table with her own dead body; pretending to herself that she can rise above the humanity that has wounded her, she not only stops the clocks and refuses to see the light of day, but "has never allowed herself to be seen doing either [eating or drinking], since she lived this present life of hers" (228).

All the kinds of frustration and rejection, like all the kinds of satisfaction and acceptance, go together.

— 2 —

There is presumably general agreement that Dickens himself shared the fascination with food and drink exhibited in the novels,[10] that, as Barbara Hardy puts it, Dickens "loves feasts and scorns fasts."[11] The records of the life amply substantiate this view. As soon after his marriage as he could afford it, Dickens made sure that none of Dora Spenlow's underdone mutton appeared on his domestic table. His biography features a virtually endless succession of splendid public banquets and lavish private parties; and the editors of the Pilgrim Edition of the letters even inform us that in the later nineteenth-century versions of Dickens' letters, edited by Georgina Hogarth and Mamie Dickens, "many references to food and drink which might be misunderstood [were] removed."[12]

This is not to say that Dickens personally was given either to overeating or heavy drinking. Dolby, his reading tour manager in America, noted: "Although he so frequently both wrote and talked about eating and drinking, I have never met with a man who partook less freely of the kindly fare placed before him."[13] If, then, Dickens' attentions to the details of the table in real life, or to the ceremony of making punch every evening, seem obsessive, it is as symbolic rather than as physical compulsions. They started, we may surmise, as projections of what Dickens dreamed about rather than of what he had experienced in his own past; and when he began writing, the tendency was probably encouraged by his audience, who loved his domestic hearthside heartiness. In either case we are dealing with wish fulfillments; and so we come, at last, to the cryptic triple pun in my title. What connection, if any, can plausibly or profitably be established between *oral* in the sense of "preoccupied with food and drink," *oral* in the sense of "spoken," and *oral* in the sense of the earliest phase of character formation described by Freud?

A good many biographical connections seem plausible, though also somewhat general and hypothetical. Not that Dickens was an infant starveling; it seems likelier that he had a difficult but not unhappy early childhood, if only because trust of others, success in work, and a great capacity for pleasure feature prominently not only in the novels but in his own character. The crucial biographical episode is more probably the five months or so at Warren's blacking warehouse. Dickens was then twelve; he would be nearing the end of the latency period when infantile sexual attitudes again come to the fore and are shaped into the basic sexual pattern of the future. But Dickens' mother had failed him on every count; he was expelled from home and family; he was hungry, and had to find his own food; all his hopes for the future were, it seemed, permanently doomed; and he seems to have laid the blame on his mother—the very mother who, in Dickens' case, had performed not only the usual maternal offices, but had taught him to read. On the other hand, it was his father—the Micawberish grandiloquent spendthrift—who eventually decided to take him out of Warren's warehouse and send him back to school. It was natural, therefore, that Dickens should have fallen back on the oral patterns of the distant past; that he should set out to achieve his early ambitions through prodigiously hard work; and that these ambitions should be connected with never going hungry, to be sure, but also with finding mother-substitutes rather than sexual experience.

As to the relationship between "oral regression" and Dickens' development as writer and oral performer, some connections seem fairly clear. We don't need Rabelais' Gargantua to teach us that what every baby would like to do at birth is shout: *"A boire! A boire! A boire!"* For most children, though, in this unlike Gargantua, or even John Henry for that matter, words normally come later, after weaning; but when words are finally mastered they provide new ways of obtaining nourishment, approval, and other modes of pleasure. The progression seems biologically natural: sucking, eating, and speaking employ the same organs and reflexes—the lips, the tongue, the jaws, the throat, the breathing apparatus. It is no doubt partly for this reason that writers in general are thought by many psychoanalysts to have strong oral personalities.[14] They are in a special case of people, in Karl Abraham's phrase, whose "longing to experience gratification by way of sucking has changed to a need to *give* by way of the mouth," and who therefore have "a constant need to communicate themselves orally to other people."[15] The contrast between these compulsive talkers, who are often professional actors, preachers, politicians, and professors as well as writers, and their opposite, the stereotype of the genital character, is tellingly enshrined in the common phrases "the stiff upper lip" and "the strong silent man." Edward Glover amusingly contrasts this stock masculine type, "the stern-jawed hero of romance," with the oral comic performer, "the darling of the music-hall with the slack jaw and loose bibulous lips."[16] Dickens, we know, was a precocious oral performer himself, in storytelling and comic songs; he began to write certainly by his early teens; and his novels, of course, proved highly suitable to oral delivery.

As to the possible connection between speech considered as a mode of erotic satisfaction and the last phase of Dickens' life, the chronology seems almost too neat. In 1857 *Little Dorrit* appeared, the novel where, in Amy Dorrit and Miss Wade, Dickens analyzed the psychic masochism of the rejected child with remarkable insight.[17] It is also in 1857 that Dickens met Ellen Ternan, and stopped play-acting. In 1858 he separated from his wife, and began the public readings, of which he gave some 470, beginning on 29 April 1858 and ending a few months before his death.[18] The readings may thus be an example of a syndrome found in such markedly oral writers as Balzac and Thomas Wolfe[19]—an obsessional and self-destructive "over-productivity."

The readings themselves were mainly taken from early works—the latest were from *David Copperfield* (1850); and they mainly feature feast scenes, comic scenes, or scenes where young children die—Nancy and Paul Dombey. In going back to an earlier stage of his development in literary subject matter, Dickens may have been enacting the same regressive impulse as in giving the readings themselves, which can be seen as reviving an earlier and more direct investment in oral satisfaction. He could burn many of the records of the past, cast off Catherine, and defy the world, but the strong oral components in his personality merely diverted their expression into an equally oral outlet in the readings: they would—and in fact did—at last persuade Dickens that he really could make the whole world hang, visibly and palpitatingly, upon his very lips.

It is not clear to me just what critical advantages would accrue if it could be established that Dickens himself was an oral-erotic character. The demonstration itself would certainly be reductive; it would have to be done most expertly not to be insufferably patronizing; and in the nature of things it would probably be impossible to find adequate evidence. For one thing, the baby's oral phase, being preverbal, is inaccessible to later introspection or analysis; for another, the kind of biographical evidence required is probably unavailable for Dickens. We can only speculate, and in my own view the advantages for literary criticism of so doing rest on rather delicate grounds. Any psychological theory may or may not help us in much the same ways as any other theoretical system may or may not help us understand a literary work more fully. At best it can serve two limited but valuable functions: either to provide a larger context of understanding which suggests possible interrelationships between various literary features that we have already observed or else to make us more sensitive to literary features which we have not previously noticed.

As to the first, the biographical hypothesis about the special nature of the psychological conflict in Dickens' last years, for instance, can provide a general perspective of psychological understanding for our literary sense that the last novels, and especially *Our Mutual Friend,* show a more inward and convincing presentation of adult sexuality; more generally it also helps us to see connections between other literary features of Dickens' work which in themselves have often been observed. For instance, the assumption that speech was itself a basic source of emotional satisfaction to Dickens may supply one reason for understanding why Dickens' whole literary style seems oral. As Robert Garis has observed, our "first impression, and a continuing one, in Dickens' prose is of a voice manipulating language with pleasure and pride in its own skill."[20] Rhetorical analysis also reveals Dickens' great reliance on many of the features of epic style: repetition, apostrophe, stock formulae of phrase and sound, extended similes, parataxis; and these features are constant in abundance, if not exactly in kind, throughout his writing life.

The same oral context would add a psychological explanation of the commonplace that, in the words of Kathleen Tillotson, Dickens was the first novelist to "put a child at the center of a novel for adults."[21] His novels reveal many of the perspectives of a child. Three obvious instances are: the amazing vividness wherever childhood experience is presented; the segregation of women characters into asexual angels or frustrating witches; and third, the relative lack of any convincing presentation of sexual love. Dickens' imaginative regression to life seen from the child's viewpoint takes many other forms. Thus Freud himself, though a great admirer of Dickens, objected to his characteristic "mannerisms," and singled out the way "all good people immediately become friends as soon as they meet, and work together throughout the whole book."[22] This is surely a youthful dream which later life, alas, rarely supports.

One can even narrow down some of the minor details of the novels to the specific viewpoint of the oral stage of character development. For instance, V. S. Pritchett includes in his anathema of Dickens' women the charge that they are "tiresome in childbirth . . . continuously breeding,"[23] and to this one can add that the only woman in the novels who is a happy mother, morally admirable, and possessed of effective eloquence, happens to be the humble Polly Toodles—Paul Dombey's wetnurse: her understanding is equal to manipulating not only Susan Nipper but even Mr. Dombey, and she consoles Florence with a moral tale that would not be out of place in the mouth of any of the published Victorian matriarchs who provided the reading public with infantile morality.

Many other commonplaces of Dickens criticism can be seen as projections of the psychic politics of the baby. The heroes and heroines are often orphans, or they are only children; or if not, they have no brothers, and their sisters die young, like David Copperfield's, or seem to have been born little mothers, like Florence Dombey, Little Dorrit, and Lizzie Hexham: one way of putting all this would be to say that in his novels Dickens permits no threatening sibling rivals at the maternal board or bosom.

The focus on the oral elements in Dickens also seems to me to have a searching power which discovers elements in his characterization and even in his plots which have not been observed before, or at least have received little critical notice. More specifically, it reveals a remarkably detailed anticipation in Dickens' novels of the theories of the oral character initiated much later by Freud and developed by Karl Abraham and Edward Glover.

The psychological concept of the oral character is itself protean and amorphous. Karl Abraham explains the main reason in "The Influences of Oral Erotism on Character-Formation": "The libidinal cathexis of the mouth which characterizes infancy can still be employed in later life," and is not repressed by the adult world, as the later anal and phallic pleasures are. These early oral traits therefore remain as more or less normal ongoing components of the personality, and do "not need to be changed into character-formation or sublimated to the same extent as the anal ones."[24]

Karl Abraham, Edward Glover, Freud himself, and various later disciples, such as Erik Erikson, are, however, substantially agreed on the main lasting effects upon individual character which are produced by the particular circumstances of the oral stage. After birth the child develops its sense of pleasure, purpose, and relation to the outside world primarily through suckling. If in its first year or so the experience is gratifying and prolonged, the child is likely to develop an optimistic character. This optimistic and ambitious character can be of two kinds. In favorable circumstances an early self-confidence may later help the child to successfully achieve its aims in life; but a second kind of character may also develop, one in which a vague optimism habituates the individual to passivity, to a life of waiting for the world as mother to give him what he needs. As Edward Glover puts it in "The Significance of the Mouth in Psycho-Analysis," behind the ambition of the oral-erotic there is often "a feeling that the silver spoon is or ought to have been in the mouth." The phrase itself surely recalls many characters in Dickens' novels; when Glover goes on to say that, "if the worst comes to the worst," the frustrated oral character falls back on "the old oral omnipotence" of his earliest experience, and then adds that this character type always assumes that "something is bound to turn up,"—Micawber himself turns up in our minds. Glover explains that such a character "doubtless . . . clings in the secret recesses of his mind to the magic formula, 'Table! Cover thyself' "[25] Mr. Micawber is ambitious, in his own way, and when catastrophe has become total, we can be sure that a table will soon appear, and cover itself with the ingredients for Mr. Micawber's punch.

Where early oral satisfaction has been denied or cut short early, the main tendencies, according to psychoanalytic theory, are toward three related types of character development. First, there are those who are always, whether modestly or aggressively, asking for something from others, the people who "cling like leeches"; secondly, there are the compulsive talkers, those earlier described by Abraham as "having a need to *give* by way of the mouth";[26] and third, we have the oral-sadistic character, where, with the double trauma of the coming of teeth and the end of weaning, biting—or later making biting remarks—becomes the way by which the frustrating world can be held and mastered.

These five oral character types can, of course, only be roughly differentiated, and they are usually found in combination with other traits; nevertheless, I hope that even this brief and simplified outline has been sufficient to transmit some ripples of recognition out into Dickens' fictional world. We surely meet examples of all these character types in the novels of Dickens, and this becomes a more convincing measure of his initiated insight when we reflect on how few other novelists even begin to supply the kind of information about physiognomy, gesture, and domestic habits that we need before we can construct such hypotheses about their characters.

The happy but independent optimists no doubt include Mr. Pickwick and Mark Tapley; for the dependent optimists a good many can be added to Mr. Micawber, with Harold Skimpole an extreme example; somewhere in between the two come Dickens' directly autobiographical characters—David Copperfield and Pip—the shy, undersized, and oral-ambitious character, the would-be mother's boy, the "jilted baby," to use Edward Glover's expressive term.[27] Among the leeches Dickens gives a host of clinging, demanding characters, usually women, like Camilla in *Great Expectations*. As for the compulsively verbal characters, they are endless: Pecksniff, Chadband, and Flora Finching, for instance. They are three obvious examples of those multitudes of urban characters of whom Pritchett writes that "Dickens saw they were people whose inner life was hanging out, so to speak, on their tongues."[28] In many cases these talkers tend to oral sadism: Sairey Gamp is presumably the classical example, but there are innumerable variants, from Mrs. Clennam to Uriah Heep. The fully developed pathology of the sadistic biter, physical or verbal, is exhibited in such horrors as Mr. Murdstone, Quilp, Arthur Gride, and Mr. Lammle; its purest manifestation is probably Mr. Carker: at Edith Dombey's wedding he approaches her "with his white teeth glistening . . . more as if he meant to bite her, than to taste the sweets that linger on her lips" (444); and it is significant that it was only because of Lord Jeffrey's objection that Dickens did not, in the event, allow Carker to sink his ever-bared teeth into Edith's white breasts.[29]

Much more could be said on how much of Dickens' characterization fits into the oral categories of psychoanalysis; and one could also make a simpler distinction, that based on the idea that the oral character types may essentially be divided into biters and suckers. Dickens could accept neither as adequate persons, but we might call many of his youthful heroes secret suckers; they are, no doubt, innocent, trusting, and benevolent, but they are also rather simple, passive, and unpracticed with women.

To pass very briefly to how Dickens' plots also reflect the oral perspective, one can say that the job of the typical Dickens plot is to find magic providers for the secret suckers. This narrative direction can be regarded as an exaggerated form of what is probably the tendency of fiction in general. Dickens' novels often begin with the hero in youth, in insecurity and frustration, in the stage, that is, where the neonate has already been separated from his mother; and, after endless vicissitudes, we find that the hero ends a step or two back from where the novel began, in a warm little haven, characterized by lots of food and drink, easily available comforts and total security.[30]

— *3* —

That Dickens creates people in his novels who are marked by residues of the oral stage according to Freudian theories of character development, does not, of course, prove anything about Dickens' own personality. On the other hand, if what has been said about the characters in his novels can be demonstrated from the text, it does not require any extraneous biographical and psychological evidence; and we already have the general support we need in the generally accepted view that Dickens' imagination remained rooted in the perceptions of childhood, perceptions which gave him an unsurpassed mastery of the internal psychological revelations which are immanent in human physiogomy, gesture, and habits of speech. The present essay could then be viewed primarily as an exploration of one particular aspect of the hallucinated clarity with which the child sees other people as larger-than-life manifestations of his own interests and perspectives.

For Dickens, and indeed for the Victorian child in general, all older people would tend to be seen in two main roles: as eaters, drinkers, and talkers themselves; and as powerful dispensers or withholders of his own oral pleasures. This itself comes close to supplying a perspective for understanding why so many of the basic conflicts in Dickens' novels can be reduced to the simple primitive choice between eating or being eaten. The sociological perspective would reinforce the psychological. We know that Victorian parents habitually used the giving or withholding of food as an instrument of religious, moral, and social discipline.[31] Presumably, therefore, the child not only categorized adults as good or bad according to whether he was being well fed or not. Giving or consuming good food was deeply equated with goodness; and this equation was reinforced by economic and class factors, since there was a much greater difference then than now between the staple diets of different classes.[32]

As for the connection between the three senses of *oral,* a few concluding generalizations seem called for. First, as regards speech, it seems that there is still much to say about the way Dickens makes speaking itself both a directly physical reality in his novels, and also an infinitely symbolic activity; more generally, that there is still much to learn about the physical, phsyiological and psychosexual functions of the act of speech.

Secondly, we should surely challenge the adverse judgment on all the oral functions which is implicit in our current terminology. The basic reason for this adverse judgment on oral satisfactions is presumably not so much the puritan objection to gluttony or the pleasures of the physical appetites in general, as it is Freud's biologically based evolutionary model for psychological development: oral satisfactions are "regressive" because they denote a deflection from, or a failure to achieve, "mature genitality," that "psychoanalytic Utopia," as Erik Erikson has called it.[33] Erikson's irony points to the reductive and pejorative connotations of such terms as *oral*, or, for that matter, *anal*. In any case, all surviving biological species have presumably achieved their genital Utopia; and though human civilization has done much with the genital component as a basis—romantic love and the family for instance—it is no more impressive than what man has done with the oral components, and it is certainly not so distinctive of man. All human societies have developed cooking, and no others have; man is indeed, as Boswell defined him, a "Cooking Animal."[34] Among the other oral components of culture which are unique to man one should at least list three that are particularly important for Dickens' novels. First, the invention of fermented beverages, which was no inconsiderable achievement; second, social laughter, which is basic to comedy; and third, of course, speech. *Homo loquens* is a reality, and were it not, we would not even have been able to christen him, however presumptuously, *homo sapiens*.

The Freudian scheme of libido development also presupposes, primarily for necessary therapeutic purposes, a contradiction between the oral and the genital impulses that is misleading as far as most human, and especially most literary, experience is concerned.[35] There is no doubt considerable truth in V. S. Pritchett's view that oral pleasures were substituted for sexual ones in the Victorian novel: "What replaced the sane eighteenth-century attitude to sex in the comic writings of Dickens? I think probably the stress was put on another hunger—the hunger for food, drink and security, the jollity and good cheer."[36] At a certain point of concentration, interest in food does exclude everything else, as Dickens reminds us in his surrealistic vignette of Lady Scadgers in *Hard Times:* "an immensely fat old woman, with an inordinate appetite for butcher's meat, and a mysterious leg which had now refused to get out of bed for fourteen years" (42). But within the more usual ranges of behavior mutual support between the oral and the genital component is the norm. We hardly need reminding of what play kissing is often a prologue to, nor of the traditional cooperation of food, drink, and laughter with Eros. Mr. Bumble understands very well one thing normally leads to another when he remarks to Mrs. Sowerberry, to explain poor Oliver Twist's sudden turning on his tormentors: "It's not Madness, ma'am . . . it's Meat."[37]

As regards literature, we must surely come to terms with the fact that the mouth is the basis for social and intellectual community: beginning with food and drink; going on to talk and laughter; ending in song and story and play. Satire, for instance, is supposed to have had its origin in the *lanx satura,* the fertility festival of the full bowl; and comedy, derived from the Greek words for song and social merrymaking, commingles all the oral pleasures, without disdaining the support of whatever anal and genital amusements society allows. As for Dickens, the hypothesis that his own personality was powerfully oral in tendency would only supply another perspective for what we know already; that there is a psychological cost for all achievement —even for the creative achievement which places Dickens among the supreme figures in the pantheon of Western comedy.

NOTE:

I am much indebted to those who, at Edmonton or elsewhere, gave me the benefit of their criticism; and especially to Philip Collins, Rowland McMaster, Steven Marcus, Thomas Moser, Robert Polhemus, Bambi Pratt, and Michael Wolff.

Philip Collins

DICKENS' PUBLIC READINGS

Texts and Performances

BEFORE DICKENS became a public reader, many of the talents and energies that went into that career had gone into his amateur theatricals, where he shared the stage with other performers but directed the whole production and organization himself and generally took the leading role. The acme of these performances, when he played Wardour in *The Frozen Deep* (a drama attributed to Wilkie Collins but largely written by Dickens), took place less than a year before his career as a reader began, and thereafter there were no amateur theatricals; the readings not only took up the time, but also (it is clear) provided much the same emotional satisfaction. At a party after one of the amateur company's performances, Dickens exclaimed, "Blow Domestic Hearth! I would like to go on all over the kingdom, . . . acting everywhere. There's nothing in the world equal to seeing the house rise at you, one sea of delightful faces, one hurrah of applause!"[1] That, it is reported, was said in a "mad-cap mood," Dickens being in the "wildest spirits"; but he was avowedly in quite sober spirits when, a few years later, he wrote to Bulwer Lytton after another such bout of theatricals: "I can most seriously say that all the sights in the world turned pale in my eyes, before the sight of three thousand people with one heart among them, and no capacity in them, in spite of all their efforts, of sufficiently testifying to you how they believe you to be right, and feel that they cannot do enough to cheer you on."[2]

Such avowals are, I suppose, both endearing, and vulgar and ignominious. Endearing, because it is a virtue—or at worst a pleasant weakness—to rejoice so heartily in making other people happy (and that includes lots of people, in public places, as well as the one or the few in private). There are other virtues, of course, moral and artistic, and Dickens possessed some of them, but he was sometimes willing to sacrifice or subordinate them to this pleasurable duty of—to quote two of his artistic manifestoes—fulfilling his "earnest and humble desire . . . to increase the stock of harmless cheerfulness," "the cheering-on of very many thousands of my countrymen and countrywomen, never more numerous or true to me than now."[3] And the

[182]

thousands mattered: not for him, only or primarily, the one judicious whose "censure . . . must o'erweigh a whole theatre of others"—he was a writer for the general, the groundlings included; he did not scorn to "make the unskil-ful laugh." For his debut as a public reader in Birmingham in 1853, he stipulated indeed that one of the three performances should be for a work-ing-class audience—and their delighted and observant response (he later re-ported) "animated me to that extent that I felt as if we were all bodily going up into the clouds together."[4] Dickens much liked to be liked, and not just by the few. Since 1836, it had been superabundantly evident that he had more of the literary talents requisite for widespread popularity than any au-thor since Shakespeare; now he showed in the public readings that, miracu-lously, he also had, more abundantly than any English writer of comparable importance, the second set of talents needed for platform popularity. A man of his disposition could hardly have resisted forever the temptation to ex-ploit the emotional and financial possibilities of this combination of talents —and certainly not in his crisis year of 1858. Friends might demur: Forster might, reasonably, argue that this was a betrayal of his genius, the substitu-tion of a lower for a higher art, or, less reasonably, that it was incompatible with the proper dignity of a great author, besides raising "a question also of respect for himself as a gentleman." Certainly it was the substitution of an ephemeral art for an enduring one, and we may lament, with Ruskin, that, had he not worn himself out and killed himself off by reading, "he might have been writing blessed books till he was eighty" (though some of us might then have been rather superannuated at the Centenary). On the other hand, we might—had we been able to hear Dickens' readings—have been won over, as was one contemporary who had not been disposed to re-gard them favorably:

> Not that we doubted their excellence; but . . . it seemed to us that a personal representation of the characters which he had created was scarcely worthy of his great genius and high place in the national literature. . . . We had not long listened to him, however, when we felt that the creations of his fancy gathered tenfold vigour from his representation, and that he . . . had the power of giving a more visi-ble and determinate embodiment to his creations, and sending to the heart with tenfold force the lessons . . . it has long been his object to inculcate.[5]

"The substitution of lower for higher aims" (to revert to Forster's phrase): I said that Dickens' sense of an audience had, besides that endear-ing side which is so significant for his art, a vulgar and igominious aspect. It is vulgar and insensitive to boast so much—as he continues to do in the let-ters about the readings—about his command of an audience; vulgar too, perhaps, to seek this regular face-to-face confirmation that he was liked;

ignominious, certainly, that a man of his genius so evidently needed to do it, and do it not once but often. There is a measure of ignominy in all actors' self-display and lust for applause, but surely the one-man-show performer puts himself into a class of his own, morally as well as artistically; he is beseeching attention and indulging vanity to a reprehensible degree *(je suis payé pour le savoir)*. And maybe too Hamlet should be granted a point, that Dickens' seeking to please all those unskilful groundlings was too easy a gratification. In 1858, when the paid readings began, there were of course special pressures, to which he alludes in a letter, that October. His provincial tour had been "wonderfully successful," netting him over a thousand guineas a month clear profit (good money, I might interject, compared with the income from his writings, which averaged under three thousand pounds a year). But, his letter continued, "the manner in which the people have everywhere delighted to express a personal affection for me . . . is (especially at this time) high and far above all other considerations. I consider it a remarkable instance of good fortune that it should have fallen out that I should, in this autumn of all others, have come face to face with so many multitudes."⁶ But it was not, of course, a matter of "good fortune": he was touring that autumn, in the aftermath of the scandal of his marital troubles, because the impulse to turn professional reader had become irresistible under the pressure of those troubles. That exclamation of ten years earlier was prophetic indeed: "Blow Domestic Hearth! I would like to go on all over the kingdom, . . . acting everywhere." But this emotional crisis cannot account for his continuing the readings throughout the 1860s (on and off); nor can financial need or cupidity, though these helped. The phrenologist Charles Bray was not surprised by Dickens' fate: "His head was very flat at the top, going straight off from the anterior lobe connected with the intellect, . . . his strongest feelings were Love of Approbation and Acquisitiveness, and he literally killed himself off in their gratification." That Love of Approbation, in particular, was central to Dickens' artistic personality, for better and for worse. Certainly one prominent American phrenologist made the unsurprising discovery that he possessed, to a very marked degree, the "organisation" which makes the poet, artist, philosopher and actor; and surely, too, percipient phrenologists must have found him large in the organ of Adhesiveness, which "disposes to friendship and society in general, and gives ardour to the shake of the hand."⁷ It was when describing his vain attempt to dissuade Dickens from performing that John Forster used one of his most-quoted phrases: "There was for him no 'city of the mind' against outward ills, for inner consolation and shelter. It was in and from the actual he still stretched forward to find the freedom and satisfactions of an ideal, and by his very attempts to escape the world he was driven back into the thick of it."⁸ The effort of touring eventually became burdensome, but he enjoyed, and forgot his sorrows in, many of these travels into the actual. The sight of a responsive audience never failed to stimulate and cheer him.

I have started by this brief reminder of some of the biographical and artistic coordinates of Dickens' reading career, before settling to the topic I have undertaken to discuss (the texts of his readings and how Dickens performed them), partly because we need to remember these matters in our discussion later; and I have kept it brief because I have already tried elsewhere more fully to elaborate their significance.[9] But also I hope we bear these matters in mind—for I think they are of primary importance to one's sense of Dickens the novelist—during much of what follows, which (to be candid) strikes me as traversing matters of secondary interest, or, as I shall suggest, perhaps interesting in that it is *not* very interesting. I have worked diligently on Dickens' reading texts, on your behalf, but cannot claim to have vitally illuminated my sense of his art—a reflection on me, no doubt—and I shall be disappointed if discussion does not throw up valuable suggestions that have not occurred to me, but I rather doubt whether there is very much of interest to be discovered about how Dickens devised his scripts that most students could not guess, without even looking at one. About my other topic, how Dickens performed, the evidence is so enormous, and inevitably so often conflicting, that any selection that I make must be, to some extent, misleading. Observers inevitably differed, in percipience, in preconceptions, and in standards of judgment; and Dickens' performances differed from night to night, let alone over the sixteen-odd years he was performing. Moreover, performances are notoriously difficult to record. One baffled reviewer of the readings aptly quoted Dickens' Dr. Marigold, confessing the inadequacy of his words: "A man can't write his eye (at least *I* don't know how to), nor yet can a man write his voice, nor the rate of his talk, nor the quickness of his action, nor his general spicy way."[10] Granted these inadequacies and conflicts, some useful reflections can, I think, arise from this evidence. Certainly the whole episode of Dickens' second career as a reader strikes me as fascinating, and as more full of suggestion than has been generally realized. Forster, who disliked it all, nevertheless went so far as to say that, in his later years, the world knew him as much by the readings as by his books;[11] for anyone wanting to consider Dickens biographically, or in his age, such an assertion should prove suggestive. We, of course, can never recapture these past performances; even if a modern performer had Dickens' talents and dedication, which is unlikely, he would still not be Charles Dickens: his performances could never enjoy the enormous extra halo effect of being delivered by the author, and a very specially loved, and long-loved, author too. And if no great author since Dickens has had his talent and zest for the platform, neither has any other great literature, written for the printed page, lent itself so magnificently to solo performance (or indeed to other forms of vocal or dramatic adaptation). As another reviewer of the readings aptly quoted, "None but himself can be his parallel."[12]

Over the years, Dickens prepared twenty-one readings. Five were never performed, another five proved relatively unsuccessful and were given only a few times. The basic repertoire was the nine readings he took to America in 1867-68 (where they were published, and thus came to constitute the collected *Readings,* which exists in several editions)—these, and *Sikes and Nancy* (devised after the American tour), and *The Poor Traveller* (an item popular during the first season but not often revived later). His charity performances between 1853 and 1858 had all been readings of *A Christmas Carol,* except for one performance of *The Cricket on the Hearth;* these two Christmas books, together with *The Chimes,* constituted his total repertoire when he began giving paid readings. They each took two hours to read, having been reduced from their earlier length. (The *Carol* had taken three hours in 1853, despite some cuts.) Dickens then devised another two-hour reading, *Little Dombey,* and a program of three short pieces *(The Poor Traveller, Boots at the Holly-Tree Inn,* and *Mrs. Gamp),* and soon began further reducing all the two-hour scripts, so that every performance would consist of at least two items. The only other two-hour script he devised and performed was *David Copperfield,* though this too was soon cut to about eighty-five minutes (and it was then Dickens' longest and most exhausting reading). Under half of the readings, in fact, came from the novels. Most came from the Christmas books and stories; there are several reasons for this, the most obvious being that these shorter narratives were easily adaptable into coherent readings of an appropriate length.

How did Dickens devise and shape his scripts? At first, when he was only working on the Christmas books, he simply had the pages of an ordinary copy inlaid into a larger page (so giving himself more margin to write in), and then marked his cuts, emphases, and rephrasings in pen or pencil. But soon, when working from the novels or from the Christmas stories in the small print of his weekly magazines, he did a quick scissors-and-paste job, indicated some cuts, and wrote in a few bridge passages, and sent this hotchpotch off to the printer—whom he used where we would use a typist— and had a few copies privately printed. Then he would start the hard work, with pen or pencil (or even with a brush, for at one period he rather fancied blocking out the major deletions with a brush and red ink). Sometimes there was a trial private performance of a reading, and this might suggest further changes; after the most famous of these—a very full-dress trial of the last reading he devised, *Sikes and Nancy,* seven weeks before the first public performance—Dickens, on the advice of Wilkie Collins and Charles Kent, extended the narrative, writing a complete extra episode. Experience with audiences, over subsequent months or years, would suggest further emendations. Or the rescheduling of programs might necessitate the drastic shortening of an item; one reading, *Nicholas Nickleby,* existed (and was printed) in two forms, a four-chapter and a "short-time" three-chapter version. Often one can trace the successive stages of the deletions and emendations by following through the prompt copy the variously colored inks which (conveniently) he used from time to time. I have not yet been able to do this for

David Copperfield (this, as we all know, is one of the limitations of photo-copying), but I shall take that reading as my main example, as it is one of Dickens' most ambitious efforts, was his favorite reading, and for many of his admirers constituted his most impressive performance, particularly in the storm scene with which it ended.

As this ending suggests, the main story line was concerned with Steer-forth—Steerforth's seduction of Emily, Peggotty's recovery of her, and the death of both her lovers in the storm. Surprising that Dickens chose *that* as his main plot—but David's career and adventures were obviously too mul-tifarious to boil down into a reading, and Dickens had evidently decided not to do with *Copperfield* what he did with *Pickwick* (which was to base read-ings on two splendid detachable episodes, the Trial and Bob Sawyer's Party, abbreviating them by about one-third), nor to center a reading on one char-acter from a novel, as he had done in *Little Dombey* and *Mrs. Gamp*. His plan for the *Copperfield* reading was devised nearly seven years before he gave it, and it shows him, just a year after giving his first charity readings in Birmingham, aware of the difficulties of creating a script from the novels.

> Having already read two Christmas books at Birmingham, I should like to get out of that restriction, and have a swim in the broader waters of one of my long books. I have been poring over Copper-field (which is my favourite) with the idea of getting a reading out of it, to be called by some such name as "Young Housekeeping and Little Emily." But there is still the huge difficulty that I constructed the whole with immense pains, and have so woven it up and blended it together, that I cannot yet so separate the parts as to tell the story of David's married life with Dora, and the story of Mr. Peggotty's search for his niece, within the time. This is my object. If I could possibly bring it to bear, it would make a very attractive reading, with a strong interest in it, and a certain completeness.[13]

This is exactly the plan he followed in the summer of 1861 when, having completed *Great Expectations,* he was making a formidable effort to refur-bish his repertoire for his big provincial tour that winter (he devised five new readings, three of them long ones, that summer).

David Copperfield, I mentioned, was originally a two-hour reading, though after a few months it was cut by over a quarter. Dickens experienced unusual difficulty over devising it. The privately printed promptbook (now in the Berg Collection, to whose Trustees I am much obliged for their per-mission to describe and quote from it) has as its title page, *David Copper-field. A Reading. In Five Chapters,* but before chapter i there is a twenty-page introduction (excerpts, mainly from chapter xxi of the novel, in which David fatefully introduces Steerforth to the Peggottys, on the evening when Ham and Emily have become engaged). The first three pages of this intro-duction are virtually identical with the first three pages of chapter i, and

some typographical oddities make it evident that, after the five-chapter version had been printed, and he had got down to revising and rehearsing it,
Dickens decided that a much fuller introduction of Steerforth and the Peggotty group was necessary—so he devised that introduction, and then re-
numbered the chapters, i to vi. Not that he tried to make this, nor his other
readings, self-explanatory. As the *Manchester Guardian* critic remarked:

> If we could suppose a person in the audience unacquainted with the
> "Life of David Copperfield," and thus unable to supply from mem-
> ory the deficiency in the narrative which the necessity of its conden-
> sation . . . occasions, we could well imagine such a person regarding
> [this reading] as a story without intelligble beginning or satis-
> factory ending.[14]

But such a person was barely supposable: one of the major delights of Dickens' readings was the pleasure of recognition, most famously instanced by
the audience's cheer, which became traditional, during *The Trial from "Pickwick"*; when Serjeant Buzfus said, "Call Samuel Weller," audiences almost
always applauded the mere mention of this character, who had not yet appeared in the reading—a moment which struck the critic in the New York
Nation as "the most impressive thing" of the evening, "such an unaffected
tribute of admiration as few authors have ever obtained. Mr. Dickens stood
before us in the flesh—listening to that voice of human sympathy and admiration which only the posterity of most other great men hear."[15] And it
was that critic in the *Manchester Guardian* who complained when Dickens
did not respect the assumption that his audience knew his books: "One
horrible suspicion alone marred our otherwise perfect enjoyment [of *The
Trial*]. Surely Mr. Dickens has been tampering with his text? . . . *Pickwick*
cannot be improved—even by Mr. Dickens."[16]

How much did Dickens tamper with his text, beyond the obvious need
to abbreviate most pieces? Surprisingly little, in fact—at least on paper.
Many of his most striking verbal additions or changes were ad libs, mainly
in the comic passages, and often made when he was stimulated by a particularly responsive audience. Some of these extempore textual emendations became a standard part of the text, though Dickens (I think) rarely if ever
went to the bother of writing them into his prompt copies: he knew the
scripts so well that he often didn't glance at them. Doubtless the great majority of these curlicues have died with their author and the audiences who
heard him; some, which became standard, were recorded. For instance, Dickens added to Mr. Squeers' confident ignorance of grammar:

> "C-l-e-a-n, clean, verb active, to make bright, to scour. W-i-n, win,
> d-e-r, der, winder, *preposition*, a casement. When a boy knows this
> out of book, he goes and does it. Where's the second boy?"
> "Please, sir, he's weeding the garden."

"To be sure. So he is. B-o-t, bot, t-i-n, tin, n-e-y, bottiney, *adjective*, a knowledge of plants. . . . Third boy, what's a horse?"

"A beast, sir."

"So it is. . . . A horse is a quadruped, and quadruped's Latin, *or Greek, or Hebrew, or some other language that's dead and deserves to be*, for beast."[17]

Neither in Dickens' novel, nor in his own reading books, does the text appear like that. The extent of Dickens' divergences even from those promptbooks was evident in America, where he had allowed the readings to be printed straight from the promptbooks—but it was a constant matter of complaint or gratification for those in his audiences who diligently followed him, book in hand, that the words he spoke were often remote from the printed text.

We, however, must rely on the printed texts, together with Dickens' marginalia in his own copies: and these texts, I said, are remarkably close to the novels. Just as, when preparing or passing a new edition of a novel for the press, Dickens rarely made any but the most trivial changes, and very few of them, so he resisted the temptation to rewrite his earlier works when creating readings from them. We all, I am sure, pity as much as admire the Clarendon editors, and other such toilers in that stony vineyard (eminently Sylvère Monod), for the enormous labor they are undertaking on Dickens' manuscripts and successive editions, with so rarely any results that even start to be interesting. Not much of the brainwork of Dickens' creation was done on paper. And so with the readings: very few additions to the *Works*, and very few new points of view, have emerged (at least from my examination of the promptbooks). A rare, and interesting, example which goes beyond the obvious process of condensation which Dickens—like myself or any other recitalist or adapter—necessarily employs is in *Sikes and Nancy*. Just when Sikes thinks he has found sanctuary in Jacob's Island, the reading goes: "Hark! A great sound coming on like a rushing fire! What! Tracked so soon? The hunt was up already? Lights gleaming below, voices in loud and earnest talk. . . ." In the novel, Sikes is fighting Charley Bates, an episode omitted in the reading, ". . . when Crackit pulled him back with alarm, and pointed to the window. There were lights gleaming below, voices in loud and earnest conversation."[18] The terrifying approach of the avengers is seen from inside Sikes' mind, and his terror is further expressed through those added ejaculatory phrases, "Hark! . . . What! Tracked so soon? . . ." —an example, incidentally, of that identification between reader and character which, in this case, seemed to go well beyond the histrionic.

That closing episode of *Sikes and Nancy*—added in manuscript after the trial performance—is a striking example of Dickens' skill in selecting and dramatizing. Only eight hundred words long, it draws upon chapters in the novel over ten times that length. But his task in devising this reading was relatively simple, for it derived from five climactic and contiguous chapters of the novel (xlv-l, omitting chapter xlix), though reducing their length by about two-thirds. *David Copperfield* set more formidable problems, and the reading lacks coherence: the Steerforth-Emily-Peggotty story holds together, but would have been dismal and have disappointed audiences who loved other things from the novel, so Dickens included those episodes about Dora and the Micawbers, though they have no relevance at all to the main plot of his reading. It is in what he once called the "streaky bacon" tradition of alternating tragic and comic scnes—what had nicely appeared in his plan for the tenth installment of *Copperfield,* "First chapter funny Then on to *Emily.*"[19] The Steerforth-Peggotty episodes proved easiest to adapt. As usual, of course, Dickens abbreviates: descriptive passages go, indications about who is speaking and how are jettisoned as unnecessary, bystanders and other irrelevant characters are written out. Thus, Martha disappears from both chapters, Mr. Peggotty taking over her lines and actions where necessary; "my dear old nurse, Mr. Peggotty's sister" was eventually eliminated from the scene of Emily's elopement; Betsy Trotwood is not present to applaud Mr. Peggotty's long narrative. Similarly, in the David scenes, the disastrous dinner ruined by Mrs. Crupp is not taken over by Littimer (he is given no entrance). The episodes about the Micawbers and Dora are very cleverly selected. Several of the best Micawber and Mrs. Micawber jokes are transferred from other chapters, and chapter v of the reading, about David's courtship and marriage, brings together many of the best passages from six chapters of the novel. In all these mechanical tasks, Dickens is as skilful, resourceful and industrious as you would expect, though his skill is sometimes baffled when he has to make drastic cuts. Thus, the final chapter opens with Mr. Peggotty's exultant cry that he had found Emily; there followed eight pages of printed script about how she had reached England and been rescued; eventually all this went, so David's ludicrously overabrupt response to this triumphant cry is a cool, "You have made up your mind as to the future, good friend?" Dickens was anxious, by this point, to get on to the great climax of the storm.

The *Copperfield* prompt copy, as it happens, is not very rich in stage directions; Dickens' practice in this varied, and sometimes he has lots of marginal indications: "Action," "Low," "Cheerful," "Terror. . . ." Nor has it many additional phrases: a happy one, though, for Mrs. Crupp, who, explaining how she knows that David is in love, adds to her "Mr. Copperfull, I'm a mother myself" the perceptive "Your boots and your waist is equally too small"; and one for Mr. Peggotty, whose delighted "such a thing as never happened before" becomes "such a merry-go-rounder. . . ."[20] The latter is one instance (of many) of Dickens' frugality: the phrase had been created for another Peggotty speech two pages later; its context there was deleted, so Dickens salvaged it and inserted it above. The revision was painstaking. The printed prompt copy contains about twenty-six thousand words, corresponding to thirty-five thousand words in the novel (or many more if one aggregated the length of all the chapters raided). Dickens then cut over ten of the twenty-six thousand words; only nine of the 120 pages of the text are unaltered. Even the *pièce de resistance,* the storm scene, had been reduced from 5,500 to 3,400 words before the printing, and then lost a further fifteen hundred in revision. But there is no substantial rewriting. Apart from condensing, and adding the rare happy phrase and a few bridge passages, Dickens' alterations are of these minor kinds: improving the diction (you may have noticed *talk* for *conversation* in *Sikes and Nancy* above); slightly thickening a speaker's characteristic idiom (Mr. Peggotty has a bit more dialect, but the best instance of this is in *Little Dombey,* where Toots' asininity is happily amplified); improving the rhythm of a phrase, for spoken delivery, and moving the punch line of a joke or comic phrase to the end of a sentence (pause for laughter); deleting phrases about stance, appearance, action, expression, which the recitalist could convey physically; omitting local references which might puzzle provincial or American audiences (thus in *Copperfield* "Kentish Town" becomes "the neighbourhood" and "Bow Street" becomes "the Police Office"[21]). "Is" becomes "was then," in a reference to customary attire: and I suspect that some other changes were updatings, to align the readings to contemporary manners: why else should Dickens alter, in *Mr. Bob Sawyer's Party,* for instance, "the punch was ready made" to "the bottles were ready"? Is it for this reason, too, that the weakness of Mr. Gamp's wooden leg is attributed, in the reading, to "its constancy of walking into public 'ouses," where in the novel it had been to ". . . wine-vaults"? Possibly offensive, or incomprehensible, phrases were removed: in *Bob Sawyer,* either or both of these reasons could account for "the scorbutic youth" becoming "the young man with a nice sense of honor." The splendid Gampism about the "Piljian's Projiss" is sadly conventionalized into "Pilgrim's Progress." Another frequent kind of alteration: jokes are pointed up, as when, in *Bob Sawyer,* Mr. Pickwick puts his foot, instead of his hat, into the tray of glasses, or, in the maudlin speeches of reconciliation after the tipsy quarrel, "Mr. Gunter replied that, upon the whole, he *rather* preferred Mr. Noddy to his own *brother*" becomes "Mr. Hopkins replied that on the whole he *infinitely* preferred Mr. Noddy to his own *mother*" (Mr. Gunter's role had been coalesced with that of Jack Hopkins, whom Dickens made, both by his revisions and his performance, the comic lead in this item). Or jokes are made: when Mr. Winkle gives his name, in *Bardell v. Pickwick,* " 'What's your Christian name, sir?' angrily inquired the little judge" becomes "COURT.—'Have you any Christian name, sir?' " Or jokes are thwacked home: for instance, in the story of *Mr. Chops the Dwarf,* Mr. Magsman says, "The gentlemen was at their wine arter dinner, and Mr. Chops' eyes was more fixed in that Ed of his than I thought good for him. There was three of 'em (in company, I mean) . . ." but, when revising his script, Dickens helped the hard-of-hearing by inserting "not his eyes—in company, I mean."[22] Or hard cases are made harder: Trotty Veck, "over sixty" in the story, becomes "over sixty-eight" in the *Chimes* reading; books at Dotheboys Hall averaged "about one to eight learners," until Dickens rounded it up, in the reading, to "a dozen."[23]

A final point about these adaptations, the significance of which I leave you to discuss. Not only did the repertoire omit all the novels after *David Copperfield,* but also Dickens—sooner or later—deleted from the readings nearly all the socially critical passages. At Birmingham in 1853, he read with particular emphasis Scrooge's vision of the terrible children Ignorance and Want. This passage, it was reported, "was magnificently given, and brought down a burst of applause that clearly indicated in what direction the sympathy of the audience lay." But, after much abbreviating, the episode was eventually omitted altogether. Similarly, the first audiences for *The Chimes,* in 1858, found Will Fern "one of the most powerfully-drawn and impressive" of Dickens' characterizations: "the whole embodiment can hardly fail to impress upon a reflecting audience a social reform lesson, which they will not easily forget." But, in the later prompt-book, both Will Fern's big social-protest speech ("To jail with him!") and his rick-burning speech in the Fourth Quarter are omitted.[24]

Before performances of *The Chimes* in 1858, Dickens reminded his audiences that this story was written a dozen years earlier, when conditions made "the utterance of a few earnest words very necessary. If there be, . . . as I hope and believe, less direct need of such utterance now than there was then, so much the better for us all." This is one of the very few comments on his writings that I know of, prefaced to his readings. In the earlier readings he often made a gruesome little speech assuring his audience that "if you feel disposed as we go along to give expression to any emotion, whether grave or gay, you will do so with perfect freedom from restraint, and without the least apprehension of disturbing me. [*Loud applause.*]" But soon he reduced the preliminaries to a bow, and would then go straight into his reading—though, as many people reported, *reading* was a misnomer, not only because the performance was so much more vivid than this term suggested (redolent, perhaps, of curates giving penny-readings to the respectable poor on Saturday nights), but also because Dickens hardly needed to glance at his script, and sometimes even ostentatiously shut it after reading the title page. His abstaining from introductory lectures was typical: he believed that good wine needed no bush, good art no preliminary explanations. Think how little he says in his prefaces, when he writes one at all—or he will acknowledge that he is writing a preface "more because I am unwilling to depart from any custom that has become endeared to me by having prevailed between myself and my readers on former occasions of the same kind, than because I have anything particular to say" (about *Martin Chuzzlewit*).[25] But the readings themselves were first-rate exercises in practical criticism—illustrations rather than readings, said one reviewer, "running critical commentaries upon his own works." Reviewers struggled for an analogy to convey the difference between their own previous apprehension of the texts, and the new world of beauty and delight revealed by his understanding and delivery: it was the difference "between a letter and a personal interview," between a photograph and a stereoscopic blow-up, between an engraving and the original of a great painting.[26] Scores of phrases and characters and moments are cited as having taken on a far sharper meaning through his rendering. There were, of course, various adverse reports; Dickens certainly had his off days, and his off audiences (to which he usually attributed them), and his skills increased with experience (though the late American tour, often taking him into even larger auditoria than he was used to, was thought to have coarsened his techniques). The overwhelming verdict, certainly, was that Dickens was not trading on his name and popularity, but as a performer was very talented, maybe a genius. After *The Frozen Deep,* Thackeray exclaimed that Dickens could earn twenty thousand pounds a year as a professional actor; during his Farewell Tour, the *Scotsman* spoke for many: "Hear Dickens, and die; you will never live to hear anything of the kind so good. . . . His works could have no more perfect illustrator; and they are worthy of his best efforts as an artist."[27]

"Let us not," wrote Ruskin in a famous passage, "lose the use of Dickens' wit and insight, because he chooses to speak in a circle of stage fire"—a happy reminder of the intrinsically dramatic, even theatrical, nature of his art, and also a literal description of his platform performances. As he remarked before a performance, "The hour has almost come when I to sulphurous and tormenting gas must render up myself!" His own stage-lighting equipment traveled with him, and was always giving trouble, besides which "the heat from the gas around him was intolerable."[28] The other accessories were simple: dark hangings behind him, a dark-colored reading desk; himself in evening dress and a buttonhole, though opinions differed about whether his evening dress was of the conventional cut and style, or whether he vulgarly overdid it (maybe he had more than one evening suit). A little flashy, perhaps: but, in this public attire anyway, Dickens was basically the respectable conventional Victorian citizen that constituted so much—though not all—of his artistic personality.

The performance was more restrained than one might have surmised. Though loving his audiences and the effects he could produce upon them, he generally impressed critics by the reserve and dignity of his execution. (It is interesting that he would very rarely return to the stage for a curtain call.) "Those who have never been present at a 'reading' by Mr. Dickens," wrote one critic,

> cannot form a correct idea of what is comprised in the term as interpreted by him. He does not only *read* his story; he *acts* it. Each character that is introduced is as completely assumed and individ-

ualized by Mr. Dickens as though he were personating it in costume on the stage. Peculiarities of voice and tricks of manner in a moment establish the identity of each new personage in the story, and when he or she again speaks, the hearer finds the conventional "said such a one" as superfluous as though the individual had actually appeared and spoken in the flesh.

But, as another pointed out, he

carefully avoids making his dramatic faculty too prominent in his reading. He does not, except on very rare occasions, act thoroughly *out;* he suggests, and suggests very forcibly; but he leaves to his hearers and readers to supply what he does not himself feel it necessary to delineate. He calls the imagination of his audience into play: they are to fill up what he leaves incomplete.

He was careful, wrote another,

not to confound the actor and the reader. Good taste and refinement mark his readings. He does not, by straining after effect and a superfluity of action, give an unnatural and lavish colouring to his descriptive passages. Generally they are given quietly and distinctly, almost in monotone. . . . His action is simple and unconstrained, but some of his effects of action, of language, and of expression are truly startling. Mr. Dickens is certainly not a noisy reader.

"No trickery in it . . . no attitudinizing, no affectation"; "calm, gentlemanly and quite without mannerism or artificial effect"; not an actor forgetting himself in a role, but a gentleman dramatically telling a story among friends, "never wholly, never, at any rate, for very long, getting away from the gentlemanly drawing-room, with its limiting conventionalities, into the wider and freer atmosphere of the stage"—these are phrases from another three reviewers. Most reports stressed that he was particularly restrained over the pathos: "He would evidently avoid all imputation of maudlin sentimentality, and where he would elicit the tears of his audience he trusts to a manly, unaffected tone."[29]

Everyone of course, in audiences as in private society, noticed his wonderful eyes. He stood still, rarely moving, except his hands—"In his everactive hand," wrote a reviewer, "an unlimited power of illustration resides. Frequently a mere motion of the hand sheds a hitherto undreamt-of meaning upon a whole passage." His face and body shape conveyed much too, of course. He had the faculty, recalled the Duke of Argyll, "which many great actors have had, of somehow getting rid of their own physical identity, and appearing with a wholly different face and a wholly different voice. I never saw this power so astonishingly exerted as by Charles Dickens." It was particularly exhibited in *Sikes and Nancy,* which in many ways differed from the other readings. Here, Dickens' performance came much closer to acting. He displayed, wrote *The Times,* "a degree of force to which nothing that he has hitherto done can be compared. He has always trembled on the boundary line that separates the reader from the actor; in this case he clears it by a leap." And this was not said in criticism: the reading "belongs to the highest order of acting," *The Times* reported. Another reporter described the trial performance, before Dickens had really rehearsed it:

> when, . . . gradually warming with excitement, he flung aside his book and acted the scene of the murder, shrieked the terrified pleadings of the girl, growled the brutal savagery of the murderer, brought looks, tones, gestures simultaneously into play to illustrate his meaning, there was no one, not even of those who had known him best or who believed in him most, but was astonished at the power and versatility of his genius.[30]

When Dickens died, Dean Stanley, who had buried him, found it appropriate to allude in his sermon to Garrick, with the inevitable splendid Johnsonianism, "his death has eclipsed the gaiety of nations." Garrick had been a frequent reference in accounts of the readings, though maybe Adolphus Ward was closer to suggesting the genesis as well as the merit of these performances when he remarked that "in the way of assumption, Charles Matthews the elder himself could have accomplished no more Protean effort." As one critic wrote, after seeing an early performance of the *Carol,* and the triple bill *Boots/Poor Traveller/Gamp:*

> "I never knew how to read a book before," was the exclamation of a friend of ours at the close of the *Christmas Carol. . . .* He only expressed what the whole audience felt. . . . If Mr. Dickens were not the most popular writer of the age, he might have been one of the greatest actors. His pathetic and humorous delineations are equally effective, and when he called both smiles and tears at pleasure, with the magical change of his voice, and with a rapidity truly marvellous, we could not help thinking of Garrick seated between tragedy and comedy—each claiming him as her own.[31]

John Forster thought Dickens' greatest strength lay in "the quickness, variety, and completeness of character," rather than in the pathos or the "graver level passages," but he acknowledged that Dickens' audiences "gave him many reasons for thinking differently."[32] Certainly, where critics were severe, it was much more often for his handling of the pathetic than for his comic or character-part effects. Probably his performance was weaker here; certainly some of his pathetic scripts, like the death of Dr. Marigold's little daughter, were inferior in writing to the other areas of his readings.

But many of the criticisms of his rendering of the pathetic came from people who, in common with most of the sophisticated during his later years, had reacted against the pathos which had been more generally acceptable a generation before. Dickens (I think) was at least a competent reader of all the kinds of writing he selected for performance, if less impressive in the grave and the sad.

The most widely admired moment in all the readings was, as I mentioned, the storm scene in *Copperfield* (a passage which was, anyway, extravagantly admired then as a piece of writing, often being cited as the most sublime and impressive thing he ever wrote). "Never shall I forget," wrote Lord Redesdale, "the effect produced by his reading the death of Steerforth; it was tragedy itself, and when he closed the book and his voice ceased, the audience for a moment seemed paralysed, and one could almost hear a sigh of relief." Thackeray's daughter Anny went to the final London performance of *Copperfield* and recalled: "It was not acting, it was not music, nor harmony of sound and colour, and yet I still have an impression of all these things as I think of that occasion."[33] Both these reminiscences were written down over forty years after the event, which does not make for precision, and may well have surrounded or eclipsed the experience with a light that never was on land or sea: but, for a performance to be remembered so ecstatically forty-odd years later, there must have been a magic at work that was not merely the magic of the great name and presence. As always, there were the dissenting voices: to quote one illustrious witness, also looking back after an interval of nearly forty years, Henry James recalling "that night of Dickens," when he was introduced to the great man during the American tour: "the *emotion,* abiding, that it left with me. How it *did* something for my thought of him and his work—and would have done more without the readings, the hard charmless readings (or *à peu près*) that remained with me." "Monstrous," James called the readings elsewhere.[34] I have quoted enough other contemporary accounts to suggest that James' dislike of the performances, like Forster's and Ruskin's dislike of the whole project, was a minority report (though the censure of a minority which, like that of Hamlet's grieving judicious, deserves attention if not acceptance). Even the curmudgeonly Carlyle could scarce forbear to cheer:

> I had to go yesterday to Dickens' Reading, 8 p.m., Hanover Rooms, to the complete upsetting of my evening habitudes and spiritual composure. Dickens does do it capitally, such as *it* is; acts better than any Macready in the world; a whole tragic, comic, heroic *theatre* visible, performing under one *hat,* and keeping us laughing —in a sorry way, some of us thought—the whole night. He is a good creature, too, and makes fifty or sixty pounds by each of these readings.

Better than Macready, the equal of Charles Matthews or of Garrick: but who now *reads* Garrick? Dickens was, said a reporter, "the greatest reader of the greatest writer of the age." As Dickens' friend Charles Kent, the official chronicler of the readings, remarked, they were "supplementary, and, certainly, very exceptional evidences of genius on the part of a great author," and the project was "a wholly unexampled incident in the history of literature."[35]

John M. Robson

OUR MUTUAL FRIEND

A Rhetorical Approach to the First Number

ONE OF the most appropriate words ever used to describe Dickens' special genius is *profusion*,[1] calling up hosts of remembrances of characters, situations, linguistic surprises; suggesting anew the Shakespearian resemblance and also the apparently wastrel character of his art. The kind of detailed reading demanded by a rhetorical approach consistently reinforces this judgment, but it also, especially when applied to a later novel, results in the somewhat contradictory, though now equally accepted, judgment that the loose baggy monsters are held together by vital tissues. The wastrel wants not a rationale for his bounteousness; Dickens' very profusion, rather than denying unity, actually serves it by giving individual details multiple purposes.

This is not the place to expatiate on the uses of classical rhetorical notions in the criticism of fiction, or to try to avoid rejection symptoms by outlining necessary modifications in rhetorical theory when explicating modern fiction. Risking misunderstanding, I shall attempt merely to show how some rhetorical considerations—to which others may well wish to give other names—help in an appreciation of Dickens' aims and achievements in *Our Mutual Friend*.

To begin, I assume that something valuable can be known about the effects Dickens sought; we can form and test hypotheses about his intention to influence his audience through the artistic manipulation of materials, controlled by his imaginative and moral vision, in a form available to that audience. An analysis of this sort releases one from reliance on comparative judgments, and enables one to approach a work as unique and as defined by understood personal, historical, and generic parameters.[2] At the very least, Dickens may be seen as attempting, like a rhetor, to change his audience's attitudes and behavior.

It has been said that Demosthenes didn't want his auditors to think, "What a splendid orator!" but to shout, "Let us march against Philip!" Dickens too aimed, through the classical endeavors to please, instruct, and move, to gather a host to strive against the Philippian evil wherever it may be found, internally as well as externally, the private recognition being essential to the public action. Make 'em weep, and make 'em laugh, certainly, but use the tears and laughter to soften hard hearts, and make them pliant and resourceful in, quite simply, the betterment of the human condition.[3]

For the nineteenth-century author, whatever may be true of our contemporaries, fictions had a beginning, middle, and end. In classical rhetoric, this same argumentative necessity is recognized in the division of orations into *exordium, narratio, confirmatio,* and *peroratio.*[4] Bringing these two descriptions together, one can see the special functions of parts of a novel. Initially one must recognize the intermingling of parts, especially of the *narratio* (the laying out of the case)[5] and the *confirmatio* (the proof—in fictional terms the main thematic development through plot narration). In many Victorian novels the *peroratio* stands distinct, giving in the final chapter, often through projected plot summary, a satisfying conclusion to individual histories, and embodying, in described or predicted futures, support and recollection of thematic argument.

The *exordium* is a tricky matter. Its function is twofold: to inform the audience, and to capture its attention. These functions combine, for the uncaptured are the uninformed. In fictional terms it may be said that the novelist makes certain attractive promises, and the rest of the novel (mainly *confirmatio*) is a fulfilment of those promises. Surprises there may be—in a great novel there certainly will be—but, at least in retrospect or on rereading, these surprises will be part of the general promise. The *narratio* and *confirmatio* will also be initiated in the *exordium,* for (unless the novelist uses a special kind of preface) there will be a flowing from information about the theme to adumbration of plot elements, and narration (the main component of *confirmatio*) normally begins almost immediately.

Do these notions help in an appreciation of *Our Mutual Friend?* I must here restrict myself for the most part to the *exordium,* which may usefully be seen as comprising the first number part, that is, the first four chapters, and particularly chapters i and ii. Here we find, not unexpectedly, the beginning of the web (the literal meaning of *exordium*). Main settings, time, principal characters, tones, themes, plot: all are brought before us. The sense of mystery and confusion that controls most of the novel is established, for much of the detail as well as the adumbration is shadowy. So much is common in fiction: what is unusual is the amount of adumbration, and, even more strikingly, the ways in which the *narratio,* so painful in inexpert hands, is charged with multiple purposes.

Before turning to analysis and interpretation, it is necessary to call to mind briefly what the first four chapters contain. The short opening chapter, "On the Look Out," presents initially a tableau, set on the Thames between Southwark and London Bridges, of a boat containing two figures, Jesse and Lizzie Hexam, on the lookout for, and eventually finding, a body.

A third character, later identified as Rogue Riderhood, comes alongside them just after the body is found, and is rebuffed by Hexam.

The second chapter, "The Man from Somewhere," contains a dinner scene at the Hamilton Veneerings, during which a wide array of Society is displayed and satirized. The desultory dinner conversation turns on a tale told by Mortimer Lightwood about John Harmon, the "Man from Somewhere," who is now returning to England to inherit from his dead father the wealth represented by great mounds of dust, on the condition that he marry a young woman chosen by his father some fourteen years earlier. The chapter closes with the arrival of a message to Mortimer, who is the solicitor employed in the search for the heir, saying that the drowned body of John Harmon has been found in the Thames.

In Chapter iii, "Another Man," the scene shifts from the Veneerings as Charley Hexam, son of Jesse, takes Lightwood and his friend Eugene Wrayburn to the Hexam home. Then, after a scene in which a bewildered man who gives his name as Julius Handford appears and asks for directions, Jesse takes them, with Handford, to a police station, where the body, unknown by sight to anyone, is identified as Harmon's. There is then a scene in the Hexam home between Lizzie and Charley. The next scene, still in Chapter iii, is set in the Six Jolly Fellowship-Porters, a riverside public house where a coroner's inquest into the death is held. The chapter concludes with the police inspector puzzling over the suspected crime, and an elaborate trope describes the gradual passing of the Harmon murder from society's eyes.

Chapter iv, "The R. Wilfer Family," moves to a new scene and set of characters: Reginald Wilfer comes from his work in the city, where he is employed by a firm owned by Veneering, to find his wife and two daughters, Bella and Lavinia, the elder of whom is the intended wife of John Harmon. They have just let a room to one John Rokesmith, who is revealed at the end of the chapter, and the number, to be none other than the Julius Handford who appeared and disappeared so mysteriously in the previous chapter.

It is perfectly apparent from this brief summary that Dickens accomplishes a great deal in these chapters: he gives three of the main settings,[6] and introduces all the central characters directly, except the Boffins.[7] The antecedent information necessary for plot development is given, and the plot itself strongly established. But, again, to say this is to say very little, for only a very incompetent novelist would fail to do as much, and many would have the plot more advanced. What is significant is the way in which Dickens rhetorically manages his materials so that every element serves to develop the reader's view of the novel's world, to move him into that world, to engage him in the thematic development, and—let it not be forgotten— to ensure that he will buy the next number, and the next, and the next.

The most comprehensive way to treat the rhetorical development is to raise a billowy spray of marginal commentary beside a thin waterfall of text, but fortunately I cannot do that here. More practicable is a selection of what seem to me important elements in the first chapter, followed by an account of contrasting and reinforcing elements in the second chapter, and to a lesser extent in the third and fourth, with the aim of showing how the *exordium* is confirmed in the rest of the novel.

First, then, the opening words: "In these times of ours, though concerning the exact year there is no need to be precise, a boat of dirty and disreputable appearance, with two figures in it, floated on the Thames, between Southwark Bridge which is of iron, and London Bridge which is of stone, as an autumn evening was closing in." The tense is past, but the time is present: we are in "these times of ours" (with a hint of "hard times for these times"?), and at any and every moment, for "there is no need to be precise." The vague present encompasses the action, and since we (as contemporary readers, that is) are in our own times, we need no historical guide to understand them; we too are engaged in them, caught in the web. In this sense, the novel takes the form of a "History of Our Times" (a popular genre in the nineteenth century), while retaining the force of the eighteenth-century fictional "Histories" to which Dickens owed so much. Less obviously, the opening phrase prepares for a central contrast in the novel: "In these times of ours" stands against "Once upon a time"—more of this later.

Between the iron and stone bridges, forming an initial frame with the banks (though not yet described, known to be slimy with mud and refuse), appears the boat, "dirty and disreputable." A closer view gives us the "two figures" in it, and the autumn evening "closes in"—the concluding *in* finishing what the opening *in* had begun.

A tableau, an engraving: with the second sentence a new paragraph begins, bringing the reader nearer, leaving him still with "figures," but now individualized and given slight characterization: a man (ragged, with grizzled hair) and his daughter (aged nineteen or twenty, dark). The action begins in the next sentence (cinema-conscious, we are likely to see the titles dissolving), as the girl rows and the father sits, eagerly looking out. A series of narrative directions serves to isolate the business he is upon: as we glance about with the narrator, we find no props to prove that he is a fisherman, a waterman, a lighterman, or a river carrier. Not often does a description depend on what isn't there, but here, we are told, there is "no clue to what he looked for"; the only clue, then, is that he looks to the river for something. The tide has turned, and they flow with it; this suggestion, a commonplace of course, is reinforced time and again, especially after the "Harmon Murder" flows on the tide and eventually out to sea at the end of chapter iii. The relation between the two figures gains definition as the girl looks with "a touch of dread or horror" at her father, while he looks only at the river. The dread and horror are transferred to us, for our sympathy goes to the girl: slightly as she has been characterized, she has already become the focus of our human engagement.

The novelist, like the rhetor, needs an appeal to ethos, to personality; this can be established through the understood character of the narrator (and Dickens makes use of this device later on, most markedly in the Social Chorus scenes and when interpreting Betty Higden's terror of the work-house); but thus far the narrator has confined himself—apart from the "our" in the first sentence—to an impressionistic rendering of what the scene itself most dominantly reveals. (It may be noted that we are not even led to this scene; we simply find ourselves in it.) Dickens is restricted, then, to entering into and forming our judgment through a character. Noticing that this as yet unnamed girl is the focus of our initial sympathy, we may recall, after finishing the novel, that it ends with discussion of her—indeed of her as a "female waterman"—and so be led to establish the center of the novel not in the Bella Wilfer-John Harmon plot, but in the Lizzie Hexam-Eugene Wray-burn plot, which has more loading of social message than the former, and comes to its climax after the former.

Having initiated his appeal to ethos, Dickens begins a major thematic development by devoting a paragraph to establishing that their unexplained and unusual search is not to them rare or inappropriate to their setting. A major thematic note is given the opening place, as the boat is seen (or inter-preted) to be "allied to the bottom of the river rather than the surface, by reason of [its] slime and ooze . . . and sodden state." The man and girl are the first of the many in *Our Mutual Friend* to seek to bring up from detritus something of value; the surface is bad enough, it is abundantly made clear, but what lies beneath it, who would habitually search for it, and what evaluatory scale can prize it?

In the next paragraph another narrative element appears, as for the first time the man speaks, giving an order to his daughter and at the same time naming her as Lizzie. He himself remains unnamed until the third character in the scene, also unnamed, identifies him as "Gaffer," then as his "pardner," and finally as "Gaffer Hexam, Esquire." This last naming, coming just after his insinuating attempt to assume a part in the enterprise of another, further serves to characterize him, and, as well as showing his prickly pride, prepares us for the implicit toadyism of his "T'other Gov-ernor" and "T'otherest Governor"; we also are prepared for parallel devel-opments in Silas Wegg, with his named hierarchy of imagined social prec-edence.

The scene is gloomily lit, the brownness of the man's face and arms and the girl's darkness being generally tonal and descriptive, rather than illu-minating, until "a slant of light from the setting sun" colors, "as though with diluted blood," a stain in the bottom of the boat that bears a "resem-blance to the outline of a muffled human form." Lizzie shivers at the sight, strengthening the impression of her "usage" of horror, while her father merely asks what "ails" her, for he sees "nothing afloat"; the "red light" goes, along with her shudder. In this frankly melodramatic sequence is thus

signalled one of the three dominant colors in the novel, which is surprisingly bare of other vivid tones. Red is almost always associated with blood, usually shed blood, though occasionally with its vital force (in contrast with
pallor). Black is a common descriptive element, as usual in Dickens, associated with fog, gloom, grief, mystery, and surfaces. The third and predomi-
nant color is gold, denoting or connoting money or gilt surfaces.

The thematic force of gold is also brought before us in the opening
chapter, when the search proves fruitful. The man, after reaching into the
water and securing what he finds there, washes (surely an inadequate
cleansing) a coin he holds in his right hand,[8] chinks it, blows and spits on
it, "for luck."[9]

Money and luck together, brought from the depths. At his point, after
the father has chastised the girl for not welcoming what the river, her "meat
and drink," the provider of her fuel and of the materials of her cradle,
brings, the other man, Rogue Riderhood, appears, strengthening the theme
of hazard by saying (and for the first time giving the first man a name): "In
luck again, Gaffer?" Rogue is, like a degenerated Pip, a man of great and
unearned expectations: the "sweat of his honest brow," emphasized by him
time and again, drops only on lucky rewards, turned up by his unending
search for the hidden, whether in the pockets of a live sailor (referred to
almost immediately, as Gaffer repudiates his "pardnership"), in the coffers of the owners of the steamer that later runs through his boat, almost
drowning him, or in the hidden reaches of Bradley Headstone's passion.
The quick and the dead are one to him—but not to Gaffer, who indignantly
"assert[s] the high moralities," and delivers himself of an angry dissertation on the distinction between taking from a dead man what he can't have
or use, and robbing a live one. The narrator's ironic comment about "high
moralities" gives this episode a lingering force: Riderhood is morally dismissed, and properly so; Gaffer's position is somewhat equivocal, for Dickens tries to save him from condemnation—he is loved by Lizzie, a "good"
character, and hated by his son Charley, a "bad" character—but his
trade, Dickens surely avers, is not an honest one.

In any case, the comment comes in the last paragraph, which is marked
by a departure from the narrator's stance as merely a percipient observer.
To this point, he has given us just what might be seen to have happened; as
he concludes his description of the Hexams' rowing off, he permits himself a
summary comment on the past and a mind's interior, unknown and un-
knowable to the reader: "A neophyte might have fancied that the ripples
passing over it[10] were dreadfully like faint changes of expression on a
sightless face; but Gaffer was no neophyte and had no fancies."[11]

Now, to dwell more fully on these matters, using the following chapters
as resource:

The world we are invited to enter is a forbidding one, drawn with that
realism in detail, but not realism in treatment, noted, I believe by Saints-

bury, as habitual to Dickens. The heavy drawing, the loaded mystery and suggestions of unexplored evil, the *outré* quality of the main character, the threat of violence, the dread and terror of the girl: all these suggest not realism but melodrama. But without committing oneself further at this stage, one can see that the melodramatic urge is in the service of genuine emotion: the horror we are invited to share is a legitimate horror, founded in the universal terror of violent death; the stock repugnance at tainted money is fed by the all-too-apparent reality of its attraction; the relation between Gaffer and Lizzie, even as here sketched, is not the hackneyed father-daughter item of the stage. And the contemporary reader, drawn into "these times of ours," would recognize the main setting as starkly but not falsely etched. This is, then, the "real" world, and its actuality is soon made more apparent by contrast.

Chapter ii begins with none of the mystery of chapter i, except in burlesque, including what I here must pass by, burlesque of the narrator's art, especially in the tale told, all unknowingly, of the background to the action of chapter i.[12] Remembering how hesitantly we are given the histories and names of the two main figures in chapter i (Riderhood isn't named until chapter vi), we cannot but note that the very first words of chapter ii give name and history, such as they are: "Mr. and Mrs. Veneering were bran-new people in a bran-new house in a bran-new quarter of London." The characters and other props are ticketed and listed as soon as the dominant tone has been sounded to full effect. Newness, varnish, stickiness; grandfather, if needed, in storage at the Pantechnicon—not needed, so here is Twemlow, an innocent but convenient piece of dinner-furniture on easy castors.[13] Some time is spent on Twemlow (a signal, in Dickens' uncondemning satire on his ineffectualness, that we are to expect well of him) to establish his confusion over a pressing problem in social relations: is he, or is he not, the oldest friend of the Veneerings? They of course have no friends, and their acquaintances have no characters. This state of nonentity has no importance for the Social Chorus that packs round the Veneerings' dinner table; only a fool like Twemlow would hold his hand to his head over such a triviality.[14]

This Social Chorus is not "real"; apart from those needed in the plot, they have no names, only functions, and even these we take for granted, for we never see them performed.[15] They are slightly differentiated by the shading of opinions that come ready made with their roles; in general, however, they have no color, only glitter, varnish, powder, and bluff. They are "new": more than once their purposeless chatter is set off by an inquiry as to "news"—and there never is any. Surface dwellers, they make ripples but are carried by the current, and like Riderhood (who is, however, flesh, and blood), they look to chance, to speculation, as a lever to raise money and themselves.[16] This impression of evanescence is strengthened by Dickens' use of the present tense in the Chorus scenes;[17] similarly, the emphasis on the impermanence of their dwellings suggests their rootlessness.

Rhetorically, the contrast between the controlling visions of chapters i and ii is a *topos,* a "commonplace," in one of its most frequently used fictional forms, though Dickens goes beyond the normal use by ringing changes on the narrative mode and does not use a single observer to give us a clear basis for comparative judgment. By placing "low" against "high" life, the Newgate threat against the Silver Fork tinkle, he is able to intensify both, as we feel suspenseful and fascinated dread of the first, and take satiric and mordant delight in the second. More, he is able to suggest the life-in-death of the former, and the death-in-life of the latter, while maintaining suspense even about his—or the narrator's—preferences. At the same time, his main purposes—to entice the reader *(exordium),* and to give him sufficient knowledge to follow the plot and enough hints to suggest the theme *(narratio)*—are well served, and the plot development begins *(confirmatio).*

But the *topos* of comparison does not exhaust the angles of vision in these chapters. In what may be viewed as a *topos* of relation, for it connects the two other worlds, being found in both in distorted forms, Dickens employs "once upon a time," the world of romance and childish vision, to suggest that even in "these times of ours" the once may be future, and even present.

In the second chapter, to get Mortimer Lightwood started on what is essential to the *narratio,* the history of the Harmon case, Lady Tippins, in a grotesque parody of coyness, coaxs him (tapping her fan on the knuckles of her *left* hand) to tell the story of "the man from Jamaica." The conversation takes a "languid"[18] and surprising course through Eugene Wrayburn's half-remembered jingle about the "man from Tobago," "our friend ["Mutual"?] who long lived on rice-pudding and isinglass, till at length to his something or other, his physician said something else, and a leg of mutton somehow ended in daygo."[19] Lady Tippins chides Eugene for "pretending" not to remember his nursery rhymes, and then cajoles Mortimer with: "Tease! Pay! Man from Tumwhere!"

Now apart from the necessity that the reader know about Harmon, this exchange, in its immediate context, has the force, first, of placing Lady Tippins and the assembled company in a strong satiric light.[20] Second, the exchange of pleasantries deepens the mystery by throwing out half-hints and mistaken assumptions about the main plot, a process furthered by different means in chapter iii. But when seen in the context of the whole novel, it has yet a further force as an exordial opening of a remarkable series of references to nursery rhymes, games, and tales, songs, ballads, adages, and images of childhood, with interspersed references to romances and (usually with strong ironic intent in Chorus scenes) to classical myth.[21]

Just how remarkable the series is could be shown by a complete catalog, not here practicable. Everyone will recall Silas Wegg's ballads and Jenny Wren's songs, and possibly the narrator's "See the conquering Podsnap

comes, Sound the Trumpets, Beat the Drums," and also the book titles:
"Cup and Lip," "Birds of a Feather," "A Long Lane," and "A Turning."
Most of the others are so embedded in the narrative, however, and serve
other purposes so immediately and convincingly, that their cumulative effect may, especially on first reading, pass by us. Let me mention some of
them of varying significance: the echo in Rogue Riderhood's name is picked
up in "little Rogue Riderhood and the wolf" about halfway through the
novel, and the tale appears frequently, with variations, in Jenny Wren's
view of Pubsey & Co., as Riah changes in her eyes from fairy godmother to
wolf and back again. Fledgeby ends as "little eyes," the fox. Tales from the
Arabian Nights[22] and the *Tales of the Genii*, both of which are explicitly
mentioned, are frequently referred to, almost always by the characters themselves, not the narrator: Aladdin's palace, the sultan's tub of water and his
buying a slave, speaking fish, ogres, and the genie, for example. Cock Rob-
in, "Bee-Bah, black sheep," Peter Piper, Jack Horner, Mrs. Hubbard's dog,
and Jack and the Beanstalk all appear, as do Gulliver, Robinson Crusoe,
"the merry greenwood of Jobbery Forest," and Don Quixote. Of games, we
see Bella getting her father's foot to the mark, hear the Boffins' narrative go
on its way to "Once! Twice! Three times and away!" and listen as Silas
Wegg comments, on Noddy Boffin's prowling round the dustheaps, that
he's "getting colder and colder! Now he's freezing!" and perhaps most
strikingly, we feel distress with Mortimer at Eugene's searching of his motives and identity with the jingle: "Riddle-me-riddle-me-ree, p'raps you
can't tell me what this may be?"

Such references are, as has been often noted, a regular feature of Dickens' imaginative projections, but their density in *Our Mutual Friend* suggests more than a habitual recurrence to stock items.[23] In other novels, as
here, we have suggestions that fairies bring up nurselings, that there are
many orphans deprived of love-cradled visions and adults similarly deprived
of imaginative needs by childlessness.[24] Dickens' use of perceptual and
imaginative magnification (another *topos*) as a symbolic device is readily
recognized in his other works. But here, it seems to me, the fully developed
rhetorical handling of these materials, in connection with two alternate
angles of vision (not one, as in *Oliver Twist*) and presented in a common
time scale (not in a retrospective one, as in *David Copperfield* and *Great
Expectations*), allows Dickens to present the child's vision as more integral
with, and hence more effectual in transforming, these times of ours.

To help make the point, let me cite what may seem a strained example. In Chapter ii the Veneerings' guests are moved from reception to
dining room when their servant (soon to be finely tagged the Analytical
Chemist) announces: "Dinner is on the table!" The narrator interprets the
announcement for us: "Thus the melancholy retainer, as who should say,
'Come down and be poisoned, ye unhappy children of men!' "[25] This is apparently a throwaway bit of characterization, which also gives a sardonic, if

incomplete, view of society's folly. But the phrase echoes, at least in my mind, to resonate with Jenny Wren's haunting call, later in the novel, to "Come up and be dead!"[26] Her invitation is not offered from the never-stilled dead center of the whirling world, but from a "garden" on top of that microcosm of the speculative chaos, Pubsey & Co., a garden high enough for Jenny at least to be clear of the City's blinding dirt and deafening noise. Here a strong Blakeian note is sounded, with children on slants of light lifting up the suffering to joy in innocence. The "poison" of the Veneerings' table is left below, and a true golden glow surrounds human love and peace.

This is the pure vision, but its broken and reflected lights gleam fitfully for most of the characters, as is seen in the mass of references to the child's world that make up, in my view, much of the *confirmatio*. Even Fascination Fledgeby is caught up, mentioning several times to Jenny her strange "game," though his clouded vision can see in it only a possibility of strategic gain for himself. The most important plot resolution, the Harmon-Wilfer marriage, both in episode and image (the baby's nursery, with birds, flowers, and gold and silver fish)[27] fulfills the fairy tale's promise. Boffin's ludicrous Bower (split between "low" comfort and "high-flying Fashion") is matched by the "golden bower" of Jenny's loosed hair, which startles the worldly and shields confidence and love.

The potential sentimentality of this device is removed by the integration of worlds that is prepared for even in the *exordium*. The child's vision does not exist as an unattainable alternative, as feeble in its true promise as it is strong in appeal. The interlocking of the characters' lives, primarily an element in the *confirmatio*, most obviously provides the needed unity, but the unity is made persuasive by a variety of tropes involving images of ascent and descent that begins, as already noted, in the opening chapters. There is of course irony, inescapable as well as powerful, because the common uses of *up* and *down*, of *surface* and *depth*, refuse easy and constant association with any such pair as *good* and *bad*, *healthy* and *diseased*, *life* and *death*, or *truth* and *lies*.

The corpse of the opening chapter, "not *much* worse than Lady Tippins,"[28] rises to be caught, though long battered by the tides; so do all the other bodies found by Gaffer (including that of Jenny Wren's grandfather, who appears on one of the bills on Gaffer's wall in chapter iii). Only Riderhood and Headstone, found "lying under the ooze and scum," do not surface.[29] Eugene floats to be rescued by Lizzie, who "by main strength took him up, and never laid him down until she laid him down in the house." Her actions, as the narrator stresses, and as we know from the opening chapter (and the number plan), are of "usage,"[30] though this time "it" becomes "he," and she has no horror. It is also usage for her to save, as we have seen in the death of Betty Higden, " 'Bless ye! *Now* lift me, my love.' Lizzie Hexam very softly raised the weather-stained grey head, and lifted her as high as Heaven."

The primary effect of this imagery is not, however, apocalyptic (or, to the cynical, sentimental); the real world of these, our times, is not devoid of transforming, though mundane, promise. The power of love can reconcile depths and surfaces. One of the most effective *topoi* Dickens uses for this effect is the parallel between Lizzie Hexam and Bella Wilfer, approaching finally a doubling. Betty Higden, in the scene last cited, mistakes Lizzie for "the boofer lady," Bella, who has irradiated the dying hours of her great-grandson, Orphan Johnny. The instinctive empathy of Bella and Lizzie is brought out in their confiding together their motives and hopes—an unusual scene for Dickens, showing how differently and more powerfully he is able to treat young women in this novel.[31] As this device is developed later in the novel—Bella and Lizzie do not meet in the first Number—I shall not pursue it here, though it may be mentioned that hints in chapter iii enable us to forecast Bella's hiding her fundamental attractiveness by a glitter of money, which draws the wrong prey; she finally moves upward into joy only by apparently descending socially.

Lizzie's thematic importance, however, is strongly suggested in the early chapters. She is, like her father and their boat, not allied to surfaces, and her drawing is explicitly like a magnet's. In chapter iii, as soon as Charley mentions his sister, Eugene grabs him roughly by the chin; later in the same chapter, Lizzie quietly exits when she finds Eugene staring at her; he is driven by her not only to seductive pursuit, but to pursuit of his own elusive nature, hidden even from himself by his languid, "absurd" surface.[32] This power of Lizzie's is substantiated later in the novel when Eugene's rival, Bradley Headstone (another double), reacts in parallel fashion. His destructive unexplored depths are similarly brought out by Lizzie; he too is unaccountably interested in Charley's first mention of his sister; and after his first sight of her he is plunged into schizoid pursuit of incompatible goals. In his schoolmaster's role he is eminently "respectable," though he looks as though he is wearing another man's clothes; in his role as vengeful lover, he descends to the depths of masquerading as Rogue Riderhood, and appears for the first time as though in his own dress.

Charley too is important in these early chapters, as his inchoate attitudes prepare us for further developments in him and also in Lizzie and Bradley. The boy bitterly strives to attain the surface Bradley reflects, angrily rejecting any attempts to cloud his respectability with the mist of human affections. Charley is determined to raise Lizzie so that he will not sink; Bradley is driven to seek a damaging marriage that will lower him (his odd proposal coming in a churchyard in which the dead are raised above the living); Lizzie tries to evade her love for Eugene because he is so far "above" her. One cannot refrain from noting that, in the eyes of Society, Lizzie is right: the Voice of Society says a female waterman can never be a lady. She has not the requisite surface to reflect, as respectable Bradley does even to the Reverend Frank Milvey, what society expects.

Dickens makes splendid use of surface reflections, again introducing the trope in the *exordium*. An important part of the second chapter gives us the gathering around the Veneering's table as in a glass sparkling. Each of the mirrored fragments is introduced by the bare word *Reflects:*[33] the most startling item is Lady Tippins, doubly reflected and distorted into reality. "Reflects charming old Lady Tippins on Veneering's right; with an immense obtuse drab oblong face, like a face in a tablespoon. . . ." Who sees these reflections from the mirror? Not the Chorus itself, confident in its surfaces, and knowing when repairs are necessary, as is witnessed by "the mature young lady's" powder epaulette, Lady Tippins' varnishing, and even poor Twemlow's hair preparation of egg yolks. All the members of Society know that the surfaces they face desire only to reflect other surfaces. It is the reader, through the narrator, who sees what they are too negligent to see.[34]

The gilt surrounds and silvered backing of the mirror indicate that which supports the surface respectability. What the Veneering mirror first reflects are the "new" crest, "in gold and eke in silver, frosted and also thawed, a camel of all work," and the crest's offspring, the table ornaments, a caravan of gold camels, finally and characteristically bearing salt.[35]

The surface, frozen by cold speculation, on which Podsnap's "skaters" cut arabesques, is perilous, even Veneering having, like the Lammles, to flee across the Channel to maintain a fiction; Twemlow keeps his head up over a stable, while Lady Tippins struggles with hers over a milliner's shop.[36]

Dickens makes it clear that genuine support is hard to find, there being a lot of fool's gold about, and true wealth being hidden deep. Actual coins appear but seldom in the novel; three times there are small piles, and these are all in the hands of the poor.[37] Twice money changes hands as part of a bribe, and the drowned corpses, as we see first in the opening chapter, yield a measure from their turned-out pockets. The main center of the frenzied search is, of course, the dust heaps of the Golden Dustman, eventually valuable as material, but hiding in reality nothing but the paper proof of the fluctuating maliciousness of a dead man's will, frustrated finally by living affection. (It is interesting to note that Mortimer tells Society that Old Harmon made certain unspecified conditions to guarantee against his resurrection.) The dead can bury only the dead-in-life, who are numerous, and active enough in helping bury themselves through digging and delving in moral as well as physical refuse.[38] The most assiduous delver, Wegg, appropriately ends with a splash in the scavenger's dust cart, but his dusty-haired former partner, Venus, emerges with a haircut, bringing with him Pleasant Riderhood, whose back hair may cease to tumble down once she is out of Limehouse Hole. More importantly, the attempt by "Sexton Rokesmith" to bury John Harmon's identity leads to a triumphant resurrection through love. The most significant rising, however, is that of the money itself; heaped up by the miserly Old Harmon, it comes to be burnished in use by John Harmon and the Boffins, whose benefactions bring "Harmony" finally out of the "Jail."

The working out of this theme needs the full scope of the novel, but the first Number sets it on course. The sinister and false aspects of money-getting having been hinted at in the first two chapters, its real threat of moral distortion is brought before us in the fourth chapter, when Dickens begins his characterization of Bella as petulant, wilful, and self-seeking. Complaining of having been willed away as though she were "a dozen of spoons, with everything cut and dried beforehand, like orange chips," she exclaims: "I love money and want money—want it dreadfully." Dickens carefully hedges this characterization, for the Wilfers are poor, and the disappointment of Bella's expectations contributes, understandably, to her desire. But when she reaches the stage (after for the first time itemizing her secrets)[39] of declaring: "the whole life I placed before myself is money, money, money, and what money can make of life!"[40] the strong medicine of Boffin's pretended miserliness is needed to cure her.

Boffin's behavior, like Handford-Rokesmith-Harmon's, proves that pretence in itself is not evil. Two linked rhetorical devices, masks and games, have to be examined before the truly damaging pretences connected with status and money can be adequately condemned. In the opening chapter, it will be recalled, we approach only hesitantly the crucial matter of naming characters, while in the second the names are given as a starter. In the fourth chapter the introduction of a new set of characters, the Wilfers, begins with a disquisition on the name of Reginald Wilfer, alias R. Wilfer (to himself), R. W. (to his wife), Rumty (to his fellow clerks and companions), but most commonly (to the narrator) "the cherub."[41] Dickens, of course, is always redolent of nicknames, allegorical suggestions, personal personifications, and metonymies, but surely, as with allusions to the child's world, he outdoes himself in *Our Mutual Friend,* the very title of which is a reaching after an identity.

Hardly a character escapes some transformation through naming. Leaving aside the minor characters, one finds John Harmon not only as Julius Handford and John Rokesmith, but also as "the Man from Somewhere" (as well as from Jamaica and Tobago), the "Secretary" (with the suggestion that he is a piece of furniture), "Our Mutual Friend," "Jack a Manory," "Chokesmith" and "Artichoke," the "Fortune-teller," "Blue Beard," and the "Mendicant"; he also appears in disguise as George Radfoot, the man who actually was murdered.[42] Bella is the "Boofer Lady," the "Mendicant's Wife," the "Home Goddess," the "Cook," "£.s.d.," and, without capitalization but characteristically, "the lovely lady," and "a certain mercenary person." Not so much is done with the other two lovers, whose tale is less open to play, but Eugene does appear as "Eligible on View," a "lime merchant," and "T'other Governor," and his father is only "M. R. F.," while Lizzie's name (cited by Jenny lovingly as "Lizzie-

Mizzie-Wizzie") at least gives the jealous Miss Peecher an opportunity to tell her pupil Mary Anne that "Lizzie" is not "a Christian name" but a "corruption" of Elizabeth or Eliza, and that it is very doubtful that there were any Lizzies in the early Christian Church.

In this instance one sees obviously what actually goes on throughout: the names are given almost always by characters to themselves and others, with the narrator chiming in only to complete the chorus, as he does with the cherub, Pa (to Bella and Lavvy) Wilfer. So it happens with Nicodemus Boffin: he is "Noddy" or "Nick" to himself; the "Golden Dustman" to most; "Whatshisname," "Spoffin," "Doffin," "Moffin," and "Poffin" to Mrs. Wilfer (who appears as "Ma," "Mrs. R. W.," the "Tragic Muse," and "a Savage Chief") and to Lavinia (who is "Lavvy" or the "Irrepressible").[43] To Wegg, Boffin is the "Worm and Minion of the Hour," the "ursurper," "Dusty Boffin," and "Bof-fin." For a time Noddy is the "Miser" to all but his wife and John Harmon.[44] Even Mortimer Lightwood, who seems to appear *in propria persona* throughout, takes some minor turns: he is first introduced—and he is the only one to be so introduced—in the morror's reflection as "a certain 'Mortimer,' " with the name in quotation marks, as though assumed;[45] he too is a "lime merchant," and he appears as "Mr. Mortimer Lightwood" in the narrator's pseudo-newspaper police report in chapter iii.[46]

The members of the Social Chorus, being for the most part interchangeable anyway, do not bother much with pseudonyms, their seemingly transparent names being sufficiently opaque to hide the nothingness within. As the *exordium* makes apparent, they do not know, and do not wish to know, one another, beyond the stage of being everyone's "oldest friend."[47] So they have, just as we have, Boots and Brewer, who merge with two other Buffers as required, "a Member, an Engineer, a Payer-off of the National Debt, a Poem on Shakespeare, a Grievance, . . . a Public Office" (and their unnamed wives), later to be joined by a "Bank Director," a "Ship Broker," and a "General Officer," and other bathers, and still later by those "Fathers of the Scrip Church," who, "like astronomical distances, are only to be spoken of in the very largest numbers," a "Contractor" (or "five hundred thousand men"), a wandering "Chairman" (or "three thousand miles a week"), and a financial genius (or "three hundred and seventy-five thousand pounds, no shillings, and no pence"). (One change is made: when Veneering is elected for Pocket Breeches, his wife becomes "W. M. P.")

What this masking and the many disguises suggest,[48] in addition to their functions in immediate contexts, is the extraordinary difficulty of knowing who one is and who others are in relation to one's dreams and expectations. The search is virtually endless. (Will "Jenny Wren"—"The Dolls' Dressmaker," "The Court Dressmaker"—revert to Fanny Cleaver when "He"—Sloppy?—comes along to change her name?) In the absence of inner definition, all fall back on their reflections in the eyes of others, and vanity ensures that "respectability" will make the largest claims. And in a world floated on evanescent golden dreams, the search for defining bouyancy is inevitably without end.

And so the games are played. The children's games, an acting out of fantasies drawn from deep needs, are positively beneficial, shadowing out mythic patterns. But not so the adult games, full of "moves" (that term beloved of modern philosophers), traps, and trains of powder (which tend to "blow up" under their layers). Some favorite games are blackmail (indulged in by Wegg and Riderhood), bribery (Eugene, Fledgeby), betrayal (Mr. Dolls, Riderhood, Sophronia Lammle, and Venus), extortion (Fledgeby, Riderhood), and deception (almost everyone, but most markedly Fledgeby, Riah, Headstone, Radfoot, Boffin, Venus, and, of course, John Harmon). Some of these games (Sophronia's and Venus' betrayals; Boffin's and Harmon's deceptions, for example) are not self-seeking, but these tend to prove the rule. Much could be made of these adult games, with their aim of getting up by putting down, their assessment of human beings as commodities, and their dependence on prey, but, as their development depends largely on secondary characters and situations not introduced in the first number, I shall not dwell on them here.

One child's game that is prepared for, however, justifies mention, the bittersweet game of family, with its inversion of normal roles and abnormal assumption of functions. Lizzie, herself nursed by the river, is a mother-sister to Charley; Podsnap becomes a "new" godfather to the "new" Veneering baby; and the boyish character of Rumty Wilfer being established, his daughter Bella can begin, as early as chapter iv, to play with him as with a child. The most telling inversion comes only with the introduction of Jenny Wren in the first chapter of Book II.[49] The narrator having described the school of Headstone as in a "toy" neighborhood,[50] we are ready for the chapter to move to a dolls' dressmaker, clothing her creatures according to fashion (weddings, not funerals; and not too near the light), and having, for her own child, a disastrously "prodigal father."[51] As *confirmatio* of the early hints, Jenny's games can be seen not only as a compensation for her own twisted existence, but also as properly attracting three characters who lack mothers: Lizzie, who takes her own turn as seer and fortuneteller looking into the glow of ashes (drawing gold out of red and gray), accomodates easily to Jenny's world, taking up the needle and learning her letters; Eugene, who on his apparent deathbed needs Jenny's vision of children who deliver us from pain, responds to her motherly nursing; and, as already noted, Feldgeby, who is queerly fascinated by her life-in-death call, finally is ministered to by Jenny with "vinegar and brown paper"[52]—and pepper.

Though much more remains to be said about the opening number of *Our Mutual Friend* in rhetorical terms, perhaps enough has been outlined to make the main point. If I may chance the image about a novel so much concerned with gold, Dickens literally loads every rift with ore, preparing the attentive reader for the development and resolution from the first words of the novel. His genius is revealed by an analysis of his opening number, which shows, along with the classical requirements for *exordium, narratio,* and the beginnings of *confirmatio,* a marvellous ability to infuse details with multiple purposes, so that for him, as for the dolls' dressmaker, there is no waste, and, as in the dust heaps, there is finally found true value in the detritus.

A brief word about the conclusion may help reinforce my argument. In the penultimate chapter, "Persons and Things in General," rhetorically the *peroratio,* with the final chapter, "The Voice of Society," an epilogue, the different worlds of the novel are resolved into one. There are darkness and bitterness enough, but surely *Our Mutual Friend* is not, as Edgar Johnson would have it, "the darkest and bitterest of Dickens' novels."[53] The world is swirling, confused, fluid; those who frantically strive to stay afloat at the cost of others sink in their own thrashings, but those who, learning the usage of love and affection, save others, also save themselves. The archetypal force of the child's vision, seemingly vulnerable in the hard glare of selfishness, triumphs, flooding the "real" world, threatening and labyrinthian in its first view, with promise and even fulfilment. The "Voice of Society" does not triumph. We open in "these times of ours"; we end, with Mortimer, turning our backs on Society and wending our way to the Temple, "gaily."

Sylvère Monod

CONFESSIONS OF AN UNREPENTANT CHESTERTONIAN

BY CALLING this paper "Confessions of an Unrepentant Chestertonian," I am implicitly admitting that I am a Chestertonian, and I am posing a number of questions, such as the following: how does one become a Chesterton addict and eventually a Chestertonian? And why should a Chestertonian be normally expected to feel repentant?

I cannot undertake to answer for all Chestertonians, but I can at least say that in my own case an appetite for Chesterton seems to have been hereditary, and that in two ways. On the one hand, I clearly inherited this appetite from my father—as I did my yet more rewarding Dickensophagy— for my father translated Chesterton's *The Everlasting Man* and *St. Thomas Aquinas* into French while I was a boy, and I thus breathed in the Chesterton atmosphere in the paternal home at an early age. On the other hand, both my father's and my own instinctive, enthusiastic reaction to Chesterton was probably due to his repeated assertion that joy was of the essence of Christianity, that, as he said in *Orthodoxy,* "Joy . . . is the gigantic secret of the Christian."[1] This exhilarating doctrine was not quite what the long dynasty of Calvinist ministers in the Monod family had preached; nor was it likely to be impressed on converts to a Jansenist brand of Roman Catholicism.

However that natural leaning came into existence, I have always had the impression that reading Chesterton was good for me, in the sense in which Guinness is said to be good for you, that he did me good. And I always found him extraordinarily stimulating.

But, like Guinness again, or, to take a more apposite comparison, like rye whisky, Chesterton can be intoxicating as well as stimulating. And doubtless a protracted intimacy with his writings is not without its perils. One may begin to write, and even think, Chestertoniously, and to unconsciously emulate Chesterton's mannerisms. What probably remains the most illuminating book on Chesterton, Hugh Kenner's admirable *Paradox in Chesterton,* is not free from this tendency in its preliminary section.

[214]

Kenner writes, for instance: "There is a penultimate stage of disillusion in the study of Chesterton wherein he merely seems to be saying the same thing over and over again; the ultimate stage is to realize that he says it so often because it can never really be said; in fact, because there is nothing else to say."[2] At the hands of a first-rate critic like Kenner, such comments are an analysis of Chesterton in Chestertonian terms. But inferior writers achieve no more than what I call Chestertoniousness. I have more than once caught myself feebly Chestertonizing. And this can be very bad for us as writers, as speakers, and more specifically as Dickens critics.

I am aware that my own early criticism of Dickens—radically altered, I am glad to say, in my more recent publications—had been dangerously influenced both by Chesterton and by John Forster, who is, incidentally, in my opinion, another underrated Dickens critic. And if I still claim that as a Chestertonian, I am unrepentant, it is not merely out of a perverse (and diabolical) delight in persevering in error; it is because I believe the advantages of reading Chesterton to overweigh the perils immensely.

I cannot hope to make everybody share my views. W. W. Robson, in his sensitive *Southern Review* article,[3] is undoubtedly right when he says that "For many readers . . . Chesterton is a dead writer. His name recalls only noisy showmanship, out-of-date class attitudes, Edwardian jolliness, foaming tankards. He is at best a period piece." Nor can one forget that the compilers of the useful *Pelican Guide to English Literature* simply ignore Chesterton in their final volume, perhaps because they call it "The Modern Age." But if I cannot hope to convince—or convert—all my hearers, I can at least honestly expound my opinions, which are based on a certain notion of Chesterton as a man and as a writer, of the state of Dickens criticism in his days, of his merits and achievement as a Dickens critic, and, finally, of what his example may teach us as to criticism in general.

— *1* —

It would be futile to claim that G. K. Chesterton was a great creative artist, and especially that his writings possessed the even quality of serenely, carefully elaborated prose that one tends to associate with the enjoyment of literature. For one thing, he wrote far too much and far too fast. Like Tennyson, he has seriously harmed his reputation by the mere size of his output. The bibliography in Christopher Hollis' valuable pamphlet on Chesterton lists eighty-seven separate works; and these do not include his literally innumerable articles, of which nearly thirteen hundred appeared as his weekly contributions to the *Illustrated London News* alone, from 1905 to 1930. In this mountainous quantity of print it was inevitable that even the most fertile writer and thinker should occasionally both contradict and repeat himself. In partial mitigation of this reproach, it must be admitted that Chesterton is seldom uninteresting, and would even nearly always be worth reading if one could give a lifetime to the study of a single author not of the very first order. Also, that Chesterton sincerely believed in the value of quantity as such and showed, in his introduction to the *Pick-wick Papers,*[4] that he saw nothing wrong in writing to order: "The larger the man's mind, the wider his scope of vision, the more likely it will be that anything suggested to him will seem significant and promising; the more he has a grasp of everything the more ready he will be to write anything." Such a view may account for the deficiency we are discussing; he did not see the difference between motivated writing and mere writing.

If a readiness to write anything be a virtue, it is not one that leads to the creation of literary masterpieces. So there are very few among Chesterton's scores of books, of which the most widely acclaimed have been, *Heretics, The Everlasting Man, Charles Dickens,* and the best of the Father Brown stories—for which I share W. W. Robson's whole-hearted admiration and which I think their author underrated. His other books are, though not great, often delightful and always intelligent. His fiction is full of stimulating essays; his poetry has plenty of vitality and vigor and he had an obvious gift for versification, but he was neither a poet nor a novelist. A more irritating weakness in Chesterton's writing is his indulgence in mannerisms. I am not referring to his tendency to intrude his theological views into the most unexpected contexts (such as the detective adventures of Father Brown); Chesterton had every right to revert to what he regarded as essential; and in *Heretics* he wrote: "There are some people . . .—and I am one of them—who think that the most practical and important thing about a man is still his view of the universe."[5] But there *are* mannerisms; there is the general attitude which W. H. Auden has so shrewdly denounced by referring it back to "the aesthetes of the eighties and nineties," whom Chesterton heartily detested, but from whom Auden says he nevertheless inherited "the conviction that a writer should be continuously 'bright' and epigrammatic."[6] This frequent confusion of brightness with real brilliancy, of wit with wisdom, is unpardonable in a man who could praise Aquinas because "the very dullness of [his] diction . . . was enormously convincing. He could have given wit as well as wisdom; but he was so prodigiously in earnest that he gave his wisdom without his wit."[7] Of Chesterton it must be admitted that he always gave his wit, and in his eagerness to give it, all too often left his wisdom behind.

The two most obvious forms assumed by this—purely external—levity are paradox and verbalism. In the age of the great paradoxmongers Wilde and Shaw, Chesterton succeeded in becoming identified with paradox. But the title of Hugh Kenner's *Paradox in Chesterton* does no more than point to his intention of studying both the core and the surface of Chesterton's achievement, its matter as well as its manner. Chesterton himself asserted his dislike of paradox for its own sake: "I know nothing so contemptible," he wrote in *Orthodoxy,*[8] "as a mere paradox; a mere ingenious defence of

the indefensible." Yet the paradoxical view of things as well as the paradoxical expression of ideas had the strongest possible hold upon his mind
and his pen; paradoxes are all over his pages and they come all sizes.
Picking up a few almost at random—others will crop up later on—we find
that Chesterton's paradoxical mode very often hits on an unsuspected truth,
on a truth unsuspected because it is so evident that we normally regard it as
beneath our notice. In the introduction to Dickens' *American Notes* there is
a phrase about the novelist's quarrel with America: "This old Anglo-Ameri-
can quarrel was much more fundamentally friendly than most Anglo-
American alliances."⁹ In the introduction to *A Tale of Two Cities*, Dickens'
fatigue is said to have been due "not to the slowing down of his blood, but
rather to its unremitting rapidity," and then comes the typical and, it seems
to me, unanswerable, paradox: "He was not wearied by his age; rather he
was wearied by his youth."¹⁰ And in *Orthodoxy*, as part of his demonstration that "imagination does not breed insanity," Chesterton writes,
"Critics are much madder than poets. . . . Shakespeare is quite himself; it is
only some of his critics who have discovered that he was somebody else."¹¹

Chesterton's use of paradox is connected with his religion. To him
Christianity was, among other things, based on the paradoxical situation of
a God—an Immortal—who died, and, before He died, had expressed Himself in exemplary paradoxes: blessed are the poor; blessed are they that
mourn. An apt pupil at that highest of all possible schools, Chesterton had
understood that paradox is both a valid rhetorical weapon, often the shortest way to the truth, and always a thought-compelling process. But of
course the unremitting use of paradox is wearisome and fallible. The magic
does not always work. The truth is not always hidden under its obverse.
And when it does not hit upon the unsuspected truth, the Chestertonesque
paradox sometimes hits upon a platitude; do we need its help to realize that
"exploration and enlargement make the world smaller. The telegraph and
the steamboat make the world smaller. The telescope makes the world
smaller; it is only the microscope that makes it larger."¹² And many a
reader's appetite for Chesterton has died of an overdose of paradox.

As for verbalism, it too often assumes the form of wordplay or down-
right punning, about which Kenner has to admit that it is "strictly speaking
a major blemish on his literary style."¹³ There is nothing intrinsically
wrong in being fascinated by words; toying with them, playing around
them, piling them up or turning them upside down is a way of probing them
and getting to know their meaning. This is what Chesterton did with words
like *innocence* and *incredulity* when he used them in the titles of two of
his Father Brown volumes. But he is apt to play that game too boisterously;
not much is gained by saying of Dickens that "his ignorance of France went
with amazing intuitive perception of the truth about it. It is here that he has
most clearly the plain mark of the man of genius; that he can understand
what he does not understand,"¹⁴ or by asserting of Dr. Johnson that "he

was not a despot, but exactly the reverse. It was his sense of the democracy of debate that made him loud and unscrupulous, like a mob."[15] One is tempted to exclaim, Hamlet-like, "Words, words, words!" and leave it at that.

But leave it at that is, in my opinion, just what we should not do, because we should thus deprive ourselves of all the enjoyment and profit to be derived from reading Chesterton. When people speak of the neglect and oblivion into which he seems to have fallen, they are apt to produce an impression that is not quite, or that is no longer, valid. He has always had a number of admirers, some of them, like Hugh Kenner, as we saw, being themselves admirable and percipient critics. Kenner's book had an introduction by a native of Edmonton, one Herbert Marshall McLuhan, who stressed Chesterton's clear-sightedness with regard to "the heart of the contemporary chaos" or to "every kind of confused moral and psychological issue of our time."[16] And the recent tributes paid by Wallace Robson, Steven Marcus,[17] W. H. Auden and C. P. Snow[18] amount to no less than a Chesterton revival, and a brilliant one at that. And that is easily understandable, for Chesterton had several valuable qualities to recommend him.

However flippant or impish many of his minor writings or occasional articles and essays may appear, they cannot obscure what Kenner calls "the astonishing consistency of his thought."[19] The contradictions affect only the details; as to the essentials, Chesterton is a coherent thinker. Then his scope, especially as a literary critic, is much broader and—if one can use the word unambiguously about him—more catholic than many people are ready to believe until they actually read him; when they do, they find that he has written finely about Dr. Johnson, Browning, and Henry James, as well as Chaucer, Dickens, and Aquinas. Another of his unquestionable assets is his unfailing sense of wonder; there was literally nothing that seemed ordinary and therefore uninteresting to him; this attitude led him to write of "the thrilling romance of Orthodoxy" and to explain that "people have fallen into a foolish habit of speaking of Orthodoxy as something heavy, humdrum, and safe. There never was anything so perilous or so exciting as Orthodoxy."[20] And, as usual, he meant what he said; nothing was so exciting to him as orthodoxy, unless it was, well, anything else, whatever he happened to be contemplating at the time, a tree, the fall of a man, the word *dog*, or an elephant's trunk, about which he wrote, "One elephant having a trunk was odd, but all elephants having trunks looked like a plot."[21] This unusual capacity for wonder was partly an innate privilege, no doubt—for it made life constantly joyful and exciting—but it was also cultivated with care and pertinacity.

Finally, the critics who have studied him most carefully and thus know him best recognize Chesterton's essential sanity and true modesty. No doubt it is easy enough to quote statements that sound arrogant, as when he defined a heretic as "a man whose view of things has the hardihood of differing from mine."[22] But, apart from the tip of his tongue perceptibly protruding through his cheek at this juncture, this can be seen as a mere prank, as Chesterton at his most Shavian, trying to out-Shaw Shaw and taking, as it were, a mountebank holiday. But there is much more of the real Chesterton in this self-definition: "I am the man who, with the utmost daring, discovered what had been discovered before."[23] Thus does he disarm criticism. As for his sanity, we need do no more than refer to the "noted psychologist" who, "asked to define sanity, simply said: 'Read Chesterton.' "[24]

— *2* —

Such, then, were the mind and the pen that began to grapple with Dickens criticism early in this century. It was not a propitious period for that purpose. Steven Marcus has shown that Dickens' popularity, and his reputation abroad, were as great as ever, but that he "had fallen into disrepute within a particular group in the English-speaking world,"[25] that is, the group of academic critics and professional literary men. In that group, any serious study of Dickens' art was almost bound to enjoy the regal position proverbially awarded to the one-eyed man in the kingdom of the blind. Almost, but not quite. Admittedly, there had been very little serious Dickens criticism before 1900. The Frenchman Hippolyte Taine had produced the earliest profound analysis of Dickens as far back as 1856; but he had written an essay, not a full-scale book; besides, Taine labored under the tremendous disadvantage of being a Frenchman. I have sometimes claimed that John Forster was not a contemptible Dickens critic, but I am not prepared to claim that he was a great one. So that the solitary star in the firmament of Dickens studies before Chesterton began to write was a man to whom I must now give a few minutes, George Gissing.

Gissing's criticism of Charles Dickens was perhaps too soon eclipsed by Chesterton's, yet it remains eminently worth reading. A superficial view of the relationship between the two writers tends to present Chesterton's book as a protest against Gissing's and more specifically against an unduly gloomy view of Dickens. That Gissing was a pessimist and Chesterton an optimist is, of course, by and large true. Outside of their work on Dickens, their respective writings support this sharp distinction. But Chesterton's book was not a protest against Gissing's, as he took care to show by calling his immediate predecessor "the soundest of the Dickens critics, a man of genius."[26] And as Dickens critics the two men had, together with inevitable differences, more in common than is often realized. They communed, it seems to me, not only in the extent, but also in the manner of their admiration and enjoyment of Dickens.

Let us begin with the differences. On the whole, Gissing is far more methodical than Chesterton: the third chapter of his *Charles Dickens: A Criti-*

cal Study[27] is called "The Story-Teller" and is an elaborate study of the evolution of Dickens' craftsmanship, a task that is entirely beyond Chesterton's powers. Gissing deals with Dickens all the time and provides an index at the end of his book. He is not entirely methodical and does not avoid, for instance, repetitions; his valid remark that many of Dickens' characters, like Mrs. Gamp or Mr. Pecksniff, while delightful in fiction, would be merely disgusting or odious in real life, is reiterated in at least four sections of his book. Yet, compared with Chesterton's whimsicality, Gissing's sins of that kind appear venial indeed. His book is also far more literary than Chesterton's and he devotes a whole chapter to "Comparisons," impatiently dismissing the traditional parallel with Thackeray in order to concentrate on Balzac, Hugo, and Dostoevsky. His study of Dickens himself is much more comprehensive and he shows intelligent appreciation of all the minor writings, like *George Silverman's Explanation, The Holly-Tree Inn,* and even Dickens' speeches. His ideas about diction are sometimes too dogmatic, but he was capable of passing balanced judgments. He took too rosy a view of Dickens' character and of his happiness in life; Chesterton was not to be so easily deceived by appearances. Nor did Chesterton write in the vein of unexpectedly chauvinistic patriotism that led Gissing to glory in Dickens' art having "made visible to all mankind the characteristic virtues, the typical shortcomings, of the homely English race."[28] Gissing also yields to the temptation of looking for "gentlemen" in Dickens' novels, perhaps the most absurd preoccupation of his early critics. But the most glaring distinction between Chesterton and Gissing still is, of course, the somber view of life in the latter. Chesterton could not have written, as Gissing did, somewhat needlessly: "Statisticians tell us that London families simply die out in the third generation; on the whole, one is glad to hear it."[29] Gissing did admit that "Dickens has as much right to his optimism in the world of art, as Balzac to his bitter smile."[30] But whenever he touches on the subject of women, Gissing writes with grim relish; I have found nine passages that are characteristic in that respect and leave the reader under the impression that Gissing had an itch to reveal that he had been familiar mostly with vulgar shrews and derived from them his idea of womanhood; it is out of the question to quote all passages, but I have selected one that is an apology for Old Orlick's savage assault on Mrs. Gargery; it is something like Gissing's "Shortest way with shrews" and reads thus: "Dickens understood by this time that there is no other efficacious way with these ornaments of their sex. . . . A sharp remedy, but no whit sharper than the evil it cures."[31] A very un-Dickensian as well as un-Chestertonian sentiment! Finally, Gissing hated the Victorian age which he regarded as a "time of ugliness" and one "in which the English character seemed bent on exhibiting all its grossest and meanest and most stupid characteristics."[32]

But all these differences should not obscure the many resemblances between Gissing and Chesterton. The very size and form of their contributions to Dickens studies brings them together: each of them wrote one self-contained critical study, a series of introductions to separate works, and several articles. Gissing is not proof, any more than Chesterton, against mistakes and other signs of ignorance: he has not explored the Forster Collection, and Forster's word in the *Life of Dickens,* even when it is deliberately misleading, remains unquestioned by him, as by Chesterton. He calls Mr. Wickfield "Wickham";[33] he invents a chapter in *David Copperfield* which he calls "Our Domestic Life";[34] he is addicted to misquotations, the worst of which probably consists in making Mr. Bumble declare "The law is an ass!"[35] Like Chesterton again, Gissing by and large prefers the earlier to the later Dickens novels. But, like Chesterton also, he is capable of combining common sense with uncommon shrewdness, in statement after statement like the following: Dickens "never desired freedom to offend his public."[36] Like Chesterton's also—as I hope to show in a moment—Gissing's criticism is apt to sound an occasional note of modernity, as when he writes about *Copperfield:* "So far as we are permitted to judge, there is much reason for the insults hurled at Emily by the frantic Rosa Dartle."[37] Both his shrewdness and his modernity derive from his refusal to accept the commonplaces of traditional readership and criticism, an attitude whose intense Chestertonianity is obvious. Lastly, the author of such somber novels as *The Odd Women* and *New Grub Street* is surprisingly stimulated by Dickens to lyrical enthusiasm and near-Chestertonious gusto: of Todgers' Gissing has this to say, "It is inconceivable that any age which has not outgrown our language should forget this priceless description; every line close-packed with humorous truth,"[38] and of the Jolly Sandboys in *The Old Curiosity Shop* he asks, "What exquisite dyspeptic but must laugh with appetite over such a description?"[39] If this is not Chestertonese, what is?

Clearly, then, we can bring this brief excursion in Gissingland to a close by observing, on the one hand that, had there been no Chesterton, Gissing's Dickens criticism would be read and enjoyed by more people today, but that on the other hand, as there had been only one Gissing, there was room, there was indeed a crying need for another man of genius to write about Dickens when Chesterton did.

— *3* —

The best of Chesterton's Dickens criticism, all its essential tenets, is to be found in his 1906 book, *Charles Dickens.*[40] W. H. Auden took all four of the Dickens essays in his selection from that book alone. Yet the introductions collected in *Appreciations and Criticisms of the Works of Dickens* in 1911 are also worth reading; they do not add much to the critical image presented in the earlier book, but they provide interesting additional illustrations of Chesterton's manner.

It must be admitted that all the defects enumerated at the beginning of this paper tell very heavily on Chesterton's criticism of Dickens and, here as elsewhere, often repel the reader. The most obvious of these is his lack of methodical organization. Like Dick Swiveller, with whom he has much in common (and about whom, as we shall see, he writes glowingly), Chesterton says what comes uppermost in his mind. As Steven Marcus puts it: "He ruminates, he associates, he lets his pen carry him where it will."[41] He is thoroughly incapable of concentrating his attention on Dickens. Even within the limited scope of an introduction, he is apt to branch off into the most unexpected directions. His introduction to *Pickwick* begins with an elaborate discussion of theological problems; and the first page of the six making up his introduction to *A Tale of Two Cities* is entirely devoted to Shakespeare. Contradictions can easily be detected; for instance in his comments on exaggeration in Dickens: now it seems that Dickens did not exaggerate, now that he exaggerated all the time; but it does not really matter, since in that case, it means that exaggeration is truer than ordinary truth.

Chesterton is probably the least scholarly of critics. He does not analyze Dickens' text; indeed he gives very few quotations, and they are always unidentified and almost infallibly inaccurate; he trusted his memory implicitly, and he certainly had a fantastically retentive memory, but he impoverished many of the passages he used for purposes of illustration. He was not properly informed; his biographical sections, insofar as they aim at telling the story of Dickens' life, have very little value; his comment on the Little Nell type of girl with "a sort of saintly precocity" consists of questions asked with extraordinary innocence: did Dickens, Chesterton wonders, "know some little girl of this kind? Did she die, perhaps, and remain in his memory in colours too ethereal and pale?"[42] He had made passing mention of Mary Hogarth less than ten pages before, but he did not connect the two! He speaks of "the rescue of Miss Lammle"[43] in terms which make one suspect that he is thinking of Georgiana Podsnap. He even seems to miss a very obvious Shakespeare reference when he says that "supping on horrors" is "a good popular phrase."[44] And, in his introduction to *Our Mutual Friend,* he supports his point about "the real jerk and spurt of good spirits with which [Dickens] opens that novel"[45] by treating chapter ii (the Veneerings' dinner party) as the first and forgetting about the real chapter i, which is all concerned with corpse-fishing in the Thames!

These are all more or less sins of omission, and they do not seriously affect Chesterton's critical vision. His positive faults, like the indulgence in wordplay and verbalism and in the expression of arbitrary opinions, are perhaps more damaging. He cannot resist a verbal contrast and writes, for instance, that if Dickens "learnt to whitewash the universe, it was in a blacking factory that he learnt it."[46] When he tells us that "The Seven Poor Travellers" was planned for seven stories, he adds, "we will not say seven poor stories";[47] "we will not say" is both a feeble disclaimer of a poor joke and evidence of the irresistible leaning of Chesterton's mind and pen toward juggling with words. This is harmless enough. But sometimes his thinking becomes involved in this ballet of words. He writes more than once about optimism and reforms. He says, for instance, that "the optimistic reformer reforms much more completely than the pessimistic reformer. People produce violent changes by being contented, by being far too contented."[48] Yet a dozen pages later we are told of "the essential truth, that the true optimist can only continue an optimist so long as he is discontented."[49] Where, then, *is* the essential truth? Or are words interchangeable at will? In mitigation of this minor caviling, I should like to show that Chesterton's proclaimed attitude to words and speech accounts for much in, after all, a satisfactory way. He is alive to what he calls—in a comment on Molière's Monsieur Jourdain—"the miracle of language."[50] He is not unlike Lewis Carroll, in his fascinated delight with this profound mystery; nor is he, as I have already hinted, unlike Dick Swiveller in his gay worship of the intoxication of speech. What Chesterton says of Swiveller could perhaps be applied to him: "Great draughts of words are to him like great draughts of wine—pungent and yet refreshing, light and yet leaving him in a glow. In unerring instinct for the perfect folly of a phrase, he has no equal"[51] Such a talent covers a multitude of sins.

Perhaps it does not, however, cover the arbitrariness, the near waywardness of many random assertions, though when some of them are carried just a little too far, it may be through the mere momentum of the words rolling along in a Chesterton paragraph. I do not feel at all convinced by his disclosure of Napoleon's secret: "The modern world with all its subtleness will never guess his strange secret, for his strange secret was that he was very like other people."[52] I am merely puzzled, not enlightened, by a statement like: "the only way to remember a place for ever is to live in the place for one hour; and the only way to live in the place for an hour is to forget the place for an hour."[53]

Yet, when all is said and done about Chesterton's defects, he remains a highly intelligent writer. Even when he goes wrong, he forces us to reconsider our views. He was aware of the difficulty of discussing Dickens and remarkably frank about it; his passing mention of Dickens' genius was followed by the admission that it is "the thing which every one has to talk about distinctly and directly because no one knows what it is."[54] Chesterton enjoyed the advantage of being unusually close to Dickens in many ways; I am not referring merely to the phenomenon of sympathy—for he could write sympathetically about artists who were entirely unlike himself, Browning and James, for instance—but to a real kinship, both intellectual and emotional, between the two men. And he unquestionably had superb gifts of his own. He was able without apparent effort to coin any number of telling phrases. The quality which *A Midsummer Night's Dream* and *A Christmas Carol* have in common he calls "farcical occult-

ism."[55] He tells us that Dickens' least convincing characters must have
been "copied from the wild freakshow of real life."[56] And of the Clennam mystery in *Dorrit* he writes that "the secrecy is sensational; the secret
is tame."[57] More than once it seems that the way Chesterton phrases his
statement has a considerable share in making it suggestive whereas it would
seem ordinary or excessive if expressed in more commonplace terms. Thus
when he says of Dickens that "his wisdom is at the best talent, his foolish-
ness is genius."[58] Or when he compares Dickens' and Carlyle's advantages as historians of the French Revolution, he hits on this terse phrase:
"Dickens knew less of the Revolution, but he had more of it."[59] Of this
talent he is so lavish that he can delight us even when he seems to be wast-
ing his time and ours over unimportant issues, like Mrs. Robert Seymour's
claim that her husband had been the real inventor of *Pickwick:* five pages on
such a theme are more than anyone wishes to read, but they contain this
gem: "To claim to have originated an idea of Dickens is like claiming to
have contributed a glass of water to Niagara."[60] Chesterton's amazing gift
of expression is nowhere so evident as when he is saying something we have
felt and tried, dimly, to express to ourselves; this happened to me with regard to Cruikshank's illustrations for *Oliver Twist*. Like Chesterton, I
think them very poor; but unlike Chesterton, I could never have defined
what is wrong with them in my eyes: "There was about Cruikshank's art
a kind of cramped energy which is almost the definition of the criminal
mind. He . . . does not only draw morbidly, he draws meanly. . . . [His Fagin in the condemned cell] does not merely look like a picture of Fagin; it
looks like a picture by Fagin."[61]

In the same way it might almost be said that the felicities of Chesterton's humor make his pages read not like a criticism of Dickens, but like a
criticism by Dickens. His praise of the death scene of Tony Weller's wife is
based on what he shudders to think Dickens might have made of it if he had
been in his maudlin mood: "For all I know Mrs. Weller might have asked
what the wild waves were saying, and for all I know Mr. Weller might have
told her."[62] Nor is there anything unkind or untrue in the following statement: "A definite school regarded Dickens as a great man from the first
days of his fame: Dickens certainly belonged to this school."[63]

But the brilliant manner of Chesterton's Dickens criticism should not
blind us to the frequent soundness of its matter, to the wealth of its insights.
He was the first to discover aspects of Dickens with which more recent critics have familiarized us. And his perceptions about the personality and the
art of Charles Dickens amount to a lucid and original vision. Let us take a
few examples, out of a long list of possibilities. "Dickens," he writes, "had
all his life the faults of the little boy who is kept up too late at night. . . .
Dickens was always a little too irritable because he was a little too
happy."[64] And again, "He had this supreme character of the domestic
despot—that his good temper was, if possible, more despotic than his bad

temper."[65] Against the charge of pandering to the lower tastes of his public—a charge proffered, among others, by Walter Bagehot—Chesterton's
defence of Dickens may be a trifle noisy, but isn't it fundamentally sound?
"Dickens was not like our ordinary demagogues and journalists. Dickens
did not write what the people wanted. Dickens wanted what the people
wanted. . . . Dickens never talked down to the people. He talked up to the
people."[66] And he analyzes, in his discussion of Pumblechook, what he
calls "the one weak point of Dickens," that "he nowhere makes the reader
feel that Pumblechook has any kind of fundamental dignity at all."[67] Of
course Chesterton does see other weak points in Dickens, but they are often
connected with this major deficiency, as when he asserts, truly, I think, that
"Dickens did have a disposition to make his characters at all costs happy, or,
to speak more strictly, he had a disposition to make them comfortable rather than happy" so that "there are cases at the end of his stories in which
his kindness to his characters is a careless and insolent kindness."[68]

Particularly honest and useful is Chesterton's attitude to the obvious,
so different from ours, and yet so necessary in Dickens criticism, since much
of Dickens lies at the obvious level, not to be disregarded without warping
the picture. W. H. Auden rightly says that "Chesterton's literary criticism
abounds in observations which, once they have been made, seem so obviously
true that one cannot understand why one had not seen them for oneself."[69]
One had not seen them, I venture to suggest, because one regards the obvious as stale and insignificant; Chesterton regards it as wonderful. Nothing is beneath his attention. This is what makes him an independent critic;
he is not afraid of saying what has been said before or what will never
again be thought worth saying by others; C. P. Snow, somewhat wistfully,
sees Chesterton as "utterly unmoved by pressures either from the mass-
media or English Departments."[70] In any case Chesterton blithely dis-
misses the truly uninteresting problems that fascinated his contemporaries:
"It has been said (invariably by cads) that Dickens never described a gentleman; it is like saying that he never described a zebra."[71] He is so unconcerned with received ideas that he dares to write sacrilegiously, about
Scrooge—for instance: "Scrooge is not really inhuman at the beginning any
more than he is at the end. There is a heartiness in his inhospitable sentiments that is akin to humour and therefore to humanity; he is only a
crusty old bachelor, and had (I strongly suspect) given away turkeys all his
life."[72]

As I do not wish to make claims that I cannot substantiate, I have to
admit that Chesterton's view of Dickens is distinctly old-fashioned. He believes that "those who most truly love Dickens love the earlier Dickens"[73]
and that "those who have any doubt about Dickens can have no doubt of the
superiority of the later books."[74] And there is much truth in W. W. Robson's words: "Even though writers whom he admired, and who influenced
him, like Browning and Dickens, are coming back into favor, they are not

seen as Chesterton saw them."[75] But isn't there something to be said for Chesterton even in that respect? On the one hand his rollicking enjoyment of the early Dickens is responsible for many delightful pages in his book. On the other hand, when we call him old-fashioned, we admit that there are fashions in criticism; they are bound to be only temporary (and only temporarily old); being old-fashioned is thus not intrinsically worse than being new-fangled at all costs (the costs may even mount higher in the latter case). Chesterton was not unaware of the transitoriness of any critical approach; he denounced "that besetting sin or weakness of the modern progressive, the habit of regarding the contemporary questions as the eternal questions and the latest word as the last."[76] And, when preparing to discuss "the future of Dickens," he wrote, "The hardest thing to remember about our own time, of course, is simply that it is a time; we all instinctively think of it as the Day of Judgment."[77] Thirdly, old-fashioned as he is, Chesterton nonetheless has some of the intuitions of more modern criticism. He sees, for instance, that "Dickens was a mythologist rather than a novelist"[78] and boldly speaks of "the incurable poetic character, the hopelessly non-realistic character of Dickens' essential genius."[79] He perceives that Dickens was revolutionary, both as an artist and as a social critic, though he wisely refrains from exaggerating the novelist's success in the latter capacity: "Dickens as a Radical," Chesterton writes, "would I fancy, much prefer that we should continue his battle than that we should celebrate his triumph; especially when it has not come."[80]

Besides, even the old-fashioned parts of Chesterton's Dickens criticism contribute in its overall value. As Steven Marcus says, "It remains important in itself and in the challenge it offers to the reader today."[81] And the challenge must be accepted and taken up. It is, by and large, the challenge of the optimist and it is clearly expressed in the following words: "If . . . you are a pessimist, in reading this [book], forego for a little the pleasures of pessimism. Dream for one mad moment that the grass is green."[82] Optimism—Dickens' own optimism—is Chesterton's key to Dickens; we may occasionally feel that he overdoes it, but it will seldom be without also feeling that he has something useful to tell us, and to tell us supremely well. In any case, we can never be—or we never ought to be—entirely sure that we are right and Chesterton wrong. A. O. J. Cockshut calls Chesterton "a penetrating though one-sided critic of Dickens."[83] Of course, he is one-sided, but then, who isn't? The critics of the present day may well be more profound than Chesterton, but they are—quite deliberately, it seems to me— far more single-minded than he was.

After all, there are moments when his *Charles Dickens* makes the professional Dickens scholar echo the words of Etienne Gilson on reading Chesterton's St. Thomas Aquinas: "Chesterton makes one despair. I have been studying St. Thomas all my life and I could never have written such a book."[84] When I am tempted to complain of Chesterton's lack of scholarliness I am reminded of what Walter W. Crotch once wrote about Dickens' characters being inartistic; if, he said, they "are inartistic, let us pray that inartistry may overtake, and at once, every contemporary writer."[85] If a book like Chesterton's is the fruit of unscholarliness, should we not likewise pray that unscholarliness may overtake, and at once, every contemporary critic of Dickens? And when our prayer is heard, perhaps we shall suffer less from what Steven Marcus slyly calls "the admirable austerity of modern criticism."[86]

— 4 —

On the whole, then, it seems to me that Chesterton's criticism of Dickens teaches us many things. On what it shows us of Chesterton's ebullient, buoyant, even blatant personality, it is needless to expatiate, because the same facts would be discoverable by reading any other work from the same irrepressible pen.

About Dickens, Chesterton suggests to us that a whole-hearted, large-souled appreciation does not preclude useful insights. I believe that we disregard Chesterton on Dickens at our own peril; the worst peril of ignoring him lies in the probability of our laboriously rediscovering through huge volumes of dry scholarship points that Chesterton had lightly thrown off, as if without effort, through the intuitions of genius, by simply formulating his individual reactions. I am therefore convinced that we still need Chesterton. Let us take him with as many grains of salt as we feel may be needed to make him acceptable or to make him safe, but let us take him.

Yet the most interesting thing we may find out by reading Chesterton's Dickens criticism concerns the nature of scholarship and criticism. A serious discussion of Chesterton, like W. H. Auden's, is bound to come up against this problem and I must take the liberty of quoting at some length Auden's remarkable comments:

> Our day has seen the emergence of two kinds of literary critics, the documentor and the cryptologist. The former with meticulous accuracy collects and publishes every unearthable fact about an author's life, from his love-letters to his dinner invitations and laundry bills, on the assumption that any fact, however trivial, about the man may throw light upon his writings. The latter approaches his work as if it were an anonymous and immensely difficult text, written in a private language which the ordinary reader cannot hope to understand until it is deciphered for him by experts. Both such critics will no doubt dismiss Chesterton's literary criticism as out-of-date, inaccurate and superficial, but if one were to ask any living novelist or poet which kind of critic he would personally prefer to write about his work, I have no doubt as to the answer."[87]

It would certainly not be a satisfactory solution to have the critics and their methods chosen by the artists themselves. And of course we do need the modern forms of criticism urgently; we need the wonderful Pilgrim edition of Dickens' letters and we need J. Hillis Miller's analyses and Rowland Mc-Master's introduction to *Little Dorrit* at least as much as we need Chesterton. My point is that they are not mutually exclusive, and that Chesterton's mode is, though less painstaking than ours, more difficult to practice successfully. Each of us does at least one thing better than Chesterton ever attempted to do it, but it would take a round dozen of us to achieve something like the global result of his critical achievement. Each of us thrives on one or two ideas; Chesterton generated ideas like a kind of spontaneous-combustion engine. As I said before, he is not infallible. But then, who is? G. B. Shaw, in one of his rare outbursts of modesty, had to admit that "even I am not infallible, at least not always."[88]

You may remember some comments on Shaw which are equally applicable to Chesterton; Chesterton himself paid Shaw the compliment of saying that he combined being always intelligent with being always intelligible,[89] and Maurice Colburn wrote that he was "always serious, never solemn."[90] Chesterton similarly was both intelligent and intelligible, always serious and never solemn. And that is a very proper attitude in which to approach the study of Dickens. As to his major fault of verbal intoxication, it has its source in his belief that "the moment our souls become serious, our words become a little wild."[91] The verbal wildness not only does not detract from the intellectual and moral seriousness, it is intimately connected with it, it wraps it up in a delightful garment; it acts like the sugar coating of the pill, but the pill itself, the gist of Chesterton's criticism, is wonderfully free from bitterness.

So, you see that I am unrepentant. I confess that reading Chesterton has been and is one of the great joys of my literary and intellectual life. He has been, and he is, to me a teacher of joy and a powerful stimulus. If I had not, because I was speaking with due severity of Chesterton's indulgence in verbalism, been exceptionally chary of wordplay, I might have been tempted to say that the best epithet to be formed from Chesterton's name is none of those I have used so far—Chestertonian, Chestertonious, and Chester-tonesque—but Chestertonic, for that expresses what he is to me, a Chester-tonic; but I must heroically resist the temptation to the very last. I am not only unrepentant, but also unblushing, because I have by now convinced myself, if no one else, that an addiction to Chesterton is nothing to be ashamed of.

Notes

Index

NOTES

LANCE SCHACHTERLE: *Oliver Twist and Its Serial Predecessors*

¹ *Oliver Twist* appeared in *Bentley's Miscellany* between February 1837 and April 1839, with three interruptions (June and October 1837, September 1838). For additional information on its serial publication, see Gerald Giles Grubb, "On the Serial Publication of *Oliver Twist*," *MLN* 56 (1941), 290-94.

² See "Dickens' Reading," (Ph.D. diss. UCLA, 1955).

³ The anonymous and unreprinted *The Man-of-War's Man* is attributed to David Stewart by Alan L. Strout, *A Bibliography of Articles in Blackwood's Magazine, 1817-1825* (Lubbock, Texas: Texas Technological College Press, 1959), p. 179. The last part of *The Man-of-War's Man* ends with an old sailor promising to continue his story on the next occasion. But no more installments appeared, and the serial, which had been published at very irregular intervals, remains unfinished.

⁴ *Blackwood's*, 12 (November 1822), 650. Three other installments, the seventh, eighth, and fourteenth, end suspensefully.

⁵ Before Marryat's novels, Chamier's *Life of a Sailor* (May 1831-April 1832) had appeared in nine numbers of the *Metropolitan Magazine*. Marryat himself contributed a long series of separate stories, *The Pasha of Many Tales*, but this serial scarcely qualifies as a novel. Between March 1834 and July 1837, the anonymous *Scenes from the Life of Edward Lascelles, Gent.* offered readers a more refined version of Michael Scott's popular sea novels. But none of these have significance as an innovator of serial techniques.

⁶ *Metropolitan Magazine,* 8 (September 1833), 69-70.

⁷ "In the serial-writer's relation to his public there is indeed something of the stimulating contact which an actor or a public speaker receives from an audience. Serial publication gave back to story-telling its original context of performance, the context that Chaucer, for example, knew and exploited." *Novels of the Eighteen-Forties* (Oxford: Clarendon Press, 1954), p. 36.

⁸ *Metropolitan Magazine* 8 (September 1833), 70. For Trollope's similar comment, see his *Autobiography* (New York: Harpers, 1883), p. 130.

⁹ Commenting on the serial publication of *Middlemarch*, George Eliot remarked that "the slow plan of publication has been of immense advantage to the book in deepening the impression it produces." Letter to John Blackwood, 4 August 1872, in *The George Eliot Letters*, ed. Gordon Haight (New Haven: Yale University Press, 1955), V, 297.

¹⁰ *Metropolitan Magazine* 9 (January 1834), 57.

¹¹ Lionel Stevenson, *The English Novel: A Panorama* (Boston: Houghton Mifflin, 1960), p. 231.

¹² This passage was dropped from all the book-form reprints of *Oliver Twist*, and may be found only in the

[231]

original serial and in the Clarendon edition of *Oliver Twist,* ed. Kathleen Tillotson (Oxford: Clarendon Press, 1966), p. 106, n. 3. All my quotations from *Oliver* are from the Clarendon edition, and will be acknowledged by the appropriate page number in parentheses directly after the reference.

ALAN R. BURKE: *The House of Chuzzlewit and the Architectural City*

1   All quotations from *Martin Chuzzlewit, A Child's History of England, American Notes,* and *David Copperfield* are from *The New Oxford Illustrated Dickens* (London: Oxford University Press, 1948-58). All subsequent chapter and page references to these works are enclosed within parentheses after the citation and refer to this edition.
2   For a detailed history and description of the Monument, see William Kent, F.S.A., ed., *An Encyclopaedia of London,* rev. Godfrey Thompson (London: J. M. Dent & Sons, 1970), pp. 367-69. One of Dickens' earliest references to the Monument is contained in a letter to Thomas Beard dated, Saturday night, January 1837. Dickens writes: "I want a walk—we can have a stroll on Monday, if you are not engaged. The top of the Monument is one of my longings, the ditto of Saint Paul's another." In Walter Dexter, ed., *The Letters of Charles Dickens* (Bloomsbury: The Nonesuch Press, 1938), I, 101.
3   Samuel Pepys, *Diary,* 3 December 1667.
4   Alexander Pope, *Moral Essays,* III, 339-40.
5   Kent, *London,* p. 369.
6   See Dorothy Van Ghent, "The Dickens World: A View from Todgers'," *Sewanee Review* 58 (1950), 419-38.
7   Alexander Welsh, *The City of Dickens* (Oxford: The Clarendon Press, 1971), p. 70.
8   Kent, *London,* pp. 367-68.
9   See Saul Steinberg, *The Labyrinth* (New York: Harper & Brothers, 1960), n. pag.
10   Kent, *London,* p. 368.
11   Northrop Frye, *Anatomy of Criticism: Four Essays* (Princeton, New Jersey: Princeton University Press, 1957),

p. 150. Jorge Luis Borges, "The Immortal," in *Labyrinths* (New York: New Directions Press, 1964), p. 110.
12   Sir Christopher Wren (1632-1723) was born at East Knoyle in Wiltshire. He conducted a survey of Salisbury Cathedral at the request of Seth Ward, Bishop of Salisbury (1667-89). See R. L. P. Jowitt, *Salisbury* (London and New York: B. T. Batsford Ltd., 1951), pp. 42, 46.
13   Borges, "The House of Asterion," *Labyrinths,* p. 139.
14   For a description of the "long winding staircase" and of a view from the top of the Monument, see "All Night on The Monument," *Household Words* 17, no. 410 (30 January 1858), 145-48.
15   Kent notes that "there was a suicide from the Monument in 1788, two in 1810, two in 1839 (one a boy of 15), and one in 1842. After the last tragedy it was temporarily closed, and the gallery at the summit . . . was enclosed with an iron cage" (p. 369). In a letter to Forster, Dickens complains that newsworthy events happen in London only when he leaves it: "I almost blame myself for the death of that poor girl who leaped off the Monument upon my leaving town last year. She would not have done it if I had remained, neither would the two men have found the skeleton in the sewers" (Dexter, *Letters,* I, 259). Concerning the two men and the finding of the skeleton, see *Martin Chuzzlewit* (xlvi, 719).
16   J. Hillis Miller, *Charles Dickens: The World of His Novels* (London: Oxford University Press, 1959), pp. 98-103.
17   Lewis Mumford, *The Culture of Cities* (New York: Harcourt, Brace and Company, 1938), p. 4.
18   Ibid.
19   Kent, *London,* p. 368.

20   Jowitt in *Salisbury* writes that on one of the walls of Salisbury Cathedral Close, there is "a mark inscribed 'Meridies,' and this is a sundial, which tells the time only at noon, the spire of the Cathedral acting as a gigantic gnomon" (p. 51).

21   Lewis Mumford, *Technics and Civilization* (New York: Harcourt, Brace and Company, 1934), p. 14.

HARLAND S. NELSON: *Staggs's Gardens*

Quotations from Dickens' novels follow the text of *The New Oxford Illustrated Dickens* (London: Oxford University Press, 1948-1958). For quotations from Dickens' *Household Words* articles I have used the text in the volume entitled *Miscellaneous Papers* in the National Library Edition of *The Works of Charles Dickens* (New York: Bigelow, Brown & Co., n. d.), a reprint of the National Edition, ed. B. W. Matz (London: Chapman and Hall, 1906-1908).

1   *Household Words* 10 May 1856.

2   *Dombey and Son,* lv.

3   There is a passage in *Bleak House* too about the coming of the railroad, in chapter lv, where Mrs. Rouncewell, Sir Leicester Dedlock's housekeeper at Chesney Wold in Lincolnshire, is on her way to London by post-chaise to see her son George: "Railroads shall soon traverse all this country, and with a rattle and a glare the engine and train shall shoot like a meteor over the wide night-landscape, turning the moon paler; but, as yet, such things are non-existent in these parts, though not wholly unexpected. Preparations are afoot, measurements are made, ground is staked out. Bridges are begun, and their not yet united piers desolately look at one another over roads and streams, like brick and mortar couples with an obstacle to their union; fragments of embankments are thrown up, and left as precipices with torrents of rusty carts and barrows tumbling over them; tripods of tall poles appear on hilltops, where there are rumors of tunnels; everything looks chaotic, and abandoned in full hopelessness. Along the freezing roads, and through the night, the post-chaise makes its way without a railroad on its mind." A man-made meteor that pales the moon by comparison hints of fatal pride, and the reassuring footnote in the *Dombey* passage about civilization and improvement (reassuring, that is, if one ignores the possible ambiguity of tone) is absent here.

4   Edgar Johnson, *Charles Dickens: His Tragedy and Triumph* (New York: Simon and Schuster, 1952), pp. 526, 751-52.

5   *The World of Charles Dickens* (New York: Viking Press, 1970), p. 192.

6   Cited in Monroe Engel, *The Maturity of Dickens* (Cambridge, Mass.: Harvard University Press, 1959), p. 68; and in Stephen Marcus, *Dickens: From Pickwick to Dombey* (New York: Basic Books, 1965), p. 306. The text is that of the Nonesuch Edition.

7   Humphry House, *The Dickens World,* 2nd ed. (London: Oxford University Press, 1942), p. 35.

8   "Old Lamps for New Ones," *Household Words* 15 June 1850.

9   *Hard Times,* I, iii.

10   *The World of Charles Dickens,* p. 118.

11   *Dickens: From Pickwick to Dombey,* p. 309. Alexander Welsh says something to the same effect about "An Unsettled Neighbourhood": "Dickens rather approves these signs of progress than otherwise, hence there is no kind of attack in the entire essay" ("Satire and History: The City of Dickens," *Victorian Studies* 11 [1967-68], 384). Distinguishing as he does between Dickens as satirist and as humorist, Welsh is certainly right to say there is no *satiric* attack here. But he means also to say there is no criticism at all; there I think he is

wrong.

12   Ch. xv. Marcus quotes almost all of the passage, but not this part.

13   *Dickens: From Pickwick to Dombey*, pp. 306-7.

14   *The Dickens World*, p. 137. Just the same, Dombey is not much different in spirit, if at all, from Thomas Gradgrind; in settling the terms with Mrs. Toodle to wet-nurse Paul, he is just as insistent upon defining the relation to exclude human feeling as Gradgrind would have been: "It is not at all in this bargain that you need become attached to my child, or that my child need become attached to you. I don't expect or desire anything of the kind. Quite the reverse. When you go away from here, you will have concluded what is a mere matter of bargain and sale, hiring and letting: and will stay away. The child will cease to remember you; and you will cease, if you please, to remember the child" (ii).

15   *Dickens: From Pickwick to Dombey*, p. 310. I have really been arguing with Marcus in much of my essay; he says that when the railroad is brought into the novel at the point where Paul is dying, "the miraculous alteration it has wrought upon Staggs' Gardens, 'originating wholesome comforts and conveniences' (xv), stands again in ironic contrast to the great change about to be inflicted upon the Dombeys" (p. 310). I think this is a considerable mistake in interpretation, worth setting right; but I also think that taken as a whole Marcus' treatment of *Dombey and Son* is criticism of the highest order.

16   *The World of Charles Dickens*, p. 229.

17   The Sleary horse-riding in *Hard Times*—an emblem of art, surely, especially since the company lodges at the Pegasus' Arms—is shabby not by nature, but because Coketown does not support it. Marcus points out that Carker is an artist of sorts, "almost the only person in the novel to whom art means anything" (p. 349. There is something wrong about his relation to art, though, as Marcus also says). It is consistent with the meaning that I think the railroad has in *Dombey and Son* that Carker is killed by a train.

R. RUPERT ROOPNARAINE: *Time and the Circle in* Little Dorrit

1   F. R. and Q. D. Leavis, *Dickens the Novelist*, (New York: Pantheon Books, 1970), p. ix.

2   George Henry Lewes, "Dickens in Relation to Criticism," *The Dickens Critics*, ed. George H. Ford and Lauriat Lane, Jr. (Ithaca, N.Y.: Cornell University Press, 1961), p. 63.

3   George Santayana, "Dickens," *The Dickens Critics*, pp. 136-37.

4   Charles Dickens, *Little Dorrit*, (London: Oxford University Press, 1953), p. 720. All subsequent page references are enclosed within parentheses after the citation and refer to this edition.

5   J. Hillis Miller, *Charles Dickens: The World of his Novels* (Cambridge, Mass., 1958), p. 239.

6   In his recent study of Dickens, *The Narrative Art of Charles Dickens: The Rhetoric of Sympathy and Irony in His Novels* (Oxford: Clarendon, 1970), Harvey Peter Sucksmith argues that "though Dickens' vision reflects authentic tragic experience, it is rarely the pure vision of high tragedy" (p. 301). Working from the Aristotelian definition which he expands to include irony, Sucksmith claims that the compassionate vision in Dickens is at variance with authentic tragic experience, and consequently, "what we often find is compassion without terror or terror without compassion, though irony is a fairly constant factor." My own concern here is less with the complex interrelation between pity, terror, and irony, than with the spectacle of Olympian malevolence forever contriving to entangle man in a web of destruction.

7   Miller, p. 239.

8   John Wain, "Little Dorrit," in *Essays on Literature and Ideas* (London: Macmillan, 1963), p. 220.

[9] Sergei Eisenstein, "Dickens, Griffith and the Film Today," in *Film Form. Essays in Film Theory,* trans. and ed. Jay Leyda (London: Dobson, 1963), pp. 195-255. See for example his breakdown of chap. xxi of *Oliver Twist* into a shooting script.

[10] David Gervais, "The Poetry of *Little Dorrit," Cambridge Quarterly* 4 (Winter 1969), 40.

[11] Ibid., p. 48.

[12] John Henry Raleigh, *Time, Place, and Idea: Essays on the Novel* (Carbondale: Southern Illinois University Press, 1968), pp. 43-55.

[13] Ibid., p. 45.

[14] Ibid., p. 51.

[15] Ibid., p. 47.

[16] K. J. Fielding, "Dickens and the Past: The Novelist of Memory," in *Experience and the Novel: Selected Papers from the English Institute,* ed. Roy Harvey Pearce (New York: Columbia University Press, 1968), p. 124.

[17] Raleigh, p. 49.

[18] Lionel Trilling, "Little Dorrit," in *Dickens,* Twentieth Century Views, Martin Price (Englewood Cliffs, N.J.: Prentice-Hall, 1967), p. 155.

[19] I have borrowed this suggestive word from Monroe Engel, *The Maturity of Dickens* (Cambridge, Mass: Harvard University Press, 1959), p. 129.

[20] The phrase is R. D. McMaster's. I am indebted to his essay, "Dickens, The Dandy, and The Savage: A Victorian View of the Romantic," for some of the points used here to illustrate my argument. See *Studies in the Novel,* 1 (Summer 1969) 133-46.

[21] Raleigh, p. 50.

ANGUS EASSON: *Marshalsea Prisoners*

[1] All references (by part, chapter and page) to *Little Dorrit* are from the *New Oxford Illustrated* Dickens (London: Oxford University Press, 1953).

[2] All documents drawn on for this account are in the Public Record Office, *Palace Court,* ix,8, except for John Cruchley's surrender of office, *Palace Court* ix,5 (pt. II). The two main manuscripts are the statements of Giles and Elizabeth Hemens. Crown Copyright material appears by permission.

[3] See, as well as his blackmailing of Amy touched on below, his reactions when told of his fortune (I, xxxv); and his behavior to his valet and to John Chivery when out of the prison (II, v,xviii).

[4] From a letter to John Forster, quoted in John Forster, *Life of Dickens,* ed. J. W. T. Ley, (1928), pp. 727-28 (I owe this quotation originally to G. H. Ford, *Dickens and his Readers* (1955; reprint ed., New York: Norton, 1965), pp. 134-35.

STANLEY TICK: *The Sad End of Mr. Meagles*

[1] *The New Oxford Illustrated Dickens* (London: Oxford University Press, 1953), pp. 813-14. All quotations are from this edition and will be indicated in the text.

[2] This essay evolved from my speculations about the relationship of *Little Dorrit* to "Nobody's Fault," the sketch or the germ from which the novel developed. Forster gives the following as Dickens' original notion, expressed in the summer of 1855: "A leading man for a story who should bring about all the mischief in it, lay it all on Providence, and say at every calamity, 'Well, it's a mercy, however, nobody was to blame, you know!' " *The Life of Charles Dickens,* new ed., ed. A. J. Hoppé [London: Dent 1966], II, 179. We know, from Forster and the extant Number Plans, that he was at about the present chapter xi when he altered the title from "Nobody's Fault" to *Little Dorrit.* My original speculation had to do with whether or not Dickens changed his story when he changed the title. We note that in chapters xvi, xvii, xxvi, and xxviii Dickens still used the "Nobody's . . ." as a

formula for the title; furthermore, the phrase, in one form or another, is employed repeatedly throughout the novel, one of the more familiar locutions being "Nobody's heart" as a way of referring to Clennam's passive and unstated affection for Pet Meagles. Some consideration is given to this matter in John Butt and Kathleen Tillotson, *Dickens at Work* (London, 1957), pp. 222-33. My hypothesis, based on the fact that Meagles brought a disconcerting and incongruous pathos to the novel, was that the Meagles story originated in the discarded theme of "Nobody's Fault," and that Dickens, for some inexplicable reason, continued with that story even after he changed the title and novel to *Little Dorrit*. Forster was not the only reader to find *Little Dorrit* incoherent; recall his criticism: "The defect of the book was . . . the want of ease and coherence among the figures of the story, and of a central interest in the plan of it. . . . Some of the most deeply-considered things that occur in it have really little to do with the tale itself" (II, 184). Yet how odd that Forster, aware of the discarded theme and the changed title (and, of course, ever the apologist for Dickens), did not ascribe the incoherence of the novel to Dickens' false start.

3   At which point Dickens was writing under the title of "Nobody's Fault."

4   Our first view of Meagles is remarkably like that of Mr. Cheeryble (see chapter xxxv of *Nicholas Nickleby*): Dickens uses many of the same words to describe both men.

5   The relevant memoranda Dickens compiled in preparation for the first number of "Nobody's Fault," including the full notes for chapter ii, make much of "practical"; clearly the term was meant to be laudatory, perhaps as an antidote to the Gradgrind sense of "practical" satirized in *Hard Times*. Below are the outline notes:
New sort of
PRACTICAL PEOPLE <All small-capped
                      letters had double
                      underlining in

original >
Meagles

Father—Mother—Baby
  Tattycoram

CHAPTER II
[Baby. Practical People]
QUARANTINE.

Bring in Father—Mother—Baby Meagles
  Arthur Clennam. From China.
Indicate his story.

"Practical people"—New and better
                      aspect thereof
                      than usual:
                      shewing how to
                      be practical, *not*
                      politico-
                      economically.

Miss Wade   <All italicized words
underscored in original >

Tattycoram
          Travellers disperse—thus
          all travellers through life

See Paul D. Herring, "Dickens' Monthly Number Plans for *Little Dorrit*," *Modern Philology* 64 (August 1966), 28-29.

6   An illustration of this kind of self-discipline urged onto others, i.e., of Dickens' reliance on practical resolution as a way of dealing with grief, is coincidentally associated with *Little Dorrit* itself. Late in the spring of 1855, not long after Dickens had begun work on the novel, an infant of Mrs. Winters unexpectedly died (the mother was the ex-Maria Beadnell, portrayed as the Flora Finching of the novel). Dickens' letter to Mrs. Winters is a model of his practical compassion:

I am truly grieved to hear of your affliction in the loss of your darling baby. But if you be not, even already, so reconciled to the parting from that innocent child for a little while, as to bear it gently and with a softened sorrow, I know that not unhappy state of mind must soon arise. The death of infants is a release from so much chance and change—from so many casualties and distresses—and is a thing so beautiful in its serenity and peace—that it should not be a bitterness, even in a mother's heart. The simplest and most affecting passage in all the noble history of our Great Master, is his consideration for little children. And in reference to yours, as many millions of bereaved mothers poor and rich will do in reference to theirs until the end of time, you may take the comfort of the gracious words "And he took a child, and set it in the midst of them."

In a book by one of the greatest English writers, called A Journey from this World to the Next, a parent comes to the distant country beyond the grave, and finds the little girl he had lost so long ago engaged in building a bower to receive him in, when his aged steps should bring him there at last. He is filled with joy to see her —so young—so bright—so full of promise —and is enraptured to think that she never was old, worn, tearful, withered. This is always one of the sources of consolation in the deaths of children. With no effort of the fancy, with nothing to undo, you will always be able to think of the pretty creature you have lost, *as a child* in Heaven.

See *Charles Dickens and Maria Beadnell: Private Correspondence,* ed. G. P. Baker (Boston, 1908), pp. 117-18.

[7]   Reasonable formulations of these charges can be found in: A. O. J. Cockshut's *The Imagination of Charles Dickens* (London: Collins, 1961), pp. 147-48; Lionel Trilling's famous eassy on *Little Dorrit* in *Kenyon Review* 15 (1953) 577-90; and John Wain's *"Little Dorrit,"* in *Dickens and the Twentieth Century,* ed. J. Gross and G. Pearson (London, 1962), pp. 175-86. The only extensive treatment I know (and an excellent study it is) is that by Robert Garis in his *The Dickens Theatre* (Oxford, 1965). Garis concludes his analysis by saying that "Dickens' grasp on the whole Meagles family and what they represent is always uncertain and often distinctly inept" (p. 174); I do not agree with this conclusion.

[8]   The affected heart of one of these spoiled young women, Dolly Varden in *Barnaby Rudge,* is described thus: "A little, gentle, idle, fickle thing; giddy, restless, fluttering; constant to nothing but bright looks and smiles, and laughter" (chapter lxxi).

[9]   Trilling, p. 586.

[10]   See Humphry House, *The Dickens World* (London: Oxford University Press, 1942), pp. 64-65.

ANTHONY WINNER: *Character and Knowledge in Dickens*

[1]   Quoted in Walter Jackson Bate, *From Classic to Romantic* (New York: Harper Torchbooks, 1961), p. 162.

[2]   *Charles Dickens: The World of His Novels* (Cambridge, Mass.: Harvard University Press, 1965), p. 277.

[3]   Given the number of editions, references are to chapter. The texts are those of the *New Oxford Illustrated Dickens.*

[4]   *"Oliver Twist:* Things as They Really Are," *Dickens and the Twentieth Century,* ed. John Gross and Gabriel Pearson (London: Routledge & Kegan Paul, 1962); reprinted in *Dickens,* Twentieth Century Views, ed. Martin Price (Englewood Cliffs, N.J.: Prentice-Hall, 1967), p. 96.

[5]   Philip Collins also finds this passage significant. See *Dickens and Crime*

(Bloomington: Indiana University Press, 1968), p. 214.

[6]   See Kathleen Tillotson, "The Lighter Reading of the Eighteen-Sixties," in Wilkie Collins, *The Woman in White* (Boston: Riverside Editions, 1969), pp. xv-xvi.

[7]   See Miller, pp. 168-77.

[8]   *Dickens, Money, and Society* (Berkeley: University of California Press, 1968), p. 207.

[9]   Ibid.

[10]   *The English Novel: Form and Function* (New York: Rinehart & Co., 1953), p. 134.

[11]   "Introduction," Charles Dickens, *Great Expectations* (Middlesex: Penguin English Library, 1965), p. 25.

[12]   Unless otherwise noted, all subsequent quotations in this section are

from chapter li.

13 *Dickens: The Dreamer's Stance* (Ithaca: Cornell University Press, 1965), pp. 119, 118.

14 "The Complexity of Dickens," in *Dickens 1970*, ed. Michael Slater (New York: Stein and Day, 1970), p. 46.

15 Miller, p. 277.

16 Hardy, p. 42.

17 "Paul Féval says of Dickens' reading of contemporary French novelists, that 'he knew us all'. He had a particular admiration for Balzac, though he deplored the unrestrained development of his personality." K. J. Fielding, *Charles Dickens: A Critical Introduction,* 2nd ed. (Boston: Houghton, 1965), p. 172.

18 Honoré de Balzac, *Père Goriot,* trans. Henry Reed (New York: New American Library, Signet Classics, 1962), p. 243.

HENRI TALON: *Space, Time, and Memory in* Great Expectations

1 See *Post-scriptum aux miettes philosophiques* (Paris: Gallimard, 1949), pp. 78-83, 125-66.

2 Nietzsche, *Prefaces inédites,* quoted by L. Gullermit et J. Vuillemin, *Le sens du destin* (Neuchatel, 1948), p. 136.

3 Thomas Hill Green, *Works,* vol. 3., *The Value and Influence of Works of Fiction,* ed. R. L. Nettleship (London, 1888), p. 29.

4 *Confessions of An English Opium-Eater,* ed. Malcolm Elwin (London, 1956), p. 315.

5 See *Confessions,* XI, XXVI.

6 *La dialectique de la durée* (Paris, 1963), p. 33.

7 See Mary Edminson, "The Date of the Action in *Great Expectations,*" *Nineteenth-Century Fiction* 13 (June 1958), 22-35; also J. H. Raleigh, *Time, Place and Idea: Essays on the Novel* (Carbondale: Southern Illinois University Press, 1968), pp. 131, 133-34.

8 Husserl and Heidegger, of course, but also, Durckheim, "Untersuchungen zum gelebten Raum," *Neue psychologische studien* 6 (1932), 383-480; Minkowski, *Le temps vécu* (1933; reprint ed., Neufchâtel: Delachaux & Niestlé, 1968); Merleau-Ponty, "L'espace," *Phénoménologie de Perception* (Paris: Gallimard, 1945), pp. 330, 331-39.

9 See *Du côté de chez Swann,* Collection Pléiade (Paris, 1968) I, 135, 183.

10 "Primordial Time and Final Time," *Man and Time* (Papers from Eranos Yearbooks), ed. J. Campbell (1958), p. 329.

11 E. Minkowski, pp. 74-75: "cet espace qui ne vient plus disséquer et immobiliser le temps, en le modelant à sa façon, mais que le temps, au contraire, porte en lui, en le vivifiant au plus haut degré, en le remplissant de tout ce qu'il y a de mobile et de dynamique en lui."

12 *The Prelude,* II, livre 271 (1850).

13 On this spatiotemporal association, see also ch. xxix: "It was like pushing the chair itself back into the past, when we began the old slow circuit round about the ashes of the bridal feast."

14 See E. Benveniste's illuminating distinction between two modes of enunciation "celui de l'historie et celui du discours," the latter being the autographer's. *Problèmes de linguistique générale* (Paris, 1966), pp. 237 ff.

15 *Philosophie* (Berlin, 1932) III, 211-12. See M. Dufrenne and P. Ricoeur, *Karl Jaspers et la philosophie de l'existence* (Paris, 1947).

16 *Les Confessions,* ed. van Bever, 3 vols. (Paris, 1946), I, 235.

17 *Rêveries d'un promeneur solitaire,* (Paris: Pléiade,1951), p. 651.

18 *Physics,* IV, 14, 223a.

19 George H. Ford, "Dickens and the Voices of Time", *Nineteenth-Century Fiction* 24 (March 1970), 437.

20 Dufrenne and Ricoeur, p. 22.

DEBORAH ALLEN THOMAS: *The Equivocal Explanation of Dickens' George Silverman*

1   George Saintsbury, "Dickens," *Cambridge History of English Literature,* ed. A. W. Ward and A. R. Waller, XIII, ii (Cambridge: Cambridge University Press, 1916), 334.
2   *The Works of Charles Dickens,* 36 vols. (London: Chapman & Hall, 1897-1908), XXV, xiii.
3   Edmund Wilson, "Dickens: The Two Scrooges," *The Wound and the Bow* (1941; reprinted., New York: Oxford University Press, 1965), pp. 3-85; J. Hillis Miller, *Charles Dickens: The World of His Novels* (Cambridge: Harvard University Press, 1958); Taylor Stoehr, *Dickens: The Dreamer's Stance* (Ithaca: Cornell University Press, 1965); Sylvère Monod, *Dickens the Novelist* (Norman: University of Oklahoma Press, 1968), pp. 382, 472; Kenneth J. Fielding, *Charles Dickens: A Critical Introduction,* 2nd. ed. (Boston: Houghton, 1965), p. 202. Jack Lindsay gives some attention to this work as an indication of Dickens' feelings about his sister Fanny *(Charles Dickens: A Biographical and Critical Study* [London: Andrew Dakers, 1950], pp. 33-34, 169-70); however, Lindsay's remarks do not deal with the complex portrayal of a carefully created personality which the work contains.
4   Harry Stone, "Dickens's Tragic Universe: 'George Silverman's Explanation,'" *Studies in Philology* 55 (1958), 95.
5   Barry D. Bart, " 'George Silverman's Explanation,' " *The Dickensian* 60 (1964), 50.
6   Dudley Flamm, "The Prosecutor Within: Dickens's Final Explanation," *The Dickensian* 66 (1970), 23.
7   Flamm observes that Dickens uses the form of a first-person confession not only in "George Silverman's Explanation" but in "A Madman's Manuscript" in *Pickwick Papers* and "The History of a Self Tormentor" in *Little Dorrit* (p. 21).
8   Stone describes Silverman as a "saintly" (p. 90) person who suffers from "a flawed society" (p. 95). Bart attributes Silverman's troubles to the fact that the world fails to understand "his selflessness" (p. 50) and "his humility" (p. 50). Flamm perceptively calls attention to the discrepancy between a reader's vision and that of Silverman; however, Flamm also contends that this discrepancy lies in the fact that while a reader is aware of "the truth that George Silverman was victim and those around him the oppressors, he himself is not in full command of this knowledge" (p. 22).
9   Citations from *Little Dorrit* in my text are to the Oxford Illustrated Edition (London: Oxford University Press, 1953).
10   Lionel Trilling, *"Little Dorrit,"* introduction to *Little Dorrit* (London: Oxford University Press, 1953), reprinted in *The Dickens Critics,* ed. George H. Ford and Lauriat Lane, Jr. (Ithaca, New York: Cornell University Press, 1961), p. 287.
11   Robert Langbaum, *The Poetry of Experience* (1957; reprinted., New York: Norton, 1963), p. 85. As my discussion indicates, I disagree with Flamm's contention that Miss Wade's "days of self-torment are over" (p. 21).
12   The second section of "Holiday Romance" still possesses a surprising degree of popularity. George H. Ford notes that over three thousand copies of it, under the title of the "Magic Fishbone" were apparently sold in the United States in 1968 ("Dickens in the 1960s," *The Dickensian* 66 [1970], 170).
13   *The Letters of Charles Dickens,* ed. Walter Dexter (Bloomsbury: The Nonesuch Press, 1938), III, 535, to John Forster, 2 July 1867; III, 539, to James T. Fields, 25 July 1867. See also the letter of 21 July 1867 to Percy Fitzgerald in this edition (hereafter referred to as *NL)* cited below.
14   Citations from "Holiday Romance" and "George Silverman's Explanation" in my text are to the Oxford Illustrated Edition of *The Uncommercial*

Traveller and Reprinted Pieces (London: Oxford University Press, 1958).
[15]   Flamm, p. 21.
[16]   John Forster, *The Life of Charles Dickens,* ed. A. J. Hoppé, new ed. (London: J. M. Dent & Sons, 1966), II, 297.
[17]   *NL,* III, 538, to Percy Fitzgerald, 21 July 1867.
[18]   Edgar Johnson, *Charles Dickens: His Tragedy and Triumph,* 2 vols. (New York: Simon and Schuster 1952), II, 1071.
[19]   M. K. Bradby, "An Explanation of *George Silverman's Explanation,*" *The Dickensian* 36 (1940), 17. Despite a few perceptive comments, much of Bradby's discussion seems vague or insuffi-

ciently substantiated.
[20]   *NL,* III, 533, to W. H. Wills, 28 June 1867.
[21]   Flamm and Bart perceptively explore connections between "George Silverman's Explanation" and *The Mystery of Edwin Drood,* but they neglect an important implication raised by these connections: the implication that Silverman's motives may not be so straightforward as he believes them to be.
[22]   Philip Collins, "Dickens's Reading," *The Dickensian* 60 (1964), p. 149.
[23]   Ibid., p. 150.
[24]   George H. Ford, *Dickens and His Readers* (1955; reprinted., New York: Norton, 1965), p. 67 and note.

IAN WATT: *Oral Dickens*

[1]   *A Room of One's Own* (London, 1935), p. 16.
[2]   Though food figures vitally and frequently in such travel books as Lawrence's *Sea and Sardinia* (New York, 1936), pp. 40-41, 65, 78-79, 98-107, 144-45.
[3]   Though a *côtelette de veau à l'oseille* at the *Cheval Blanc* is specified *(Ambassadors,* XI, iii).
[4]   Cited in William Ross Clark, "The Hungry Mr. Dickens," *Dalhousie Review* 36 (1956), 251. The article's general purport is to use Dickens' "tenacious interest in groceries and the wine-list" as evidence of his "good vulgar zest for food" (pp. 256-57).
[5]   Margaret Lane, "Dickens on the Hearth," in *Dickens 1970: Centenary Essays,* ed. Michael Slater (London, 1970), p. 166.
[6]   *A Christmas Carol,* in *Christmas Books, New Oxford Illustrated Dickens* (Oxford, 1954), p. 45. Unless otherwise specified, all subsequent quotations from Dickens are from this edition, and are cited by page number in the text.
[7]   Claude Lévi-Strauss, *Les Structures élémentaires de la parenté* (Paris, 1949), p. 71.
[8]   *Essays in Criticism* 13 (1963), 351.

[9]   P. 354.
[10]   The drinking has been studied in Ross Wilson's "The Dickens of a Drink," *The Dickensian* 63 (1966), 46-61.
[11]   "Food and Ceremony in *Great Expectations,*" p. 351.
[12]   *The Letters of Charles Dickens, Volume One 1820-1839,* ed. Madeline House and Graham Storey, The Pilgrim Edition (Oxford, 1965), I, x.
[13]   Cited in Alfred H. Holt, "The Drink Question as Viewed by Dickens," *The Dickensian* 27 (1931), 170.
[14]   See especially Edmund Bergler, "On a Clinical Approach to the Psychoanalysis of Writers," *Psychoanalytic Review* 31 (1944), 40-70; Abraham Brill, "Poetry as an Oral Outlet," *Psychoanalytic Review* 18 (1931), 357-78.
[15]   In what is still the standard treatment of the subject, "The Influence of Oral Erotism on Character-Formation" (1924), *(Selected Papers of Karl Abraham,* ed. Ernest Jones, trans. Douglas Bryan and Alix Strachey [New York, 1953], I, 401.)
[16]   "The Significance of the Mouth in Psycho-Analysis," *British Journal of Medical Psychology* 4 (1924), 154.
[17]   See Edmund Bergler, *"Little Dorrit* and Dickens' Intuitive Knowledge of Psychic Masochism," *American Imago*

14 (1957), 371-88.

18   See Philip Collins, "Dickens' Public Readings: the Performer and the Novelist," in *Studies in the Novel* 1 (1969), 118-32.

19   See Joseph Katz, "Balzac and Wolfe: A Study of Self-Destructive Over-productivity," *Psychoanalysis* 5 (1957), 3-20.

20   Robert Garis, *The Dickens Theatre: A Reassessment of the Novels* (Oxford, 1965), p. 16; "the performer is 'there' in the sense that he is displaying his skill" (p. 9); opening a Dickens novel the reader "knows, without consciously defining it as such, that humorous writing is theatrical in nature" (p. 40).

21   Kathleen Tillotson, *Novels of the Eighteen-Forties* (Oxford: Clarendon Press, 1954), p. 50.

22   Ernest Jones, *The Life and Works of Sigmund Freud* (New York, 1963-67), I, 174 (5 October, 1883). Another youthful residue, perhaps, was Dickens' "easy toleration of feeblemindedness," which also irritated Freud.

23   "The Comic World of Dickens," *The Victorian Novel: Modern Essays in Criticism*, ed. Ian Watt (New York, 1971), p. 30.

24   *Selected Papers of Karl Abraham*, I, 394.

25   *British Journal of Medical Psychology* 4 (1924), 154. See also Abraham on the over-indulged, whose "whole attitude towards life shows that they expect the mother's breast to flow for them eternally" (p. 399).

26   *Selected Papers of Karl Abraham* pp. 400-401.

27   *British Journal of Medical Psychology*, p. 140.

28   "Histrionic and self-made myth-makers are not simply odd 'characters' but are pretty well the norm in the myth city" *(George Meredith and English Comedy. The Clark Lectures for 1969* [New York, 1969], p. 21).

29   Edgar Johnson, *Charles Dickens: His Tragedy and Triumph*, 2 vols. (Boston: Simon and Schuster, 1952), II, 622.

30   Dickens' tendency to "miniaturize" the habitations of his good characters is analyzed in an interesting phenomenological study by Lucien Pothet, "Sur quelques images d'intimité chez Dickens," *Etudes Anglaises* 23 (1970), 136-57.

31   There are many examples in Augustus Hare's autobiography of how not only his mother but his aunt and his grandmother used the withholding of food as moral weapons, treatment varying from being put on "bread and water" to "break my spirit," to administering a "forcing spoon" of "rhubarb and soda" to punish his "carnal indulgence" in sweets. (Augustus J. C. Hare, *The Years with Mother*, ed. Malcolm Barnes [London, 1952], pp. 16, 21, 60-62. Hare was born in 1834.)

32   See John Burnett, *Plenty and Want: A Social History of Diet in England from 1815 to the Present Day* (London, 1966), especially the chapters on the food of the town workers and of the rich in the early Victorian period.

33   Erik Erikson, *Childhood and Society*, 2nd ed., (New York, 1963), pp. 92, 76.

34   *Journal of a Tour to the Hebrides with Samuel Johnson, LL.D*, ed. R. W. Chapman (London, 1961), pp. 179-80. Burke replied, "Your definition is good, and I now see the full force of the common proverb, 'There is *reason* in roasting of eggs.' "

35   The association is manifest, for example, in what is perhaps Dickens' most orgiastic scene, and one which might have been used by Michael Steig in his "Dickens' Excremental Vision," *Victorian Studies* 13 (1970) 339-54. In *The Christmas Carol*, poor anal Scrooge sees his own room transformed, with holly and mistletoe and yule logs and gorgeous groceries: "Heaped up on the floor, to form a kind of throne, were turkeys, geese, game, poultry, brawn, great joints of meat, sucking-pigs, long wreaths of sausages, mince-pies, plum-puddings, barrels of oysters, red-hot chestnuts, cherry-cheeked apples, juicy oranges, luscious pears, immense twelfth-cakes, and seething bowls of punch, that made the chamber dim with their delicious steam.

In easy state upon this couch, there sat a jolly Giant, glorious to see; who bore a glowing torch, in shape not unlikely Plenty's horn, and held it up, high up, to shed its light on Scrooge" (p. 39). American idiom, fortunately, makes it superflous to explicate the symbolism of Plenty's horn.

[36]   P. 30. Pritchett continues: "Domestic life means meals. Good food makes people good. To our taste now this doesn't seem very amusing. Half of

Victorian England was disgustingly overfed, and since Dickens was an extremist he pushed the note of jollity much too far. The jolly Dickens is the one part of him that has become unreadable."

[37]   *Oliver Twist*, ed. Kathleen Tillotson, The Clarendon Dickens (Oxford, 1966), p. 41. Bumble continues: "You've overfed him, ma'am. You've raised a artificial soul and spirit in him, ma'am, unbecoming a person of his condition."

PHILIP COLLINS: *Dickens' Public Readings*

[1]   Mary Cowden Clarke, *Recollections of Writers* (London, 1878), p. 324.

[2]   *Letters of Charles Dickens*, ed. Walter Dexter (Bloomsbury: Nonesuch Press, 1938), II, 377: cited hereafter as *NL*.

[3]   "Address" prefaced to the Cheap Edition, 1847; Edinburgh speech, 25 June 1841, *The Speeches of Charles Dickens*, ed. K. J. Fielding (Oxford: Clarendon Press, 1960), p. 9.

[4]   *NL*, II, 533.

[5]   John Forster, *Life of Charles Dickens*, ed. J. W. T. Ley (London, 1928), pp. 641, 709; John Ruskin, *Works*, ed. E. T. Cook and Alexander Wedderburn (1902-12), XXXIV, 517; *Aberdeen Journal*, 6 October 1858.

[6]   *NL*, III, 65. The statement about Dickens' income derives from Robert L. Patten's Appendix to my *Charles Dickens: the Critical* Heritage (London, 1970), p. 620.

[7]   Charles Bray, *Phases of Opinion and Experience* (London, 1884), p. 28; *Cheltenham Examiner*, 10 April 1867; George Combe, *Elements of Phrenology*, 3rd ed. (London, 1881), p. 69.

[8]   Forster, p. 641.

[9]   "Dickens' Public Readings: the Performer and the Novelist," *Studies in the Novel*, 1 (Summer 1969), 118-32; revised and abbreviated in *The Listener*, 25 December 1969.

[10]   *The Scotsman*, 19 April 1866, quoting *Dr. Marigold's Prescriptions*, ch. i *(Christmas Stories, New Oxford Illustrated Dickens*, [London, 1956],

p. 452). All references to Dickens' fiction are to this edition of the *Works*.

[11]   Forster, p. 363.

[12]   *Clifton Chronicle*, 27 January 1869.

[13]   *NL*, II, 619 (to Arthur Ryland, 29 January 1855).

[14]   *Manchester Guardian*, 16 December 1861 (reprinted in *Dickensian* 34 (1938), 141).

[15]   *The Nation* (New York), 12 December 1867, p. 483.

[16]   *Manchester Guardian*, 4 February 1867 (reprinted in *Dickensian* 34 (1938), 143. The critic was obviously Adolphus W. Ward, for much of this critique is echoed in Ward's *Charles Dickens* (London, 1882), pp. 152-53.

[17]   *Nicholas Nickleby at the Yorkshire School* (privately printed, n.d.; copy in the Berg Collection), p. 22, amended on information from Kate Field, *Pen Photographs of Charles Dickens' Readings* (London, 1871), p. 57. The words italicized are the variants from the printed text. I thank the Trustees of the Berg Collection, New York Public Library, for their kind permission to describe and quote from the prompt copies in their possession.

[18]   *Sikes and Nancy* (privately printed, n.d.; copy in the Berg Collection), p. 114; *Oliver Twist*, 1, 387.

[19]   *Oliver Twist*, xvii, 118; John Butt and Kathleen Tillotson, *Dickens at Work* (London, 1957), p. 144.

[20]   *David Copperfield. A Reading* (privately printed, n.d.; copy in the Berg

Collection), pp. 21, vi, viii; both phrases added in autograph. "Merry-go-rounder" had appeared, in another context, in one of Mr. Peggotty's speeches in the novel (vii, 103).

21 Ibid, pp. 75, 78.

22 *Nicholas Nickleby at the Yorkshire School. A Reading* (privately printed, n.d.; copy in the collection of the Comtesse de Suzannet), p. 13, amended in autograph; *Bardell and Pickwick. Mr. Chops the Dwarf. Mr. Bob Sawyer's Party. Three Readings* (privately printed, n.d.; copy in the Suzannet collection), pp. 64, 55, 69, 78, 17, 43; *Pickwick Papers*, xxxii, 438, 444, and xxxiv, 477; *Mrs. Gamp* (Boston, 1868; prompt copy in the Suzannet collection), p. 14 for both references; *Martin Chuzzlewit*, xl, 625, and xxv, 404. "Projiss" went first, as the earlier prompt copy shows: see *Mrs. Gamp*, ed. John D. Gordan (New York Public Library, 1956), pp. 42, 50, 97. I thank the Comtesse de Suzannet for her kind permission to describe and quote from the prompt copies in her possession.

23 *The Chimes: A Reading* (privately printed, n.d.; copy in the Berg Collection), p. 22; *Christmas Books*, p. 100; *Nicholas Nickleby at the Yorkshire School* (Suzannet collection), p. 21.

24 K. J. Fielding, *Charles Dickens: a Critical Introduction*, 2nd ed. (Boston: Houghton, 1965), p. 158; *A Christmas Carol* (1844; Dickens' prompt copy in the Berg Collection), pp. 116-20 ("Cut over twice"); [John Hollingshead], "Mr. Charles Dickens as a Reader," *The Critic*, 4 September 1858, p. 538; *The Chimes*, pp. 49, 65; *Christmas Books*, pp. 127-33 (the whole Bowley episode is omitted), and 147-48.

25 *Saunders' News-Letter* (Dublin), 25 August 1858; *Speeches of Charles Dickens*, p. 169 and elsewhere; Preface to *Martin Chuzzlewit*, 1st ed. (London, 1844).

26 [John Hollingshead], p. 537; *Preston Guardian*, 14 December 1861; *Yorkshire Post*, 1 February 1867; *Birmingham Gazette*, December 1861.

27 William Howitt, letter of 15 January 1857, in Carl Ray Woodring, *Victorian Samplers* (Lawrence, Kansas, 1952), p. 184; *Scotsman*, 8 December 1868.

28 *Unto this Last (Works*, XVII, 31n); Mrs. James T. Fields, *Memories of a Hostess*, ed. M. A. DeWolfe Howe (London, 1923), pp. 152, 181.

29 *Edinburgh Courant*, 28 November 1861; *Northern Whig* (Belfast), 21 March 1867; *Brighton Gazette*, 22 October 1868; *National Republican* (Washington), February 1868 (quoted in *Speeches of Charles Dickens* p. 376); *Ipswich Journal*, 9 November 1861; *The Nation* (New York), 12 December 1867, p. 482; *Times*, 1 July 1857, p. 12.

30 *Belfast News-Letter*, 9 January 1869; George Douglas, 8th Duke of Argyll, *Autobiography and Memoirs* (London, 1906), I, 417; *Times*, 17 November 1868, p. 8, and 8 January 1869, p. 7; Edmund Yates, "Mr. Charles Dickens's New Reading," *Tinsley's Magazine* 4 (February 1869), 62.

31 Dean Stanley, quoted by Forster, p. 842; A. W. Ward, *Charles Dickens* (London, 1882), p. 153 (Ward names Garrick, instead of Matthews, in the corresponding passage in his *Manchester Guardian* critique, 4 February 1867); *Hampshire Independent*, 13 November 1858.

32 Forster, p. 667.

33 Lord Redesdale, *Memoirs* (London, 1915), cited in *Dickensian* 33 (1937), 136; Lady Ritchie, *From the Porch* (London, 1913), p. 44.

34 Henry James, *Notebooks*, ed. F. O. Matthiessen and Kenneth B. Murdock (New York, 1947), p. 319; *Autobiographies*, ed. Frederick W. Dupee (London, 1956), p. 390.

35 J. A. Froude, *Thomas Carlyle: a History of his Life in London 1834-1881* (London, 1884), II, 270; *Freeman's Journal* (Dublin), 14 January 1869; Charles Kent, *Charles Dickens as a Reader* (London 1872), pp. vii, 36. My apparent omniscience of British provincial press reports of the Readings is not to my credit at all; the credit belongs to Mr. John Greaves, Honorary Secretary

of the Dickens Fellowship, for his diligence in collecting these cuttings and his generosity in allowing me to use them.

JOHN M. ROBSON: *Our Mutual Friend*

1   See G. M. Young, "Portrait of an Age," in *Early Victorian England* (London: Oxford University Press, 1934), II, 493, where the point is made with reference to *Our Mutual Friend:* " 'I want,' said Bella Rokesmith to her husband, 'to be something so much worthier than the doll in the doll's house.' In the profusion of Dickens, the phrase might pass unnoticed. Twelve years later Ibsen made it the watchword of a revolution."

2   It should be emphasized that what is here offered is not in any sense a full rhetorical analysis. Such an analysis would involve a consideration of all the rhetorical variables bearing on a particular work, including speaker, audience, occasion, subject, theme, argument, resistance, and materials. One major omission is the consideration of "invention," one of Dickens' great powers; when it is seen in the classical context, as involving intrinsic and extrinsic "proofs," one can bring to bear the biographical evidence. A mere mention of other omissions would bulge this note into another paper.

3   See, for example, "Heaven knows we need never be ashamed of our tears, for they are rain upon the blinding dust of earth overlying our hard hearts" (*Great Expectations*, ch. xix).

4   This is the standard division, though some theorists introduced other parts (and used other names) to deal with special cases and refinements. One other part often referred to is *confutatio,* worth mentioning here because Dickens embodies it in his "Postscript, In Lieu of Preface" to *Our Mutual Friend,* which, like his added prefaces to other novels, engages his critics in battle.

5   In some novelists, for example Scott, the *narratio* is isolated, giving anguish to readers whose expectations have been differently trained.

6   There are some seven in all, including "Boffin's Bower," "Our House,"

Mortimer's and Eugene's chambers in the Temple, and up-river, plus some half-dozen less important ones.

7   They appear, with Silas Wegg, in the opening chapter of No. II which, like other similarly placed chapters, takes on some of the tasks of an *exordium.* (Others, like the closing chapters of the Numbers, serve in part as transitions.)

8   At various places in the novel, the right hand is identified as the "business" hand, used for mucky tasks, including insincere handshaking. The most important episode is when Boffin, rudely bidding farewell to the disgusted Bella, offers her his left hand, saying "it's the least used." Also, Sophronia Lammle takes the £100 given to her as "Cashier" in her left hand. The right hand can, however, also be the conveyor of love; Lizzie kisses hers to her father half a page after he washes his.

9   The words "for luck," appear in quotation marks, followed by "he hoarsely said," though they come in the midst of the narrator's external description of Gaffer's actions. I here cannot deal with unusual variants on reported and direct speech. Attention should also be drawn to a descriptive term that becomes a thematic signal in the next paragraph of description: "He was a hook-nosed man, and with that and his bright eyes and his ruffled head, bore a certain likeness to a roused bird of prey." The associated symbolic pattern having been so well treated by others, I need refer only to R. D. McMaster's "Birds of Prey: A Study of *Our Mutual Friend,*" *Dalhousie Review* 40 (1960-61), 372-81, and Richard A. Lanham's *"Our Mutual Friend:* The Birds of Prey," *Victorian Newsletter* 24 (Fall 1963), 6-11. Professor McMaster also touches on the question of disguises and roles, treated below, as do Robert Morse, *"Our Mutual Friend,"* *Partisan Review* 16 (1949), 277-

89, and Masao Miyoshi, "Resolution of Identity in *Our Mutual Friend,*" *Victorian Newsletter* 26 (Fall 1964), 5-9.

[10] "It" is, of course, the corpse, never so identified in the chapter. In the Number plan (now in the Pierpont Morgan Library), a note reads: "It in tow," with "It" underlined three times; in the chapter notes, however, Dickens permits himself to write "the body." The Number plans are printed in Ernest Boll's "The Plotting of *Our Mutual Friend,*" *Modern Philology* 42 (1944), 96-122; the cited notes are on 102.

[11] In the earlier passage mentioned as dwelling on the habitual behavior of Gaffer and Lizzie, the narrator infers their "usage" from their present behavior; he knows no more than any percipient viewer—the reader—would know.

[12] Some of the phrases used by Mortimer in his tale will, without comment, establish the point: he is "sorry to destroy romance by fixing [John Harmon] with a local habitation"; he sees the story (which obviously has its fascination for him) as "not at all statistical and . . . rather odd"; Old Harmon "lived in a hollow in a hilly country," he says, as he finally launches into the story; he goes on to say that Harmon's daughter was "secretly engaged to that popular character whom the novelists and versifiers call Another," and that they "lived in a humble dwelling, probably possessing a porch ornamented with honeysuckle and woodbine twining"; and, after one of the many interruptions, he continues, "We must now return, as the novelists say, and as we all wish they wouldn't, to the man from Somewhere."

[13] Once again a critic's acuteness makes analysis of a trope unnecessary: see, as a gloss on *Our Mutual Friend,* Dorothy Van Ghent's comments on thing as man and man as thing in "The Dickens World: A View from Todgers's," in *Dickens: A Collection of Critical Essays,* ed. Martin Price, (Englewood Cliffs, N.J.: Prentice-Hall, 1967), 24-38 (reprinted from *The Sewanee Review*).

[14] Another character in *Our Mutual Friend* has to give way to puzzled head-holding: Jenny Wren, when she can't distinguish between Fledgeby and Riah as component elements in Pubsey & Co. Like Twemlow, she is unaware of the rules of the game, and so is bewildered by false fronts.

[15] Dickens in fact seldom shows people actually at work; his plots, like those of most novelists, take place in the interstices of the workaday world. Usually only his professional men perform their functions on stage: clergymen, doctors, teachers, lawyers (Mortimer, even, does some of what little work he has to do in front of us), and then the description is normally perfunctory or summary. Exceptions in *Our Mutual Friend,* each of them instructive thematically, include Gaffer, Rogue, Fledgeby, and Jenny Wren.

[16] Podsnap is marked as at least a partial exception. He starts off with "a fatal freshness" (cf. note 47 below), but is finally seen as, like his plate, solid—and his friends are not the friends of Veneering, though the latter's good table attracts their greed. Is Podsnap, unlike Sydney Smith, who sank by his levity, like Smith's brother, who rose by his gravity? Or is it that his particular speculation, Marine Insurance, is, in the world of the novel, a sound one?

[17] In chapter ii the action begins in what may be called "past-present," but shifts to the present as the Chorus is assembled.

[18] The relevant note in the Number plan reads: "Languid story of Harmon the Dust Contractor" (Boll, p. 102).

[19] The source is a limerick from *Anecdotes and Adventures of Fifteen Gentlemen* (London, 1822), possibly by R. S. Sharpe, that first inspired Edward Lear's adoption of the form:

> There was a sick man of Tobago,
> Who liv'd long on rice-gruel and sago;
> But at last, to his bliss,
> The physician said this—
> "To a roast leg of mutton you may go."

See William S. Baring-Gould, *The Lure of the Limerick* (London: Panther Books,

1970), 39, 41. I am indebted for the reference to my colleague, Michael Laine.

20   The four Buffers join in with "You can't resist!" and Mortimer says he feels "immensely embarrass[ed] to have the eyes of Europe" upon him, when his story—a tale of suffering, life, and death—is such a bore.

21   One may mention—without any intention of upsetting the standard view of Dickens' small Latine, and lesse Greeke—some of the classical references, normally applied by the narrator for satiric purposes: Antinous, Argus, the Colossus at Rhodes, Cupid, Cymon, the Fates, the Graces, Hymen, Jupiter, Mercury, the Muses, Neptune, Pegasus, Priam, Romulus and Remus.

22   Dickens often referred to novelists as responsible for a thousand and one tales, in an interesting amalgam of childhood memory and professional duty. See, e.g., Edgar Johnson, *Charles Dickens: His Tragedy and Triumph,* 2 vols. (New York: Simon and Schuster, 1952), 364, 749.

23   The commentator closest to my view is Robert Morse in *"Our Mutual Friend,"* see pp. 280-81.

24   This lack is not sentimentally treated in *Our Mutual Friend,* and anyone who feels inclined to sorrow greatly over the Boffins' childlessness might well remember that Dickens himself was only too aware of the perils of overfecundity. See, for example, his contemporary comment to Lytton: "What a wonderful instance of the general inanity of Kings, that the Kings in the Fairy Tales should have been always wishing for children! If they had but known when they were well off, having none!" (Letter of 16 July, 1866, quoted in Johnson, II, 1065.)

25   There is no room here to comment on Dickens' use of mock-epic and mock-biblical phrases, especially in conjunction with reported speech. Also worthy of notice, but ignored here, are his hypothetical tropes (in this case, "as who should say"), which are frequent enough (though not so frequent as in, for example, Hawthorne's *Scarlet Letter*) to give a sense that speech and gesture

need interpretation, and also that interpretation is likely to be somewhat askew.

26   Jenny also calls Riah to "come back and be dead!" in the garden, and, dismissing Fledgeby because he is not "dead," tells him to "get down to life!" And when Bradley Headstone wrestles Riderhood into the water and death, he cries, "Come down!"

27   Another example is the Children's Hospital where Orphan Johnny dies. Its description may be compared, as another example of rhetorical use of materials, with Dickens' comments on the hospital in Great Ormond Street. See K. J. Fielding, ed., *The Speeches of Charles Dickens* (Oxford: Clarendon Press, 1960), p. 251.

28   This is again apparently a throwaway line, illustrating Eugene's flippant morbidity, but its further importance is indicated by its being on cue from an entry in the Number plan (Boll, p. 102).

29   Riderhood's "eyes were staring upward"; since they were locked face to face, Headstone's burning gaze must have been relentlessly downward.

30   Dickens' notes for the Number include "Back to the opening chapter of the story" [underscored in notes]; for the chapter they include "Back to the opening chapter of the book, Strongly," with "Strongly" underlined three times (Boll, p. 118).

31   As has been suggested before, this ability may reflect Dickens' new knowledge, gained from his liaison with Ellen Ternan.

32   Concerning his table manners, it might be noted that, unlike Gaffer, who violently strikes downward at the table with his all-purpose knife, Eugene merely "trifles quite ferociously with his dessert-knife."

33   Another example of Dickens' manipulation of syntactic speech structures; in the Chorus scenes the narrator frequently omits initial "It" and "The."

34   Bella's mirror, which makes its first appearance in chapter iv, is a great trial to her, initially because, having to share it with Lavvy, she has only "one

flat candle and a few inches of looking-glass!" Later she tests her upward rise in the world by looking into her more commodious and accommodating glass in "Our House," but it never shows her exactly what she wants to see, though it brings out hints of what the reader wants to see.

35 The Herald's College has "found out" a Crusading ancestor for the Veneerings; their quest is ironically revealed in their "bran-new pilgrims on the wall, going to Canterbury in more gold frame than procession," and fascinating Charley, whose quest is just beginning.

36 As mentioned above, the "homes" of the members of Society are typically impermanent, just as they themselves are rootless; the search for a true home is a subsidiary theme throughout, seen, for example, in Eugene's attempt to cultivate the goddess of domesticity when Lizzie's magic is working on him.

37 In chapter xiii we see the "mysterious paper currency" of the streets blown about with the "dust."

38 Even the boys at Greenwich show a practised willingness to plunge into the mud for sixpences.

39 She later happily itemizes secrets for her husband, ending with the "ship" bringing her baby. In itemizing, she is following a characteristic practice of Dickens' characters, who often indulge in inventoried lists (see, for example, Venus in chap. vii, Lady Tippins in chap. x, Rokesmith in chap. xv, Fledgeby and Lammle in Book II, chap. v, and Eugene in Book II, chap. vi).

40 J. Hillis Miller uses this outburst as the theme-note of his fine "Afterword" to *Our Mutual Friend* in the Signet Classic edition (New York: New American Library, 1964); reprinted in Price, 169-77. His perceptive treatment of the theme of money makes it, yet again, unnecessary for me to go into much detail. I do not, however, agree with him if a narrow and literal meaning is to be put upon his opening comment: "*Our Mutual Friend* is about 'money,

money, money, and what money can make of life.'" But the rest of his essay makes such an interpretation unlikely. If asked to take one speech as an emblem of *Our Mutual Friend*'s themes, one could do worse than seize on Boffin's explosive riposte—as astonishing, Dickens makes clear, to Boffin and his pretended conspirators as to the reader, and repeated with evident relish—to Rokesmith's effusive but genuine statement that he wishes to "win [Bella's] affections . . . and possess her heart." Boffin bursts out with "Mew says the cat, Quack-quack says the duck, Bow-wow-wow says the dog!"

41 This does not exhaust the list: "the facetious habit had arisen in the neighbourhood surrounding Mincing Lane of making christian names for him of adjectives and participles beginning with R. Some of these were more or less appropriate: as Rusty, Retiring, Ruddy, Round, Ripe, Ridiculous, Ruminative; others, derived their point from want of application: as Raging, Rattling, Roaring, Raffish." Later, telling Bella of his fellows' playfulness, R. W. exclaims: "What does it matter? It might be Surly, or Sulky, or fifty disagreeable things that I really shouldn't like to be considered. But Rumty! Lor, why not Rumty?"

42 In chapter viii, as Rokesmith, he seems to catch the sound of his real name imperfectly, trying "Harmoon" and "Harmarn."

43 The Harmon baby becomes the "Inexhaustible"—behind them both is of course the "Inimitable" himself.

44 His name also appears in an imaginary list of clients (reminiscent of more familiar lists in other novels) prepared by Mortimer's "dismal" clerk ("whose appropriate name was Blight"): "Mr. Aggs, Mr. Baggs, Mr. Caggs, Mr. Faggs, Mr. Gaggs, Mr. Boffin"; and then: "Mr. Alley, Mr. Balley, Mr. Calley, Mr. Dalley, Mr. Falley, Mr. Galley, Mr. Halley, Mr. Lalley, Mr. Malley. And Mr. Boffin."

45 In the Number plan, the notes for chapter iii (though not for chapter ii, where his name first appears) give Eu-

gene's name in quotation marks (Boll, p. 102).

46   In view of the recent discovery that T. S. Eliot first thought of "He Do the Police in Different Voices" as a title for *The Waste Land,* it should be noted that this ability of Sloppy (no other name) permits him to pass himself off to Wegg as a "dustman"; this masking is prepared for in chapter xvi.

47   Dickens hits on a splendid phrase to express their eagerness, as Podsnap, mistaking Twemlow for Veneering, concludes his insincere greeting with "So glad of this opportunity, I am sure!" He expresses the same sentiment on the part of his wife, repeats it to Veneering (still not knowing who he is), and then, when the confusion is dispelled, says to Twemlow: "Ridiculous opportunity—but so glad of it, I am sure!"

48   They are supported by the orphan theme, and by such mysteries as Silas Wegg's not knowing why Silas, or why Wegg, and the late Mrs. Riderhood's not being able to explain why her daughter is "Pleasant." Riderhood is himself much more fixed (though he objects to Headstone using his name "as if it was a street pump"), insisting on his first name being proper like Jesse Hexam's, just as he insists that he, like Hexam, has a daughter. Also worth mention is Fascination Fledgeby's inability to capture Georgiana Podsnap's first name; he tries "Georgina" and even (running after echoes of "concertina" and "scarlatina" to "parach—") "Georgeute." Is there here a hint of Christiana Weller? See Johnson, pp. 497-98, and passim.

49   This is another *exordium,* bringing before us two new settings, the schools and Jenny's house, introducing Bradley Headstone, with Miss Peecher and Mary Anne, adding a new element to the "respectability" theme (the chapter is entitled "Of an Educational Character"), and so reinforcing the *narratio;* by tying loose strands (Jenny as granddaughter of the drowned old drunkard in list slippers, for example), and introducing Eugene's rival-double, it also advances the *confirmatio.*

50   Edgar Johnson (p. 1023) is slightly misleading on this point, implying that the whole city is toy.

51   It would be extravagant to add to poor John Dickens' staggering load of identifications that of Mr. Dolls; still, Dickens did think of him as "a prodigal father." See, e.g., Johnson, pp. 350, 452. The tremulous hands of the drunken Dolls, especially when he is unable to hold the coins Eugene throws at him, suggest yet another biographical gloss; see the reference to Dickens' early experience with the tipsy bookseller in Hampstead Road (Johnson, p. 31).

52   Brown paper is curiously applied to the human form in two other situations: Miss Peecher cuts out a pattern for herself, and Venus returns Wegg's leg wrapped like a brown-paper truncheon.

53   *Charles Dickens,* p. 1043. This view is much less misleading, of course, than G. K. Chesterton's strangely contrary opinion, expressed in his introduction to *Our Mutual Friend:* "The opening of a book goes for a great deal. The opening of *Our Mutual Friend* is much more instinctively energetic and lighthearted than that of any of the other novels of his concluding period. . . . Dickens, in his later years, permitted more and more his story to take the cue from its inception. All the more remarkable, therefore, is the real jerk and spurt of good spirits with which he opens *Our Mutual Friend.*" *Appreciations and Criticisms of the Works of Charles Dickens* (London: Dent, 1921), pp. 210-11.

SYLVÈRE MONOD: *Confessions of an Unrepentant Chestertonian*

1   (London: Lane, 1908), p. 296.

2   With an introduction by Herbert Marshall McLuhan (London: Sheed and Ward, 1948), p. 9.

3   "G. K. Chesterton's 'Father Brown' Stories," *Southern Review* 5

(Summer 1969) 612.

4   (London: Dent, Everyman's Library, 1907), p. x.

5   *Heretics* (London: Lane, 1905), p. 15.

6   *G. K. Chesterton. A Selection from his Non-Fictional Prose,* ed. W. H. Auden (London: Faber and Faber, 1970), p. 13.

7   Reprinted in Auden's *G. K. Chesterton,* p. 163.

8   *Orthodoxy,* p. 15.

9   (London: Dent, Everyman's Library, 1908), p. vii.

10   (London: Dent, Everyman's Library, 1909), p. x.

11   Reprinted in Auden's *G. K. Chesterton,* p. 171.

12   From *Heretics.* Reprinted in Auden's *G. K. Chesterton,* p. 77.

13   Kenner, p. 50

14   Introduction to *A Tale of Two Cities,* p. x.

15   From *The Common Man,* 1950. Reprinted in Auden's *G. K. Chesterton,* p. 84.

16   Kenner, pp. xviii-xix.

17   In his introduction to a reprint of *Charles Dickens* (New York: Shocken Books, 1965).

18   See Lord Snow's review of Auden's *G. K. Chesterton* in *Financial Times,* London, 26 February 1970.

19   Kenner, p. 66.

20   *Orthodoxy,* p. 183.

21   *Orthodoxy,* p. 105.

22   *Heretics,* p. 22.

23   From *Orthodoxy;* quoted in Maurice B. Reckitt, *G. K. Chesterton. A Christian Prophet for England To-Day* (London: S.P.C.K., 1950), p. 29.

24   Quoted in Maisie Ward, *Return to Chesterton* (London, 1952), p. 5.

25   Marcus, p. vii.

26   *Charles Dickens* (London: Methuen, 1906), p. 5.

27   George Gissing, *Charles Dickens: A Critical Study* (1898; reprint ed., London: Gresham, 1903).

28   Ibid., p. 95.

29   Ibid., p. 251.

30   Ibid., p. 261.

31   Ibid., pp. 168-69.

32   Ibid., pp. 9,12.

33   Ibid., p. 60.

34   Ibid., p. 227.

35   *The Immortal Dickens,* (London: Palmer, 1925), p. 71.

36   *Charles Dickens: A Critical Study,* p. 75.

37   Ibid., p. 187.

38   Ibid., p. 206.

39   Ibid., p. 216.

40   London: Methuen, 1906.

41   Marcus, p. xi.

42   *Charles Dickens,* p. 122.

43   Ibid., p. 188.

44   Ibid., p. 112; see *Macbeth,* V, v, 10.

45   Introduction to *Our Mutual Friend* (London: Dent, Everyman's Library, 1907), p. viii.

46   *Charles Dickens,* p. 40.

47   Ibid., p. 118.

48   Ibid., p. 272.

49   Ibid., p. 285.

50   Ibid., p. 96.

51   Ibid., p. 123.

52   Ibid., p. 9.

53   Ibid., p. 46.

54   Introduction to *A Tale of Two Cities,* p. x.

55   *Charles Dickens,* p. 21.

56   Ibid., p. 121.

57   Ibid., p. 168.

58   Introduction to *American Notes and Pictures from Italy,* p. xvi.

59   Introduction to *A Tale of Two Cities,* p. xi.

60   *Charles Dickens,* p. 78.

61   Ibid., pp. 110-11.

62   Introduction to *Pickwick Papers* (London: Dent, Everyman's Library, 1907), p. xiv.

63   *Charles Dickens,* p. 4.

64   Ibid., p. 27.

65   Ibid., p. 206.

66   Ibid., p. 106.

67   Ibid., pp. 247, 252.

68   Ibid., pp. 264, 266.

69   Auden, *G. K. Chesterton,* p. 15.

70   *Financial Times* (London) 26 February 1970.

71   *Charles Dickens,* p. 235.

72   Ibid., p. 170.

73   Introduction to *Our Mutual*

Friend, p. v.

74   *Charles Dickens,* p. 181.

75   Robson, p. 614.

76   *Charles Dickens,* p. 159.

77   Ibid., p. 288.

78   Ibid., p. 87.

79   Ibid., p. 184.

80   Ibid., p. 62.

81   Marcus, p. x.

82   *Charles Dickens,* p. 23.

83   *The Imagination of Charles Dickens* (London: Collins, 1961), p. 95.

84   Quoted in Christopher Hollis, *G. K. Chesterton* (London: Longmans, 1950), p. 20.

85   *The Soul of Dickens* (London: Chapman and Hall, 1916), p. 77.

86   Marcus, *Charles Dickens,* p. xi.

87   Auden, *G. K. Chesterton,* p. 13.

88   *Shaw. A. Prose Anthology,* ed. H. M. Burton (London: Longmans and Constable, 1954), p. 73.

89   *George Bernard Shaw* (London: Bodley Head, 1909), p. 239.

90   *The Real Bernard Shaw* (London: Dent, 1949), p. 252

91   *Charles Dickens,* p. 19.